All-sorts Worship

Complete all-age services for every Sunday of Common Worship Year C

Claire Benton-Evans

Illustrations by Melody-Anne Lee

kevin mayhew

kevin mayhew

First published in Great Britain in 2012 by Kevin Mayhew Ltd
Buxhall, Stowmarket, Suffolk IP14 3BW
Tel: +44 (0) 1449 737978 Fax: +44 (0) 1449 737834
E-mail: info@kevinmayhewltd.com

www.kevinmayhew.com

© Copyright 2012 Claire Benton-Evans.

The right of Claire Benton-Evans to be identified as the author of this work has been asserted by her in accordance with the Copyright, Designs and Patents Act 1988.

The publishers wish to thank all those who have given their permission to reproduce copyright material in this publication.

Every effort has been made to trace the owners of copyright material and we hope that no copyright has been infringed. Pardon is sought and apology made if the contrary be the case, and a correction will be made in any reprint of this book.

All rights reserved. Except for the photocopiable cover sheets (see page 19 for details), no part of this publication may be reproduced, stored in a retrieval system, or transmitted, in any form or by any means, electronic, mechanical, photocopying, recording, or otherwise, without the prior written permission of the publisher.

Scripture quotations are taken from *The New Revised Standard Version of the Bible*, copyright © 1989 by The Division of Christian Education of the National Council of Churches in the USA. Used by permission. All rights reserved.

ISBN 978 1 84867 530 8
Catalogue No. 1501238

Cover design by Rob Mortonson
© Images used under licence from Shutterstock Inc.
Illustrations by Melody-Anne Lee
Edited by Nicki Copeland
Typeset by Richard Weaver

Printed and bound in Great Britain

*To the many talented people with whom I have worked
on the following all-age, all-sorts services:*

*Open Door at St Margaret's, Northam
Second Sunday at St John's, Ivybridge
'It's church, Jim, but not as we know it' at St Thomas', Camelford
Tea at Tetha's at St Tetha's, St Teath*

With special thanks to John, Chris and Jim

Contents

	About the author	7
	Introduction	9
Advent	First Sunday of Advent	28
	Second Sunday of Advent	34
	Third Sunday of Advent	40
	Fourth Sunday of Advent	46
	Christmas Eve	54
Christmas	Christmas Day	62
	First Sunday of Christmas	68
	Second Sunday of Christmas	76
Epiphany	Epiphany	82
	First Sunday of Epiphany	88
	Second Sunday of Epiphany	96
	Third Sunday of Epiphany	104
	Fourth Sunday of Epiphany	110
	Candlemas	116
Ordinary time	Proper 1	124
	Proper 2	132
	Proper 3	140
	Second Sunday before Lent: Pets' service	146
	Sunday next before Lent	152
Lent	Ash Wednesday	160
	First Sunday of Lent	168
	Second Sunday of Lent	176
	Third Sunday of Lent	184
	Fourth Sunday of Lent: Mothering Sunday	190
	The Annunciation	198
Passiontide	Fifth Sunday of Lent	206
	Palm Sunday	214
	Maundy Thursday	220
	Good Friday	226
Eastertide	Easter Day	232
	Second Sunday of Easter	238

	Third Sunday of Easter	246
	Fourth Sunday of Easter	254
	Fifth Sunday of Easter	260
	Sixth Sunday of Easter	268
	Ascension Day	274
	Seventh Sunday of Easter	280
	Pentecost	288
Ordinary time	Trinity Sunday	296
	Proper 4	302
	Proper 5	310
	Proper 6	318
	Proper 7	326
	Proper 8	334
	Proper 9	342
	Proper 10	348
	Proper 11	354
	Proper 12	362
	Proper 13	372
	Proper 14	378
	Proper 15	384
	Proper 16	392
	Proper 17	400
	Proper 18	408
	Proper 19	414
	Proper 20	422
	Proper 21	430
	Harvest Thanksgiving	438
	Proper 22	444
	Proper 23	450
	Proper 24	458
	Proper 25	468
	All Saints' Day	474
	Fourth Sunday before Advent	482
	Third Sunday before Advent	488
	Remembrance Sunday	496
	Second Sunday before Advent	502
	Christ the King	510
Appendix	Resources for Activities	517
Index	Index by theme	567

About the author

Claire Benton-Evans studied English at Oxford before teaching English and Drama in London, North Devon and Cornwall. Claire's consultancy work includes all-age worship workshops and children's spirituality training for clergy, worship leaders, head teachers and school governors. The creative arts inspire her, exclusion makes her angry and family life keeps her feet on the ground. Claire likes long walks, good food, live theatre and the Greenbelt festival. She lives with her husband – now a minister in the Scottish Episcopal Church – and three children in the Scottish Borders.

All-sorts Worship for Years A and B are already available. Details of Claire's other titles can be found at the end of this book and also on her website at: www.clairebentonevans.com

Introduction

What do we mean when we talk about all-age worship? This question can stir up some strong opinions, as these comments on a Christian website[1] have shown:

> You don't make a normal Eucharist into an all-age worship service by throwing in a children's sermon and an action song.

This kind of service is familiar to all those of us who have struggled to contain bored and fidgety children in a pew during a long Old Testament reading or full-length intercessions. Neither is it all-age worship when the regular service runs parallel to a separate 'children's church' service or Sunday school, traditionally the home of craft, worksheets and Bible-story colouring. This mother of boys aged four and two has this to say:

> My children get enough craft-quizzes-colouring at home and kindergarten. It does very much seem that children are 'tidied away'; I would prefer them to grow up experiencing the full range of what goes on at a service, accepted as they are but given a chance to learn to be quiet when called for, a real part of the congregation.

There is such longing here for real, shared worship and a sense of belonging; her feeling that children are 'tidied away' in church is one that many of us may recognise. When we send our children out of the service at the beginning and invite them back in at the end, we marginalise their role in our church; we reduce their spiritual journey to a five-minute 'show and tell' spot after the notices, in which they present what they have learnt. (How many of us could do this at the end of a Sunday service?) This state of affairs is noted by the Church of England's National Children's Adviser, the Revd Mary Hawes, who has said that children in church are often treated as 'Christians in waiting rather than disciples in training. We still tend to see

---

1. www.ship-of-fools.com, 'The magazine of Christian unrest', 11.11.09.

them as needing to be taught and kept out of the way until they have learnt how to behave.'[2]

This view of children as 'Christians in waiting' reflects the fact that until recently, children's spirituality was assumed to be an immature, incomplete version of adult spirituality. Research which has sought to examine it on children's own terms has found that it has its own rich and complex character. Rebecca Nye has summarised the key features of children's spirituality.[3] First of all, it is rooted in ordinary, everyday experience; it is an integrated part of their lives, so that an experience of God may be discussed as freely and excitedly as an encounter in the playground or a discovery in the garden. From this comes the seemingly erratic nature of children's spirituality: Nye says, 'One minute they are having profound, sacred experiences, and the next they are thinking about custard.'[4]

There are two further aspects of children's spirituality which are particularly significant for those of us seeking to involve them in worship. Children's spirituality is both verbal and non-verbal: like so much of their play and learning, their spiritual life is experienced and expressed not only through words but also through actions, through all their senses, their emotions, imagination and intuition. When we recognise this, we may realise that our own spirituality is not so different, and that we also need opportunities to explore it non-verbally. Finally, Nye says that all these features of children's spirituality combine to surprise and challenge adults. Our own experience gives us plenty of examples of this. Every parent is familiar with children's God-related questions which ask, 'Why?' about everything from cancer to headlice; my young daughter asked me, crossly, 'What's the point of church?' and I heard recently about a teenager who came upon a group of youth leaders in prayer before the start of a holiday club: 'What are you doing?' he asked. 'Why are you all looking at the floor? Have you lost something?' Nye describes this as children's ability 'to speak out, to be prophetic, to articulate (not necessarily through words

---

2. *Church Times*, 1.5.09.
3. Rebecca Nye, 'Spirituality' chapter in *Through the eyes of a child*, ed. Anne Richards and Peter Privett, Church House Publishing 2009.
4. *Church Times*, 1.5.09.

alone) the need for a change or to offer a new way of seeing things.'[5] Children are unafraid to wonder aloud and they challenge us directly with their questions about the fundamentals of faith, worship and church practice.

If we agree that children's spirituality is both a force to be reckoned with and a challenge to all of us to do church differently, then what we need is a bold re-imagining of what all-age worship can and should be. We need to create a way of joining people of all ages together in *worship*, not just tolerant co-existence. Since becoming involved with all-age worship almost as soon as I became a parent, I have been privileged to work with teams of talented and creative people in different churches; we have been blessed with open-minded clergy and congregations who allowed us to experiment and offered us generous feedback. My thinking about all-age worship has also been inspired, in recent years, by the hands-on practicality of Messy Church and by the child-centred spirituality and reflective storytelling of Godly Play.[6] Through these years of shared debate, experiment and exploration, and as I began regularly to devise and lead my own all-age worship services, I have found myself returning again and again to my daughter's question: 'What is church *for*? What's the point of it?'

This question goes to the heart of why we do what we do on a Sunday morning – and on the other six days of the week. Archbishop Rowan Williams describes the Church like this:

> . . . the Church is first of all a kind of space cleared by God through Jesus in which people may become what God made them to be (God's sons and daughters), and that what we have to do about the Church is not first to organise it as a society but to inhabit it as a climate or landscape. It is a place where we can see properly – God, God's creation, ourselves.[7]

---

5. *Through the eyes of a child*, p.72.
6. See Jerome Berryman, *Godly Play*, Augsburg Books, 1995 and Lucy Moore, *Messy Church*, BRF, 2006 or www.godlyplay.org.uk and www.messychurch.org.uk. See also *The Spirit of the Child* by David Hay with Rebecca Nye, Jessica Kingsley Publishers, 2006.
7. Rowan Williams, 'The Christian Priest Today', quoted by Justin Lewis-Anthony, *If You Meet George Herbert on the Road . . . Kill Him!*, Mowbray, 2009, p.81.

The Church as a space in which to live and grow and see more clearly – how many of us recognise our own place of worship in that description? Yet at the centre of this wonderful vision is a practical direction: '. . . what we have to do about the Church is not first to organise it as a society but to inhabit it as a climate or landscape.' Like tracing the source of the Nile, we need to move through our contemporary landscape of Synods and Sunday schools, pews and flower rotas, and find our way back to our Church's origin: Jesus, a small band of followers and some heady days which we now celebrate as the Ascension and Pentecost. This is where the Church was born, when Christ entrusted his disciples with his mission:

> 'You will receive power when the Holy Spirit has come upon you; and you will be my witnesses in Jerusalem, in all Judea and Samaria, and to the ends of the earth.' *(Acts 1:8)*

After all their questions about when Christ would accomplish the work he came to do, they are told, 'It's up to you, now.' This was their mission and our mission in the Church today: to do Christ's work in the world. And what is the first act of the embryonic Church? On the day of Pentecost, when the disciples are filled with the Holy Spirit, they tell all sorts of people about Jesus in a language which each can understand. This is a Church which embraces variety ('from every nation under heaven' – Acts 2:5), which responds to different needs ('We hear, each of us, in our own native language' – Acts 2:8) and which, above all, communicates the truth about Jesus: 'Therefore let the entire house of Israel know with certainty that God has made him both Lord and Messiah' (Acts 2:36). This is not so far, after all, from Dr Williams' vision of a Church in which we may see God and ourselves properly, and have the space to become what God made each of us to be.

The Church was not created as a fixed, inward-looking, self-serving institution which focuses on its own ways of doing things. It is a living body of believers, a Church made of 'living stones' which is both upward-looking – to Christ, its head – and outward-looking, to the world which it was made to serve. This Church springs up between Ascension and Pentecost: it stands

INTRODUCTION

with one foot on the holy mountain and the other in the crowded marketplace.

In our worship we express what we believe the Church is for. Firstly, our worship should be *welcoming* to people of all sorts, not just those who are used to our way of doing things. Secondly, if we wish to engage a wide variety of people in worship, then it needs to be as *varied* as possible; we also need to use as many channels of communication as we have available to us, which means using not just words but all the senses. Like the disciples speaking in many different languages, we need to communicate in *multi-sensory* ways, through actions, visual stimuli, music, tactile objects and food. Finally, we should aspire to be a church which is 'a place where we can see properly – God, God's creation, ourselves.' In our worship we need *clear* teaching, but also opportunities to *explore* our own responses to God and our own place in the church and in the world. The services in this book are shaped by these principles: they are designed to be *welcoming, varied, multi-sensory, clear* and *exploratory*.

Welcoming

These services must welcome and include not only people of all ages, but – as *The Book of Common Prayer* has it – people of 'all sorts and conditions of life'[8]: children at all educational stages, grown-ups of any age, people who are single, part of a childless couple or part of a family – all together in church. These services should engage people who are new to church and those who are returning to church after many years' absence. They should also involve those who have different physical and mental abilities, like the profoundly disabled teenagers who regularly attend a church I know well. They come in their electric wheelchairs with their carers and they, too, are part of the church family. That family should be characterised by its variety, inclusivity and unity, as described by Paul in his letter to the church at Corinth:

> For just as the body is one and has many members, and all the members of the body, though many, are one body, so it is with Christ. For in the one Spirit

---

8. *Collect or Prayer for all Conditions of men* in Prayers and Thanksgivings, BCP.

we were all baptised into one body – Jews or Greeks, slaves or free – and we were all made to drink of one Spirit.

Indeed, the body does not consist of one member but of many. If the foot were to say, 'Because I am not a hand, I do not belong to the body', that would not make it any less a part of the body . . . As it is, there are many members, yet one body. The eye cannot say to the hand, 'I have no need of you', nor again the head to the feet, 'I have no need of you'. *(1 Corinthians 12:12–15, 20, 21)*

If we truly believe our Church to be one body, then all of us – all ages and all sorts – need to be welcome to worship together as one. Everything about the way one of these services is designed, planned and conducted should shout, 'Welcome!' from beginning to end:

- Before the service, posters in local schools, toddler groups and shops should invite everyone in the community, not just the church. For those leaders who are online, social networking sites such as Facebook are increasingly useful for publicising services.
- On the day, leaders should greet people at the door, and outside on the church steps, to welcome them in and help with access if necessary. Heavy church doors are not very welcoming – especially for people with prams, buggies or wheelchairs!
- In the church, seating should be arranged in a way that encourages people to feel relaxed and unconfined, because the activities are mostly designed to get them moving around. (This can be the single thing which makes parents of young children feel most welcome, given the impossibility of keeping a toddler still in a pew for any length of time.)
- These services have been designed to be easy for newcomers to follow, without the need for service sheets or for more than one hymn book.
- 'Feed my lambs . . . feed my sheep', Jesus commanded Peter. Taken literally, his words remind us that there should *always* be food at these services. Hospitality welcomes people to our churches, and the promise of food will invariably keep my own children in church. I have called the post-service

refreshments 'a feast', and so they should be. It is as easy to provide several kinds of shop-bought cake as it is to open packets of mixed biscuits; better still, invite your church's best bakers to contribute cakes. At our Sunday tea-time service we have even provided hot buttered toast, crumpets and cocktail sausages. It is important to allow time for the feast: we usually plan on 90 minutes for an all-age service, of which one half is worship and the other half is hospitality. There is absolute continuity between the service which talks about loving your neighbour and the opportunity, afterwards, to drink tea, eat cake together and ask each other, 'How are you?'

Clear These services follow *The Common Worship Lectionary*, because it provides a common thread which links our individual churches together as we progress through the year. The Lectionary readings for each Sunday inspire a single clear theme which integrates every detail of the service from the title to the concluding prayer. I would suggest that this theme is expressed visually on your church's publicity posters. In following this single, clear idea, I have kept three questions in mind for each service:

- *'What is the story?'* This reminds us simply to tell and retell the stories of our faith through the Church year. Just as Jewish families at Passover recount the story of the Exodus in answer to a child's question, 'Why is this night different?', so we should imagine a child at every service asking us, 'Why is this day different?' We answer them by telling the story.

- *'What does it mean?'* This question is asked of all of us. It provides opportunities for teaching as well as individual reflection and shared discussion. It gives us a chance to explore our faith together.

- *'What does it tell us to do?'* This question turns our attention outwards: it encourages us to keep our faith active and real in our lives outside church.

Maintaining a clear focus in our worship also requires a certain economy. The services in this book are designed to last approximately 45–50 minutes. No single component lasts longer than about 15 minutes; there is usually a change of activity every five or ten minutes, in order to encourage concentration and engagement. These services have been tried and tested in my local parish church and subjected to the critical judgements and various attention spans of my own children, their friends and families. This process has encouraged me to keep our worship clear, concise and to the point.

Varied

Within each element of these services, I have created as much variety as possible from week to week. For example, the storytelling might involve puppets one week, a dramatised dialogue the next and a reading accompanied by audio-visual aids the week after. In each case I have chosen the medium to suit the message. The range of prayers which I explored in *All-sorts Prayer 1 and 2*[9] has informed the wide variety of prayer actions offered here. They give people the opportunity to confess, to wonder, to give thanks, offer intercessions and be contemplative; they may involve writing, a creative act, movement, stillness, words, sound or silence. Finally, even the structure of the service itself might be varied to suit a particular purpose. In general, our worshippers should come to expect the unexpected!

Multi-sensory

It is in this respect that children can best help us transform what we do in church. I recently invited children to design their ideal church. The many and varied responses to this challenge were a revelation: they depicted worship in hot air balloons, in tents lined with cushions and rugs, in hi-tech spaces with plasma screen TVs and disco lights, in tree houses and on beaches. These churches featured tasty snacks, drinks and other home comforts such as pews which convert into beds. The detailed design by Phoebe, aged ten, epitomises many children's desire for a multi-sensory worship space in which they might relax, explore and discover. The addition of an 'escape pod' also speaks volumes about her own response to traditional church services!

Children remind us that our spiritual selves are intertwined with our hearing, seeing, smelling, tasting, feeling bodies, and that our worship might be more

---

9. Kevin Mayhew, 2010 and 2011.

INTRODUCTION

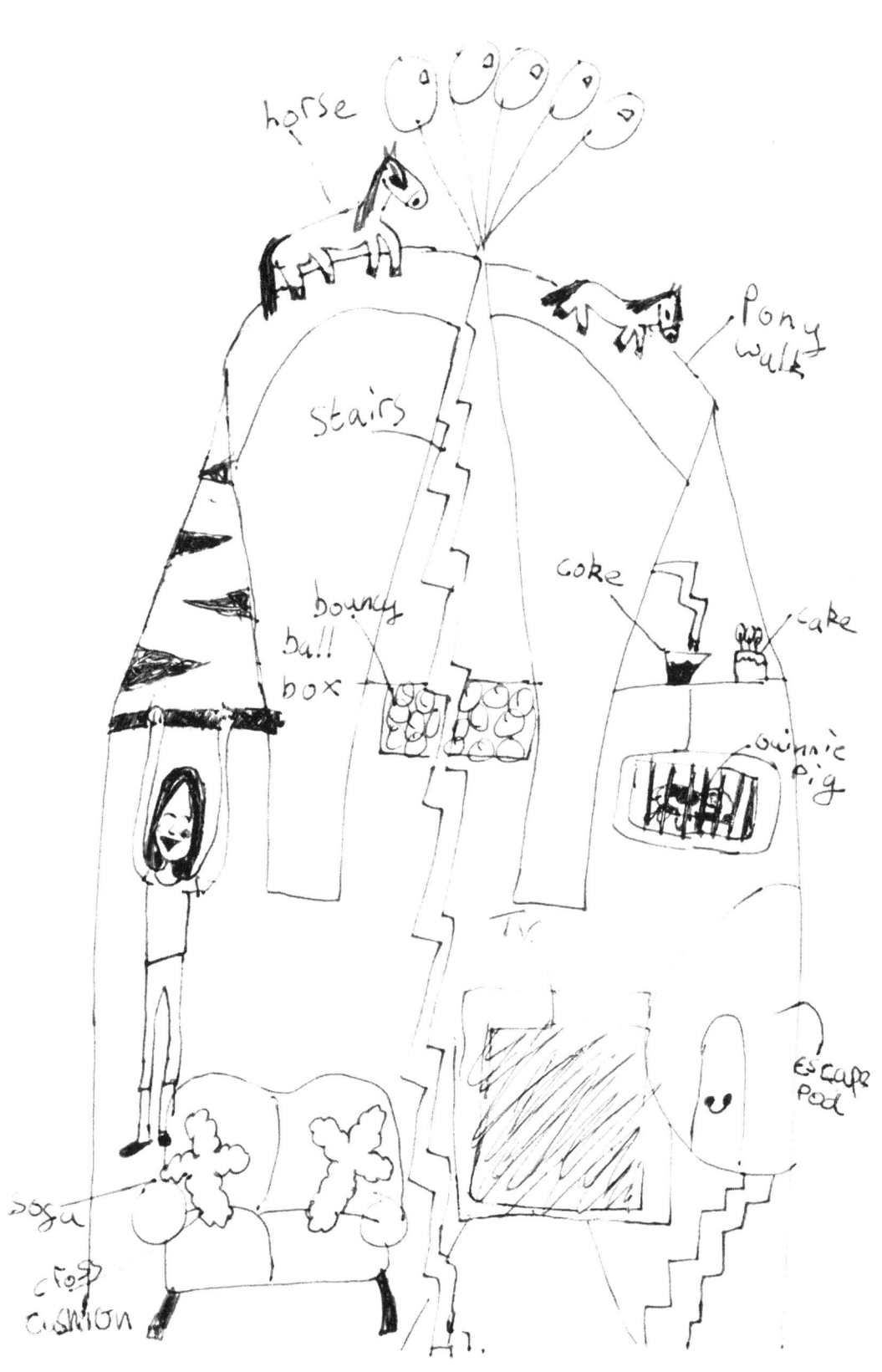

'Design for a brilliant church' by Phoebe (10)

wholehearted if we adopted a more holistic approach. In our prayer and worship, we seek to tune in to God, and so these services appeal to the senses in an attempt to open up more channels of communication.

Exploratory

In these services, I have moved away from the traditional 'educational' model of children's church, which presupposes that the (spiritually mature and well-versed) teacher instructs the (spiritually less knowledgeable and less developed) children. The services in this book embrace the new understanding of children's spirituality and acknowledge that all of us – leaders and congregation, adults and children – are fellow travellers on our spiritual journey. Consequently, the 'Teaching' element is now part of 'Exploring', which is more creative, interactive and shared. This exploratory approach is more in sympathy with Godly Play's 'wondering' and with the freely chosen responses to Bible stories it encourages.

When knowledge and information are shared in these services, there is no testing or assessment. God is not an educational Attainment Target, and we can't presume to know whether those we have led in worship have 'achieved' a certain level of spiritual development. What the exploratory approach recognises is that any such development is – wonderfully – out of our control and in the hands of the Holy Spirit, who is active in the space between the worship which is offered and the people of all ages and abilities who engage in that worship. It is a space for spiritual adventure and wondering exploration – a space which I hope may help us 'to see properly – God, God's creation, ourselves'.

What about Holy Communion?

These are services of the Word; however, there is certainly scope to adapt them to incorporate a *Common Worship* Eucharistic liturgy. Our church has tried this on occasions and the experiment has proved interesting and worthwhile, since it takes everyone involved a little way outside their comfort zone. The service is inevitably longer and wordier than our all-age congregation is used to, while being more informal and interactive than the regular Sunday worshippers expect. For details, see the section below titled '*All-Sorts* Eucharist', (page 22).

The Cover Sheet
Photocopiable Cover Sheet

This contains the essential information for everyone involved in the service, from the person designing the poster to the wonderful lady who – in one of our local churches – decorates themed cakes for the end of the service. The running order is vital for leaders, especially when several are involved: everyone needs to see at a glance where their 'bit' fits in.

Resources

A long list of resources is usually a feature of any all-age worship service, since visually rich storytelling and multi-sensory prayers inevitably involve a certain amount of kit. Please don't be put off by the length of some of these lists: firstly, they are there as comprehensive checklists for use at every stage of a service, from the first planning meeting to the last-minute checks, early on Sunday morning. Secondly, the resources themselves are not usually expensive or hard to find. If these lists were recipes (and there are some similarities), they would call for carrots and onions rather than quails' eggs and caviar. Most of the items listed can be borrowed from schools and Sunday schools or bought from local shops relatively cheaply.[10] I would only add that you should try to provide the best resources you can afford, as a box of feeble felt-tip pens with missing lids suggests that our all-age congregations deserve no better. Good-quality resources show that we value the people who will use them in their prayers and worship.

These resources lists do not include 'human resources' such as the Sunday school, the Brownies or the youth group. It is wonderful if such groups can be involved in these services, but I have never made it a requirement. Ministers and leaders have enough to do in preparation for a service, without fitting in weeks of rehearsal for a specific group's contribution.

The last thing to say about the resources lists is that they are not set in stone. They list the optimum amount of resources, and may be adapted with ingenuity and imagination to take account of particular constraints, such as the absence of a screen and projector.

---

10. Many craft materials are available in newsagents, toy shops and pound shops as well as art shops. An excellent resource is your local scrapstore: this is a centre for craft and textile bits and bobs which are donated by industry; for a small annual fee, you can go as often as you like and stock up for free on everything from gold paper to sequinned scraps to giant cardboard tubes (see national directory on www.childrensscrapstore.co.uk). The internet is your best source of audio-visual resources: for photographs, there are websites such as www.shutterstock.com which allow you to purchase copyright-free images.

Leaders These services have been written so that any designated person, lay or ordained, might lead them. A new leader can use the script straight off the page, exactly as written, but it is not at all prescriptive – experienced leaders may well wish to use their own words. The minimum leadership requirement reflects a reality of church life: often too many jobs are done by too few people. However, the optimum number should point us in a more hopeful direction. We can encourage more people to take on a leadership role, however small, and in the spirit of these services we should be welcoming and inclusive. This means inviting those who do not usually do 'this sort of thing' to play a part; in particular, it means encouraging children and teenagers to get involved. Ideally, your leadership team should be as varied as the people in your all-sorts congregation.

Music Primary school children today will often sing in assembly, even if theirs is not a Church school; at secondary level, singing in school tends to be occasional rather than the norm. Hymn practice – once a regular feature of the school week – has given way to staffing pressures and the increasing demands of the curriculum. When children do sing in school, they are likely to sing secular songs, not traditional hymns. So unless children are regular churchgoers, they do not have the opportunity to become familiar with the wealth of church music, old and new, which should be theirs to enjoy. All-age worship can offer them just such an opportunity. If many in your all-age congregation are new to church, you might like to introduce some informal music teaching of your own, perhaps with a five-minute practice of that Sunday's hymns just before the service (this also works well as a way of 'warming up' a congregation!). Alternatively, you may like to invite your musicians to play through each hymn as people are coming into church, as a way of subliminally familiarising them with the tunes.

As any church which has ever tried to woo a new organist knows, we need to cherish our musicians. There are many opportunities to celebrate musical skill and enthusiasm in all-sorts worship: in my own church, we established The Really Brilliant Music Group, featuring a skilled accordion player, junior recorders and a variety of keen percussionists. There is undoubtedly a place for musical excellence – young pianists can flourish if given the chance to play in public – but there should also be opportunities for babies and toddlers to get their hands on a tambourine and join with the rest of us in making 'a joyful noise unto the Lord'. Every resources list for these services contains the catch-all item, 'Music and words': this will depend on your own church's musical resources, and could mean anything from a piano and hymn books to the youth group's rock band and words projected from a laptop onto an overhead screen.

Get stuck in!

You may choose to use these services straight off the page, exactly as written: complete scripts and instructions lay everything out clearly from the Welcome to the Conclusion. Alternatively, you and your worship team may prefer to use a particular service as a springboard for your own ideas, adapting the various components within the outline I have provided in order to suit your own purposes and available resources. Equally, you may simply want to dip into this book as a source of bright ideas, creative prayers and interactive storytelling to engage all ages. Whatever you do, feel free to engage with these services with energy and imagination. I hope that they help us all – all ages and all sorts – to join together in joyful, wholehearted worship.

All-sorts Worship in practice

Since the publication of *All-sorts Worship Years A and B*, I have been excited and encouraged to discover how different churches have been using the services. Feedback is always welcome, as are questions from those who would like to introduce their church to all-age worship but are unsure how to go about it.[11] For those people, and for all of us who continually reassess our offering of all-age worship, here are some of the different ways in which *All-sorts Worship* is being used.

---

11. Contact me via my website, www.clairebentonevans.com or on Twitter (@CBentonEvans).

A special occasion Some churches use a one-off *All-sorts* service to introduce or re-launch all-age worship. In Year C, I have included some services which are particularly suitable for a special occasion, such as a Christingle service, a Festival of Light (Candlemas) and a Pets' service.

The bonus service Some churches offer a separate all-age service once a month, in addition to the main Sunday morning service. One church I know well held a regular Sunday tea-time service which proved popular with families bringing children for baptism. The *All-sorts* services were adapted to accommodate the baptismal rite, usually after the Exploring and before the Prayer Action. For the post-service feast, they served tea, cake and other tea-time treats.

Family Sunday Other churches turn one main Sunday act of worship a month into an *All-sorts* service. This is usually a service of the Word, although some churches offer a short service of Holy Communion afterwards. For example, in an effort to bring new all-age congregations together with the regular Sunday morning worshippers, a church in Cornwall now holds a monthly non-Eucharistic *All-sorts* service at 9.15am, with chairs and tables arranged café-style. Afterwards, there is a cooked breakfast for all.

***All-sorts* Eucharist** Some churches combine an *All-sorts* service with *Common Worship* Holy Communion. The details of a particular service and the needs of an individual congregation will vary, but broadly speaking the service can be ordered as follows. Begin with a Prayer of Penitence and the Collect before the Introduction. Then replace one or more of the readings with the Storytelling and let the Exploring and/or the Activity do the job of a sermon, to be followed by the Creed. Use the Prayer Action instead of Intercessions, then move on to the Peace and the Eucharistic Prayer as usual. For an example, see the service for Harvest Thanksgiving.

Pick and mix These services can also be used piecemeal, and an index of themes is included at the back of the book to make this easier. For example, when leading our local

INTRODUCTION

Messy Church, I have often taken the Storytelling and Prayer Action from a service which suited our theme and used them for Messy Church's brief Celebration. The pick-and-mix approach might also be the way forward for parishes that are new to all-age worship and rather nervous of it. If the only available time for a family service is the 9.15 Holy Communion, then I would suggest introducing new *All-sorts* elements occasionally, over several months – perhaps a dramatic Storytelling one month and a creative Prayer Action the next. As these tie in with each Sunday's Lectionary readings, taken in isolation they might not seem like such a frightening departure from the norm. I have known many churchgoers who, given time, have warmed to something which at first they found rather strange: sensory and interactive prayers, in particular, tend to be well received. This 'softly, softly' approach may eventually make a congregation more ready to accept a full-on, no-holds-barred all-age worship experience!

A note on the Lectionary

This book completes my journey through *The Common Worship Lectionary*, years A, B and C, and looking back I can now appreciate how profoundly it has influenced these services. The Storytelling at the heart of each service is usually based on the Gospel, although the Old Testament reading is sometimes such a dramatic story that it needs to be told, too. When two stories are told in the same service, together they deepen our understanding of their common theme or throw light on some challenging questions. The other set readings shape the service's theme and language: for example, the Exploring section may borrow Paul's explanations from an Epistle while the words of a psalm may be echoed in a prayer.

The Lectionary readings have challenged me to make these *All-sorts* services – over 200 of them – as varied as possible. The Lectionary highlights the fact that Jesus said the same thing in many different ways. Through his teaching, his stories, his miracles and – above all – the example of his own life and death, he conveyed the same message: God loves you, so love God and one other. Service by service, I have had to find fresh and engaging ways of getting this message across. There is not a wordsearch in sight! Instead I have used picnics, a piñata, a shadow play, sugar cubes, an obstacle course, a conga, building bricks, archery, graffiti, a parachute, musical chairs, a maze, kites and more – anything which, when explored in context, might help people of all ages grasp Christ's message of love.

The Lectionary has also influenced my approach to the Bible in an all-age context. Had I not used its set readings as my starting point, I might have been tempted to cherry-pick the more obviously family-friendly passages of Scripture: stories of miracles and angels would have grabbed the headlines while the slaughter of the innocents stayed hidden in a footnote. As it is, I have worked with the set readings for each Sunday, however difficult or uncompromising some of them may be. In presenting hard stories in a way that children can understand, I have not been content to gloss over the difficulties with confident adult assertions. Instead, I have found myself looking at the Bible with a child's sharp eye for inconsistency and unfairness, interrogating Scripture with the kind of direct questions that children ask: why did God tell Isaac's dad to kill him? Why didn't God save the other babies in Bethlehem from Herod's soldiers? Why did God let Jesus die? If it was good news that Jesus came back from the dead, why did his friends run away and hide? Questions like these challenge us all to explore the Bible and our faith more deeply, so I have given them centre stage in many services.

The Common Worship Lectionary leads us all on a pilgrimage through the church year, and these Lectionary-based services offer children and families a chance to join us on the journey. Whether all-age worship takes place once a month or occasionally, in the main Sunday service or outside it, each service in *All-sorts Worship A, B* and *C* will allow people to walk a little way with us, past some familiar landmarks and perhaps into new pastures. Once people have shared part of the journey, they may be encouraged to walk further: for example, if your church held a well-attended all-age Palm Sunday service this year, why not consider an all-age Holy Week in the future? As a child at a local *All-sorts* Advent service said, happily waving her glow-stick, 'If church was always like this, I'd come every week!' Now there's a challenge . . .

Advent

First Sunday of Advent

Get ready!

Theme	Being prepared for Jesus
Scripture	Luke 21:25-36

Running order	Total: 50 minutes
Welcome	Making a Christmas 'To do' list *(10 minutes)*
Introduction	Opening the theme
Storytelling	The fig tree – visual storytelling *(5 minutes)*
Music	God is working his purpose out *(5 minutes)*
Exploring	When will the kingdom come? Visual exploration *(10 minutes)*
Activity	Making Advent lights *(10 minutes)*
Prayer action	Laying a path of lights and singing the Taizé chant, 'Wait for the Lord' *(5 minutes)*
Music	Lord of the future *(5 minutes)*
Conclusion	Closing prayer and invitation

Resources

- Music and words
- A flip chart or two large sheets of card. On the first sheet: '*Getting ready for Christmas – Things to do.*'
  On the second sheet: '*Getting ready for Jesus – Things to do.*
  1. Live our lives God's way.
  2. Share God's good news.'
- Some marker pens
- A small bare tree branch with twigs
- Sticky tack
- 24 clean jam jars or glass tumblers
- Red, orange and yellow tissue paper
- Diluted PVA glue, poured into shallow dishes
- Baby wipes for sticky hands
- 24 tea lights
- Matches and tapers
- Fig tree illustration *(see appendix)*
- Timeline *(see appendix)*
- Numbers 1–24, cut out of paper *(see appendix)*

Leaders

Minimum: 1

- Leader

Optimum: 6

- Leader *(Introduction and Conclusion)*
- Storyteller
- Music Leader
- Explorer
- Activity Leader
- Prayer Leader

Suggestions for additional music

- Lo, he comes with clouds descending
- Great is the darkness

Service

Welcome *As people arrive, invite them to add items to your giant list: 'Getting ready for Christmas – Things to do.' For example, 'Write Christmas cards' and 'Order turkey'.*

Introduction Today is the first Sunday of Advent. Who has an Advent calendar at home? *(Invite responses.)* The countdown to Christmas is beginning, and as we can see from our long list of things to do, we have a lot of preparations to make. In our Advent services, as we look forward to Christmas, we think about waiting for Jesus and preparing for his arrival. Jesus' message in today's story is: get ready! Let's hear what he said.

Storytelling Before Jesus died, he made a promise. He said that a lot of bad things would happen in the world, but that he would come back one day and put everything right: he would make sure that everything was done God's way. He called this the kingdom of God and said he would come in power and glory to establish it. He told his disciples that they had to be ready! He couldn't say when God's kingdom would come, so they had to look for the signs. This is how he explained it. *(Invite a volunteer to hold up the bare branch.)* 'It's like this fig tree. It is bare all winter – then leaves start to appear. (Stick on the seven leaves with sticky tack, one by one, leaf-side outwards.) When you see the leaves sprouting, you know that summer is on its way.' *(Invite another volunteer to hold up the picture of the sun.)*

Jesus said, 'It will be like this when I come back to earth. There will be signs that it's nearly time: *(Turn over each leaf in turn to show the words.)* there will be fighting in Jerusalem; there will be wars; there will be earthquakes; there will be hunger, illness and unhappiness. People will be worried and afraid. When you see all these things happening, you will know that the kingdom of God is near and I am on my way. *(Turn over the sun to show Jesus returning in glory.)* So get ready!'

Music God is working his purpose out

FIRST SUNDAY OF ADVENT

Exploring When Jesus knew he was going to die, he told his disciples what would happen in the future. He promised that he would come back, but that in the meantime, lots of things would go wrong – and these would all be signs that God's kingdom was just around the corner. Ever since, Christians have looked at the signs of the times and thought, 'This is it! Things are looking bad – Jesus must be coming back soon.' For example, when Jerusalem was destroyed by the Romans in AD 70, Christians at the time must have expected Jesus to come back then – but he didn't. An English Archbishop[2] predicted Jesus' return when he preached a sermon about all the bad things around him: violent crime, dishonest people in power, high taxes and unusually bad weather. England was fighting a war and people had been killed. This could have been a sermon from last week – but in fact it was preached in 1014, and the war he was talking about was against the Vikings.

So if Christians throughout the last 2000 years have seen signs that Jesus is on his way, isn't it time he was here? If we are going to think about this question, we need to think about time. The earth is four thousand six hundred million years old. Let's make this huge amount of time easier to imagine by picturing the earth as 46 years old. Its life has been this long.

Invite two volunteers to unroll the timeline and hold it out so that you can point to the different years as you mention them.

It has taken all this time for the earth to become the place we know, full of forests, seas, deserts and mountains. The earth was 11 when the first microscopic blobs of life appeared. The simplest animals – such as worms – arrived when the earth was 40. Dinosaurs didn't exist until the earth was over 45 years old. In this version of earth's life, human civilisation began only two hours ago! Put like this, the time between Jesus' death and now is the blink of an eye.[3]

---

2. Wulfstan, Archbishop of York in the *Sermon of the Wolf to the English*.
3. I am indebted to Arundhati Roy for this wonderful comparison: she compared the earth to a 46-year-old woman. This Earth Woman idea and the related facts and figures can be found in her book, *The God of Small Things* (Flamingo, 1997).

We are certainly living in the time before Jesus returns, but we don't know how long that time will last. Only God knows, and from his point of view a few hundred or a few thousand years must look pretty much the same. In the meantime, Jesus left clear instructions about what we should do: be ready! He told his disciples to be prepared for his return by living good lives and spreading God's good news. So at this time of year, as our Advent calendars count us down to Christmas and we rush to make all our preparations for the big day, let's not forget that we need to get ready for the biggest day of all: the day when Jesus comes back in power and glory. Our 'To do' list for this is short and easy to remember: *(Flip over the Christmas 'To do' list to reveal a second, shorter list: 'Getting ready for Jesus – Things to do.')* We need to live our lives God's way and share God's good news, not just during Advent, but every day.

Activity

Getting ready for Jesus is often described as preparing the way. Today we will make special Advent candle holders, which we will use to light a pathway.

Invite people to gather round the craft tables and decorate the 24 plain glass jars or tumblers with flame-coloured tissue paper and a number for each one. Tear the tissue paper roughly into pieces and soak them in the diluted PVA – they will stick to the outside of the glass in colourful, overlapping layers. Stick the numbers on last, in the same way. As each glass is finished, place an unlit tea light inside it. Ask people to hold their Advent lights and move so that odd-numbered lights are on one side of the aisle and even-numbered ones on the other. Light the candles with a taper.

Now let's lay a path of Advent lights, as a reminder that we need to make way for Jesus in our lives.

Prayer action

Turn off the lights in church. Encourage people to lay down their Advent lights in order, 1–24, on either side of the aisle as it leads up to the altar.

As we look at this path of lights leading us through the days of Advent, let us pray with a simple chant: 'Wait for the Lord'.

Sing the chant together.

O Lord, show us your way.
Guide us in your truth.[4]
Amen.

Music Lord of the future

Conclusion Lord of the past, present and future,
may we remember your birth,
look forward to your coming
and know your presence with us now.
Amen.

Give notices, announce the next all-age service and invite everyone to the feast.

You may like to keep these Advent lights around the church and light the appropriate number at the beginning of your other Advent services.

---

4. 'Wait for the Lord', Taizé Community,© Ateliers et Presses de Taizé.

Second Sunday of Advent

The voice in the wilderness

Theme	God's prophets
Scripture	Luke 3:1-6

Running order	Total: 50 minutes
Welcome	Creating a wilderness landscape *(10 minutes)*
Music	Long ago, prophets knew *(5 minutes)*
Introduction	Opening the theme
Storytelling	Reading Luke 3:1-6, then a modern version *(5 minutes)*
Exploring/Activity	Where are today's prophets? Active and visual exploration *(20 minutes)*
Prayer action	Praying for the world – interactive prayer with a world map *(5 minutes)*
Music	Make way, make way *(5 minutes)*
Conclusion	Closing prayer and invitation

Resources

- Music and words
- Lots of empty boxes and containers
- Several large, plain sheets
- *(Optional)* Some pebbles and stones
- The Peters Projection map. A large, laminated version is produced by Oxfam and available from amazon.co.uk. Mount it on a portable pin board for this service
- Map pins (or spot stickers, if preferred)

Leaders

Minimum: 2

- Leader
- Storyteller

Optimum: 5

- Leader *(Introduction and Conclusion)*
- Storyteller
- Music Leader
- Explorer/Activity Leader
- Prayer Leader

Suggestions for additional music

- On Jordan's bank the Baptist's cry
- Inspired by love and anger

Service

Welcome *As people arrive, invite them to create a wilderness landscape at the front of church: use lots of different boxes and empty containers to make rough terrain, then cover the whole thing with large, plain sheets. You may like to add some pebbles and stones on top.*

Music Long ago, prophets knew

Introduction Our Advent story today takes us to the wilderness. This was a wild, empty place near Jerusalem, full of mountains and deep crevasses, rather like the landscape we have created in church this morning. It was home to John the Baptist. Let's hear his story from the Bible.

Storytelling

Storyteller — In the fifteenth year of the reign of Emperor Tiberius, when Pontius Pilate was governor of Judea, and Herod was ruler of Galilee, and his brother Philip ruler of the region of Ituraea and Trachonitis, and Lysanias ruler of Abilene, during the high-priesthood of Annas and Caiaphas, the word of God came to John son of Zechariah in the wilderness.

Leader — I'm sorry to interrupt, but there were a lot of old emperors, kings and rulers in that bit! I wonder if we could bring John's story a bit more up to date? And make it a bit more local?

Storyteller — In the *second* year of *Barack Obama's* presidency, when *Queen Elizabeth II* was on the throne and *David Cameron* was Prime Minister of Great Britain, and *Michael D. Higgins* was the President of Ireland, during the time when *Rowan Williams* was Archbishop of Canterbury, the word of God came to Zach's son, John, in the middle of *Bodmin Moor*.[5] He went into all the surrounding areas, proclaiming a baptism of repentance for the forgiveness of sins, as it is written in the book of the words of the prophet Isaiah:

---

5. Replace the italics with current leaders and the last with a local area which might be described as 'wilderness'.

'The voice of one crying out in the wilderness:
"Prepare the way of the Lord,
make his paths straight.
Every valley shall be filled,
and every mountain and hill shall be made low,
and the crooked shall be made straight,
and the rough ways made smooth;
and all flesh shall see the salvation of God."'

Exploring/Activity

Did you notice something when we updated the first part of John's story? There was a great long list of important people, but we passed by them all and ended up with a man on his own in the wilderness who had no title and no power – yet the word of God came to him. John, a wild loner, was chosen to be God's spokesman.

Let's have a closer look at what God's spokesman said. He went around 'proclaiming a baptism of repentance for the forgiveness of sins' – he told people to say sorry for the things they had done wrong, get baptised and be forgiven. In other words, he told people to *change*, because Jesus was on his way. The Gospel writer says that John was fulfilling an old prophecy about a lone voice in the wilderness, crying out for change before the Saviour comes. The prophecy used a powerful image:

Every valley shall be filled,
and every mountain and hill shall be made low,
and the crooked shall be made straight,
and the rough ways made smooth.

This voice calls for a change so radical, so momentous, it would be like a reshaping of geography. Look again at the wilderness landscape we made earlier, with all its hills and valleys. Can we transform it into a flat plain? Come and help me move mountains!

Encourage everyone to come forward and rearrange the boxes and empty containers to make a level plain. Cover it again with the sheets.

This changed landscape gives us a picture of the kind of change John was calling for. He wanted people to transform their lives by leaving their old ways behind them and starting afresh, with their sights set on Jesus. This change would cause such an upheaval it would be like moving mountains – but it would be a change for the better. This hilly desert is now a flat plain, which is much easier to cross; John wanted people to change their lives so that they would be readier to follow Jesus.

John the Baptist gives us a clear picture of what a prophet is like. As our updated version of his story showed, he was an ordinary person with no political power – and yet God chose him to call for change. He spoke with authority, 'proclaiming' what people needed to do. So this prophet was an ordinary person who spoke with authority about the need for change. Does this description ring any bells? Prophets did not die out in biblical times: all around us today there are ordinary people protesting about the way things are and crying out for change. Not all these voices are true, but we need to listen to them to decide whether God is speaking through any of them. Some call us to stop relying on fossil fuels or capitalism, and changes like this would be as massive as turning a hilly desert into a flat plain.

Let's look at just one example which, coincidentally, concerns geography. Two ordinary men worked on ideas for a new map of the world. One was a clergyman called Gall and the other was an amateur historian called Peters. The map Peters produced, using Gall's ideas, presented all the countries of the world based on exact comparisons of their surface area. It looks like this.

Hold up the Peters Projection map.

On traditional maps, Greenland looks the same size as Africa. In fact, Africa is 14 times larger, so this map accurately represents that huge difference in size. Come and have a closer look at this new way of seeing the world.

Encourage people to come forward. Allow plenty of time for them to look and ask questions.

This new map has changed the way many people think, because it challenges our assumptions about wealth and power. The richest countries are not necessarily the biggest; the countries which dominate the map contain some of the largest populations and the poorest people. Many charities and political organisations now use this map to try and change the way people think.

This map is just one example of what we might call a modern prophetic voice, calling for change. So remember John the Baptist – the lone voice in the wilderness – and keep your eyes and ears open for other prophets. They will be calling for change, calling us to move mountains, calling us to change the world!

Prayer action   We regularly say prayers for the world: today we will use this new view of the world to help us picture it accurately as we pray for particular people and places. In a time of quiet, bring before God those individuals or countries for whom you would like to pray. Come forward and place a pin in the map to mark the subject of your prayer.

Place your own pin in the map and encourage others to do so during a period of silence.

Creator God,
you hold the world in your hands.
Hear our prayers
in Jesus' name.
Amen.

Music   Make way, make way

Conclusion   Lord of the wilderness,
as we go out into the world,
may we hear the cries for change
and listen for the call of your Holy Spirit.
Amen.

Give notices, announce the next all-age service and invite everyone to the feast.

Third Sunday of Advent

What should we do?

Theme	Bearing fruits worthy of repentance
Scripture	Luke 3:7-18

Running order Total: 50 minutes

Welcome	Discovering facts and information from charities *(5 minutes)*
Music	O comfort my people *(5 minutes)*
Introduction	Opening the theme
Storytelling	John's challenge – interactive sketch *(10 minutes)*
Exploring	What should we do? *(5 minutes)*
Activity	Creating a display of charities' information *(15 minutes)*
Prayer action	Sticky-note prayers *(5 minutes)*
Music	Colours of day *(5 minutes)*
Conclusion	Closing prayer and invitation

Resources

- Music and words
- Charity information *(see appendix)*
- Two cards with the crowd's lines *(see appendix)*
- Title: 'What should we do?' *(see appendix)*
- A large piece of board
- Scissors
- Glue sticks
- Sticky notes
- Pens

Leaders

Minimum: 4

- Leader
- Cast x 3

Optimum: 8

- Leader *(Introduction and Conclusion)*
- Cast x 3:

    John, wearing a rough tunic and some fur

    Tax-collector, wearing a rich robe

    Roman soldier, wearing a tunic and items of Roman armour *(see appendix)*

- Music Leader
- Explorer
- Activity Leader
- Prayer Leader

Suggestions for additional music

- Make way, make way
- Lord Jesus Christ

Service

Welcome *As people arrive, invite them to discover facts and information from the array of charity leaflets and posters which you have displayed around the church.*

Music O comfort my people

Introduction Today is the third Sunday of Advent. Our first hymn was a wonderful Advent promise of comfort and joy: the Lord said, 'O comfort my people and calm all their fear, and tell them the time of salvation draws near.' Throughout Old Testament times, God's people expected a Saviour who would put everything right: he would feed the hungry, heal the sick, reward the good and punish wrongdoers. He would bring justice, peace and prosperity. So imagine how excited people were when they met someone who looked as if he might be the Saviour! His name was John the Baptist.

Storytelling I'm going to need your help to tell this story. This is John, and you are the people who follow him down to the River Jordan to repent, be forgiven and get baptised. You're a mixed bunch – mostly Jews, but there are some strangers amongst you and even a few unpopular but feared Roman soldiers. As the crowd, you have two lines.

Hold up the placards and encourage people to say all together, 'So what should we do?' and 'BOO!' (as if to a pantomime villain).

Now let's hear what John said to his followers.

John You 'orrible lot! Who warned you about Judgement Day? You say you're sorry for your wrongdoing. Now show that you really mean to live a good life: do some good! You've got to walk it like you talk it! And don't even begin to think, 'We're OK – we're related to Abraham!' So what? Your family tree won't save you! You're like an orchard, and the farmer's coming with his axe. Every tree that doesn't produce good fruit will be cut down and thrown on the bonfire!

All	*(hold up the sign)* So what should we do?
John	If you've got more clothes than you can wear, share them with people who don't have enough. If you've got more food than you need, share it with anyone who's hungry.
Tax-collector	I'm a tax-collector, like my brothers.
All	*(hold up the sign)* BOO!
Tax-collector	What should we do?
John	Collect your taxes fairly, and don't take an extra cut for yourself.
Soldier	Me and the boys are with the Roman Army.
All	*(hold up the sign)* BOO!
Soldier	OY! THAT'S ENOUGH OF THAT! *(to John)* What should we do?
John	Don't use violence to bully money out of people. Make do with your pay.
Tax-collector	*(to the congregation)* I reckon this one could be the Messiah!
John	You're wrong. I'm baptising you with water, but someone is coming who's much more powerful than me. I'm not worthy to lick the soles of his boots. He'll baptise you with the Holy Spirit and with fire. He's like the farmer who separates the wheat grain from the stalks: he puts the wheat in his barn and chucks the stalks on the bonfire!
Exploring	John certainly was a fiery preacher! He told people to say sorry for the things they had done wrong, and he baptised them as a sign of God's forgiveness – but that wasn't enough. He wanted action, not just words. John guessed that his Jewish followers would argue that they were a special case, because of their history as God's chosen people, but he wouldn't let them off the hook. John's strong words made people ask a really important question: 'So what should we do?' He gave some practical examples: share your clothes, share your food, be honest and fair with money, don't take more than is yours.

John's message is for us, too. In church we regularly ask for God's forgiveness, we listen to his word and we pray, but none of that is going to make any difference if it doesn't change what we do in our everyday lives. Like John's faithful Jewish crowd, we might be tempted to think, 'But we're fine as we are! We're good churchgoers!' Like them, we should listen to John's words and ask, 'So what should we do?' Remember that John gave the crowd some clear, straightforward answers that were related to their lives and their work: our activity today might give us some answers, too.

Activity

When you came into church, you had an opportunity to look at the information from charities. It shows us how many people and places need help. Everything here suggests answers to the question we should be asking ourselves as individuals, as a church and as a community: 'So what should we do?' Let's cut out information and pictures about particular needs that have caught our eye. We will cover this board with our cuttings to make a thought-provoking display.

Allow plenty of time for people to cut out pictures and clippings and stick them on the board to form a colourful, informative collage. Add the title 'So what should we do?' and display the board at the front of the church.

In a moment, we will use this display to stimulate our prayers, but I'll leave you with this thought. We began today's service with God's Advent promise of a Saviour who would put everything right. Jesus is that Saviour, but this display reminds us that a great deal is still wrong with the world. So what has happened? Why hasn't Jesus righted every wrong? A wise person once said, 'I want to ask God why he doesn't do something about poverty and injustice, but I'm afraid he will ask me the same question.'

Prayer action

We will be using sticky notes in our prayers today. Many of us use sticky notes to remind us of jobs that need doing: we might scribble 'Buy milk' on one and stick it to the fridge door. Today we are thinking about

THIRD SUNDAY OF ADVENT

our own lives, our church, our local community and our world, as we ask God this question: 'So what should we do?' Let's rest in God's presence and ask this question now.

Pause for a short time.

If you have an answer to your question, you may like to write or draw it on your sticky note, as a reminder of a job that needs doing. If you are still waiting for an answer, then leave your sticky note blank to remind you that you are still looking for something good, kind or helpful to do.

Pause for a short time.

Let us pray.

Heavenly Father,
in all that we say and do
may we look to you and ask,
'So what should we do?'
Help us to recognise your answer.
Amen.

Please take your sticky note home with you. Put it where you will notice it and be reminded of your prayer.

Music Colours of day

Conclusion In the Old Testament, there is a prophet who gives an answer to the question we have been asking today. He says, 'What does the Lord require of you but to do justice, and to love kindness, and to walk humbly with your God?'[6] Let us pray.

May we do justice,
and love kindness,
and walk humbly with you, our God.
Amen.

Give notices, announce the next all-age service and invite everyone to the feast.

---

6. Micah 6:8.

Fourth Sunday of Advent

It's you!

Theme	Recognising God's goodness
Scripture	Luke 1:39-55

Running order	Total: 50 minutes
Welcome/Activity	Making footprints to mark the Advent countdown *(10 minutes)*
Introduction	Opening the theme
Music	Like a candle flame *(5 minutes)*
Storytelling	Mary and Elizabeth – sketch *(10 minutes)*
Exploring	What happens when Mary meets Elizabeth? *(10 minutes)*
Music	Tell out, my soul *(5 minutes)*
Prayer action	Glitter prayer *(5 minutes)*
Music	Lord, the light of your love *(5 minutes)*
Conclusion	Closing prayer and invitation

FOURTH SUNDAY OF ADVENT

Resources

- Music and words
- Thin card for Advent footprints
- Scissors
- Felt pens
- Stick-on numbers, 1–24
- *(Optional)* Christmas stickers, self-adhesive stars and glitter glue for decorating the footprints
- At least two bowls of loose gold or silver glitter

Leaders

Minimum: 3

- Leader
- Cast x 2

Optimum: 8

- Leader *(Introduction and Conclusion)*
- Storyteller
- Cast x 2 (wearing traditional robes):
  Mary
  Elizabeth
- Music Leader
- Explorer
- Activity Leader
- Prayer Leader

Suggestions for additional music

- See him lying on a bed of straw
- The angel Gabriel from heaven came

Service

Welcome/Activity *As people arrive, invite them to make footprints to mark the Advent countdown. You will need 24 footprints (individual or pairs). Encourage people to draw round their feet, with shoes on or off, then cut out the footprints and decorate them with a Christmas theme. Stick numbers on the finished footprints. Invite everyone to return to their seats as you and some volunteers lay out the footprints in order, leading from the church door to the front. If your church has a crib scene, end the line of footprints there.*

Introduction Today is the fourth Sunday of Advent and our Advent countdown is almost over! This line of footprints leads us through the church and reminds us that Christmas is nearly here.

Music Like a candle flame

Storytelling

Leader Previously in the Christmas story... Mary was visited by an angel who told her she was going to have a baby – God's Son. The angel also gave Mary a second piece of amazing news: her cousin, Elizabeth, was six months pregnant, even though she was an old lady. Without delay, Mary hurried off to see Elizabeth. This meant a five-day walk from Nazareth to Elizabeth's home in the Judean hills. In our story today, the two cousins remember what happened.

Mary I couldn't talk to anyone about the angel's visit without them shouting at me. My parents were horrified that I was pregnant before I was married. Joseph was furious. People in the market place yelled insults at me.

Elizabeth So you came to see me. I couldn't talk to anyone, either, since my husband, Zechariah, was struck dumb after a visit from an angel. Whenever he needed anything, he scratched out messages on a writing tablet, but that's no way to hold a conversation. He was left speechless because he didn't believe the angel's news that I would have a son. Me! At my age! We'd both given up hope of ever having children. But

FOURTH SUNDAY OF ADVENT

	the angel said it was so, and sure enough, in the weeks that followed my body began to change.
Mary	By the time I arrived, you were six months gone and you looked radiant!
Elizabeth	And you looked as white as a sheet, bless you. I think you were still in shock.
Mary	I was so relieved to have arrived in one piece, I called your name across the fields!
Elizabeth	And my boy gave the most enormous kick! As if he was leaping for joy.
Mary	You called me over and I tried to tell you what had happened to me –
Elizabeth	But I wanted you to feel my baby move. What a welcome for you and your son!
Mary	I wanted to explain, so you wouldn't judge me and shout at me like everyone else did, but –
Elizabeth	I understood, and I told you that you were blessed!
Mary	And my baby was blessed, too!
Elizabeth	I was right. Suddenly all those extraordinary promises which Zechariah had scratched out on his tablet made sense. My son was filled with the Holy Spirit, and he was going to prepare people for the Lord! Even before our boys were born, my John recognised your Jesus!
Mary	I was so happy! I knew I was welcomed by you and completely loved by God. My joy overflowed in a great rush of words. Do you remember what I said?
	My soul magnifies the Lord,
	and my spirit rejoices in God my Saviour,
	for he has looked with favour on the lowliness of his servant.
	Surely, from now on all generations will call me blessed;
	for the Mighty One has done great things for me,
	and holy is his name.
Elizabeth	His mercy is for those who fear him
	from generation to generation.
	He has shown strength with his arm;
	he has scattered the proud in the thoughts of their hearts.

> He has brought down the powerful from their thrones,
> and lifted up the lowly;
> he has filled the hungry with good things,
> and sent the rich away empty.

Mary and Elizabeth

> He has helped his servant Israel,
> in remembrance of his mercy,
> according to the promise he made to our ancestors,
> to Abraham and to his descendants for ever.

Exploring

This meeting between Mary and her cousin Elizabeth was very special.

Bring forward Elizabeth.

First of all, there was Elizabeth, six months pregnant in her old age. Her baby was miraculous: he had been announced by an angel, who told his father that he was to be called John. The angel promised that John would be filled with God's Holy Spirit and would prepare his people for the coming of their Saviour. Elizabeth knew this, but she didn't know where or when the promised Saviour would arrive. Then Mary turned up, out of the blue, and Elizabeth's unborn baby *leapt* at the sound of Mary's voice. All heavily pregnant women feel their babies move, but there must have been something special about that kick! As Mary's news tumbled out, Elizabeth knew for certain that Mary was carrying the Saviour – the One whose arrival her own son was destined to herald.

Bring forward Mary.

Then there was Mary, exhausted from four or five days' walking. She had set off, the Bible tells us, 'with haste' as soon as she had received the angel's life-changing news. The journey would have given her time to wrestle with the things she was now required to believe. Could she, a virgin, really be pregnant? There were no pregnancy tests in those days! And as for her elderly cousin Elizabeth, also expecting her first child – could that really be true? But as soon as Mary saw Elizabeth, and saw her great round belly, she knew that the angel had been right. She had real proof

FOURTH SUNDAY OF ADVENT

that God's miracles were taking place, and that the biggest miracle of all was happening inside her own body: God's Son was getting ready to be born into the world.

For both Mary and Elizabeth, this meeting was a wonderful moment of recognition. They both suddenly realised that God had kept his promises to them and to their people. That realisation was like a great big wonderful 'YES!' It was so big that Mary couldn't keep it in: elsewhere in the Bible she is quiet, pondering things in her heart, but at this moment she overflowed with a song of praise.

This moment of recognition marks the real beginning of the Christmas story. Before long it was the turn of the wise men to realise that God had kept his promise to send a Messiah. Then it was the world's turn, and ours. At Christmas we celebrate that wonderful moment when we know, beyond all doubt, that God loves us and keeps his promises to us. We know it because he gave us his Son. That is what our Advent countdown looks forward to: in church today, our numbered footprints lead us towards Christmas and our celebration of the moment when human beings first met God in the baby Jesus. We can still meet him today and, like the baby leaping in Elizabeth's womb, say, 'It's you!'

Music   Tell out, my soul

Prayer action   When Mary poured out her joy in a song of praise, she described God's great goodness and rejoiced at how much he had done for her and her people – far more than anyone could possibly deserve. In our prayers today, we will give thanks for God's goodness, and to help us we will use this glitter.[7]

Hold up a handful of glitter and let it fall from your fingers.

---

7. Thanks to Jim Benton-Evans for this inspired idea.

Like loose glitter, God's goodness gets everywhere. It shines in the light and in the darkest corners. Like glitter that sticks to our fingers and clothes, or turns up unexpectedly in our hair, God's goodness won't give up on us. Even if we don't notice it at first, we may suddenly be surprised by the realisation that his love has never left us.

Pass the bowls of glitter to the people sitting closest to you.

Pass round these bowls of glitter and let some run through your fingers. As you do so, give thanks for the good things in your life. Let us pray.

Pass round the bowls of glitter and pause for a moment of silence.

God of love,
in your goodness, you shower us with the shining gifts of your grace.
We thank you for your lavish generosity.
Amen.

Music   Lord, the light of your love

Conclusion   After this service, when you find bits of glitter stuck to your clothes, remember that those sparkling fragments are like God's goodness, which finds its way into all our lives. Let us pray.

God of grace,
help us to recognise you
wherever we may find you,
in Jesus' name.
Amen.

Give notices, announce the next all-age service and invite everyone to the feast.

Christmas Eve

Christingle

Theme	The light of the world
Scripture	Luke 1:67-79; Matthew 5:14-16

Running order — Total: 50 minutes

Welcome	Dressing up the Christingle volunteers *(5 minutes)*
Introduction	Opening the theme
Music	Once in royal David's city *(5 minutes)*
Exploring	What does Christingle mean? Visual exploration *(5 minutes)*
Activity 1	Creating living Christingles *(10 minutes)*
Music	It's rounded like an orange *(5 minutes)*
Prayer action	Sharing the oranges – active thanksgiving *(5 minutes)*
Activity 2	Distributing and lighting Christingles *(10 minutes)*
Music	Away in a manger *(5 minutes)*
Conclusion	Closing prayer and invitation

Resources

- Ordinary Christingles, made in advance, enough for one each (see The Children's Society website for further details: www.childrenssociety.org.uk)
- Giant Christingle (visit www.childrenssociety.org.uk to download a useful guide on how to make these)
- Music and words
- Christingle costumes: at least three, but as many as you can manage. Each child will need:
  – a simple white tunic or extra-large white T-shirt
  – a flame headdress *(see appendix)*
  – a small bowl or basket of satsumas, clementines or mandarin oranges. You will need enough oranges for everyone
- A very large map of the world *(see appendix)*
- A wide red ribbon or strip of red fabric
- Several collection plates
- Matches and tapers
- Containers for orange peel

Leaders

Minimum: 1

- Leader

Optimum: 6

- Leader *(Introduction and Conclusion)*
- Activity Leader 1 and 2
- Music Leader
- Explorer
- Prayer Leader

Suggestions for additional music

- While shepherds watched
- Hark, the herald-angels sing
- Mary had a baby

Service

Welcome *As people arrive, invite some children to dress up as Christingle candles (as many as you have costumes). Explain that they will be helping you later on in the service.*

Introduction Welcome to our Christingle celebration. Everyone will have a chance to join in today's service: there will be things to look at, things to listen to and things to think about. Of course, there will also be treats to eat!

Music Once in royal David's city

Exploring Who has been to a Christingle service before? *(Invite responses.)* I wonder if you can tell me what the different parts of the Christingle mean?

Hold up your giant Christingle. Invite children to come up and point to the different parts and tell you what they mean. Elicit the following answers, which you may like to repeat when the children have finished.

The familiar meaning of the Christingle is this.

- The orange represents the world.
- The sweets and fruit represent the fruits of creation – all the good things that God has given us.
- The red ribbon represents Jesus' love and the blood he shed for us.
- The candle represents Jesus, the light of the world.

We are used to this way of understanding the Christingle. However, there is another way. Could I have my volunteer Christingle candles, please?

Activity 1 *Bring forward your volunteers.*

The Christingle candle reminds us that Jesus is the Light of the world. Today's Bible reading looks forward to Jesus' birth, saying, 'the dawn from on high will break upon us, to give light to those who sit in darkness.' Yet Jesus told us that *we* are the light of the world, too. He said this to his followers: 'You are the light of the world . . . let your light shine before others, so that they may see your good works and give glory to your Father in heaven.' So my helpers here have dressed up as Christingle candles to remind us that each one of us is the light of the world. It's our job to show God's goodness to other people.

Now the Christingle candle stands in an orange, which represents the world. Here is another representation of the world for our living Christingle candles to stand on.

Show the map of the world and lay it down.

This reminds us that we live in the real world – we have our feet on the ground. We must show God's love in our everyday lives.

Invite your volunteers to stand on the map.

The Christingle has a red ribbon around the orange, representing Jesus' love. Here's a red ribbon for our living Christingles.

Lay the big red ribbon on the map.

Now this red ribbon looks as if it is marking out a path. Jesus' love shows us the way to go, because we have his loving example to follow.

Invite the volunteers to stand on the ribbon.

Finally, the Christingle has sweets and fruit sticking out of it, reminding us of the fruits of creation.

Hand the baskets or bowls of little oranges to your volunteers and encourage them to hold the fruit out at arm's length.

These living Christingles are holding out their tasty treats not for one person to munch, but for us all to share. Please keep your little oranges when you get them, because we will share them out later as part of our prayers.

Encourage your volunteers to move among the congregation, handing out the oranges, then return to their positions at the front.

So these living Christingles are here to remind us that we all have a job to do. We are shining lights who live in the real world. Our job is to follow Jesus' loving example and share the good things we have been given.

Give your volunteers a round of applause and ask them to sit down.

This Christingle service is raising money for The Children's Society, which helps vulnerable children and young people. Our living Christingles have reminded us to be the light of the world, to love others and to share what we have. Today we have a chance to do just that. However little money we have, let's share some of it with children who really need our help.

Take a collection for The Children's Society during the next hymn.

Music It's rounded like an orange

Prayer action Today we will use these little oranges in our prayers. These sweet and tasty fruits are at their best at this time of year. They remind us of all the good things that God's creation produces for us to enjoy. We'll hold these oranges in our hands as we rest quietly in God's presence. Let's say thank you in our hearts for all the good things he has given us.

Pause.

Now let's peel the oranges.

Allow time for everyone to do this.

Before we eat our oranges, we remember what we have learnt today. Let's share! Please give a piece of your orange to the person next to you, then let's all enjoy this fruit.

People exchange pieces of orange and then eat. Pass round containers for the peel.

Let us pray.

God of all good things,
thank you for your great goodness.
Help us to share your gifts.
Amen.

Activity 2 *Distribute and light the Christingles according to your church's custom. Turn off the lights and sing the following carol by candlelight.*

Music Away in a manger

Conclusion God of Love,
let us be living Christingles.
May we be the light of the world,
making a difference to people around us.
May we live in the real world,
keeping our feet on the ground.
May we be guided by your love,
following your way.
May we be thankful for your gifts,
sharing them with all.
Amen.

Give notices, announce the next all-age service and invite everyone to the feast.

Christmas

Christmas Day*

God is with us

Theme	The Nativity
Scripture	Luke 2:1-20
Running order	Total: 50 minutes
Welcome/Activity	Preparing the manger and swaddling the baby Jesus *(5 minutes)*
Introduction	Opening the theme
Storytelling 1	The angel visits Mary – DVD clip *(4 minutes)*
Music	The angel Gabriel from heaven came *(5 minutes)*
Storytelling 2	The shepherds hear the news – DVD clip *(1 minute)*
Music	While shepherds watched *(5 minutes)*
Storytelling 3	The wise men follow the star – DVD clip *(2 minutes)*
Music	We three kings *(5 minutes)*
Storytelling 4	Jesus is born – DVD clip *(3 minutes)*
Music	Silent night *(5 minutes)*
Exploring	What did the people in the stable come to know? *(5 minutes)*
Prayer action	God is with us – tangible prayer *(5 minutes)*
Music	O come, all ye faithful *(5 minutes)*
Conclusion	Closing prayer and invitation

* This service is a visual, all-age version of the familiar 'Nine lessons and carols' format. It could be used at any time during the Christmas season.

Resources

- Music and words
- Laptop, projector and screen
- Speakers
- A DVD of the *The Nativity* (BBC, 2011). This is available from amazon.co.uk. You will need the following clips (DVD timings given in minutes):
  – the angel visits Mary (26:58–31:19)
  – the shepherds hear the news (1hr 42:13–1hr 43:29)
  – the wise men follow the star (1hr 14:45–1hr 16:25)
  – Jesus is born (1hr 49:21-1hr 52:26)
- A manger or wooden fruit box
- Some hay
- A baby Jesus doll
- Lots of rough strips of white cotton fabric
- Lots of short pieces of white ribbon
- Two bowls

Leaders

Minimum: 1

- Leader

Optimum: 6

- Leader *(Introduction and Conclusion)*
- Activity Leader
- Storyteller/IT technician
- Music Leader
- Explorer
- Prayer Leader

Suggestions for additional music

- Ding dong, merrily on high!
- O little town of Bethlehem
- See him lying on a bed of straw

Service

Welcome/Activity *As people arrive, invite children to prepare the manger by filling it with hay. Then give them the baby Jesus doll and lots of strips of white cloth. Explain what 'swaddling' is and invite them to have a go.*

Introduction Happy Christmas! Welcome to our joyful celebration today. This morning, some of you have been helping to recreate the most important part of our Christmas story: the baby Jesus, wrapped in swaddling clothes, lying in the manger. *(Show the manger and child.)* Every Christmas, schools put on Nativity plays to tell the wonderful story of Jesus' birth. Today we are going to enjoy a fresh version of the Nativity story, which was made by the BBC. Let's begin at the beginning, with Mary. She is about to meet an angel.

Storytelling 1 *Show the first clip: the angel visits Mary.*

Music The angel Gabriel from heaven came

Storytelling 2 *Show the second clip: the shepherds hear the news.*

Music While shepherds watched

Storytelling 3 *Show the third clip: the wise men follow the star.*

Music We three kings

Storytelling 4 *Show the fourth clip: Jesus is born.*

Music Silent night

Exploring The final moments of *The Nativity* showed us the scene which sums up Christmas: the baby in the manger, watched over by Mary and Joseph, worshipped by shepherds and kings. During this version of the story, we learned why all those people were there. Mary and Joseph had been rejected by the people of Bethlehem, who thought Mary's pregnancy was shameful. They were in the stable with the animals because it was the only houseroom anyone would give them. Joseph was by his fiancée's side, even though he had been so angry about her pregnancy that he had come close to leaving her.

The shepherds were there because an angel had promised a Saviour who would care for poor people like them. They wondered if such a thing could really be true. The wise men were there because their study of the stars showed that an old prophecy was about to be fulfilled: the king of the Jews, the Messiah, was to be born in Bethlehem.

When Jesus was born, all these people came to know the truth. Mary knew that God had kept his promise to her. Joseph looked around at the strangers worshipping Jesus and knew that the child in the manger was indeed God's Son – and his beloved Mary had told him the truth. The shepherds knew that God had not forgotten them, because he had sent his own Son to save them. The wise men knew that God's ancient promises had been fulfilled: this baby was the long-awaited Messiah.

We celebrate Christmas because it is the moment when we, too, know the truth. God became a human being and lived among us. As the angel in our first clip put it, Jesus formed 'a bridge between heaven and earth for all time'. Through Jesus, we can know God. We know that he loves us and is always with us. What news could be better than that?

Prayer action In our prayers today, we give thanks that God is with us. We remember the reality of the baby in the manger. As a focus for our prayers, please take a piece of this white ribbon to remind you of the swaddling clothes that Mary wrapped around her child.

Hand round the bowls of ribbons and encourage everyone to take one.

Let us pray.

Heavenly Father,
thank you for the gift of your Son.
The body that Mary swaddled with such love
was the same body he sacrificed with such love
for our sake on the cross.
We give thanks today for the birth of Jesus,
our Saviour and friend,
the Light of the world.
Amen.

Please take home your ribbon – your piece of swaddling cloth. Keep it in your purse or wallet as a reminder of Jesus' birth.

Music O come, all ye faithful

Conclusion May the love of God
and the peace of Christ
fill our hearts and homes this Christmas.
Amen.

Give notices, announce the next all-age service and invite everyone to the feast.

First Sunday of Christmas
Missing!

Theme	Jesus shared our humanity
Scripture	Luke 2:41-52

Running order — Total: 50 minutes

Welcome/Activity	Exploring the abandoned campsite *(10 minutes)*
Introduction	Opening the theme
Storytelling	Visual and interactive retelling of Luke 2:41-52 *(10 minutes)*
Music	Born in the night, Mary's child *(5 minutes)*
Activity	Speech bubbles – imagining the family conversation *(10 minutes)*
Exploring	What does this story tell us about Jesus? *(5 minutes)*
Prayer action	'In my Father's house' – contemplative prayer *(5 minutes)*
Music	Who would think that what was needed *(5 minutes)*
Conclusion	Closing prayer and invitation

Resources

- Music and words
- The contents of Jesus' family campsite *(see appendix)*
- Speech bubbles, in every pew or row of seats *(see appendix)*
- Pens and pencils
- A board for displaying the speech bubbles
- Sticky tack or drawing pins

Leaders

Minimum: 1

- Leader

Optimum: 6

- Leader *(Introduction and Conclusion)*
- Storyteller
- Music Leader
- Explorer
- Activity Leader
- Prayer Leader

Suggestions for additional music

- It came upon the midnight clear
- Lord, I lift your name on high

Service

Welcome/Activity *As people arrive, invite them to explore the scene you have laid out at the front of the church. It is a hastily abandoned family campsite on the pilgrim route to Jerusalem – but don't announce this yet!*

Introduction We've got a strange, untidy scene in front of us today. Can you help me puzzle it out? *(Invite responses to the following questions, valuing all contributions. The aim is to engage interest rather than elicit the correct answers.)*

- I wonder what all this is for?
- I wonder where in the world this scene might belong – in this country, or somewhere else?
- I wonder who this belongs to?
- I wonder what has happened here?

Storytelling This is what happened. Jesus and his family often went on a pilgrimage to Jerusalem. It was a long, long way: four solid days of walking and three nights camping out under the stars. They went on foot, with all their friends and neighbours, through the hill country of Galilee, along the fertile Jordan Valley and then up the steep, rocky road that led to Jerusalem. They made this journey three times a year, but no one in Jesus' family ever forgot what happened on the Passover pilgrimage when Jesus was 12.

The whole family set off early with the rest of the village. There was Mary and Joseph, Jesus, his brothers and sisters. The youngest was still a baby – she was wrapped in a shawl and strapped safely onto Mary. The toddlers took it in turns to ride on the family's donkey or on Joseph's shoulders. Sometimes they begged piggybacks from their big brothers. Like all the other families, they took with them everything they needed for the journey. The long-suffering donkey carried the cooking pot, food supplies and rugs for the tent.

Who would like to try carrying this lot?

Invite a selection of volunteers – two adults and some children, if possible – to come and pack up the campsite and carry it to the end of the aisle, then around the church, as you continue telling the story.

It was like a travelling festival. Neighbours chatted as they walked. Families met up with their cousins from nearby villages. People told jokes and stories, teased each other and shared their food together in the evenings. Jesus and the older boys went off with their own friends and picnicked with other people's parents, but no one minded and everyone looked out for each other.

Then they reached Jerusalem – noisy, crowded, smelly Jerusalem: a sweating mass of dusty pilgrims; the farmyard stench of animals for sacrifice on sale in the temple courtyard; the jingle of foreign coins and the gabble of incomprehensible haggling; the hot, white stones of the temple and the smoky, prayer-filled hush near the holiest place; the quiet talk of people gathered around tables on Passover night, eating lamb, bitter herbs and unleavened bread.

Then the festival was over and the Galilee crowd regrouped, gathered together the stragglers and headed home. What a relief to be going downhill this time, through the rocky landscape around Jerusalem! After a long day's walking, Jesus' family found a favourite spot by the river to set up camp.

Bring your volunteers back to the front of the church and help them to set up camp there. They can sit or lie around the camp as you continue with the story.

As they made their shelter for the night and lit a fire, the older boys drifted back from their groups of friends and settled down. By the time it was dark, Jesus still hadn't returned. Joseph was sure he was with his uncle – he'd be along once he got tired. His brothers thought they'd seen him earlier with his friends. He'd be back soon enough. Only Mary stayed awake, waiting for him.

By dawn, he still hadn't come back. Mary went from camp to camp, shaking bleary-eyed relatives awake and demanding, 'Have you seen Jesus? Was he with you yesterday?' Mary was gripped by cold panic as she realised that no one had seen her son since they left Jerusalem. Where on earth was he? There was nothing for it but to retrace their steps. Joseph hastily arranged for his brother's family to take the rest of the children home while he and Mary headed back the way they had come. No time to pack – they left their camp in a big hurry, like this.

Ask your volunteers to return to their seats, then arrange the camp so that it looks as hastily abandoned as it did at the beginning of the service.

Mary and Joseph set off, dreading at every turn in the road that they would find Jesus, perhaps lying terribly injured, beaten and robbed by bandits. They found nothing except pilgrims' footprints in the dusty earth. In Jerusalem, they went everywhere they could think of and asked everyone, 'Have you seen our boy, Jesus? He's 12 – about this tall.' They were searching for three days. Three days! At last they went to the Temple – and there he was, sitting quietly with the teachers, listening and asking questions. The learned rabbis nodded as he spoke. A crowd had gathered, astonished by the young boy's wisdom.

Mary and Joseph gawped for a moment before Mary stormed through her son's circle of admirers. 'Son, why have you treated us like this? Look, your father and I have been worried sick! We've been looking everywhere for you!'

And Jesus replied, 'Why did you look everywhere? Didn't you know I'd be here, in my Father's house?'

Well – we can only imagine what Mary and Joseph said to that! All the Bible tells us is that they didn't understand, and that they took Jesus back to Nazareth with them. I wonder what they said to each other on the long journey home? Let's think about that as we sing together.

FIRST SUNDAY OF CHRISTMAS

Music Born in the night, Mary's child

Activity We left our story when Mary and Joseph were setting off for Nazareth at last, having found the missing 12-year-old Jesus. We've been wondering what they might have said to each other on the way home. Remember, they were travelling for about four days, so there would have been plenty of opportunity for discussion – and maybe some arguments! Let's take some time to think and talk about what Jesus' parents might have said to him, and what he might have replied. If you would like to, you can write or draw your ideas in these speech bubbles.

Allow plenty of time for discussion and writing. Then invite people to share their suggestions and pin up their speech bubbles on the display board.

Exploring Today's story is unique because it is the only one in the Bible that tells us about Jesus as a growing child. In all the other stories about him, he is either a baby in Bethlehem or an adult. This story about the 12-year-old Jesus gives us a glimpse of his family life and his normal, nearly teenage behaviour. His family is going on the Passover pilgrimage to Jerusalem; he knows the way, because they make this trip three times a year, every year. Jesus is the eldest so, of course, he doesn't want to walk with his parents or his little brothers and sisters. Naturally, he'd rather find his friends in the crowd and walk with them. Are there any 12-year-olds or teenagers here who would do the same? *(Invite responses.)* Clearly his parents trust him, because on the way home they don't even worry that he's missing until they have been walking for a whole day. Then look what happens when they finally find him: the parents say, 'Where have you been? We've been worried sick!' and the 12-year-old replies, in effect, 'Why are you making such a fuss?' Does this conversation sound familiar to any parents and growing children here? *(Invite responses.)* The words with which we've filled these speech bubbles today show that we sympathise with Jesus and his parents in this situation!

Jesus' words in this story are interesting because while they are recognisably the kind of thing a nearly teenager would say to his panicking parents, they also show that Jesus is growing up. The Bible gives us this brief conversation:

> When his parents saw him they were astonished; and his mother said to him, 'Child, why have you treated us like this? Look, your father and I have been searching for you in great anxiety.' He said to them, 'Why were you searching for me? Did you not know that I must be in my Father's house?'

Jesus shows a calm, clear understanding of who he is and where he belongs. He is God's Son and so he is in God's house, the Temple. It is significant that he is 12 in this story, because 13 is when Jewish boys celebrate their coming of age, their Bar Mitzvah. Jesus' words in this story show that he is becoming the man he will be. Much later, when he is on trial for his life before the Roman Governor, Jesus shows exactly the same calm authority. Pilate demands, 'Are you the King of the Jews?' and Jesus replies, 'Do you ask this on your own, or did others tell you about me? . . . My kingdom is not from this world.'[8] This man sounds very like the boy who asked, 'Why were you searching for me? Did you not know that I must be in my Father's house?' By the end of today's story, it seems that Mary sees something new in her son, because the Bible tells us that she 'treasured all these things in her heart.' Perhaps she realises that her boy is becoming a man.

In this Christmas season we celebrate the fact that God was born as one of us: the Word became flesh. Today's story reminds us how human he was – how, as a 12-year-old, he made his parents worried and cross. Yet Jesus was also God's Son who came to save us. This Jesus, who is both God and man, is the One we can trust and turn to in any circumstances, because he knows from experience what human life is like. Whatever we're feeling, whatever we're going through, he has been there too. God is always with us, and we can always rely on him.

---

8. John 18:33-36.

FIRST SUNDAY OF CHRISTMAS

Prayer action Jesus told his parents that his place was in his Father's house. We are in his Father's house today, and he left us this promise: 'where two or three are gathered in my name, I am there among them.'[9] For our prayers today, we will simply rest in God's presence and know that he is with us.

Pause for a short time of silence.

Emmanuel, God with us,
keep us company
today and always.
Amen.

Music Who would think that what was needed

Conclusion Heavenly Father,
your Son grew like us,
died for us,
lives in us.
We praise you!
Amen.

Give notices, announce the next all-age service and invite everyone to the feast.

---

9. Matthew 18:20.

Second Sunday of Christmas
God's plan

Theme	God's plan for us
Scripture	Ephesians 1:3-14; John 1:1-9

Running order — Total: 50 minutes

Welcome	The Creation story, as told by The Brick Testament *(5 minutes)*
Introduction	Opening the theme
Activity	Lego building *(20 minutes)*
Exploring	What is God's plan for us? *(5 minutes)*
Storytelling	Visual retelling of Ephesians 1:3-14, using illustrations from The Brick Testament *(5 minutes)*
Music	God is working his purpose out *(5 minutes)*
Prayer action	Lego brick prayer *(5 minutes)*
Music	Take this moment *(5 minutes)*
Conclusion	Closing prayer and invitation

Resources

- The Brick Testament. This is the Bible illustrated with Lego, available at www.thebricktestament.com. The website gives details of how you can legally use Brick Testament images in your church
- Laptop, projector and screen
- Lots of Lego, plus Duplo for younger children (ask local playgroups if they could lend theirs)
- A large mat or rug
- Boxes for Lego bricks
- Music and words
- Church set-up:
  – an empty table at the front of the church
  – a mat on the floor covered with Duplo
  – *either* place tables and chairs café-style, with a pile of Lego on each table
  – *or* have one or two large tables at the front, loaded with Lego

Leaders

Minimum: 1
- Leader

Optimum: 6
- Leader *(Introduction and Conclusion)*
- Activity Leader
- Explorer
- Storyteller
- Music Leader
- Prayer Leader

Suggestions for additional music

- Lord of all life and power
- In the bleak mid-winter

Service

Welcome — *As people arrive, show the Creation story from The Brick Testament.*[10]

Introduction — Our opening story of the Creation was from The Brick Testament – the Bible illustrated with Lego. As you can see, we are going to be creative in church this morning! All this Lego is here for us to build things with. Later, we'll be wondering how it might help us to think about God, but first we need to get building. What do you think you might like to make?

Invite responses from children and grown-ups alike. Encourage them to be specific about what they plan to make: if they are going to build a house, will it be a cottage or a mansion?[11]

Activity — *Encourage everyone to gather round the Lego and start building. As pieces are finished, display them on a table at the front.*

Exploring — *Start by inviting people to explain their creations.*

Here are all our original Lego creations. It is wonderful to see how a random collection of plastic bricks can be turned into all these different things! Our Lego builders have one thing in common: you had a plan. You knew what you wanted to make and you put it together by finding all the bricks you needed. Those of you who had new boxes of Lego for Christmas will know that each new Lego set comes with its own plan – an instruction booklet which tells you exactly how to fit the pieces together.

God has a plan, too. It involves all of us: we are like Lego bricks and God is the master builder who collects us all together and makes something wonderful out of us. Today we are going to hear more about God's plan, with the help of some pictures from The Brick Testament.

---

10. It begins at www.bricktestament.com/genesis/creation/00_gn01_01-02.html
11. Some children will need no encouragement to be specific: they will inform you that they are going to make a *Star Wars* T-16 Skyhopper and a Jedi Interceptor!

SECOND SUNDAY OF CHRISTMAS

Storytelling   God has blessed us in Christ. God chose us in Christ before the world was created.

Show the picture of God saying 'Let there be light.'[12]

He chose us to be holy and perfect in love.

Show the picture of Jesus and the angels.[13]

God chose us to be his adopted children through Jesus Christ.

Show the picture of the Nativity.[14]

Because of Jesus, God has forgiven our sins and given us new life.

Show the picture of the angels in the empty tomb.[15]

Through Jesus, God has shown us his plan: in the fullness of time, he will gather to himself everything in heaven and earth.

Show the picture of all creation praising God.[16]

Through Jesus we have become children of God. We will inherit eternal life.

Show the picture of Jesus talking to the crowd.[17]

Before we built something out of Lego, we had a plan, and we searched out the bricks we needed. God had a plan before he created anything at all. Jesus was part of that plan from the start: as today's Bible reading puts it, 'He was in the beginning with God.' God's plan is to gather us all up and make us part of his everlasting kingdom: he gave us his Son so that we could know him and belong to him forever. So whatever happens,

---

12. www.bricktestament.com/genesis/creation/01_gn01_03.html
13. www.bricktestament.com/the_life_of_jesus/the_end_of_the_world/mt24_29-30p16_27.html
14. www.bricktestament.com/the_life_of_jesus/jesus_is_born_02/lk02_07.html
15. www.bricktestament.com/the_life_of_jesus/the_empty_tomb/lk24_04-06.html
16. www.bricktestament.com/revelation/heaven_revealed/rv05_13.html
17. www.bricktestament.com/the_teachings_of_jesus/on_love/lk06_17p20p27.html

we can trust that God loves us. He searches us out and wants to keep us close to him. He will never leave us.

Music — God is working his purpose out

Prayer action — For our prayers today, we will each take a Lego brick.

Pass round some boxes of Lego bricks.

We each have a single brick. It is one of thousands here today: some are similar and some are very different. In the same way, each one of us is an individual and a member of the wonderfully varied human race. We are one of billions, but God knows us and loves us. Just as we picked out the Lego bricks we needed, God has chosen us. He has a place for each of us in his plan. In a moment of quiet, let's say thank you to God for his love. Then we'll gather all our individual bricks together to build a tower, as a reminder that we all have a place in God's kingdom.

Pause for a moment of quiet. Then encourage people to come forward and join their Lego bricks together to make a tower.

Let us pray.

God, our Creator,
from the beginning we were part of your plan.
Keep us always in your sight, and at the end,
gather us to yourself,
in Jesus' name.
Amen.

Music — Take this moment

Conclusion — God, our Maker,
take us and build our lives
into the fabric of your kingdom,
in the name of Christ.
Amen.

Give notices, announce the next all-age service and invite everyone to the feast.

Epiphany

Epiphany

Gifts

Theme	What the Epiphany gifts mean for us
Scripture	Matthew 2:1-12

Running order — Total: 50 minutes

Welcome	Treasure hunt – collecting the gold, frankincense and myrrh *(5 minutes)*
Introduction	Opening the theme
Activity	Dressing up the three wise men and retelling their story *(10 minutes)*
Music	We three kings *(5 minutes)*
Storytelling	Reading *Three Wise Women* by Mary Hoffman *(10 minutes)*
Exploring	What do these gifts mean? *(5 minutes)*
Music	In the bleak mid-winter *(5 minutes)*
Prayer action	Gift-tag prayers *(5 minutes)*
Music	Lord, the light of your love *(5 minutes)*
Conclusion	Closing prayer and invitation

Resources

- Items for treasure hunt: gold, frankincense and myrrh *(see appendix)*
- Three 'treasure chests': jewelled or carved wooden boxes, or ordinary shoe boxes covered with shiny paper
- Basic costumes for three wise men: cloaks and crowns
- A manger, some straw and a baby Jesus doll
- A copy of *Three Wise Women* by Mary Hoffman *(see appendix)*
- Gift tags, enough for one each
- Insert for each gift tag *(see appendix)*
- Bowls or collection plates for gift tags
- Music and words

Leaders

Minimum: 1

- Leader

Optimum: 6

- Leader *(Introduction and Conclusion)*
- Activity Leader
- Storyteller
- Music Leader
- Explorer
- Prayer Leader

Suggestions for additional music

- Brightest and best
- We bow down
- From the eastern mountains

Service

Welcome — *As people arrive, invite them to look for the gold coins, small bags of incense and bottle of myrrh that you have hidden around the church. (Don't tell them exactly what they are yet.) Collect the items together at the front and place them in the treasure chests.*

Introduction — Today we celebrate Epiphany, and we have begun by collecting some treasure for three precious presents that were given to the baby Jesus. Who can tell me what these presents are?

Hold up each gift in turn and invite suggestions, eliciting the correct answers.

Activity — Who gave Jesus these presents?

Elicit the correct answer.

I need three volunteers to dress up as wise men. Who would like to wear a crown and a cloak?

Invite volunteers to come forward and help them to dress up. Then place the manger and the baby Jesus doll at the front of church. Ask each of your wise men to choose a treasure chest. Now retell their story with the congregation's help, by asking these or similar questions.

- Where did these wise men come from?
- Why did they travel to Bethlehem?
- How did they know the way?
- Why did they bring presents for Jesus?

Then ask your volunteers to move to the back of the church. Explain that during the following hymn, they will walk slowly to the front, place their gifts in front of the manger and kneel down until everyone has finished singing.

Music — We three kings

Storytelling — *Ask your volunteers to return to their seats and give them a round of applause.*

EPIPHANY

Our volunteers have re-enacted for us the familiar story of the three wise men. Today we will hear a different Epiphany story. It's called *Three Wise Women*.

Read Three Wise Women *by Mary Hoffman.*

Exploring

'Epiphany' means 'showing' or 'revealing'. We call the wise men's visit the Epiphany because it marked the moment when Jesus was revealed to the wider world. Our Epiphany stories today have shown us something else, too. Traditionally, Christians have understood that the wise men's gifts revealed particular things about Jesus. Gold is a rich gift, fit for a king: it reminds us that Jesus was King of the Jews. Frankincense was burnt in the Temple, and its white, sweet-smelling smoke represented holiness, so it reminds us that Jesus is God. Lastly, myrrh is a resin or oil which was rubbed on dead bodies: it reminds us that Jesus was a mortal man who died for our sake.

The wise men's gifts show *who Jesus is*: God, King and man. What gifts did the wise women give in our modern story?

Invite responses and elicit the correct answers: bread, a story and a kiss.

The wise women's gifts show *what Jesus did*. The bread reminds us that Jesus shared bread with anyone who was hungry; he shared bread with his disciples at the Last Supper, and he continues to share bread at the Communion table with all who believe in him. The storytelling reminds us that he spread the good news by telling simple, memorable stories which anyone could understand. And the kiss reminds us that he loved us so much, he died for us.

The gifts given by the three wise women reveal Jesus' great gifts to us: his sharing, his storytelling and his loving. But the gift-giving doesn't stop there, because Jesus wants us to give these gifts to everyone else. We are called to share bread with each other, not only by sharing Communion in church but by sharing what we

ALL-SORTS WORSHIP

have – our food, our money, our time – with people who are in need. We are called to spread the good news about Jesus by telling his story and recounting the stories he told. Finally, Jesus told us to love one another as he loved us. We have to share his gift of love with everyone.

Music In the bleak mid-winter

Prayer action For our Epiphany prayers today, we think about the gifts Jesus received. Please take one of these gift tags as a token of the gifts he gave us, and a reminder of the gifts he asks us to give each other.

Pass round the bowls of gift tags.

Let us pray.

Jesus, our God and King,
for our sake you were born as one of us.
May we share our bread,
tell your story
and love one another,
for your sake.
Amen.

Music Lord, the light of your love

Conclusion God of Love,
as the wise men did at Epiphany,
may we go out into the world
and tell people the good news.
May we show your love in our lives
in Jesus' name.
Amen.

Give notices, announce the next all-age service and invite everyone to the feast.

First Sunday of Epiphany

You are my Son

Theme	The Baptism of Christ
Scripture	Isaiah 43:1-7; Luke 3:15-17, 21, 22

Running order	Total: 50 minutes
Welcome	Meditation montage based on Isaiah 43:1-7 *(5 minutes)*
Introduction	Opening the theme
Storytelling	An eyewitness story from the River Jordan – monologue *(10 minutes)*
Music	Christ, when for us you were baptised *(5 minutes)*
Activity	Guess who? An interactive identification game *(15 minutes)*
Exploring	What does Christ's baptism reveal? *(5 minutes)*
Prayer action	Feathers – tangible prayer *(5 minutes)*
Music	Do not be afraid *(5 minutes)*
Conclusion	Closing prayer and invitation

Resources

- Laptop, projector and screen
- Meditation montage based on Isaiah 43:1-7 *(see appendix)*
- Music and words
- Lots of clean white feathers: I recommend taking apart a cheap feather boa

Leaders

Minimum: 2

- Leader
- Cast x 1

Optimum: 6

- Leader *(Introduction and Conclusion)*
- Cast x 1:
  Baptised man, wearing traditional tunic or robe (wet hair optional)
- Music Leader
- Explorer
- Activity Leader
- Prayer Leader

Suggestions for additional music

- Breathe on me, breath of God
- Spirit of the Living God (Iverson)

Service

Welcome *As people arrive, show the following as a slideshow of words and pictures.*

A picture of a beautiful sunrise.

But now thus says the Lord,
Do not fear, for I have redeemed you;
I have called you by name, you are mine.

A picture of a mixed crowd of people.

For I am the Lord your God,
the Holy One of Israel, your Saviour.

A picture of the sun shining through clouds.

Because you are precious in my sight,
and honoured, and I love you . . .
I will bring your offspring from the east,

A picture of an Asian baby.

and from the west I will gather you;

A picture of a white woman.

I will say to the north, 'Give them up',

A picture of an Inuit man.

and to the south, 'Do not withhold';

A picture of some young African girls playing.

bring my sons from far away

A picture of teenage boys.

and my daughters from the end of the earth –

A picture of old women.

> everyone who is called by my name,
> whom I created for my glory,
> whom I formed and made.

A picture of a mixed crowd of people.

Introduction What a wonderful way to begin today's service! Those words from the Bible showed God the Father saying to us, his sons and daughters, 'I love you'. Listen out for God saying 'I love you' in today's story, which will tell us what happened when Jesus was baptised. Baptism in those days took place outdoors, in the river. Here is someone, fresh from the River Jordan, to tell us all about it.

Storytelling You'll never believe what I've just done! I've gone and got baptised! Me! Jacob from Bethsaida! There's not a Roman soldier in the district who hasn't had to break up a fight I started. My dad said I was born looking for trouble – and somehow I always managed to find it. Or it found me. That's what I was doing down by the river this morning – I was out with my brothers, looking for the lowlife who's been saying I cheat my customers. The place was heaving! So we were shoving our way through the crowds, on the lookout, when I spotted this hairy bloke who looked as if he'd just killed a camel with his bare hands and then skinned it. All covered in furs, he was – but that wasn't the strangest thing about him. He was yelling at people! It sounded like he called them a nest of snakes! He had more guts than most of these travelling preachers you see, who just tell people what they want to hear. He was shouting about the Day of Judgement and telling people to repent of their sins. He reminded me of my grandmother, who used to say to me, 'Say sorry, Jacob!'

Then I heard a Roman soldier ask what he should do. A Roman – asking advice from a wild local preacher! This I had to hear. So I pushed in a bit closer and listened to what the preacher said. He told the Roman to stop threatening people to get money out of them! Well, that sounded just like me. I've always managed to get some ready cash with my fists. I kept listening, and this man – John, they called him, John the Baptist – was telling people to come and get baptised in the river. He said God would forgive them and wash all their sins away. Well, he had me, then. I thought of all the bad stuff I'd done over the years, all the things I regretted and the fights that gave me bad dreams, and I thought, 'Wouldn't it be great to start again? To say sorry – and mean it, this time – and get rid of all that badness?'

Suddenly I just had to get in that river. I pushed through the people and waded out to where John was standing. I blurted out, 'I'm sorry – for everything!' and John grabbed my shoulders and tipped me back. I went right under, and for a moment the noise of the crowd disappeared and it was quiet under the water. Then John brought me up again and said, 'Son, your sins are forgiven.' I felt like a newborn baby, crying and gasping for air.

I waded back to dry land, where people I didn't know cheered and patted me on the back. There was a buzz around me: folk were saying, 'I reckon this John might be the One!' Someone started yelling, 'He's the Messiah!' Then John looked towards us and shouted, 'I'm not the Messiah! I'm not worthy to untie his sandals. Someone much more powerful than me is coming, who will baptise you with the Holy Spirit!'

The man who had been baptised after me was coming out of the water, when he suddenly stopped and knelt down. Then the most amazing thing happened: the sky opened and there was this bright light, and in the light a white dove fluttered down and landed on the praying man. Then – and I swear this is true – we all heard this voice from heaven. I've never heard anything like it: it was loud and soft at the same time. It said, 'You are my Son and I love you. I am well pleased with you.'

I still can't get my head around it all, but I know that everything's different now. I've got a new life to live, thanks to John the Baptist. And as for that praying

FIRST SUNDAY OF EPIPHANY

man – his name's Jesus of Nazareth and he's the real deal. You can't tell me he's not the Messiah, not after what I've seen. And he's going to change everything, for all of us!

Music Christ, when for us you were baptised

Activity In our story today, we got a glimpse of how expectantly people were waiting for their Saviour, the Messiah. They didn't know what he would look like or when he would come, and John can't have been the first impressive preacher who made people wonder, 'Is this God's Son?'

Today we will play a game which involves trying to identify the right person. I need a volunteer who is a parent, and whose son or daughter is also in church today.

Bring your volunteer to the front.

Now, we are going to try and identify your child through a series of questions, to which you can only answer 'Yes' or 'No'. This is like a live, interactive version of the game called *Guess Who?* First of all, I need everyone to stand up.

Encourage everyone in the congregation to stand.

(*To the volunteer.*) Is your child female?

If the answer is yes, everyone male can sit down. If the answer is no, everyone female can sit. Continue by asking simple questions about appearance, for example:

- Does your child have blond hair?
- Does s/he wear glasses?
- Is s/he wearing trainers?
- Does s/he have blue eyes?

By a process of elimination, you should end up with only a few people of similar appearance left standing.

ALL-SORTS WORSHIP

Now we've only got a few people left, and some of them seem pretty likely candidates. There's only one thing for it. You'll have to tell us which one is your child.

The parent points out their child and gives him/her a hug. Applaud your volunteers and ask everyone to sit down.

Exploring

In Jesus' time, people looked at the preachers, teachers and prophets around them and tried to work out which one was God's Son. As in our game of *Guess Who?*, they identified the most likely candidates – and for many, John the Baptist seemed to fit the bill. But in our game, the best way to get what the police call a positive ID was for the parent to step forward and say, 'That's my child.'

That is exactly what God did in today's story: he intervened directly and left hundreds of witnesses in no doubt. There was the strange sight of the sky opening and an unearthly dove which the Bible describes as 'the Holy Spirit in bodily form'. Then there was that voice from heaven: 'You are my Son and I love you. I am well pleased with you.' In effect, this was God's first official, public announcement that Jesus was his Son.

The story of Jesus' baptism shows us who Jesus is, and it also reminds us who we are: we are God's sons and daughters. In the Old Testament reading that began our service today, God said, 'you are precious in my sight . . . and I love you.' Just as the Holy Spirit came down upon Jesus at his baptism, so the Holy Spirit came to his followers – and that means us, too. Today's story reminds us that we are God's children and he loves us. We can trust that his Holy Spirit is with us.

Prayer action

No one can say what God's Holy Spirit looks like. The Bible often describes the Spirit as a powerful wind: it comes and goes and you can't see it, but you can feel its power and see the effects it has. In today's story the Spirit appeared as a dove, fluttering briefly down from heaven and perhaps leaving behind nothing but a feather or two to show where he'd been.

Hold up a feather or two and let them drift down.

See how light and soft these feathers are! They are hardly there at all, yet they remind us of the bird whose powerful wings beat the air. For our prayers today, we will use these white feathers to remind us that the Holy Spirit comes and goes in our lives, too. We may not see him, but we can feel his power and recognise him by the signs he leaves behind. Let's rest in God's presence and invite his Holy Spirit.

Invite everyone to take a feather or two and allow some time for people to sit quietly in prayer.

Come Holy Spirit,
fly down to us.
May we know you
by the inspiration and
transformed lives
you leave behind.
Amen.

Please take your feathers home with you. May they remind us all to look out for signs of God's Holy Spirit at work in the world and in our lives.

Music   Do not be afraid

Conclusion   Heavenly Father,
may we recognise your Son
wherever we may meet him
and know your Spirit's power.
Amen.

Give notices, announce the next all-age service and invite everyone to the feast.

Second Sunday of Epiphany

Water into wine

Theme	God's gifts for the common good
Scripture	John 2:1-11; 1 Corinthians 12:1-11

Running order Total: 50 minutes

Welcome	Lighting candles on the tables *(5 minutes)*
Introduction	Opening the theme
Storytelling	Interactive retelling of John 2:1-11 *(10 minutes)*
Music	Jesus' love is very wonderful *(5 minutes)*
Activity	Discovering the gifts of the Holy Spirit using visual aids *(10 minutes)*
Music	Filled with the Spirit's power *(5 minutes)*
Exploring	Why did Jesus turn water into wine? Why does the Holy Spirit give us gifts? *(5 minutes)*
Music	One shall tell another *(5 minutes)*
Prayer action	Edible sharing prayer with grapes *(5 minutes)*
Conclusion	Closing prayer and invitation

Resources

- Church set-up: café-style or with long banqueting-style tables at the front. Lay tables with party food, plates and glasses or clear plastic beakers
- Tall candles in candlesticks or candelabras on the tables
- Matches and tapers
- Music and words
- An empty blackcurrant squash bottle
- A clear plastic camping water carrier
- A china or opaque plastic jug, with a large measure of good quality blackcurrant squash in the bottom (If you expect lots of thirsty people, have several more such jugs in reserve)
- A glass jug
- A chalice
- Bowls of red grapes
- Wrapped parcels, placed at intervals along the tables, containing:
  - a microphone
  - a magnifying glass
  - a lantern (candle, oil or electric)
  - a bandage
  - a bottle of water
  - a bottle of red wine (screw top)
  - a megaphone (one made from a roll of cardboard is fine)
  - two speech bubbles *(see appendix)*

Leaders

Minimum: 1
- Leader

Optimum: 6
- Leader *(Introduction and Conclusion)*
- Storyteller
- Music Leader
- Explorer
- Activity Leader
- Prayer Leader

Suggestions for additional music

- Joy to the world!
- Sing of the Lord's goodness

Service

Welcome — *As people arrive, invite them to light a tall candle on the table, as a way of saying, 'Here I am, Lord.'*

Introduction — We're having a party in church this morning! There's room for lots of people. Who would like to help themselves to some party food?

Storytelling — *Encourage people to gather round and fill their plates. Allow some time for eating.*

Now, who is getting thirsty? Who would like a drink?

Invite responses, then go and fetch the empty squash bottle.

Oh no – this is embarrassing! We've put out all this lovely party food for you, but we've run out of nice things to drink! There is only plain old tap water. I'm really sorry.

Bring forward the camping water carrier and the china jug. Put the water carrier on a table.

I'll just fill up this jug, then I can give you all a drink of water. I'm sorry it's nothing more special.

Fill the china jug with water, then hold up the first glass and pour out what is now blackcurrant squash.

Hang on a minute – what's this? It smells like blackcurrant squash! I don't understand – I put water in this jug. You all saw me do it! Who would like to taste this?

Invite a volunteer.

How does it taste?

Invite a response.

It *is* blackcurrant squash! And it's delicious! It's the really good stuff we'd usually give our party guests first, not the cheap stuff we're left with when all the other drinks have run out! Who else would like some?

SECOND SUNDAY OF EPIPHANY

Share out the blackcurrant squash. Fill more china jugs if necessary.

There's plenty more! Anyone for seconds?

Pour out more blackcurrant squash and continue speaking as people finish eating and drinking.

This is what happened at a party Jesus went to. It was a wedding reception and the host ran out of wine. Without any fuss, Jesus asked the servants to fill several big containers with water – and when they poured some out to drink, the water had become fine wine. This was Jesus' first miracle: it was the first sign that God's power was working through him. We can sum it up with this rhyme:

They poured in water,
he poured out wine,
Jesus proved his power divine.

Music   Jesus' love is very wonderful

Activity   Our second story today is also about God's power at work. Another name for this power is the Holy Spirit, and it can work through us. The Bible describes the special gifts that the Holy Spirit can give, and today we have got some objects to represent each of these gifts. Who would like to unwrap these presents and help us discover what they are?

Invite a volunteer to unwrap the first gift: a microphone.

What's this for? *(Invite responses.)* This microphone helps you to be heard and understood. It represents the gift of wise words.

Invite a volunteer to unwrap the second gift: a magnifying glass.

What would you use this for? *(Invite responses.)* This magnifying glass represents the gift of knowledge – the ability to look at the world with insight and deep understanding.

Invite a volunteer to unwrap the third gift: a lantern.

This lantern can light the way at night. It represents the special gift of strong faith, which shines like a guiding light in the darkness.

Invite a volunteer to unwrap the fourth gift: a bandage.

Who uses one of these? *(Invite responses.)* This represents the gift of healing. God's Holy Spirit doesn't only bring about physical healing; he can heal broken spirits and mend relationships, too.

Invite a volunteer to unwrap the fifth gift: a bottle of water and a bottle of wine.

These remind us of Jesus' miracle at the wedding. The Holy Spirit continues to work miracles: we may never see someone turn water into wine, but we may witness a miraculous change for the better in our world or in the life of someone we know. Such transformation is the work of the Holy Spirit.

Invite a volunteer to unwrap the sixth gift: a megaphone.

What would you use this for? *(Invite responses.)* This megaphone is useful for enabling a whole crowd of people to hear your voice. It represents the gift of prophecy: this is the gift of being God's spokesperson and speaking his truth.

Invite a volunteer to unwrap the seventh and eighth gifts: a speech bubble with scrambled symbols and a speech bubble with a translated prayer.

Finally, here are two gifts that belong together. The first is the gift of speaking in tongues: this means praising God and praying with strange, inspired words. The second gift is the ability to interpret this mysterious speech.

Ask all your volunteers to hold up their objects.

According to the Bible, all these are the special gifts of the Holy Spirit. God has the power to give them to us if he chooses.

Music   Filled with the Spirit's power

Exploring   Both our stories today told us about God's amazing gifts, which exceed all our hopes and expectations. The wedding guests received more fine wine than they could drink; the Holy Spirit gives gifts that empower people far beyond their own abilities. Today we are going to wonder about these generous gifts.

Pour the wine into the glass jug.

First of all, what would have happened if Jesus hadn't turned the water into wine? A wedding reception would have fizzled out disappointingly early and a bridegroom would have been embarrassed because he'd let his guests down. It's not as if anyone was ill, or dying, or in danger. Yet this was where Jesus chose to perform his first miracle: he turned water into wine, and as a result, the celebrations could continue. He made gallons and gallons of the best wine the steward had ever tasted, and he did it for the common good, regardless of whether people deserved it or not.

This generous giving reminds us that Jesus himself is like the miraculous new wine in this story.

Pour the wine into the chalice.

He gave his life for our sake when he died on the cross, in spite of the fact that none of us could ever deserve such a precious gift as eternal life. Nevertheless, it was his gift to us all, as freely and generously given as the miraculous wine in our first story.

Now let's look at those powerful gifts of the Holy Spirit.

Ask all your volunteers to hold up their objects.

We can see that God grants these gifts to some people. We may be able to think of someone who is undoubtedly blessed with great wisdom or inspirational faith. But the Bible is clear that these gifts are not given to make individuals feel special or important; they are given 'for the common good' – to build up the Christian community and strengthen people in faith and love.

So today's stories give us a clear message. However we use God's gifts, we should use them for the common good, to help and strengthen other people. That is what the gifts of the Holy Spirit are for, and all the other God-given gifts and talents we have received. The miraculous wine at the wedding was created for the common good, too, and it reminds us that Jesus gave his own life for the good of all humanity. Whoever we are and whatever we've done, because of him we can be forgiven and find eternal life.

Music One shall tell another

Prayer action Today we remember that God's gifts are ours to share. As a focus for our prayers, we will use these grapes – the fruits of creation that we turn into wine. Let's share these gifts now.

Pass the bowls of grapes around and encourage everyone to take one and eat it.

Generous Lord,
help us to recognise the gifts we have received
and to use them for the common good.
Help us to share,
in Jesus' name.
Amen.

Conclusion God of power and might,
send us out into the world
in the company of your Holy Spirit.
May we use your gifts
to love and serve others.
Amen.

Give notices, announce the next all-age service and invite everyone to finish the feast.

Third Sunday of Epiphany
One body

Theme	Being the Body of Christ
Scripture	1 Corinthians 12:12-31a

Running order — Total: 50 minutes

Welcome	Lighting a variety of candles *(5 minutes)*
Introduction	Opening the theme
Storytelling	Visual retelling of 1 Corinthians 12:12-31a *(10 minutes)*
Music	One is the body *(5 minutes)*
Activity	What gifts do we have? Labelling the members of the body *(10 minutes)*
Music	O Lord, all the world belongs to you *(5 minutes)*
Exploring	How can these members work together? Musical exploration *(10 minutes)*
Prayer action	Singing in harmony – 'Thuma mina' *(5 minutes)*
Conclusion	Closing prayer and invitation

Resources

- A variety of candles in different colours and shapes
- Matches and tapers
- A 2m long piece of lining paper
- A small piece of white card
- Lots of marker pens
- Music and words

Leaders

Minimum: 5

- Leader
- Four singers

Optimum: 9++

- Leader *(Introduction and Conclusion)*
- Storyteller
- A choir: anything from a quartet with soprano, alto, tenor and bass to a fully robed church choir. They should be prepared to sing 'Thuma mina' (or something else) in four-part harmony
- Explorer
- Activity Leader
- Prayer Leader

Suggestions for additional music

- Christ is the King!
- I come with joy

Service

Welcome — *As people arrive, invite them to light one of a variety of candles.*

Introduction — We have lit these candles as a way of saying, 'Here I am, Lord.' They are a mixed bunch: different colours and different sizes, some with tall flames and others with pools of liquid wax. They remind us that we are all different, too. Our story today is about diversity in the church.

Storytelling — A man named Paul was a leader of the early Church. His congregation was a very mixed bunch indeed: Jews and Greeks, who had always seen themselves as opposites, now both worshipped Jesus. Slaves worshipped alongside free men and women. Paul wanted to help them overcome their differences and work together for the sake of the Church, so he compared them to the human body.

Ask for a volunteer to lie on a piece of lining paper while a second volunteer draws around them. Make sure their arms and fingers are slightly outstretched. Ask the two volunteers to hold up the picture of the body. Have a piece of white card in your hand to mask the body parts you mention doing without: feet, ear, hand and thumb.

Paul said to his church, 'Think of the human body: although there are many different body parts, they all belong to the same body. There is one God and we have all been baptised into one body, and have shared in the same Holy Spirit.

Now, this body has many different body parts, but they are all necessary. The foot can't say, 'No one needs me, because I'm not a hand.' *(Cover up one foot.)* The ear can't say, 'I don't belong here, because I'm not an eye.' *(Cover up one ear.)* You couldn't have a body that was just made up of eyes! So we have one body but many body parts.

These body parts can't do without each other. The eye can't say to the hand, 'I don't need you!' *(Cover up one hand.)* The head can't say to the feet, 'I can manage without you!'*(Cover up the feet.)* In fact, some of the smallest body parts are the most vital: look at your thumb! Where would your hand be without it? *(Hide your own thumb in your palm and encourage others to do the same.)* And if one bit of your body hurts, your whole body suffers.'

Paul said to his church, 'This body is like all of you. You are the body of Christ and individually you are the members of that body. Each of you has your own God-given abilities and your own job to do. For example, God has chosen people in his church to be prophets and teachers; some can work miracles and others have the gift of healing. But does everyone have these gifts? No! That would be like having a body which is nothing but eyes and ears. Make the most of what you have been given and ask God to grant you even greater gifts.'

Music   One is the body

Activity   *Hold up the picture of the body again.*

This picture of the body reminds us that we are all different, but we are all members of the body of Christ, the Church. Paul talked about the gifts that are given to different people, and how they each help the whole body. I wonder what gifts we have in our church? Let's take some time now to think about what we are good at. You may think of something that you can do, or a gift that has been given to someone else. It could be something that everyone notices, like a gift for teaching or leading, or it might be a more quietly appreciated gift, like a talent for making friends or listening to people. Let's write or draw our gifts on this body.

Allow plenty of time for people to think and write or draw. Read out some of the contributions and point out the variety of gifts in your church.

Music   O Lord, all the world belongs to you

Exploring

We have learnt that we are different members of the body of Christ, and we have seen what a variety of gifts we possess. The point of all these gifts is that they help us to do Christ's work in the world – to love and serve others – and that requires the whole body to work together. Paul gave us some clear advice about how to make this happen, so now we're going to look at that advice with the help of a musical illustration.

Bring forward the choir.

Here is our choir. This choir sings together, but it has four different parts: soprano, alto, tenor and bass. The singers' voices suit their parts. They each need to be themselves and sing their own musical line.

Ask each to sing their part in turn.

The harmony won't work if everyone tries to sing the same part, like this.

All sing the alto line.

The different parts can't do without each other. Listen to what happens if we lose the soprano and bass.

The altos and tenors sing their lines together.

We are like this choir. We have to be ourselves, singing the part that suits our gifts. We can't all try to be the same, and we can't do without each other.[18] When we all work together, great things happen.

The choir sings the whole piece through in four-part harmony.

Prayer action

Today we will pray a South African musical prayer. Its Zulu words remind us that, together, we have to do Christ's work in the world: 'Thuma mina, Somandla' means 'Send me, Lord.' Let us pray.

---

18. At this point, you could demonstrate what happens when a choir doesn't work together: all the different parts sing at once, but each at their own speed. Whoever finishes first shouts, 'I win!' Thanks to Emma Herd and the choir of St Peter's, Peebles for this lovely idea.

Sing 'Thuma mina' together, with the choir providing harmony.

Send us and lead us, Lord.
Amen.

Conclusion Heavenly Father,
as we go out into the world,
may we celebrate our diversity
and work together as one body,
in the name of Christ.
Amen.

Give notices, announce the next all-age service and invite everyone to the feast.

Fourth Sunday of Epiphany

The greatest gift

Theme	Love
Scripture	1 Corinthians 13

Running order	Total: 50 minutes
Welcome	Heart-shaped prayers *(5 minutes)*
Introduction	Opening the theme
Music	Wide, wide as the ocean *(5 minutes)*
Storytelling	Reading 1 Corinthians 13 *(1 minute)*
Exploring	How do we love each other? Interactive exploration *(10 minutes)*
Music	Help us to help each other, Lord *(5 minutes)*
Activity	Making symbols of love: everlasting roses and the cross *(14 minutes)*
Music	Jesus' love is very wonderful *(5 minutes)*
Prayer action	Knitted heart – active prayer *(5 minutes)*
Conclusion	Closing prayer and invitation

Resources

NB Advance preparation needed for knitting!

- A knitted heart *(see appendix)*
- A drawing board or flip chart
- A marker pen
- A blindfold
- Music and words
- *Optional:* laptop, projector and screen to display 1 Corinthians 13:4-7
- On tables, spread out equipment for roses/crosses *(see appendix)*
- In every pew or row of seats:
  - heart-shaped pieces of paper *(see appendix)*
  - A5 sheets of paper or smaller
  - pens and pencils

Leaders

Minimum: 1

- Leader

Optimum: 6

- Leader *(Introduction and Conclusion)*
- Storyteller
- Music Leader
- Explorer
- Activity Leader
- Prayer Leader

Suggestions for additional music

- Love divine, all loves excelling
- A new commandment

Service

Welcome — *As people arrive, invite them to take a heart shape, write or draw on it a prayer for someone they love and leave it on the altar.*

Introduction — Our service today is all about love. The shops are starting to fill up with pink and red hearts in preparation for Valentine's Day, persuading us that on 14 February we need to show people how much we love them. Jesus believed in *always* showing people how much he loved them, and today we'll be wondering how we follow his example.

Music — Wide, wide as the ocean

Storytelling — Paul was a leader of the early Church, whose advice to the first Christians is recorded in the Bible. Today we will hear his most important teaching.

Read 1 Corinthians 13 and, if possible, display verses 4-7 on a screen to remain as a focal point.

Exploring — Those beautiful words may sound familiar: they are a favourite at weddings. They remind us that whatever we do, love needs to come first. It should be the foundation of everything else in our lives. Paul's words are also a challenge: however much we love people, do we always manage to be patient? I wonder whether any of us can honestly say we are never irritable with our nearest and dearest. Today we have an activity which will help us think about how we love each other.

In the days before industrial machines and computers, it used to be said that the test of a true artist was whether or not he could draw a perfect circle, freehand. Today we are going to try a similar test by drawing a perfect heart. Can I have a volunteer, please?

Invite your volunteer forward and stand them in front of the drawing board or flip chart with a marker pen.

We're going to make this a little more challenging.

Blindfold your volunteer and lead their hand to the board, then invite them to draw the best heart shape they can manage. Applaud the result, whatever it may be!

Now it's your turn. You'll find paper and pens where you are sitting. Use the hand you *don't* normally write with and try to draw a heart shape.

Allow enough time for everyone to draw, including you. Then compare the results.

We all know what a perfect heart shape looks like, but it's really hard to copy it, especially when we are hampered by not being able to see properly, or by not using our best drawing hand. Trying to love each other is like this. We all know what perfect love is: today's reading describes it beautifully. But none of us is perfect, and in our lives we often find it difficult to live up to the ideal. If we are stressed, it is hard to be patient. If someone we love has an annoying habit, it is hard not to be irritated. And if those we love let us down badly, it can seem almost impossible to 'bear all things, believe all things, hope all things, endure all things.'

Yet love is at the heart of the Christian gospel, and we are called to keep trying. In our drawing challenge, none of us managed to draw a perfect heart shape, but we all had a go – and every drawing that we made was recognisably heart-shaped. In our daily living, we need to keep practising loving each other so that our lives – and our churches – are recognisably love-shaped. This will take time and effort: it's a life's work, but it is the most important work we will ever do. As Paul reminds us, 'And now faith, hope and love abide, these three; and the greatest of these is love.'

Music   Help us to help each other, Lord

Activity   One of the most popular symbols of love is the red rose. However, many Valentine's roses fade quickly, sometimes without even opening their petals. They are not a very good symbol of long-lasting love, or the never-ending love described by Paul. So today we will make some red roses that will last.

Encourage everyone to gather around the activity tables and create roses out of red paper. When everyone is ready, hold up a finished rose.

This red rose won't fade; it is a good symbol of love that never ends. What is more, its long, green stem suggests another symbol of everlasting love: the cross.

Tie a second, shorter stick across the stem to form a cross.

Jesus loved us so much that he gave up his life for us on the cross, and his love formed a bridge which connects us forever to God's love. So let's turn these roses into something special for us all to take home and keep: a double symbol of never-ending love.

Allow time for everyone to make their roses into crosses.

Music Jesus' love is very wonderful

Prayer action *Hold up the knitted heart.*

For our prayers today, we will use this labour of love: a knitted heart. It represents the time and effort that goes into loving others, and reminds us of Jesus' love – his life's work. Together we give thanks for God's love, which reaches all of us, wherever we are. As a sign of our prayer, we will unravel this knitted heart and stretch the wool right around the church so that it surrounds us all.

Pull the last stitch on the heart and start to unravel it. As you hold the heart, invite volunteers to pull the wool and walk with it so that it reaches around the church.

Let us pray.

Loving Lord,
we give thanks for your love,
reaching us, whoever we are,
surrounding us, wherever we may be,
infinitely extending from heaven to earth.
We thank you for your love that never ends.
Amen.

Conclusion	God of Love,
show us how to make our lives love-shaped
and our church Jesus-shaped,
for your Son's sake.
Amen.

Give notices, announce the next all-age service and invite everyone to the feast.

Candlemas*

Festival of Light

Theme	Welcoming the Light of the world
Scripture	Luke 2:22-40

Running order Total: 50 minutes

Welcome	Letting the light shine – glow-sticks *(5 minutes)*
Introduction	Opening the theme
Storytelling	Shadow play – Christ's presentation in the temple *(10 minutes)*
Music	Hail to the Lord who comes *(5 minutes)*
Exploring	What is revealed at Candlemas? Active exploration *(10 minutes)*
Activity	Preparing the sky-candles *(10 minutes)*
Prayer action	Candlemas blessings – releasing the sky-candles *(5 minutes)*
Music	Christ, whose glory fills the skies *(5 minutes)*
Conclusion	Closing prayer and invitation

* This is a service for the late afternoon or evening.

Resources

- Church set-up: a dark church with two long rope lights lying switched off along the length of the aisle. (For rope lights, see online retailers of Christmas lights, including Amazon)
- Lots of glow-sticks. These are available cheaply from pound shops and in bulk on the internet: see www.glowsticks.co.uk
- A screen and bright light for the shadow play: a large white sheet and the light from a projector would work well
- Props:
  - silhouettes of two pigeons *(see appendix)*
  - a realistic baby doll, wrapped in a blanket
- A single church candle
- Matches
- Sky lanterns *(see appendix)*
- Felt pens
- Music and words

Leaders

Minimum: 5

- Leader
- Non-speaking cast x 4

Optimum: 10

- Leader *(Introduction and Conclusion)*
- Storyteller
- Non-speaking cast x 4 *(wearing robes or cloaks – to be seen in silhouette only)*:
  Mary
  Joseph
  Simeon
  Anna
- Music Leader
- Explorer
- Activity Leader
- Prayer Leader

Suggestions for additional music

- Faithful vigil ended
- Jesus bids us shine

Service

Welcome — *As people arrive in the dark church, invite them to activate lots of glow-sticks. They may like to keep them as sticks or join some together to make crosses, crowns, necklaces or bangles. Don't turn on the lights until after the Storytelling.*

Introduction — We've come into a dark church tonight and have started to fill it with light, because today is Candlemas: our festival of light. We celebrate a special occasion in Jesus' life, which was his first visit to the Temple in Jerusalem, forty days after his birth. This is what happened.

Storytelling — *Turn on the light behind the screen.*

It was the done thing: Mary and Joseph, proud new parents of a bouncing baby boy, had to take him to the Temple in Jerusalem. Quite a trip with a newborn! They took an animal for the sacrifice. A lamb was out of their league, so the best they could manage was a pair of pigeons.

The actors enter and hold the first tableau: Mary, Joseph, the baby Jesus and two pigeons.

As Mary and Joseph picked their way through the crowded streets, an elderly man was also heading for the Temple.

Simeon walks on.

His name was Simeon and he was a good man. That day, he was very excited: the Holy Spirit had told him to hotfoot it to the Temple. He had no idea why, but he knew it was going to be something special. When he saw the baby in Mary's arms, he knew he had found what he'd been looking for.

The actors hold the second tableau: Mary, Joseph; the baby Jesus in Simeon's arms.

Long ago, the Holy Spirit had whispered in Simeon's ear, promising that he'd live to see the Messiah – and at last, that promise had come true. He said, 'Lord, now I can die a happy man. I've seen your Saviour! He's the glory of Israel and a beacon of light for the whole world!' Mary and Joseph were stunned. Simeon blessed them both.

The actors hold the third tableau: Simeon's hand raised in blessing over Mary and Joseph.

Then Simeon said to Mary, 'There's a lot in store for this little one. He's going to turn the world upside down. Many will be against him; many more will show their true colours – and your own heart will be broken.'

Pause before Anna enters and breaks up the scene, creating the fourth tableau: the baby in Anna's arms, with Mary, Joseph and Simeon looking on.

Suddenly an old lady arrived and asked to hold the baby. She was Anna, a prophet and faithful worshipper at the Temple. She knew exactly who she was cuddling. The Messiah! She called out to anyone who would listen, 'This is him! Praise the Lord! The Saviour is here!'

Simeon and Anna leave, creating the fifth tableau: Mary and Joseph holding up their baby in wonder.

Mary and Joseph took their baby home. Jesus grew up big and strong: he was wise beyond his years and God loved him.

Music Hail to the Lord who comes

Exploring We've heard the story of Christ's presentation in the Temple. This is celebrated as Candlemas because it is all about light and enlightenment. To help us think about this, we're going to remind ourselves what it's like to be left in the dark.

Turn off all the lights.

In the years before electric light, and the time before gas lights, darkness was a force to be reckoned with.

Work had to be done and journeys had to be made before dark, and especially in the winter, darkness hemmed people in at both ends of the day.

Light a single candle.

Light was precious. Candles cost money and so did oil for lamps. You had to cherish the little light you had, or give in to the dark until the sun rose. Who would like to try walking down the aisle with just the light of this candle to guide them?

Invite a volunteer to try and find their way in the near darkness. When they are halfway, stop them.

What our volunteer really needs is this.

Turn on the rope lights so that the path down the aisle shines clearly. When the volunteer gets to the end, turn on all the lights.

When people described Jesus as the Light of the world, they were using one of the most powerful images of their time. We have seen what a difference light makes in the darkness, and how bright light shows us the way. Light changes the way we see everything. In today's story, Jesus was described as a beacon of light. In the Bible, Simeon calls him 'a light for revelation' and in a modern version of the Bible, the meaning is even clearer: Simeon says, 'I've seen your Liberator, the eye-opener of outsiders, the pride and joy of Jews.'[19] Jesus the eye-opener! This description reminds us that, like our rope lights in church today, the Light of the world helps us to see clearly and shows us the way forward.

Candlemas is a time for seeing clearly and looking forward. In our story, we heard two prophets, Simeon and Anna, speak about what was to come. Anna foresaw the redemption of God's people, while Simeon could see the great upheaval that would be caused by

---

19. *the street bible*, Rob Lacey, Zondervan, 2003.

the Messiah's arrival, and the trouble that was in store for Jesus himself. He could see the grief that was heading Mary's way, too.

Over the years, Candlemas traditions have drawn on this idea of looking forward into the future. There are old rhymes about predicting the weather to come, based on whether it is cloudy or fair on Candlemas day, and this tradition is still celebrated in parts of America as Groundhog Day. The behaviour of a small mammal on that day is supposed to predict the end of winter, or more bad weather in store.

For us, today, we celebrate the Light of the world, the Eye-opener who shows us the way. As a church, we turn from Christmas to look forward to Easter, when the light of Christ's love overcame the darkness of death forever.

Activity There is a Candlemas tradition of blessing candles, which people then take home and use throughout the year to come. It is a way of spreading the light of Christ out into the local community. Today we are going to do the same, by asking for God's blessing on these sky-candles. These are Chinese flying lanterns: we can write on them, then light them and release them into the night sky, taking the light of Candlemas out into the parish and beyond. Let's take some time now to remember all those for whom we would like to ask God's blessing.

Invite people to write or draw their prayer requests on the sky lanterns. Allow plenty of time for this, so that the lanterns are covered with words and pictures.

Prayer action *Take the lanterns outside and gather everyone around. Light the fuel and release the lanterns.*

Let us pray.

Heavenly Father,
we ask your blessing on these sky-candles.
May you bless all those for whom we pray,
and bless our local community
as we spread the light of Candlemas tonight,
in Jesus' name.
Amen.

Music Christ, whose glory fills the skies

Conclusion Jesus, Light of the world,
open our eyes,
enlighten our minds
and show us the way.
Amen.

Give notices, announce the next all-age service and invite everyone to the feast.

Ordinary time

Proper 1

Fish galore!

Theme	God's goodness and his call
Scripture	Luke 5:1-11

Running order	Total: 50 minutes
Welcome	Naming those for whom we pray *(5 minutes)*
Introduction	Opening the theme
Storytelling	Visual retelling of Luke 5:1-11 *(10 minutes)*
Music	I, the Lord of sea and sky *(5 minutes)*
Exploring 1	How did Jesus call his first disciples? *(5 minutes)*
Activity	Reckoning God's goodness *(10 minutes)*
Exploring 2	How does Jesus call us? *(5 minutes)*
Prayer action	Catching people – gathering them up in prayer *(5 minutes)*
Music	Jesus Christ is waiting *(5 minutes)*
Conclusion	Closing prayer and invitation

Resources

- A fishing net (a shrimping net would be ideal)
- An inflatable dinghy *or* two sides of a large cardboard box, cut to suggest the prow of a rowing boat
- Two large pieces of netting (garden netting will do)
- A quantity of blue fabric to suggest the sea
- A large box covered with fish shapes *(see appendix)*
- Lots of small paper carrier bags with handles *(see appendix)*, each containing something heavy – I suggest tins. Tape each bag shut at the top: the point is the weight, not what is inside. Make enough for at least one each and use them to fill the fish box (see above)
- A large plastic container with handles, such as a flexitub (available from hardware shops and large supermarkets)
- Music and words
- In every pew or row of seats:
  - lots of small pieces of thin card, about the size of business cards
  - pens and pencils

Leaders

Minimum: 1

- Leader

Optimum: 7

- Leader *(Introduction and Conclusion)*
- Storyteller
- Music Leader
- Explorers 1 and 2
- Activity Leader
- Prayer Leader

Suggestions for additional music

- I will worship
- We'll walk the land with hearts on fire

Service

Welcome *As people arrive, invite them to take some of the small cards and write on them the names of people for whom they would like to pray.*

Introduction Our story today takes place on the shore of Lake Galilee. This is a large, freshwater lake with a good supply of fish. Fishing is a thriving local business round here – most of the time.

Storytelling *Stand in the boat with the loose net in your hands.*

Simon Peter had been fishing all night with his brother and his business partners, James and John. They owned a couple of boats between them and usually they made a good enough living. That night was different. They'd started out in the evening when the fish were rising, but hadn't caught a single one. Hour after hour they cast their nets into the water, and still they came up empty.

Hold up the empty net.

By dawn they were tired and fed up. They landed on the other side of the lake and set about checking their nets for holes. However, they soon had company – and how! A huge crowd of people was gathering on the beach, and the fishermen could hear one man's voice above the rest. He sounded as if he were preaching. Soon the press of people was so great that the fishermen and the preacher backed down to the water's edge. The preacher caught Simon's eye: 'Lend me your boat, brother!' he said. So Simon steadied the boat while the preacher got in and sat down. He spoke to the crowds in a firm, clear voice. There were no flourishes or fancy words, just stories and straightforward teaching. In spite of his worries, Simon listened.

When the preacher had finished, he turned to Simon. 'Put out into deep water and cast your nets.'

Simon replied, 'Sir, we've been fishing all night and we've still come back empty-handed. See?' He held up

PROPER 1

the empty nets. The preacher just looked at him until finally, he relented. 'All right then! I'll do it, if you say so.' He and his brother headed back out in their boat and cast the net over the side.

Cast the net at the back of the boat.

Then they tried to pull the net back in, and found that they couldn't!

Try to pull in the second net from the back of the boat (the one that is pinned down by the fish box).

If was so stuffed full of fish, it was starting to break under the strain! They called to their friends for help. *(To the congregation:)* Who can help me land this enormous catch?

Invite volunteers to help you lift the load of fish into the boat.

There were so many fish, the catch filled both boats and they began to sink! When Simon saw this, he realised that the preacher was Jesus. He fell at his feet, saying, 'You should go, Lord. Don't waste your time on me – I'm not good enough!'

Jesus looked at all the fishermen, up to their knees in fish, and said to Simon Peter, 'Don't be frightened; from now on you'll be catching people.' Then the men landed their boats, left everything and followed him.

Music	I, the Lord of sea and sky

Exploring 1	Today's story was from Luke's Gospel. In other versions of this story, Jesus simply turns up on the beach and calls the fishermen to follow him. Only this version gives us a miracle. How heavy was that load of fish we brought into the boat?

Invite responses from your volunteers.

The miraculous catch was so huge that it almost broke the nets. It took four men to lift it and then it nearly sank the boats. Jesus didn't simply give them the fish they had failed to catch that night; he gave them a hugely generous, bumper catch that was almost more than they could manage.

Today we will be wondering what this story has to say to us. Not many of us have been given a boatload of fish, but let's start by considering what God *has* given us.

Activity   *Open the fish box and hand out the heavy bags.*

We are going to create a physical image of all the good things we have received. Each of these heavy bags represents a gift from God: please take one and ask yourself, 'What is good in my life? What do I have to be thankful for?' Whatever it is, please write or draw it on the bag.

Allow plenty of time for people to do this.

Now let's gather together all the good things that we have been given.

Put all the heavy bags in the tub.

Now, how heavy is this pile of good things? Who would like to try and lift it?

Invite individual volunteers to try, then ask for their comments on the weight of the tub.

This heavy weight is more than we can lift! It reminds us that the sum total of all the good things God has given us, and continues to give us, is greater than any of us can comprehend.

Exploring 2   So what do we do in response to all this goodness? In our story, Simon Peter immediately felt that he didn't deserve it. He didn't feel good enough or holy enough. He even told Jesus to leave him alone! We might feel like that, too, sometimes. The thought of all the good things that God has done might overwhelm us. But Jesus' reply to Peter was simple: 'Don't be frightened.' With those words he accepted all Peter's insecurity and feelings of inadequacy – and wanted him, just the same. Jesus continues to offer us that same reassurance and acceptance. He wants us to belong to him, however unlikely or unworthy a follower we might feel ourselves to be.

Finally, Jesus gave Peter and his fellow fishermen a job to do: 'From now on, you'll be catching people.' In other words, he wanted them to help bring as many people as possible to God through him. And just look at how they responded! Those fishermen, blessed with the catch of their lives, moored their boats then simply left them, fish and all, and went with Jesus. They became his first disciples.

We may find it hard to follow their example in dropping everything, but we are still called to follow Jesus and help him fish for people. By telling others the good news of Jesus, and by showing his love in our lives, we may help them turn to God and know that good news and that love for themselves.

Prayer action

One way in which we can 'catch people' like fishermen is by gathering them up in prayer, as a fisherman collects fish in his nets. When we arrived in church this morning, we wrote the names of people for whom we would like to pray. Let's gather those people together now.

Pass the fishing net around the church to collect all the prayer cards.

Fishermen talk about 'the one that got away', and there are many people who may have slipped through this net of prayer. We need to catch them, too. Let's take a moment to think of anyone we have forgotten, or who may have no one else to pray for them.

Pause while everyone writes more names on cards, then pass the net around again.

Lastly, we'll put these blank cards in the net as we pray for those no one has remembered, and those whose needs are known only to God.

Place the blank cards in the net.

Let us pray.

Lord Jesus, Fisherman of humankind,
we have caught these people in our net of prayer;
we bring them before you now.
May you bless us all.
Amen.

Music   Jesus Christ is waiting

Conclusion   Lord Jesus,
as we go out into the world,
keep calling us to follow you,
saying to us, 'Don't be frightened.'
Amen.

Give notices, announce the next all-age service and invite everyone to the feast.

Proper 2

Good news for the poor

Theme	The Beatitudes
Scripture	Jeremiah 17:5-10; Luke 6:17-26

Running order Total: 50 minutes

Welcome	Exploring the props and costumes for today's story *(5 minutes)*
Introduction	Opening the theme
Storytelling	Visual and interactive retelling of Luke 6:17-26 *(10 minutes)*
Music	The kingdom of heaven *(5 minutes)*
Exploring	What impact did Jesus' words have then? Visual exploration with video clip *(10 minutes)*
Music	Alleluia! Alleluia! Raise the Gospel *(5 minutes)*
Prayer/Activity	Trusting and growing – planting a rose bush *(10 minutes)*
Music	Be bold, be strong *(5 minutes)*
Conclusion	Closing prayer and invitation

PROPER 2

Resources

- Props and costumes, spread out at the front of church:
  - lots of bandages
  - a begging bowl with a couple of copper coins
  - a bowl with a crust of bread
  - a black head-cloth and a hanky
  - a rich cloak and two full purses or money bags
  - some Roman armour *(see appendix)*
  - a rich robe and a crown
  - a plain white robe and sandals
- A sign: 'Which people might these things belong to?'
- Music and words
- Video clip of Narayanan Krishnan *(see appendix)*
- Laptop, projector and screen
- A rose ready for planting *(see appendix)*
- *Either* a spot outside the church for planting *or* a very large container with soil (in which case, place it on a tarpaulin inside the church)
- A spade and trowels
- Watering cans

Leaders

Minimum: 2

- Leader
- *Jesus*

Optimum: 7+

- Leader *(Introduction and Conclusion)*
- Storyteller
- *Jesus*
- Music Leader
- Explorer
- Activity Leader(s)
- Prayer Leader

Suggestions for additional music

- Blest are the pure in heart
- All my hope on God is founded

Service

Welcome — *As people arrive, invite them to explore the props and costumes you have laid out at the front of church, and think about who they might belong to.*

Introduction — Today we have lots of costumes and props in church to help us tell our story. I wonder who they belong to?

Hold up each set of props in turn and invite suggestions, then ask a volunteer to take on each part. By the end, you should have the following, dressed as in Jesus' time:

- *An ill person (wrapped in lots of bandages)*
- *A poor person (give them the begging bowl with a couple of copper coins)*
- *A hungry person (give them the bowl with a crust of bread)*
- *Someone in mourning (cover their head with the black cloth and give them a hanky to dry their tears)*
- *A tax-collector (dress him and tell him to jingle his money bags)*
- *A Roman (dress him and tell him to pat his belly as though he has just eaten a good meal)*
- *A king (dress him and tell him to smile smugly!)*
- *Jesus (bring forward your actor and dress him)*

Storytelling — Now we have our cast, let's set the scene. We're on a flat plain in Galilee and we've come here to listen to Jesus. Here he is.

Bring Jesus to the front.

Word about Jesus has spread far and wide, so there is a huge crowd pressing around him.

Invite your congregation to stand and ask your volunteers to mix in with the crowd.

You've come from the surrounding towns and villages, from the coast and even from the big city! There are all sorts of different people here. Lots are sick, like this person.

Bring forward your first volunteer.

Everyone has heard that Jesus can heal people, so the ill and the dying are trying to touch to him, hoping his power will cure them. And do you know what? It works! Jesus heals everyone he can reach.

Jesus touches the first volunteer, who tears off the bandages and cheers.

Then Jesus tells everyone to listen. *(Jesus holds his hands up.)* The people sit down and pay attention.

Invite your congregation to sit down.

Jesus   *As he speaks, he invites forward each volunteer in turn. He gathers the poor person, the hungry person and the mourner to him, and addresses the last blessing to them as a group. He speaks to the rich tax-collector, the well-fed Roman and the complacent king and sends them off to the back of church, calling the last 'woe' after them.*[20]

Blessed are you who are poor,
for yours is the kingdom of God.
Blessed are you who are hungry now,
for you will be filled.
Blessed are you who weep now,
for you will laugh.
Blessed are you when people hate you, and when they exclude you, revile you, and defame you on account of the Son of Man. Rejoice on that day and leap for joy, for surely your reward is great in heaven; for that is what their ancestors did to the prophets.
But woe to you who are rich,
for you have received your consolation.
Woe to you who are full now,
for you will be hungry.
Woe to you who are laughing now,
for you will mourn and weep.
Woe to you when all speak well of you, for that is what their ancestors did to the false prophets.

---

20. This is taken directly from Luke's gospel (NRSV). You may prefer to use a different translation.

Music The kingdom of heaven

Exploring Jesus' words in today's story may be familiar to us, but what impact did they have on the first people who heard them? Let's look at the groups of people he mentioned. First, there were the poor.

Bring forward the poor person.

For these people, there was no government support and little education or training. Since wealth was seen as a blessing from God, many people at that time may have believed that their poverty was their own fault, a sign that they lived unworthy lives. To these people, Jesus promised, 'Yours is the kingdom of God.' Now a kingdom is the greatest gift a king can give: remember Shakespeare's Richard III, so desperate for a mount that he cried, 'A horse, a horse! My kingdom for a horse!'? Then there was King Herod, who was so delighted by his stepdaughter's dancing that he promised to give her anything she asked, even half of his kingdom. Jesus promised an entire kingdom to the poor – and not just any kingdom, *God's* kingdom!

Then there were the hungry.

Bring forward the hungry person.

These people were starving. They never had enough to eat, and what little they did get, they could never choose. They had to steal leftovers and rotten food from the market place, or they were dependent on the charity of others. Their empty bellies ached from lack of food and their bodies were weakened by poor nutrition. Jesus promised them that they would be full! They couldn't remember what that felt like, but the thought of it kept them awake at night.

Then there were those in mourning.

Bring forward the mourner.

In Jesus' time, if someone in your family died, you had to follow a strict set of rules for mourning. In the week following the death, you were not allowed to work, change your clothes or even bathe. In the following month, you were not allowed to socialise or go to any kind of celebration. If you had lost a parent, these restrictions continued for a whole year. Mourning affected your entire life. There must have been people who lost several relatives and entered into years of mourning which, in effect, isolated them from society. Imagine how they must have felt when Jesus promised them joyful laughter!

All these people to whom Jesus spoke were in some way pushed out by society. The poor and hungry were seen as an inconvenience or as objects of pity and charity. The mourners were socially excluded. Most of all, there were the sick who surrounded Jesus in huge numbers. They were treated as unclean and untouchable. Let's imagine how Jesus' blessings and promises affected all these people. To help us do this, we will watch this video of an ordinary man in India who is changing the lives of the sick, poor and hungry.

Play the video of Narayanan Krishnan.

If it were possible to see a video clip of Jesus at work in Galilee, it might look something like this. This inspirational man is not a Christian, but he embodies the spirit of Christ in his care for the poor. He shows us the kind of difference Jesus made to the lives of ordinary people.

But Jesus' promises didn't end with blessings. When he talked about the prosperous who would come to nothing – those who were rich, full and laughing – his audience would have had some clear ideas about who he meant.

Bring forward the tax-collector, the Roman and the king.

Among the rich were the hated tax-collectors, who extorted unfair taxes and prospered at the expense of the poor. Famously well-fed were the Romans, the occupying power, notorious for their lavish feasts. And when Jesus mentioned 'those who laughed', people may have thought of local kings like Herod, who were cruel, self-satisfied despots. Jesus promised the downfall of all these people, which must have been music to the crowd's ears.

Finally, when Jesus promised these blessings and woes, he was making a big announcement. All Jews were familiar with God's promises of a Saviour. They knew the words of the prophet Isaiah:

> The Spirit of the Lord is upon me,
> because he has anointed me
> to bring good news to the poor.
> He has sent me to proclaim release to the captives
> and recovery of sight to the blind,
> to let the oppressed go free,
> to proclaim the year of the Lord's favour.

Shortly before today's story, Jesus had read these words in the synagogue and declared that he was the fulfilment of this promise – he was the Messiah, the Lord's anointed.[21] When he then healed the sick and brought good news to poor, hungry people, he was publicly demonstrating that he was their Saviour. No wonder they followed him!

Music Alleluia! Alleluia! Raise the Gospel

Prayer/Activity We have been exploring the impact that Jesus' words had on those who first heard him. As a result of his healing and preaching, they believed and trusted that Jesus was their Saviour. Today's Old Testament reading suggests that trust is key for us, too.

> Blessed are those who trust in the Lord,
> whose trust is the Lord.
> They shall be like a tree planted by water,
> sending out its roots by the stream.
> It shall not fear when heat comes,
> and its leaves shall stay green;
> in the year of drought it is not anxious,
> and it does not cease to bear fruit.

---

21. Luke 4:18-19.

If we trust in Jesus, we are like a firmly rooted tree, able to withstand all weathers. But the crucial thing is that a tree like this can grow. If we trust fully in Jesus, then we, too, will grow and become more like him. We, too, can bring good news to the poor, help the hungry and comfort the isolated. Jesus' work of salvation is ongoing, and we have our own part to play in it.

Today we will pray to root our lives in our trust of Jesus, so that we might grow more like him in all that we do. As a sign of our prayer, we will plant this rose. May it be for us and our church a sign of our firmly rooted faith and growing lives.

The people gather round as the rose is planted. Everyone helps to fill in the hole and water the earth.

Let us pray.

Lord Jesus,
may you bless us all.
May our trust take root in you
and bear fruit in our lives.
Amen.

Music   Be bold, be strong

Conclusion   Loving Lord,
send us out into the world to bring your good news
to those who need it most,
in your name.
Amen.

Give notices, announce the next all-age service and invite everyone to the feast.

Proper 3

The challenge of love

Theme	Loving our enemies and turning the other cheek
Scripture	Genesis 45:3-11, 15; Luke 6:27-38

Running order

Total: 50 minutes

Welcome	Decorating cakes with hearts *(10 minutes)*
Introduction	Opening the theme
Storytelling 1	Visual retelling of Joseph's reunion with his brothers *(5 minutes)*
Storytelling 2	Memo from HQ: Jesus' instructions to his followers *(5 minutes)*
Music	A new commandment *(5 minutes)*
Activity	How did the crowd around Jesus react to his teaching? Interactive exploration *(10 minutes)*
Exploring	What does Jesus' teaching mean for us? *(5 minutes)*
Prayer action	'Give, and it will be given to you' – edible prayer *(5 minutes)*
Music	Brother, sister, let me serve you *(5 minutes)*
Conclusion	Closing prayer and invitation

Resources

- Music and words
- A laptop, projector and screen
- Joseph's story in pictures *(see appendix)*
- Jesus' email from HQ *(see appendix)*
- Pictures of people from the crowd in Galilee *(see appendix)*
- Sticky notes shaped like speech bubbles (available from stationers and Amazon)
- Pens and pencils
- Spread the following on some wipe-clean tables:
  - ready-made plain sponge cakes and/or fairy cakes
  - ready-mixed icing
  - cake decorations in the shape of hearts (there should be plenty in the shops around Valentine's Day)
  - some plates for finished cakes
  - some knives for spreading, cutting and serving

Leaders

Minimum: 1
- Leader

Optimum: 7
- Leader *(Introduction and Conclusion)*
- Storytellers 1 and 2
- Music Leader
- Explorer
- Activity Leader
- Prayer Leader

Suggestions for additional music

- Lord, we come to ask your healing
- Make me a channel of your peace

Service

Welcome — *As people arrive, invite them to decorate ready-made cakes with icing and hearts and then leave them on the altar.*

Introduction — These delicious-looking cakes will play their part in our service today, but first we have a story. It begins with a very special coat.

Storytelling 1 — *Show the picture of Joseph in his multicoloured coat.*

Who did this coat belong to?

Invite responses.

Joseph was one of twelve brothers, but he was their father's favourite. The multicoloured coat was his special treat. Was that fair?

Invite responses.

Joseph's brothers were so jealous that they planned to kill him. Instead, they grabbed his coat and dumped him in a pit in the desert, then sold him to some passing slave traders. Did he deserve that?

Invite responses. Show picture of Joseph in chains.

The brothers returned home and told their father that his precious son was dead. Joseph became a slave in Egypt. Time passed, and Joseph did well – so well that he ended up working for Pharaoh himself. Joseph was put in charge of all Egypt's farming and produce: during seven years of bumper harvests, he organised storage of all the spare food. When seven years of famine came, the people of Egypt still had enough to eat, thanks to Joseph.

Show the picture of overflowing baskets of food.

Unfortunately, Joseph's family back home wasn't so well off. His father and brothers were starving.

Show the picture of the hungry brothers with empty bowls.

So they went to Egypt to beg for food. They were met by Pharaoh's right-hand man, Joseph – but they didn't recognise their own brother! However, he knew exactly who they were.

Show the picture of Joseph facing the brothers, remembering himself in chains.

He tested them to see if their hearts were true. When he found that they were, he declared, 'I am Joseph, your long-lost brother!' He opened his arms and hugged them all.

Show the picture of Joseph embracing his brothers.

He forgave them everything they had done to him, and shared his home, his food and his money with them. The whole family settled in Egypt with Joseph.

Storytelling 2 Joseph's story began with unfairness, jealousy, hatred and cruelty, but it ended with loving, giving and sharing. Our second story today takes up the same theme. Jesus taught hundreds of his followers by speaking to large crowds. If he were giving us God's instructions today, he might well do it like this.

Display and read the email from HQ: Jesus' instructions to his followers.

Music A new commandment

Activity *Display the email again, then keep it on the screen for the rest of the service.*

Jesus' instructions are quite a challenge, aren't they? Loving people who hate us, turning the other cheek, giving to everyone who asks – none of this is easy! These words would have made a big impression on the people who first heard them. Today we're going to explore some of the reactions in Jesus' crowd of followers.

Around the church today are some of the people from that crowd in first-century Galilee. Each of them is cross or upset about something. For example, here is someone who is fed up of being bossed about by Roman soldiers. He sees the Roman occupying army as the enemy. He's thinking, 'Those horrible Romans have taken over *our* country!' I wonder what he might say when he hears Jesus say, 'Love your enemies'.

Invite responses and write them on the sticky notes shaped like speech bubbles, then stick them around the figure. For example: 'Love that lot? No way!' and 'They don't deserve it!'

Let's take some time now to consider the other people in the crowd and wonder what they would say in response to Jesus' teaching. Write your ideas in speech bubbles and stick them around the figures, like this.

Allow plenty of time for people to circulate, think and write.

Exploring

Begin by reading out a selection of the responses from the Activity.

Many of us will sympathise with these responses from Jesus' first followers! They remind us how hard it has always been for people to love, do good and share in the face of hatred, unkindness and injustice. It is still hard for us, today. We may not think of ourselves as having enemies like the Romans, but we may have rivals or bullies in our lives. We may well know people who take without asking or who can be unkind and hurtful. Jesus calls us to love them – but why? The answer lies in the second set of instructions he gave:

- Don't judge others, and you won't be judged.
- Don't condemn others, and you won't be condemned.
- Forgive, and you will be forgiven.
- Give, and it will be given to you in return (more than you can imagine!).

None of us is perfect, and we are all in need of love. Sometimes we feel judged: we worry what people think of us. We may feel condemned, because it seems as if we can never get it right. We may feel as if we will never be forgiven for something we did wrong, or as if we have nothing worthwhile in our lives. God meets all our worries, inadequacies, failures and emptiness with his overflowing love, which is freely given and more than we could ever deserve.

So every time we try to love someone who is hard to love, or help someone who doesn't deserve it, we are trying in our own small way to love other people in the way God loves us. We are doing things God's way. We may not always manage it, but we are called to try.

Prayer action

Jesus said, 'Give, and it will be given to you in return.' Our prayer today is an active prayer that will remind us about giving and receiving. Who would like to share some of this delicious cake?

Invite one half of the congregation to come forward, to take a piece of cake and then give it to someone who is still sitting down. When those people have eaten, they come forward and take a piece of cake to someone who has not yet had any.

Let us pray.

Loving and giving God,
may we generously give,
as we have received in abundance;
may we forgive,
as we have been forgiven,
in Jesus name.
Amen.

Music

Brother, sister, let me serve you

Conclusion

God of Love,
as we go out into the world,
help us to love those who are hard to love.
May we do things your way.
Amen.

Give notices, announce the next all-age service and invite everyone to the feast.

Second Sunday before Lent

Pets' service

Theme	Being caretakers of God's creation
Scripture	Genesis 2:4b-9, 15-25

Running order	Total: 50 minutes
Welcome	Meeting and greeting the pets *(10 minutes)*
Introduction	Opening the theme
Storytelling	Visual retelling of the creation of Adam and Eve and the naming of the animals *(5 minutes)*
Music	Who put the colours in the rainbow? *(5 minutes)*
Activity	Creating a global collage of all God's creatures *(10 minutes)*
Exploring	How do we look after our pets? Show and tell *(10 minutes)*
Prayer action	The life of the world in our hands – creative prayer *(5 minutes)*
Music	All things bright and beautiful *(5 minutes)*
Conclusion	Closing prayer and invitation

Resources

NB advance notice needed! Invite people to bring their pets to church.

- Illustrations for the story, shown as a slideshow *(see appendix)*
    - God making Adam
    - a wild, exotic garden
    - an exotic fruit tree
    - a slideshow of many different animals and birds
    - Adam and Eve
- A large circle of black card (A1 size)
- Animal outlines *(see appendix)*
- Scissors
- Glue sticks
- Music and words
- Table tennis balls, enough for one each (available cheaply in bulk from sports shops and Amazon. Make sure they are plain white)
- Blue and green felt pens
- *(optional)* Cat and dog treats

Leaders

Minimum: 1

- Leader

Optimum: 6

- Leader *(Introduction and Conclusion)*
- Storyteller
- Music Leader
- Activity Leader
- Explorer
- Prayer Leader

Suggestions for additional music

- All creatures of our God and King
- O Lord of every shining constellation

Service

Welcome *As people arrive, encourage them to mingle and meet each other's pets.*

Introduction Welcome to our special service in celebration of all God's creatures, especially our pets. Our story today will take us right back to the beginning, when God was busy creating the world.[22]

Storytelling Then the Lord God formed man from the dust of the ground, and breathed into his nostrils the breath of life; and the man became a living being.

Show the picture of God making Adam.

And the Lord God planted a garden in Eden, in the east;

Show the picture of a wild, exotic garden.

and there he put the man whom he had formed. Out of the ground the Lord God made to grow every tree that is pleasant to the sight and good for food, the tree of life also in the midst of the garden, and the tree of the knowledge of good and evil.

Show the picture of an exotic fruit tree.

The Lord God took the man and put him in the garden of Eden to till it and keep it. And the Lord God commanded the man, 'You may freely eat of every tree of the garden; but of the tree of the knowledge of good and evil you shall not eat, for in the day that you eat of it you shall die.' Then the Lord God said, 'It is not good that the man should be alone; I will make him a helper as his partner.'

As you read the next section, show a slideshow of many different animals and birds.

---

22. The text is taken from the NRSV; you may prefer to use a different translation.

SECOND SUNDAY BEFORE LENT

So out of the ground the Lord God formed every animal of the field and every bird of the air, and brought them to the man to see what he would call them; and whatever the man called each living creature, that was its name. The man gave names to all cattle, and to the birds of the air, and to every animal of the field; but for the man there was not found a helper as his partner. So the Lord God caused a deep sleep to fall upon the man, and he slept; then he took one of his ribs and closed up its place with flesh. And the rib that the Lord God had taken from the man he made into a woman and brought her to the man.

Show the picture of Adam and Eve.

Then the man said,
'This at last is bone of my bones
and flesh of my flesh;
this one shall be called Woman,
for out of Man this one was taken.'

Music Who put the colours in the rainbow

Activity Today's story is just one part of the Bible's great Creation story. It gives us a way of understanding how we all came to be here. At first there was nothing, and then God created something out of nothing. Over millennia – in our story, a matter of moments – his work of creation evolved, producing an extraordinary variety of creatures, including us and the pets that are with us today.

To help us celebrate God's creation, we are going to build up a picture of this global variety.

Encourage everyone to come forward and create the collage by adding animal shapes to the globe to form continents, seas and icecaps. Display the finished piece.

Exploring This collage has been inspired by a design used by the environmental charity, Greenpeace.[23] It shows us the wonderful variety of creatures that God has made. In

---

23. On a recent T-shirt: see www.greenpeace.org.uk.

today's story, he brought them all to Adam for naming; elsewhere in the Creation story, God made human beings the masters of all living things. So Adam's first job was to name the animals and be in charge of them. Now, many of us here today have shared Adam's experience in a small way: when we decided to own a pet, we gave it a name and we became responsible for it. Who would like to introduce us to their pet and tell us how they look after it?

Invite volunteers to come forward, show their pet and explain the care it needs, such as feeding, exercise, grooming, training, etc.

All these owners set us a wonderful example. They are responsible for their pets and they care for their needs: they remind us how we should look after the world that God made for us and all the creatures in it. In today's story, we heard that 'The Lord God took the man and put him in the garden of Eden to till it and keep it.' Those words 'till' and 'keep' are translations of Hebrew words that also mean 'serve' and 'preserve'. They emphasise that God made human beings the caretakers of his creation: it is our job to look after the world. This is a bigger challenge today than it has ever been, because as well as looking after the pets we love and the local countryside we enjoy, together we are also responsible for global problems like the changing climate, our use of fossil fuels and the amount of rubbish we produce. We are creation's caretakers, and the life of the world really is in our hands.

Prayer action Our prayers today will help us think about creation and remind us that the life of the world is in our hands. Please take one of these balls and use green and blue pens to colour in land and sea. Make your own tiny planet earth.

Allow plenty of time for people to create their models.

Let's hold the world in our hands as we pray.

Creator God,
thank you for the beautiful, fragile, evolving world
you have given us.
Help us to be good caretakers of your creation,
in Jesus' name.
Amen.

Please take your model of the earth home with you, to remind you that you are one of its caretakers.

Music All things bright and beautiful

Conclusion *Invite people to bring their pets forward for a blessing.*

God of all living things,
thank you for the world's creatures.
May you bless our pets
and help us to cherish them.
Amen.

Give notices, announce the next all-age service and invite everyone to the feast. Give out animal treats, too.

Sunday next before Lent
Shining bright

Theme	The Transfiguration; showing God's glory
Scripture	Exodus 34:29-35; Luke 9:28-36

Running order	Total: 50 minutes
Welcome	Adding sequins to the shining picture of God's glory *(5 minutes)*
Introduction	Opening the theme
Storytelling 1	Mime with music – Moses and his shining face *(5 minutes)*
Music	O raise your eyes on high *(5 minutes)*
Storytelling 2	Dramatised retelling – the Transfiguration *(5 minutes)*
Activity	Torch-lit treasure hunt for shining letters *(10 minutes)*
Exploring	What does this shining brightness show us? *(5 minutes)*
Music	Jesus bids us shine *(5 minutes)*
Prayer action	High-visibility crosses – creative prayer *(10 minutes)*
Conclusion	Closing prayer and invitation

Resources

- A shining tabard *(see appendix)*
- Sequin strings: gold, silver or hologram, available from fabric shops and online craft suppliers
- Scissors
- PVA glue
- A screen (a white sheet) held taut by volunteers, ready to drop it on cue
- Two spotlights, one behind the screen and one in front
- A recording of the closing minutes of 'O Fortuna' from *Carmina Burana* by Carl Orff, plus audio equipment to play it on
- A microphone
- Several torches
- Music and words
- Stone tablets *(see appendix)*
- High-visibility letters, spelling out 'THE GLORY OF GOD' *(see appendix)*
- Craft tables with equipment for making high-visibility crosses *(see appendix)*

Leaders

Minimum: 7

- Leader
- Cast x 6

Optimum: 13

- Leader *(Introduction and Conclusion)*
- Storytellers 1 and 2
- Cast x 6 *(wearing traditional robes)*:
  Moses, wearing the shining tabard, holding a mallet and chisel
  Jesus, wearing a white tunic and the shining tabard, covered by an outer robe
  Elijah/Voice of God
  Peter
  James
  John
- Music Leader
- Explorer
- Activity Leader
- Prayer Leader

Suggestions for additional music

- Meekness and majesty
- Lord, the light of your love

Service

Welcome — *As people arrive, invite them to add strings of sequins to the shining tabard in a radiating pattern.*

Introduction — Today's service is full of light. It's not just any light – this is shining, bright, dazzling light. For our first story, we will go back to the time of Moses.

Start the music, quietly.

A long time ago, Moses led God's people into the desert. There God gave him a set of rules to help his people live good lives: these were called the Ten Commandments. Moses spent a long time on a high mountain with God, learning about the Commandments, before he was ready to come down and speak to the people.

Storytelling 1 — *On the screen, backlit by the first spotlight, we see a silhouette of Moses. He listens and then chisels the tablets of stone.*

As the music builds to a climax, Moses stands and holds up the tablets of stone. He is preparing to speak to the people.

At the climax of the music, the screen drops to the floor to reveal Moses. He is wearing the shining tabard. Both spotlights shine on him as the music ends.

Music — O raise your eyes on high

During the hymn, Moses gives the shining tabard to Jesus, who puts it on under his outer robe. All the actors wait at the back of the church.

Storytelling 2 — Our second story took place many, many years later. Jesus called his closest disciples, Peter, James and John. Together they climbed a high and lonely mountain to pray.

The actors walk down the aisle as if climbing a steep mountain slope. At the front of the church, the disciples kneel down and Jesus stands facing the congregation with his arms raised, looking upwards.

SUNDAY NEXT BEFORE LENT

Then something strange began to happen.

The back spotlight is turned on.

Jesus' face began to shine. Then two men appeared in the glow: they were Moses and Elijah.

Moses and Elijah stand on either side of Jesus. They take off his outer robe, revealing the shining tabard. The front spotlight is turned on them all.

Jesus' clothes became dazzling white. The disciples could hardly look at him.

The disciples stagger, clutching their eyes.

Peter blurted out the first thing that came into his head.

Peter   Master, it's just as well we came! We should make a shelter for each of you: one for you, and one for Moses, and one for Elijah!

Storyteller   Suddenly, they were overshadowed by a strange cloud.

Turn off the spotlights and all the other lights in church. Moses and Elijah leave. Jesus takes off the tabard and kneels.

From the cloud came an unearthly voice.

Voice of God   *(unseen, amplified)* This is my Son, my Chosen; listen to him!

Turn on the ordinary church lights.

Storyteller   Then, just as suddenly, the disciples found themselves alone with Jesus on top of the mountain. They were stunned into silence.

The disciples clutch each other and look astonished.

Activity   In both our stories, there was dazzling brightness. This was not a gentle glow – it was the kind of light which was impossible to miss. Our activity today will help us discover what this bright, shining light means. We are going to have a torchlit treasure hunt in the dark: who would like to join in?

Bring forward some volunteers and give them each a torch.

Hidden around the church are some bright letters, like this. *(Hold up a high-visibility letter G.)* When a torch beam reflects off it in the dark, it really shines.

Turn off the lights and ask a volunteer to shine their torch on the letter G to demonstrate.

How many shining letters can you find?

Allow plenty of time for the volunteers to search the church. Invite them to bring the letters to the front and rearrange them, propped up on the altar, to spell out 'THE GLORY OF GOD'. Turn on the lights and ask the volunteers to shine their torches on these words during the next part of the service.

Exploring

In the Bible, bright light is a sign of God's glory. It is a visible reminder of his power and goodness. When Jesus' appearance became dazzling in front of his disciples, he showed them the glory of God himself. This was reinforced by everything else that happened at the same time: Moses the law-giver and Elijah the great prophet appeared with Jesus, confirming that he was the fulfilment of everything that the law and the prophets had promised. Then the voice of God spoke and identified Jesus as his Son. The three disciples who were present never forgot the glory of God they witnessed that day.[24]

In our first story, when Moses' face shone brightly it was a visible sign that he had been in the presence of God. He was changed by the experience: he began to reflect God's glory. In fact, the light in his face was so dazzling that he had to cover it with a veil when he left God's presence to speak to his people.

24. See 2 Peter 1:16-18.

Together, these stories give us a clear message. When God's people were in the desert, no one but Moses was allowed into the presence of God. Things are different now: since Jesus came among us, we can all know God and enter his presence, because Jesus is God – and when we have been in God's presence, we should reflect a little of his glory, as Moses did. If we know Jesus, then we should be shining his light into the world. We should be like the letters in our treasure hunt, which reflected the torch beams so brightly that they could easily be found. We may not physically shine with light, but as followers of Jesus we should be easy to spot: everyone we meet ought to be able to see the difference in us.

Music Jesus bids us shine

Prayer action For our prayers today, we will each make a high-visibility cross, like this.

Demonstrate how to stick strips of high-visibility tape on the plain cardboard cross. You could also decorate it further with sequins and glitter.

This cross reflects light very brightly: please make one and keep it as a reminder that we are called to reflect the light of God's glory in our lives.

Allow plenty of time for people to make their own crosses.

Let us pray.

Lord Jesus,
shine in our hearts.
May our lives reflect your light.
Amen.

Conclusion God of glory, light and life,
may we know your presence with us
today and always.
Amen.

Give notices, announce the next all-age service and invite everyone to the feast.

Lent

Ash Wednesday

Looking towards Lent

Theme	Fasting and repentance
Scripture	Isaiah 58:1-12; Matthew 6:1-6, 16-21

Running order	Total: 50 minutes
Welcome	Wondering about the sackcloth and ashes *(5 minutes)*
Introduction	Opening the theme
Activity	Ashing *(10 minutes)*
Music	Forgive our sins as we forgive *(5 minutes)*
Storytelling 1	Reading Isaiah's words on fasting, with visual aids *(2 minutes)*
Storytelling 2	Visual retelling of Jesus' teaching on fasting, prayer and charity *(3 minutes)*
Exploring	What should we give up for Lent? Interactive exploration *(15 minutes)*
Prayer action	Cleansing fire – active confession *(5 minutes)*
Music	God forgave my sin *(5 minutes)*
Conclusion	Closing prayer and invitation

ASH WEDNESDAY

Resources

- Sackcloth and ashes *(see appendix)*
- Music and words
- A large purse or money bag
- A board or flip chart with the first title on the front: *Giving something up = FAST* and the second title on the back (or second sheet): *Giving something away = FAST*
- Lots of marker pens
- A box of chocolates
- A bag of sweets
- A bottle of wine
- A DVD of a TV series
- In different places around the church, place four large boards or pieces of card, each with a heading:
  - *Giving something away to God*
  - *Giving something away to another person*
  - *Giving away something we'd miss*
  - *Giving time*
- Two boxes of tissues
- Outside, a small bonfire or brazier, lit before the service begins

Leaders

Minimum: 2

- Leader
- *Penitent*

Optimum: 8

- Leader *(Introduction and Conclusion)*
- Storytellers 1 and 2
- *Penitent,* wearing traditional robes
- Music Leader
- Explorer
- Activity Leader
- Prayer Leader

Suggestions for additional music

- Lord Jesus Christ
- I believe in Jesus

Service

Welcome — *As people arrive, invite them to feel the sackcloth, rub their hands in the ashes and wonder, 'What are these things used for?'*

Introduction — Today is the beginning of Lent: it is known as Ash Wednesday. The name comes from these things. *(Hold up the sackcloth and ashes.)* This is sackcloth and these are ashes: in ancient times, people wore both as a sign that they were sad and sorry. The ashes are all that is left after something has been consumed by fire, so they were a reminder of loss and sadness. The sackcloth is rough and itchy, so people wore it to show that they were sorry for things they had done wrong.

The actor who will play the penitent in the Storytelling takes away the sackcloth to drape around his shoulders and a pinch of ashes to smear on his face.

Activity — Lent is a season for remembering that none of us is perfect, and we begin it by showing that we are sad and sorry for the things we have done wrong. We don't wear sackcloth and ashes; instead, we mark the sign of the cross in ash on our foreheads. If you would like to, come forward and be marked with ash. May these ash crosses be a sign that we say sorry to each other and to God for all we have done wrong.

Encourage everyone to come forward and be marked with an ash cross. As you make each mark, say:

May this be a sign that you are sorry.

Music — Forgive our sins as we forgive

Storytelling 1 — Long before Jesus lived, this is how God's people showed that they were sad and sorry.

Bring forward your penitent, dressed in sackcloth and ashes, with his head bowed, clutching his stomach.

They dressed in sackcloth and ashes – but that wasn't all. *(to the penitent)* What have you eaten today?

Penitent	Nothing!
Storyteller	This person is fasting, which means he has made a sacrifice by eating little or no food. So here we have sackcloth, ashes and fasting – all signs that this person is sorry for his sins. However, let's hear what God had to say about this particular sort of penitent, through the words of his spokesman, Isaiah.

> Such fasting as you do today
> will not make your voice heard on high.
> Is such the fast that I choose,
> a day to humble oneself?
> Is it to bow down the head like a bulrush,
> and to lie in sackcloth and ashes?
> Will you call this a fast,
> a day acceptable to the Lord?
> Is not this the fast that I choose:
> to loose the bonds of injustice,
> to undo the thongs of the yoke,
> to let the oppressed go free,
> and to break every yoke?
> Is it not to share your bread with the hungry,
> and bring the homeless poor into your house;
> when you see the naked, to cover them,
> and not to hide yourself from your own kin?
> Then your light shall break forth like the dawn . . .

According to Isaiah, God wants a different kind of fasting. We'll look more closely at that once we've heard what Jesus had to say on the same subject.

Storytelling 2 Jesus also pointed to the example of someone who was showing that he was sorry for his sins.

Bring forward your penitent again.

Here he is, still fasting – everyone can see that, by the look on his face.

The penitent clutches his stomach and grimaces.

He is also doing other good things. Look – he's giving money to the poor.

The penitent hands a large money bag to the Storyteller.

Penitent (*to the congregation*) Look! I'm giving money to the poor!

Storyteller Look – he's praying.

Penitent Don't talk to me now – I'm praying! (*He closes his eyes and raises his arms heavenward.*)

Storyteller Jesus said, 'Don't be like this. If you do things to help others, don't advertise the fact. When you pray, don't draw attention to yourself – keep it between you and God. And when you fast, don't moan and make a big deal out of it. Keep it to yourself and behave normally.'

Exploring In our stories, both Isaiah and Jesus challenged particular ways of showing that you were faithful to God and sorry for your wrongdoing. Jesus criticised certain people for being attention-seeking, and Isaiah told his listeners that they had gone astray and in fact they were being self-serving when they fasted, because they merely pitied themselves and mistreated those who were dependent on them. The message to these people was simple: it shouldn't be about you. Jesus wanted people to focus their attention on God, not on whether others admired them for their do-gooding. Isaiah went further by stating that God wanted people to turn their fasting into action against injustice, hunger and poverty in the world around them.

Both Isaiah and Jesus were criticising the religious practice they saw around them, so what can they have to say to us today? People no longer wear sackcloth and ashes, but the practice of fasting still survives in the habit of giving something up for Lent.

Bring forward the board with the title: 'Giving something up = FAST'.

Many people give something up for Lent. This modern fasting may involve one of these things: (*Produce the items as you name them.)* chocolate, sweets, alcohol or television. There may be something else you're thinking of giving up. Now, doing without a treat you enjoy is one way of showing that you are sad and sorry during Lent, but giving something up is all about what we ourselves are doing without. Let's apply the message of today's stories: it shouldn't be about us. What would happen if, instead of giving something up, we turned our attention to others and made Lent all about giving something away?

Turn round the board to show: 'Giving something away = FAST'.

This is a rather different kind of fast. Giving something away means: F.A.S.T.

Write the letters F A S T vertically, on the left-hand side of the board or flip chart. As you explain each letter, write the underlined words next to it.

- First: to God. He needs to be top of our list. We give him our time and attention when we pray. Second:
- Another person. We need to ask ourselves, 'What can I give that someone else needs?' The third kind of giving involves:
- Something we'd miss. This may be money, food or something else, but it is the kind of giving that costs us. Finally, there is:
- Time. This is something we all have, we all use and we can all give.

Now it's time for some practical suggestions. We've seen the kind of things many of us give *up* for Lent; now these four categories may give us ideas about what we can give *away* for Lent. There is a board for each one of these around the church: take your time to think and then write or draw some ideas about what we could do. For example, Isaiah talked about feeding the hungry and housing the homeless: we could give our time by helping at a homeless shelter, or give some food to a local food bank.

Write or draw 'donating food' and 'helping at a homeless shelter' on the appropriate boards, then allow plenty of time for people to add their own suggestions. When everyone has finished, display all four boards at the front of church and share some of the suggestions, as a way of summing up today's message: 'Let's give something away for Lent!'

Prayer action *Gather outside around the fire with boxes of tissues in hand.*

We have been wearing these ashes on our foreheads as a sign that we are sad and sorry for all that we have done wrong. During Lent, we look forward to Easter, when Jesus' death and resurrection gave us God's forgiveness for our sins. For our prayers today, we will wipe the ashes from our foreheads and throw the remains onto this fire, as a sign that we ask God to take away all our wrongdoing and all the messes we have made.

Hand round the boxes of tissues and encourage everyone to wipe away the ash, then throw the tissues onto the fire.

Merciful Lord,
may you create in us a clean heart
and renew a right spirit within us,
in Jesus' name.
Amen.

Music God forgave my sin

Conclusion Generous Lord,
this Lent, may we show that we belong to you,
not by giving things up,
but by giving things away,
in your name.
Amen.

Give notices, announce the next all-age service and invite everyone to the feast.

First Sunday of Lent

Me! Me! Me!

Theme   Selfishness and temptation

Scripture   Luke 4:1-13

Running order   Total: 50 minutes

Welcome   The Elder Wand – clip from *Harry Potter and the Deathly Hallows Part 2* (3 minutes)

Introduction   Opening the theme

Storytelling   Modern temptation in the wilderness – sketch with pictures *(10 minutes)*

Music   Lord Jesus Christ *(5 minutes)*

Activity   Identifying modern temptations: collecting pictures and objects *(12 minutes)*

Exploring   What was Jesus' response to the temptations? What should our response be? *(10 minutes)*

Prayer action   Sugar lumps – active confession *(5 minutes)*

Music   We are marching *(5 minutes)*

Conclusion   Closing prayer and invitation

Resources

- Music and words
- Laptop, projector and screen
- Clip from *Harry Potter and the Deathly Hallows Part 2 (see appendix)*
- Hidden around the church, pictures and objects to suggest modern temptations *(see appendix)*
- Downloaded pictures (free from www.dreamstime.com – use the following search terms)
  - industrial wasteland
  - fresh bread
  - skyscraper view from the top
  - Facebook page
  - St Paul's Cathedral, London (or the cathedral in your country's capital)
- Three stand-up signs (folded A4 card) on a table at the front of church:
  - 'Comfort'
  - 'Power'
  - 'Certainty about God'
- Sugar cubes, enough for one each
- A large heatproof bowl full of hand-hot water

Leaders

Minimum: 3

- Leader
- Cast x 2

Optimum: 8

- Leader *(Introduction and Conclusion)*
- Storyteller
- Cast x 2:
  Jesus, wearing jeans and a white hoody
  Devil, wearing black trousers and hoody
- Music Leader
- Explorer
- Activity Leader
- Prayer Leader

Suggestions for additional music

- Forty days and forty nights
- What a friend we have in Jesus

Service

Welcome — We will begin today with a clip from the last Harry Potter film. Many of you will know the story: Harry has finally defeated the evil Voldemort and has won the Elder Wand – the most powerful wand in the world. Now he has a big decision to make.

Show the clip from Harry Potter and the Deathly Hallows Part 2.

Introduction — In that moment, Harry had the chance to become the most powerful wizard in the world. Voldemort had killed for such power – but Harry Potter rejected it completely. He made the choice we would expect from the hero. Let's remember the temptation of the Elder Wand, and the hero's decision, as we hear today's story.

Storytelling

Show the picture of an industrial wasteland.

Storyteller: Jesus was brimful of the Holy Spirit. He was ready to go nationwide with his teaching and healing work, but first he left his family and friends and headed for the wasteland.

Jesus walks down the aisle to the front of church.

It was a no-man's-land beyond the city and the comfortable suburbs. Most people avoided it unless they were lost, mad or up to no good. Yet Jesus wandered there for forty days, alone – or was he? The devil was stalking him, waiting to trap him in a moment of weakness.

Jesus: *(groaning and clutching his belly)* Oww!

Devil: *(walking down the aisle towards him)* Hungry, aren't you? Bet you'd do anything for food right now.

Jesus: I haven't eaten for weeks.

Devil: Call yourself the Son of God? If you are who you say you are, take those lumps of old concrete over there and turn them into loaves of fresh bread.

Show the picture of fresh bread.

FIRST SUNDAY OF LENT

	Then you could eat as much as you wanted. If you're the Son of God, you've got to keep your strength up.
Jesus	One doesn't live by bread alone.
	Show the picture of skyscrapers in a major city.
Storyteller	Then the devil took him to the top of the highest building and showed him the glittering skyscrapers and neon-lit towers of the city.
Devil	Look at all the money and power in the world!
	Show the picture of the Facebook page.
	Look! Fame and followers! All this belongs to me. It can be yours, all of it: the money, the multinational corporations, the celebrity, the record-breaking numbers of Facebook friends and Twitter followers. Just think of the power, the control, the influence you could have! All you have to do is worship me.
Jesus	Worship the Lord your God, and serve him only.
	Show the picture of St Paul's Cathedral.
Storyteller	Then the devil took him to the top of the cathedral in the centre of the capital.
Devil	If you're the Son of God, we all need proof. Go on, jump. You won't come to any harm, because it says in the Bible, 'He will command his angels concerning you, to protect you' and 'On their hands will they bear you up, so that you will not dash your foot against a stone.' Go on, give it a go! Jump – and prove that you are God's Son.
Jesus	Do not put the Lord your God to the test.
	Show the picture of the industrial wasteland again.
Storyteller	At that, the devil left Jesus in the wasteland. The devil went off to bide his time, and Jesus was accompanied by angels.
Music	Lord Jesus Christ
Activity	Today we are thinking about temptation. In our opening clip we saw Harry Potter being tempted by the absolute power of the Elder Wand. In the wasteland, or wilderness, Jesus was tempted by the devil,

who offered power over the whole world. In addition, the devil played on Jesus' physical longing for food, and tempted him to seek proof of God's love.

Place the three signs on the table: 'Comfort', 'Power' and 'Certainty about God'.

Our modern retelling of this Bible story might help us think about its relevance to us today. Around the church, can you find pictures and objects that represent modern temptations?

Encourage people to find the items, bring them to the front and gather round the table with the signs.

Jesus was tempted by these three things: can we sort our modern temptations into the same groups?

Allow time for people to think, discuss and move the items. Encourage engagement rather than a search for the 'right' answer.

Exploring

The devil knew exactly which weak spots to aim at when he tried to tempt Jesus away from God. The first was very basic: Jesus was starving, so the devil tempted him to use his power to feed himself. The second temptation was calculated to work on Jesus as he prepared for his life's work of teaching, healing and spreading God's word. Why not take a shortcut and become the most powerful man in the world? Imagine how he could influence people then! The third temptation played on what the devil believed must be Jesus' deepest, darkest fear: the fear that God wasn't in charge of everything and that he wasn't watching over his Son. How much easier it would be to believe in God's love if you had solid proof, such as a rescue by angels!

Our temptations are not so different. We may not be starving, but we are still tempted to use our energy and resources to improve our own physical comfort: we want to satisfy our appetite for food, drink and pleasure, and we want stuff that makes our lives more convenient and enjoyable.

Show the pictures of smartphones, cars, etc.

We may not want to rule the world, but many of us dream of instant wealth via the Lottery, or instant fame thanks to *The X Factor*. Many of us are keen to upgrade our houses or cars, or see the number of our Facebook friends or Twitter followers increase.

Show the picture of the Facebook friends counter.

We may try to have faith, but how many of us have been troubled by atheists' demands for evidence of God, or by our own inability to prove to others that he exists? This request, taken from a book called *Children's Letters to God*, is an extreme example of our need for proof:

Dear God,
OK. I kept my half of the deal. Where's the bike?
Bert[25]

All these temptations have one thing in common: they are self-centred. Each one is like a small child screaming, 'Me! Me! Me!' They focus our minds on how satisfied *we* feel, how much *we* possess, how many people look up to *us* and how sure *we* are about God. As these temptations are like the ones faced by Jesus, we can look to his example. How did he respond?

Jesus rejected every selfish temptation by turning back to God. Bread? No – 'man cannot live by bread alone.' He quoted words from the Old Testament that continue, 'but by every word that comes from the mouth of the Lord.' In his ministry, Jesus preached the word of God and broke bread to feed others, not himself. What about worldly power, gained by serving the devil? Jesus replied, 'Worship the Lord your God, and serve only him.' Jesus challenged the authority of both the Jewish elders and the Roman governor, and he never held any official position. He knew that he possessed God's absolute authority and in his life and death, he only obeyed God's will. Finally, when tempted by the

---

25. From *Children's Letters to God*, Fontana, 1976.

devil to prove God's love, he replied, 'Do not put the Lord your God to the test.' He focused resolutely on God, not on any selfish desire for proof, and he carried on trusting God even as he died on the cross.

So what about us? Instead of pleasing ourselves, we should serve others in God's name. Instead of worrying about how important we are, we should worship God. And instead of looking for proof, we should trust in the God who loves us. The only way to resist temptation is by turning away from ourselves and back to God.

Prayer action

We have been thinking about selfish temptations today, and selfishness is behind a lot of the hurts we cause and the messes we make in our lives. This mess-making and wrongdoing is what the Bible calls 'sin', and as if to remind us, 'sin' is a little word with 'I' in the middle. Sin is selfish and self-centred.

Lent is a time for saying sorry for our sins, and in our prayers today we will say sorry to God for our selfishness. To help us think about how tempting it can be to please ourselves, we will use these sugar cubes. Please take one, and as you hold it in your hands, think about the things that tempt you.

Pause while everyone takes a sugar cube.

Let's say sorry to God in our hearts for those times when we have been selfish. Then, as a sign of our prayer, we will come forward and drop our sugar cubes in this bowl of hot water. The sugar will dissolve, just as God's love takes all our sins away. Let us pray.

After a moment, drop your own sugar cube in and stir the water so that it dissolves, then encourage everyone else to do the same.

Forgiving Lord,
take our selfishness from us.
May you dissolve our sin in your love
and make us free to serve only you.
Amen.

Music   We are marching

Conclusion   Heavenly Father,
as we go out into the world,
may our cry of 'Me! Me! Me!'
become a song of praise to you, you, only you.
In Jesus' name.
Amen.

Give notices, announce the next all-age service and invite everyone to the feast.

Second Sunday of Lent
Waiting for God

Theme	Patience and faith
Scripture	Genesis 15:1-12, 17-18

Running order	Total: 50 minutes
Welcome	Watching the sand in the hourglass *(5 minutes)*
Introduction	Opening the theme
Storytelling	Visual retelling of God's promise to Abraham *(5 minutes)*
Music	Faithful one, so unchanging *(5 minutes)*
Exploring	How long did Abraham wait for God to keep his promises? *(10 minutes)*
Activity	Making sand timers *(15 minutes)*
Prayer action	Sand timers – visual prayer *(5 minutes)*
Music	Lord, for the years *(5 minutes)*
Conclusion	Closing prayer and invitation

Resources

- Music and words
- Hourglass or home-made sand timer *(see appendix)*
- A black cloth
- A large handful of silver glitter and sequins
- Some pieces of fur
- Some feathers
- A large candle and matches
- An incense burner *(see appendix)*
- Two head-cloths and ties
- A false beard
- Two age counters *(see appendix)*
- Copies of the computer's hourglass picture, enough for one each *(see appendix)*
- On two craft tables, equipment for making sand timers *(see appendix)*:
  - empty, dry water bottles of different sizes
  - several cardboard discs, the same size as the necks of the bottles, each with a hole in the middle
  - fine, dry sand
  - a few plastic cups
  - marker pen
  - sticky tape and scissors
  - some small funnels
  - a sheet of paper and a pen

Leaders

Minimum: 1

- Leader

Optimum: 6+

- Leader *(Introduction and Conclusion)*
- Storyteller
- Music Leader
- Explorer
- Activity Leader(s)
- Prayer Leader

Suggestions for additional music

- There's a wideness in God's mercy
- All my hope on God is founded

Service

Welcome — *As people arrive, turn the hourglass and watch the sand start to trickle through.*

Introduction — This sand takes an hour to trickle from the top to the bottom. It's a long time to wait! Today's story is about someone who waited a very long time indeed.

Storytelling — There was once a man who was specially chosen by God. His name was Abram and he was to become Abraham, the father of God's people. One night, God spoke to Abram. He said, 'Don't be frightened, Abram. I will always look after you. Your reward will be great.'

But Abram said, 'What will you give me? I still have no children, and my servant's child is my only heir.'

Then God said, 'Your servant's child shall not be your heir. Your own children shall inherit everything.' God said, 'Look at the stars.'

Spread out the black cloth, then throw a handful of glitter and sequins in the air so that they fall on the cloth.

Can you count them?

Invite children to try and count the sequins and pieces of glitter.

Abram looked at the stars and couldn't count them all. God said, 'Your family members will be like this. You will have so many descendants that you won't be able to count them all.' Abram believed God; and so God knew that he was a good man.

Then God said, 'I give you this land for your own.'

Abram replied, 'Lord, how do I know it's mine?' God told Abram to sacrifice a cow, a goat, a ram, a dove and a pigeon. He laid out the animals' bodies.

Lay out the fur and feathers in a long strip.

SECOND SUNDAY OF LENT

This was how treaties were made in Abram's time. Then Abram fell into a deep, dark sleep. In the darkness, God appeared as a flaming torch and a smoking fire.

Light both. Hold the candle in one hand and the incense burner in the other, then pass them over the strip of fur.

God's fire and smoke passed through the sacrificed animals as a sign that the treaty was sealed. Then God made Abram a great promise: 'All this land is yours. It belongs to you and your descendants.'

Music Faithful one, so unchanging

Exploring Today's story showed us God's dramatic promises to Abram. What did he promise him?

Invite responses until you elicit the correct answers.

God promised Abram lots of children and a land of his own. At that point Abram was a childless nomad, so the prospect of his great-great-grandchildren living in their own land must have seemed remote, yet he trusted God to keep his promise: 'Abram believed God; and so God knew that he was a good man.' Abram's faith is an example to us all, but it is even more amazing when we discover just how long he waited for God to keep his promises.

The Bible often tells us how old people are: in today's story, Abram was 76 years old and his wife Sarai was 67. Who would like to dress up as Abram and Sarai?

Invite two volunteers forward. Dress each in a head-cloth and give Abram a beard. Ask them to hold up the age counters for Abram and Sarai, showing 76 and 67.

That's quite an age to believe that you will still have children! Even so, Abram believed God. Sure enough, his first child, Ishmael, was born – ten years later!

The volunteers flick forward 10 years: Abram is 86 and Sarai is 77.

Ishmael was the son of Sarai's slave, Hagar. Sarai herself still longed for a child, although by then she was 77. Then, *thirteen years later*, God told Abram that Sarai would give birth to their son, Isaac.

The volunteers flick forward 13 years: Abram is 99 and Sarai is 90.

He was 99 and she was 90! Even so, Abram still believed God, and Isaac was born a year later.

The volunteers flick forward one more year.

Abram, Isaac and Isaac's son, Jacob, became the founding fathers of the Jewish nation. Abram was renamed 'Abraham', which means 'father of many', and Sarai was renamed Sarah. So God did keep his promises, although Abraham had to wait 24 years to see it happen.

Applaud your volunteers and ask them to sit down.

The birth of Abraham's and Sarah's son was miraculous: Sarah herself laughed when she found out and God answered, 'Is anything too wonderful for the Lord?' However, just as wonderful is Abraham's patient faith. God promised and Abraham believed, even though for ten more years there were still no children, and after Ishmael's birth it took another fourteen years for God's promise to be fulfilled in the birth of Isaac. God takes his own time, and his time is not always the same as human time, but for 24 years Abraham waited in faith.

In contrast, we live in an impatient world. Internet searches return millions of results in a tenth of a second, and we would be hugely frustrated by a search or download that took 24 seconds. Waiting for a delayed train, waiting in a traffic jam or waiting for a company to answer our phone call drives us mad. Even 24 minutes seems like an unacceptable time to wait. Abraham's 24 years of waiting remind us that God takes his own time. He loves us and hears our prayers, but his response does not necessarily arrive as promptly as a search by Google. We need to have faith, like Abraham, that God is on our side and he will never leave us on our own.

Activity

For our activity today, we will make some sand timers like the hourglass that has been running during this service. Who would like to help me measure enough sand to last a minute?

Invite a volunteer to tip sand into a bottle and attach a circle of card with a hole, then hold an empty bottle firmly on top. Turn the bottles over as you start the minute timer. When a minute has elapsed, take the bottles apart again and remove the card. Give your volunteer a plastic cup and ask them to measure the amount of sand that travelled through the timer in a minute, by marking the cup if necessary. Use this calculation to help you work out how much sand you need for the following timers: five minutes, ten minutes, thirty minutes. Write the answers on a sheet of paper. Then invite your congregation to gather round the craft tables and make a selection of sand timers.

Prayer action

The sand timers we have made today remind us of a familiar sight. Where have you seen something like this before?

Hand out the pictures of a computer's hourglass and invite responses.

A tiny picture like this appears on a computer screen whenever we have to wait for a computer to finish doing a job. Until the sand timer disappears, we can't do anything except sit and wait in frustration. So this image reminds us how impatient we can be.

However, this picture can also represent God's different view of time. If we turn the hourglass on its side, it looks like a sideways figure of eight.

Turn your picture through ninety degrees and trace the figure of eight with your finger.

In mathematics, this is the symbol for infinity. God's time is eternity, which is infinite time, time without end. When we remember this, it puts our own impatience at a few minutes' delay into perspective.

So for our prayers today, we will consider this picture of a sand timer, which is also a picture of God's infinite time. First, hold it upright in your hands and remember the things that make you impatient.

Pause for a moment of quiet.

Then turn it on its side so that it looks like the symbol for infinity. Remember that God works in his own time, and pray for renewed trust in him.

Pause.

God of the past, present and future,
you have given us time.
May you forgive our impatience
and strengthen our faith,
in Jesus name.
Amen.

Music Lord, for the years

Conclusion Almighty God,
send us out into the world with the faithfulness of Abraham,
the hope of your chosen people
and the love of your Son, Jesus Christ.
Amen.

Give notices, announce the next all-age service and invite everyone to the feast. Keep the sand timers in a safe place for use in future all-age activities.

Third Sunday of Lent

In the wilderness

Theme	Depending on God in the wilderness
Scripture	Isaiah 55:1-9; Psalm 63:1-9; 1 Corinthians 10:1-13

Running order	Total: 50 minutes
Welcome	A slideshow of wilderness pictures with sound effects *(5 minutes)*
Introduction	Opening the theme
Exploring	Why is the wilderness so significant? *(10 minutes)*
Storytelling	Reading Psalm 63:1-9 *(2 minutes)*
Music	As the deer pants for the water *(5 minutes)*
Activity	Exploring our modern wildernesses – reading and collage *(18 minutes)*
Prayer action	Candle-lighting and Taizé chant: 'The Lord is my song' *(5 minutes)*
Music	Beauty for brokenness *(5 minutes)*
Conclusion	Closing prayer and invitation

Resources

- Music and words
- Slideshow of wilderness pictures with sound effects *(see appendix)*
- Laptop, projector, screen and speakers
- A long, blank strip of lining paper
- A cardboard sign taped to a stick:
    ⬅︎ *Civilisation*
- Lots of tea lights
- Matches and tapers
- Materials for the wilderness collage:
    - a large piece of card
    - lots of newspapers and current affairs magazines
    - some suitable pictures from the internet
      (Google 'wasteland' images)
    - glue sticks
    - scissors

Leaders

Minimum: 2

- Leader
- Storyteller

Optimum: 6

- Leader *(Introduction and Conclusion)*
- Storyteller
- Music Leader
- Explorer
- Activity Leader
- Prayer Leader

Suggestions for additional music

- Just as I am, without one plea
- Purify my heart

Service

Welcome — *As people arrive, show a slideshow of wilderness pictures accompanied by the sound of the wind. Turn the sound effects off before the Introduction, but keep the pictures scrolling until the end of the first hymn.*

Introduction — We are in the season of Lent, when we remember the time that Jesus spent alone in the wilderness. Today we will be finding out more about the wilderness in the Bible, what it meant to Jesus and his fellow Jews and what it might mean for us, today.

Exploring — We've seen some pictures of the wilderness that Jesus knew, but what was it really like? If you are planning to travel somewhere wild and exotic on holiday, you might consult the *Lonely Planet Guide*. In an entertaining book which imagines the story of Jesus in the time of the internet and Facebook,[26] there is an invented website called 'The Lonely Known World Guide to the Wilderness'. It lists the area's attractions:

Restaurants?

Storyteller	None.
Explorer	Bars?
Storyteller	None.
Explorer	Places of interest?
Storyteller	None.
Explorer	Entertainment?
Storyteller	None.
Explorer	Best time to visit?
Storyteller	Never.
Explorer	The Guide includes a helpful map of the wilderness. It looks like this:

You and the Storyteller unroll a completely blank sheet of paper.

---

26. *Jesus on Thy Face*, Denise Askew and Steve W. Parker, Simon & Schuster, 2010.

THIRD SUNDAY OF LENT

There is only one thing marked on it:

Hold up a sign reading ' ⟵ Civilisation'.

As this Guide neatly demonstrates, people rarely chose to go into the wilderness! Bandits and outlaws hid there; unpopular kings found refuge if their people threatened to overthrow them. For the Jewish people, the wilderness was a place of freedom after they had escaped from slavery in Egypt, led by Moses. They left everything behind and became refugees in a harsh landscape. Basic survival was a struggle, but God was with them. They were his chosen people and he looked after them by giving them food, water and rules for living a good life together. They often let him down, and he punished them as a parent disciplines a wayward child, but he never stopped loving them. The Jewish nation stayed in the wilderness for forty years before God led his people to the Promised Land.

This wilderness experience is key to understanding the faith of Jesus and his fellow Jews. We have seen what an empty place the wilderness is, and as a nation under Moses, that is where they gathered. They had nothing and depended on God for everything. Given this experience, it is not surprising that the Bible's poems, or psalms, often use the wilderness to describe what it feels like to lose touch with God; the joy of relying on him again is like finding water or shade in the desert. See if you can picture the wilderness through the words of this psalm.

Storytelling   *Read Psalm 63:1-9*

Music   As the deer pants for the water

Activity   So what about us? Few of us will have visited a real desert, so what can the Bible's wildernesses have to say to us? The clue lies in the psalm we heard, which used the wilderness to describe the feeling of being lost without God. Here is a modern example of someone who is experiencing wilderness as a state of mind. He is a man who is a disappointment to himself.

187

Storyteller	As you grow older, you gradually realise that the gulf between where you are now and where you had hoped to be is never going to be bridged. In your daily life you pretend that you will catch up, make up all that lost ground and suddenly be catapulted to that elusive magical place called 'Success' . . .
	I seemed to live permanently with that feeling you have when you're lost on a car journey and you just keep on driving further and further in the wrong direction hoping there'll be a turning or a signpost somewhere up ahead.[27]
Activity Leader	The wilderness is an empty space where you feel lost and alone. It can be a place or a feeling: someone who is being bullied may feel as if they are in the wilderness. When we are waiting for someone we love to get better, or when someone dies, it is like being stranded in the wilderness. Today we are going to create a picture of the wilderness. Remember, it can be a place or a feeling: we will make a collage by cutting out newspaper pictures that we think show different kinds of wilderness.
	Invite people to gather round and start selecting pictures. Encourage them to focus on wilderness as a place or a feeling: pictures could include an industrial wasteland, moorland, refugees waiting for food, a person in court. Stick the pictures on the large piece of card to create a collage, then display the finished work. You may like to invite comments on these different kinds of wilderness.
Prayer action	We have seen that there are many different kinds of wilderness, but the lesson from the Bible remains the same. The wilderness is that hard place where you realise that you can't do everything yourself – you need God's help. The good news is that God is longing to help us, if we will only trust him. The prophet Isaiah said, 'Seek the Lord while he may be found, call upon him while he is near.'[28] Paul advised the early Christians who were facing challenging times, 'God is faithful, and he will not let you be tested beyond your

---

27. John O'Farrell, *This Is Your Life*, Doubleday, 2002, p.61-2.
28. Isaiah 55:6.

strength, but with the testing he will also provide the way out so that you may be able to endure it.'[29] The advice from both the Old and New Testaments is the same: trust God and ask him for help.

So in our prayers today, we call to mind all those who are lost in the wilderness. We light a candle for them and sing as we pray for renewed trust in God.

Begin singing the Taizé chant: 'The Lord is my song'. Light your own tea light and place it in the centre of the floor in front of the altar, then encourage others to do the same, spreading the tea lights out from the centre. Repeat the song until all the tea lights are lit.

Almighty God,
all that we have comes from you.
May we trust in you to provide for us,
in Jesus' name.
Amen.

Music Beauty for brokenness

Conclusion Heavenly Father,
be with us in the wilderness,
hear us when we call
and show us the way.
Amen.

Give notices, announce the next all-age service and invite everyone to the feast.

---

29. 1 Corinthians 10:13.

Fourth Sunday of Lent
Mothering Sunday

Theme	Love and forgiveness
Scripture	Luke 15:1-3, 11b-32

Running order	Total: 50 minutes
Welcome	Handing out posies *(5 minutes)*
Music	All things bright and beautiful *(5 minutes)*
Introduction	Opening the theme
Storytelling	The prodigal daughter – a mother's tale *(10 minutes)*
Music	The King is among us *(5 minutes)*
Exploring	What does this mother's love show us? *(5 minutes)*
Prayer action	Glass pebbles – gathering prayer *(5 minutes)*
Music	God of life, God of love *(5 minutes)*
Activity	Icing biscuits for the feast *(10 minutes)*
Conclusion	Closing prayer and invitation

Resources

NB Advance notice needed! Invite people to bring a contribution for a bring-and-share Mothering Sunday party.

- Mothering Sunday posies
- Music and words
- At the front of the church, a long table laid with a tablecloth and party plates, cups, etc.
- Cash (photocopy some £10 and £20 notes – enough to make a fat pile)
- Jewels (use the coloured glass pebbles available from craft shops and online specialist retailers)
- A high-visibility tabard
- A broom
- A glamorous dress (shiny or silky, any size – it won't be worn)
- A glittery necklace
- A glass bowl or vase
- Ingredients for biscuit-decorating activity:
  – Rich Tea biscuits
  – bowls of white and coloured icing
  – cake decorations
  – tubes of writing icing
  – paper plates

Leaders

Minimum: 4

- Leader
- Cast x 3

Optimum: 8+

- Leader *(Introduction and Conclusion)*
- Cast x 3 (all in modern dress)
  The mother
  The prodigal daughter, carrying cash and jewels
  The sister
- Music Leader
- Explorer
- Activity Leader(s)
- Prayer Leader

Suggestions for additional music

- The gracious invitation stands
- Bind us together, Lord

Service

Welcome — *To begin the service, distribute the Mothering Sunday posies according to your church's custom.*

Music — All things bright and beautiful

Introduction — Our story today was first told by Jesus. It was the tale of a father and his two sons. One of them has since become known as the prodigal son: 'prodigal' means he was a waster who threw away everything he had. As today is Mothering Sunday, we will hear a modern mother's story of her prodigal daughter.

Storytelling

The mother — *(talking as she lays the table for the party)* We're just getting ready for a big party. It's a homecoming for my younger daughter – the one we thought had run away for good! She was always a tearaway. Her father called her a wild child. As soon as she was 18, she asked for her inheritance: there was a lot of money, and some jewels that were family heirlooms. She was of age, so we gave her everything that was rightfully hers. Of course, we hoped she'd invest it, maybe start her own business. But she announced that she was leaving home and going travelling. She took everything with her.

The prodigal daughter — I had a riot! I went all over the world, stayed in the best hotels and went to wild parties every night. I spent loads of money on fun, fun, fun! *(she throws her notes in the air)* When I ran out of cash, I gave away my jewels.

She distributes the jewels freely around the church and congregation, moving down the aisle as she does so.

I was really popular! The more extravagant parties I threw and the more drinks I bought, the more people seemed to like me. Until my money started to run out. Suddenly people weren't so friendly. At the same time, the banks were having big problems and people everywhere were running out of money. Friends I'd lent a fortune to couldn't pay me back, and worse, no one would lend me anything. They started avoiding me. Before long, I couldn't afford a room in even the cheapest

B and B. I was out on the streets. Then I managed to get a part-time job picking up litter outside the takeaways.

At the back of church, she puts on a high-visibility tabard and uses a broom. She moves towards the middle of the aisle as she sweeps.

I used to get so hungry that I'd look at the cold, half-eaten burgers I was sweeping up and wish I could eat them, but my supervisor was watching and I had to keep working. Because I was wearing my uniform, I wasn't allowed to beg, so no one ever gave me anything.

One day I was binning the remains of a birthday cake from some office party. I remembered the cakes my mum made for me every birthday, and how she'd decorate them just the way I wanted. I remembered my mum's cooking and my mouth watered. At home, even the man who comes to clean out the drains gets one of her home-made cookies! That was when I decided I'd go back home. I had a speech all prepared: I'd knock on the door and say, 'Mum, I've done lots of bad things. I'm not fit to be your daughter, but please just give me a job. I'll clean the drains, do the weeding – anything!'

The mother	But I saw you coming.
The prodigal daughter	Mum, I –

The daughter walks down the aisle towards her mother; the mother walks towards her with arms outstretched, ready to embrace her.

The mother	Come here.

They embrace.

Darling, I'm so glad you've come home.

The mother gives her daughter a glamorous dress and some jewellery.

Now I've got a surprise for you: these are for you. Go and get ready and then we'll throw a homecoming party in your honour!

The sister	*(entering from the side)* Hey! That's not fair! I've been here all this time, helping around the house, doing my chores and being a good daughter, but you've never given me a designer outfit! You've never thrown a

ALL-SORTS WORSHIP

	party for me and my friends – not even a barbecue! But this sister of mine goes off and wastes all her money, and you organise a big do!
The mother	My darling, you've always been here with me. Everything I have is yours, you know that. But we've got to celebrate because your sister was dead to us, and now she has come back to life; she was lost and we've found her again. And I love you both.
	The mother stretches out her arms and embraces both her daughters.
Music	The King is among us
Exploring	The mother in our story loved her child enough to give her the freedom she asked for. She kept on loving her daughter while she was far away and busy making big mistakes and bad choices. When she saw her sorry child returning empty-handed, her love reached out to her. She took her in her arms, kissed her and celebrated her return. She didn't turn her away, shout at her or say, 'I told you so!' – she welcomed her back with open arms. Today, on Mothering Sunday, we celebrate all mothers who love their children like this, with a love that simply never gives up.

Of course, our own experience of mothers and motherhood may fall short of this ideal, and for some of us Mothering Sunday may be a sad occasion. The older sister's resentment is very human, and it reminds us of the complexity of our family relationships. However, the point of this story, whether we tell it about a mother or – as Jesus did – about a father, is that the loving and forgiving parent shows us what God is like. Let's look again at the moment when the prodigal child returned home:

Ask your actors to freeze in position 1: the daughter walking towards her mother; the mother with her arms outstretched, ready to embrace her.

And let's look at the final moment of the story, when the mother rejoiced with the beloved child who was lost and the beloved child who never left:

FOURTH SUNDAY OF LENT

Ask your actors to freeze in position 2: the mother with her arms outstretched, ready to embrace both her daughters.

The physical action that expressed the mother's love was this. *(Hold out your arms as if offering a big hug, and stay in this position as you talk.)* Who else do you know who held out his arms like this?

Invite responses.

With his arms stretched out on the cross like this, Jesus died for our sake. With his arms stretched out, he still welcomes us all – those who have always been with him and those who have wandered off. No matter how far away we've been and no matter what bad choices we have made, he offers us love and forgiveness. He welcomes us home.

Prayer action All around the church are the jewels and treasure that the prodigal daughter scattered about so wastefully. They are glass pebbles like this. *(Hold up a handful.)* Can you find as many as you can and share them out so that everyone has one to hold?

Allow time for volunteers to find and distribute the pebbles.

We've gathered up the lost treasure, just as the loving mother in our story gathered up her lost child. Prayer is a way of gathering things up and bringing them home to God, so today we are going to use these jewels as a sign of our prayer. In a moment of quiet, let's hold a jewel in our hands and bring our own prayers to God.

Pause.

We pray for our mothers: those we love, those we miss, and those from whom we feel far away.

Pause.

We pray for ourselves, as we are all in need of love and forgiveness.

Pause.

When you are ready, bring forward your jewel and drop it into this glass bowl. Let's collect these jewels together as a sign of our prayers.

Encourage people to come forward and fill the glass bowl.

Let us pray.

Gather up our prayers, O Lord,
and hold us all in your open arms,
in Jesus' name.
Amen.

Music   God of life, God of love

Activity   Today's story ended with a celebration and a feast. We're going to end our service in the same way, so we need some party food. Who would like to help decorate these Mothering Sunday biscuits? There's enough for everyone! You could even decorate one especially for your own mum.

Allow plenty of time for people to ice and decorate the biscuits. Children can then present their finished creations to their mums. Arrange the rest of the biscuits on plates and add them to the feast.

Conclusion   God, our heavenly Father and Mother,
we thank you for mothers.
May we all, mothers and children,
follow the example
of your loving, forgiving embrace.
Amen.

Give notices, announce the next all-age service and invite everyone to the feast.

The Annunciation
Wonderful

Theme	Nothing is impossible with God
Scripture	Luke 1:26-38; Psalm 40:5-11

Running order Total: 50 minutes

Welcome	Viewing extraordinary pictures of nature *(5 minutes)*
Introduction	Opening the theme
Storytelling	Visual retelling of the Annunciation *(5 minutes)*
Activity	Creating the 'Wow! Corner' *(15 minutes)*
Music	To God be the glory *(5 minutes)*
Exploring	How can we be like Mary? *(10 minutes)*
Prayer action	'Here I am' – visual prayer with response *(5 minutes)*
Music	I, the Lord of sea and sky *(5 minutes)*
Conclusion	Closing prayer and invitation

Resources

- Music and words
- Laptop, projector and screen
- A table set up for the 'Wow! Corner' with a colourful cloth
- A slideshow of extraordinary pictures of nature and Christ's incarnation *(see appendix)*
- Pictures to illustrate the Annunciation story *(see appendix)*
- All around the church, items for the 'Wow! Corner' *(see appendix)*

Leaders

Minimum: 2

- Leader
- Storyteller/IT technician

Optimum: 6

- Leader *(Introduction and Conclusion)*
- Storyteller/IT technician
- Music Leader
- Explorer
- Activity Leader
- Prayer Leader

Suggestions for additional music

- For Mary, mother of our Lord
- There is a Redeemer

Service

Welcome — *As people arrive, show the slideshow of extraordinary images depicting creation and Christ's incarnation – examples of wonderful things that God has done.*

Introduction — Our theme today can be summed up by a single word: wonderful. We will be thinking about the amazing things God has done – things that fill us with wonder and make us say, 'Wow!' We begin with the wonderful story of how God came to be born as one of us. This story is known as the Annunciation, which means 'announcement': it describes the moment when an angel gave Mary a life-changing piece of news.

Storytelling — The angel Gabriel was sent to earth by God.

Show the picture of the Earth from space.

God sent Gabriel to the Middle East,

Show the picture of the Middle East.

to a region called Galilee;

Show the picture of Galilee.

to a town called Nazareth,

Show the picture of Nazareth.

to a young woman, engaged to be married, whose name was Mary.

Show the picture of Mary.

The angel said, 'Greetings, favoured one! The Lord is with you.' Mary was frightened and utterly confused. She wondered who he was and what he was talking about. The angel continued, 'Do not be afraid, Mary, for you are special to God. Now you will become pregnant with a son, and you will name him Jesus. He will be great, and he will be called the Son of the Most High, and the Lord God will give to him the throne of his ancestor, King David.

Show the picture of King David on his throne.

He will reign over the people of God for ever, and his kingdom will never end.'

Show the picture of Jesus on his throne, stretching towards eternity.

Mary said to the angel, 'How can this be possible? I've never been with a man!' The angel said to her, 'The Holy Spirit will come upon you, and the power of God will overshadow you;

Show the picture of the Holy Spirit.

and so the child who will grow inside you will be holy; he will be called Son of God. At this very moment, your elderly cousin Elizabeth is also pregnant – six months gone, though she has been childless all these years – because nothing will be impossible with God.'

Show the picture of Mary kneeling before the angel and leave it on the screen after the end of the story.

Then Mary said, 'Here I am, the servant of the Lord; let it be with me according to your word.' Then the angel left her.

Activity When the angel announced Jesus' coming to Mary, he said, 'Nothing will be impossible with God.' This story reminds us that God does more wonderful things than we can ever imagine or even understand.

We began our service today with extraordinary pictures of God's creation, and now we are going to celebrate the wonderful things that he has done by creating a 'Wow! Corner' for our church. This is a special place full of amazing things that remind us what God is capable of and make us say, 'Wow!' The first thing to go in our 'Wow! Corner' is the baby in the manger – God born as a human being.

Place the manger in the Wow! Corner.

ALL-SORTS WORSHIP

What else can we put here? All around the church[30] there are pictures and objects that might make you say, 'Wow!' Take your time to choose something special.

Allow plenty of time for people to bring things to the Wow! Corner and arrange them. You may like to invite people to explain their contributions.

Music To God be the glory

Exploring Our story today was full of wonders. First of all, our pictures illustrated the vast context of the angel's meeting with Mary. God had the whole of creation to choose from.

Show the picture of the Earth from space.

God chose a particular country,

Show the picture of the Middle East.

a particular region

Show the picture of Galilee.

and a particular town.

Show the picture of Nazareth.

He chose one ordinary young woman.

Show the picture of Mary.

God holds the whole world in his hands, yet he singled out Mary. And the wonder of this story doesn't stop here. In his words to Mary, the angel looked back in time to Jesus' ancestor, King David, who lived a thousand years earlier.

Show the picture of King David on his throne.

---

30. If your church has attractive grounds, you may like to suggest that children go outside to see if they can find anything for the 'Wow! Corner'. They may bring back anything from a wild flower to a dead stag beetle!

The angel looked forward to eternity and Jesus' kingdom that will never end.

Show the picture of Jesus on his throne, stretching towards eternity.

This shows that although Jesus was to be born to a particular young woman in a specific time and place, he belongs in God's eternity. God's time extends infinitely in all directions beyond our limited human sense of past, present and future.

Most wonderful of all, the angel announced that all God's power was to be present in the cells dividing invisibly in Mary's womb: he said, 'The Holy Spirit will come upon you, and the power of God will overshadow you; and so the child who will grow inside you will be holy; he will be called Son of God.'

Show the picture of the Holy Spirit.

What else could Mary do?

Show the picture of Mary kneeling before the angel.

The angel's presence and his words demonstrated to Mary the awesome power of God that is wider, longer, higher and deeper than we can ever grasp. He is not restricted by our human limitations: consequently, a virgin and her elderly cousin both conceived miraculous babies and – wonder of wonders – God was born as a human being. As the angel said, 'Nothing will be impossible with God.'

In response, Mary didn't argue about the problems her pregnancy would cause with Joseph, or the real risk she faced of being stoned to death for immorality: she bowed to God's greater power and said, 'Here I am, the servant of the Lord; let it be with me according to your word.' Whenever we experience the wonderful things that God does in our lives, and when we consider the amazing things we have gathered in our Wow! Corner, we need to remember Mary's response.

ALL-SORTS WORSHIP

We can only recognise God's power, say, 'OK, God – have it your way!' and be ready to serve him.

Prayer action For our prayers today, we will use words of praise from the Bible and pictures of wonderful things that God has done. Let's rest in God's presence and reflect on his goodness; then we will kneel and say Mary's words together: 'Here I am, the servant of the Lord; let it be with me according to your word.' Let us pray.

> Great are the wonders you have done,
> O Lord my God.
> How great your designs for us!
> There is none that can be compared with you.
> If I were to proclaim them and tell of them
> they would be more than I am able to express.[31]

Play the slideshow of images depicting creation and Christ's incarnation, ending on the last slide which shows Mary's words. All kneel.

All **Here I am, the servant of the Lord; let it be with me according to your word.**
Amen.

Music I, the Lord of sea and sky

Conclusion God of power and might,
make us witnesses of your love
and servants of your world,
in Jesus' name.
Amen.

Give notices, announce the next all-age service and invite everyone to the feast.
You may like to keep the Wow! Corner in church and encourage children to bring regular contributions.

---

31. Psalm 40:5, 6 (Common Worship Psalter).

Passiontide

Fifth Sunday of Lent

Sweet-smelling feet

Theme	Love and service
Scripture	John 12:1-8

Running order	Total: 50 minutes
Welcome	Comparing perfumes *(5 minutes)*
Introduction	Opening the theme
Storytelling	Mime – Mary anoints Jesus' feet *(5 minutes)*
Music	Such love *(5 minutes)*
Exploring	What does Mary's action mean? Interactive exploration *(10 minutes)*
Activity	Hand-washing, feet-washing and hand massage *(15 minutes)*
Prayer action	Incense – sensory prayer *(5 minutes)*
Music	From heaven you came *(5 minutes)*
Conclusion	Closing prayer and invitation

FIFTH SUNDAY OF LENT

Resources

- Music and words
- Several different bottles of perfume or essential oils (ask people to donate unwanted bottles of perfume, even if they are nearly empty)
- A bottle to represent Mary's bottle of nard *(see appendix)*
- Price labels for each bottle of perfume: research current prices on the internet and label the bottle of nard '300 denarii'
- A table and three chairs at the front of church
- A washing-up bowl containing a large, rough stone
- An incense burner and granular incense *(see appendix)*
- Three stations around the church *(see appendix)*

    For the hand-washing:
    - two jugs of warm water, one soapy and one clean
    - a large bowl
    - a supply of small hand towels or paper towels

    For the foot-washing: as above

    For the hand massage:
    - dishes of very light olive oil, perhaps with a drop of lavender oil added

Leaders

Minimum: 6

- Leader
- Cast x 5

Optimum: 11+

- Leader *(Introduction and Conclusion)*
- Storyteller
- Cast x 5 (non-speaking, in traditional dress):
    Mary
    Martha
    Lazarus
    Jesus
    Judas
- Music Leader
- Explorer
- Activity Leader(s)
- Prayer Leader

Suggestions for additional music

- Christ's is the world
- Jesus' love is very wonderful

207

Service

Welcome — *As people arrive, invite them to compare the perfumes on display.*

Introduction — Today's service will be very fragrant! We have begun by smelling these perfumes because in our story, some expensive perfume is given as a gift. Let's find out what happened.[32]

Storytelling — *Mary, Martha and Lazarus prepare the table together. There are no props apart from table and chairs – everything else is mimed.*

Six days before the Passover Jesus came to Bethany, the home of Lazarus, whom he had raised from the dead. There they gave a dinner for him.

Jesus enters and is embraced by the three siblings. Jesus and Lazarus sit at the table together. Jesus sits where the foot-washing will be clearly visible to the congregation. The two sisters leave. Martha re-enters with some plates of food and lays them on the table, then sits down. They start to eat and drink.

Martha served, and Lazarus was one of those at the table with him. Mary took a pound of costly perfume made of pure nard, anointed Jesus' feet, and wiped them with her hair.

Mary re-enters with the perfume. She kneels at Jesus' feet and takes off his sandals. She mimes breaking the neck off the perfume bottle and catching the overflowing perfume oil. She slowly massages the perfume into his feet and dries them with her hair.

The house was filled with the fragrance of the perfume.

The group around the table sits transfixed, then Judas bursts in, gesticulating angrily.

---

32. The text is taken directly from John's Gospel (NRSV). You may prefer to use a different translation.

But Judas Iscariot, one of his disciples (the one who was about to betray him), said, 'Why was this perfume not sold for three hundred denarii and the money given to the poor?' (He said this not because he cared about the poor, but because he was a thief; he kept the common purse and used to steal what was put into it.)

Mary looks up and Jesus lays his hands on her head.

Jesus said, 'Leave her alone. She bought it so that she might keep it for the day of my burial. You always have the poor with you, but you do not always have me.'

Music   Such love

Exploring   Let's look more closely at what happened in today's story. Mary washed Jesus' feet with perfume, which might seem a bit odd to us. However, in Jesus' time foot-washing was quite usual. These days, when you have a visitor, you might take their coat and offer them a cup of tea as a way of welcoming them to your home. In Jesus' time, a guest often had his hot, dusty feet washed, usually by a servant. Mary was the hostess, so by washing Jesus' feet herself she was making a special effort to welcome him.

But that's not all. Mary used perfume – and not just any perfume. She used the most expensive perfume in our collection this morning: nard, or spikenard, which cost about 300 denarii. In those days, an ordinary farm worker earned one denarius for a day's work, so this perfume was worth nearly a year's wages. In today's money, that's about £15,000![33] No wonder Judas said they should have sold it and got the money instead. Now, imagine that this bottle contained £15,000-worth of perfume: who would like to hold it?

Invite volunteers forward and let them pass the bottle around.

How does it feel when you hold it?

---

33. 300 days x £50 (approximate figure based on eight-hour day @ £6.08 per hour. Adjust as necessary, in line with the current minimum wage.)

Invite responses.

Mary's bottle was heavy because there was half a kilo of perfume oil in it, and it was made of fine white stone called alabaster. Be careful you don't drop it! Now, imagine you are Mary.[34] You have this valuable perfume. You have saved and saved for it. You were going to keep it for a loved one's funeral and prepare the body for burial with this wonderful perfume. It was going to be your last, best gift. But now Jesus is here and you realise how much you love him. He deserves your precious perfume and you want to give it to him right now. Quick – do it before you change your mind! But how are you going to get it out of its stone bottle? It's sealed tight at the top! Any ideas?

Invite responses, until someone suggests breaking the top off the bottle. Explain that this is probably how Mary opened the bottle, then gather your volunteers round the table on which there is a washing-up bowl containing a large, rough stone. Invite your volunteers to try and break the top off the bottle by striking it against the stone. Take it in turns until the top breaks and the thick lotion inside pours out in big messy dollops. Encourage your volunteers to try and gather up the lotion in their hands or catch it in the bowl.

This is what happened when Mary broke open her bottle of nard. Imagine £15,000-worth of perfume pouring out like this! Once the bottle was broken, she couldn't keep any back for later: the whole lot gushed out. Mary didn't want to waste any of it, so she scooped it up from the table, the floor and her clothes and used it all on Jesus' feet. Imagine the wonderful smell! Here we're using bubble bath with a light fragrance, but nard is a thick amber oil with a deep, rich, strong smell which would have been overwhelming in that little house. Everything it touched carried the smell for days: the earth floor, Mary's hair,

---

34. I am indebted to Margaret Hebblethwaite's lovely version of this story in *Six New Gospels – New Testament Women Tell Their Stories*, Cowley Publications, 1994.

FIFTH SUNDAY OF LENT

Jesus' feet. When he entered Jerusalem on a donkey the next day, Jesus still wore the wonderful smell of Mary's gift.

Mary gave Jesus the most precious thing she had, and she gave it with unstoppable generosity. She sets us an example of how to serve God and each other. Imagine that our lives are like this precious perfume: how much are we willing to give to God? Do we offer a drop here and a drop there, or do we pour out everything we have in God's service? Mary's lavish gift is a challenge to us all.

Activity   In our activity today, we will serve each other as Mary served Jesus. We can offer hand-washing, feet-washing or hand massage: take your time to choose what you would like to do, and then allow someone else to do the same for you.

Allow plenty of time for people to choose their activities. Your volunteers from the Exploring should be the first to have their hands washed! Encourage everyone both to perform and receive an act of service.

Prayer action   Our prayers today will use fragrance to remind us of Mary's gift. Her unstoppable generosity is like God's goodness, so today we thank God for all the good things he has done for us. We will use this incense: *(Show a handful of grains.)* these grains are gums and resins – including nard – that release perfume when they are burned. Please come forward and add a pinch of incense to this burner and as you do so, thank God for a gift he has given you.

Encourage everyone to come forward and add incense to the burner.

Let us pray.

God of Love,
your goodness fills our lives
as this fragrant smoke fills the air.
May we always be thankful.
Amen.

Music   From heaven you came

Conclusion   God, our Servant King,
send us out into the world
to love you and serve one another
in your name.
Amen.

Give notices, announce the next all-age service and invite everyone to the feast.

Palm Sunday

Hosanna!

Theme	Christ's entry into Jerusalem and the story of his Passion
Scripture	Luke 19:28-40; Luke 23:1-49

Running order	Total: 50 minutes
Welcome	Flag-making *(19 minutes)*
Introduction	Opening the theme
Storytelling 1	Retelling Christ's entry into Jerusalem, with flags *(5 minutes)*
Activity	Palm Sunday procession with singing *(10 minutes)*
Music	We have a King who rides a donkey
Music	Clap your hands, all you people
Storytelling 2	Active retelling of the Passion story *(5 minutes)*
Exploring	What happens in Holy Week? *(1 minute)*
Prayer action	Reflective prayer – dance with worship flags *(5 minutes)*
Music	I danced in the morning *(5 minutes)*
Conclusion	Closing prayer and invitation

Resources

NB Advance preparation needed!

- Worship flags *(see appendix)* for:
  - Jesus
  - two Pharisees
  - Pilate
  - Herod
- Equipment for making the crowd's flags *(see appendix)*
  - thin white fabric, cut into long triangles with a sleeve sewn at one end
  - green and blue fabric pens, paints or crayons
  - balsa wood sticks (sold by craft suppliers as candy floss sticks)
  - pattern templates *(see appendix)*

Leaders

Minimum: 3

- Leader
- *Jesus*
- Dancer

Optimum: 9+

- Leader *(Introduction and Conclusion)*
- Storytellers 1 and 2
- *Jesus*, in traditional dress
- Music Leader
- Explorer
- Activity Leader(s), also responsible for the Welcome activity
- Prayer Leader
- Dancer

Suggestions for additional music

- Give me joy in my heart
- Hosanna, hosanna
- I cannot tell

Service

Welcome

As people arrive, invite them to make a flag for use during the service. Find volunteers to carry the special flags for the Storytelling and explain to them briefly what they will be doing (they don't need to remember it all, as the Storyteller will cue them in).

Introduction

Today is the beginning of Holy Week: it is Palm Sunday, when we celebrate Jesus' triumphant entry into Jerusalem. Let's tell the story together. I need you to stand and hold your flags ready: you are the crowds in the streets of the city. Listen to the story and you'll hear what to do.

Storytelling 1

Jesus arrived in Jerusalem like a king.

Jesus – starting at the back of church – waves his white flag with the gold crown and starts to walk down the aisle.

Although he rode on a humble donkey instead of a white steed, he was surrounded by adoring crowds who cheered him on his way.

Encourage everyone to cheer.

People waved palm leaves in celebration. They blessed Jesus, declared peace in heaven and shouted words of praise: 'Hosanna!'

Encourage everyone to shout 'Hosanna!' and wave their white flags with palms and doves. Keep cheering and waving as Jesus walks to the front of church. As he arrives at the front, two Pharisees enter, waving a black flag with a red cross and a red flag with a black crown of thorns. They block Jesus' path.

Not everyone cheered. Some wanted to silence Jesus and his crowds of followers. The Pharisees said, 'Order your fans to be quiet!' But Jesus said, 'Listen, if they stopped yelling, the rocks all around us would cheer instead!'

PALM SUNDAY

The Pharisees sweep down the aisle with their red and black flags. The crowd continues to wave their white flags.

The crowd was unstoppable! People filled the streets of Jerusalem, singing God's praises.

Activity That is exactly what we are going to do now. We will take our flags, go out into the streets and sing.

Jesus leads the Palm Sunday procession out of the church and into the street, taking a circular route that leads back to the church. Remind everyone to take their hymn books and flags so that they can sing and wave as they go.

Music We have a King who rides a donkey

Music Clap your hands, all you people

Storytelling 2 *People are now back in their places in the church.*

After the celebrations of Palm Sunday, the story of Holy Week continues with those who wanted to silence Jesus forever.

The Pharisees enter at the front with their flags. In between them stands Pilate with his red flag bearing the black Roman motif.

The chief priests plotted to get rid of Jesus. They bribed his friend to betray him and then they arrested him. They took him to Pilate, the Roman Governor.

Jesus with his flag kneels before Pilate.

Pilate sent him to Herod, the local king.

Pilate leaves and Herod enters, carrying a black flag with a red crown.

Herod sent him back to Pilate in disgust.

Pilate returns and Herod leaves.

ALL-SORTS WORSHIP

Pilate wanted to let Jesus go but the chief priests stirred up the crowds to shout, 'Crucify him! Crucify him!'

Encourage the Pharisees to lead the shouting of 'Crucify him! Crucify him!' Everyone stands.

The people turned against Jesus.

Encourage everyone to throw down their flags in the aisle.

So Pilate condemned him to death.

Pilate leaves. The Pharisees raise their flags up high and wave them triumphantly until the end of the story.

Jesus was tortured and nailed to a cross. He died and was buried in a borrowed stone tomb.

Jesus lowers his flag and lies down with his arms outstretched. The Storyteller covers Jesus' face and upper body with the flag. Pause for a moment.

Exploring   In Holy Week, we remember the events that led to Jesus' death on the cross. Our flags have reminded us that there was a battle going on between the light and life of Christ and the power of darkness and death. In our retelling of the story, Jesus carried the white flag of peace with the crown of a king, and the crowd waved white flags with the dove of peace and the palms of victory; the powerful people who put Jesus to death carried red and black flags, the colours of death and darkness. By the end of today's story, only those flags were waving, like the flags of a victorious army at the end of a battle. When Jesus died on the cross, it looked as though he had been well and truly beaten. No one knew then that Easter morning would be his final victory.

For our prayers today, a dancer will help us reflect on this battle between life and death, good and evil, which is known as Christ's Passion.

Prayer action   *As the tune of 'I danced in the morning' is played slowly and thoughtfully, a dancer performs with flags: one is Jesus' white flag with the gold crown, the other is the black flag with the red cross.*

Let us pray.
God of light and life,
for us you took on the power of death
and won.
May we follow you wherever you lead.
Amen.

Music I danced in the morning

Conclusion Lord Jesus,
as we celebrate with palms today
and remember your Passion,
we look forward to celebrating your Easter victory.
May we be faithful witnesses.
Amen.

Give notices, announce the next all-age service and invite everyone to the feast.

Maundy Thursday

Loving to the end

Theme	Love and sacrifice
Scripture	Exodus 12:1-14; 1 Corinthians 11:23-26; John 13:1-17, 31b-35

Running order Total: 50 minutes

Foot-washing

Welcome/Activity 1	Foot-washing *(10 minutes)*
Introduction	Opening the theme
Music	Great God, your love has called us here *(5 minutes)*

Bread-breaking

Storytelling/Activity 2	The first Passover meal / making unleavened bread *(15 minutes)*
Exploring	What does the Last Supper mean to us? *(10 minutes)*
Music	One whose heart is hard as steel *(5 minutes)*
Prayer action	Breaking unleavened bread – active prayer *(5 minutes)*
Conclusion	Closing prayer and invitation

Resources

- Equipment for foot/hand-washing:
  - two jugs of warm water, one soapy and one clean
  - a large bowl
  - a supply of small hand towels or paper towels
- Music and words
- Two wipe-clean tables for bread-making
- Ingredients for making unleavened bread *(see appendix)*
  - plain flour
  - water
  - measuring cups
  - mixing bowls
  - baking trays lined with greaseproof paper
  - rolling pins
  - some forks
- A cooker. If your church doesn't have a kitchen, you could use a tabletop mini oven
- Plates
- A plain cup (such as an earthenware cup or goblet)
- Unleavened bread (some you made earlier)
- The chalice
- Communion bread or wafers (unconsecrated)

Leaders

Minimum: 1

- Leader

Optimum: 7

- Leader *(Introduction and Conclusion)*
- Storyteller
- Music Leader
- Explorer
- Activity Leaders x 2
- Prayer Leader

Suggestions for additional music

- Let there be love
- The world is full of smelly feet

Service

Welcome/Activity 1 *Anyone involved in leading the service should be ready with water and towels. As people arrive, invite them to have their feet or hands washed. Hold each foot or hand over a large bowl and carefully pour warm soapy water over it, then rinse with clean water and pat dry.*

Introduction Today is Maundy Thursday. 'Maundy' comes from the Latin word for 'commandment' and today we remember when Jesus gave us a new commandment. Many of the original Ten Commandments tell us what *not* to do, such as do not steal, do not kill and do not tell lies. Jesus' new commandment gave his disciples, and us, something positive to do: love each other. Jesus said, 'Just as I have loved you, you also should love one another. By this everyone will know that you are my disciples, if you have love for one another.'

Jesus practised what he preached by rolling up his sleeves, taking off his disciples' sandals and washing their dusty, smelly feet. This was usually a servant's job, so Jesus' disciples were shocked to see him getting down on his hands and knees, but Jesus explained that he was setting them an example. Loving other people means helping them, serving them, putting yourself out for them.

This morning we've followed Jesus' example: we have washed each other's feet and hands as one small way of loving each other as he loved us. Whenever we remember today's service and recall what it was like to wash someone else's feet, or have our own feet washed, let's think what else we might do to love and serve each other.

Music Great God, your love has called us here

Storytelling/Activity 2 *Invite everyone to gather round the bread-making tables and show them how to mix the dough and press it out onto a baking sheet, then prick it all over. Encourage everyone to make their own small loaves of unleavened bread as you tell the story.*

Imagine that you're making this bread in a big hurry. You're living in the slave camp in Egypt and all your relatives are Pharaoh's slaves. Terrible things have happened in Egypt, and last night was the most terrible of all. God's spokesperson, Moses, gave you special instructions about killing and eating a perfect lamb, marking your doorposts with its blood and getting packed and ready for a long journey. During the night, God's angel of death killed all the eldest children in Egypt, but the children in your families were saved. God passed over your houses that were marked with the lamb's blood, so last night was called 'Passover'.

Now Pharaoh has finally agreed to give you your freedom. You've got to go straight away, before he changes his mind. You're going to escape into the desert, and after that, who knows? You've packed up everything you can carry and now you've just got to make some food for the journey. You've got a long way to walk, and who can say when your next meal will be? So you're making this bread without yeast – there's no time for it to rise. Just mix it, flatten it, bake it and go. It's time to escape – time to be free!

Quickly finish making the bread and then have volunteers ready to bake it during the rest of the service. It should only take a few minutes, so more than one batch can be cooked.

Exploring When Jesus washed his friends' feet, they were about to celebrate Passover together. This was the special meal that reminded them of their ancestors' escape from slavery in Egypt. They ate lamb and unleavened bread, just like the flat loaves we have made today, and there were cups of wine on the table.

Hold up the unleavened bread and the plain cup.

Because it was the last meal Jesus shared with his friends before he died, we call it the Last Supper. It is special because Jesus took the Passover bread and wine and gave them a new meaning. This is what happened:

> The Lord Jesus on the night when he was betrayed took a loaf of bread, and when he had given thanks,

he broke it and said, 'This is my body that is for you. Do this in remembrance of me.' In the same way he took the cup also, after supper, saying, 'This cup is the new covenant in my blood. Do this, as often as you drink it, in remembrance of me.'

Jesus knew he was going to die and he used the bread and wine to show what his death would mean for us. His body would be broken and his blood would be spilled on the cross so that we would receive a new promise, or covenant, from God: the promise of forgiveness for all our wrongdoing and the gift of eternal life.

At the Passover meal, the Jews remembered the night God gave them their freedom, when they killed a perfect lamb and were saved by its blood on their doorposts. Jesus used the Passover bread and wine as a sign that he was like the perfect lamb – he was going to die so that God's people might live. God freed his people from slavery in Egypt; Jesus freed us all from sin and death.

Hold up the chalice and the Communion bread.

Whenever Christians share bread and wine together, we remember the sacrifice Jesus made for our sake.

Music One whose heart is hard as steel

During the hymn, take the bread out of the oven and put it on plates on the altar, ready for sharing during the prayer.

Prayer action For our prayers today, we will share this unleavened Passover bread. May it remind us of the love of Christ and the new life he gave us through his death and resurrection.

Pass round the fresh bread and invite everyone to eat a piece.

Living Lord,
may this bread remind us that your body was broken for us,

and your blood was shed for us,
so that we might be freed from sin and death.
We thank you for life and liberty.
Amen.

Conclusion Lord Jesus,
you loved your own who were in the world
and you loved them to the end.
Help us to follow your example
and love one other in your name.
Amen.

Give notices, announce the next all-age service and invite everyone to the feast. This should include the unleavened bread baked during the service.

Good Friday

Life and death

Theme	Christ's death and our redemption
Scripture	John 18:1—19:42

Running order	Total: 50 minutes
Welcome	Building the Easter garden *(9 minutes)*
Introduction	Opening the theme
Storytelling	Modern version of the Good Friday story – news stations of the cross *(10 minutes)*
Music	There is a green hill far away *(5 minutes)*
Exploring	Why is Good Friday 'Good'? *(1 minute)*
Prayer action	Building a cross out of confessions *(5 minutes)*
Activity	Bringing the Easter garden to life *(15 minutes)*
EITHER	
Music	Such love *(5 minutes)*
Conclusion	Closing prayer and invitation
OR	*(If you are not holding an all-age service on Easter Day)*
Storytelling 2	The Resurrection *(1 minute)*
Music	Led like a lamb to the slaughter *(4 minutes)*
Conclusion	Closing prayer and invitation

Resources

NB Advance preparation needed!
Collect lots of clean egg shells – neat halves are best

- Materials for the Easter garden, according to your church's custom (inside or outside)
- Music and words
- News stations of the cross *(see appendix)*
- Lolly sticks *(see appendix)*
- Felt pens (ideally, for the egg-decorating activity, some of these should be permanent markers)
- Clean egg shells
- Cotton wool
- Cress seeds
- Some small jugs of water
- *(Optional)* Some budding flowers in pots

Leaders

Minimum: 1
- Leader

Optimum: 6+
- Leader *(Introduction and Conclusion)*
- Storyteller(s)
- Music Leader
- Explorer
- Activity Leader(s)
- Prayer Leader

Suggestions for additional music

- At the cross she keeps her station
- It is a thing most wonderful

Service

Welcome — *As people arrive, invite them to help construct the Easter garden. At this stage you are aiming to get stones and earth or other materials in place: the plants and flowers will be introduced during the Activity.*

Introduction — Today is Good Friday. We are nearly ready to celebrate Easter, but today we remember the day Jesus died. We are going to tell the story of what happened as if it were taking place today, in a world with TV cameras, newspapers and mobile phones. All around the church are things to look at, listen to and hold: they tell us what happened when Jesus died. Take your time to explore, then we'll come together to tell the story.

Storytelling — *Allow plenty of time for people to circulate around the 'news stations of the cross', then gather everyone at each station in turn.*

Station 1: Condemned — Jesus was so popular with the crowds that they nearly rioted wherever he went. He was so unpopular with the religious leaders that they wanted to kill him. The Romans were in charge of Jerusalem and they wanted peace, so the Roman soldiers arrested Jesus and the Roman Governor, Pilate, decided that Jesus had to die.

Station 2: Surrounded — The crowds in the streets yelled at Jesus. Some felt sorry for him, but others shouted that he deserved to die.

Station 3: Stripped — The soldiers took Jesus' clothes away.

Station 4: Killed — The soldiers nailed Jesus to a cross and left him there until he was dead.

Station 5: Buried — Jesus was buried in a stone tomb. A big rock sealed it shut.

Music — There is a green hill far away

Exploring — The Good Friday story is all about bad things happening to Jesus. He was innocent but he was treated like a criminal; he is God but he was killed as a man –

GOOD FRIDAY

so why is today called 'Good'? It's because today is not the end of the story. Jesus suffered and died on Friday, but on Sunday he rose from the dead and was alive again: he went through terrible things but then came out the other side, into life. He did this so that we can follow him: when we do bad things, we can be forgiven, leave them behind us and enjoy new life. When we go through death we can follow him out the other side, into eternal life.

So Good Friday is good because Jesus let all of these bad things happen to him for a reason – and that reason is us. He died so that we can leave sin and death behind us and find life.

Prayer action

For our prayers today, we will say sorry for the things we have done wrong. In a time of quiet, think what you would like to say sorry for. Then write or draw it on one of these lolly sticks, or simply write the word 'sorry'. Then we will collect all our stick confessions together and make a wooden cross to remind us that Jesus died for our sins.

Allow plenty of time for people to think and make their confessions. Encourage each person to bring their stick forward and add it to the others (face down if preferred) to form the shape of a large cross on the floor.

God of Love,
we are sorry for the hurt we have caused,
for the messes we have made,
for all we have done wrong.
May you forgive us
and take our sins from us,
in Jesus' name.
Amen.

Activity

As we think about Jesus in the tomb today, and look forward to Easter, we remember that Good Friday is good because it is about life as well as death. Now our Easter garden needs some new life.

Encourage people to gather round and decorate the egg shells, then fill them with damp cotton wool and sow them with cress seeds. These can then be placed in the Easter garden. You could also decorate the garden with budding flowers in pots. By Sunday, the cress should have started growing and the flowers should have opened.

EITHER *(If you are holding an all-age service on Easter Day)*

Music Such love

Conclusion Lord Jesus,
by your death you opened for us
the new and living way.
May we always follow you.
Amen.

OR *(If you are not holding an all-age service on Easter Day)*

Storytelling 2 On Sunday we will celebrate Jesus' coming back to life. This is called the Resurrection and it is the Easter story's happy ending.

Show Station 6: Alive!

Music Led like a lamb to the slaughter

Conclusion Lord Jesus,
by your death you opened for us
the new and living way.
Now you are alive!
May we always live in you.
Amen.

Give notices, announce the next all-age service and invite everyone to the hot cross bun feast.

Eastertide

Easter Day*

Full of life

Theme Christ's resurrection

Scripture Luke 24:1-12

Running order Total: 50 minutes

Welcome — Lighting candles around the bonfire *(10 minutes)*

Introduction — Opening the theme

Music — All in an Easter garden *(5 minutes)*

Storytelling — Visual and sensory retelling of Luke 24:1-12 *(5 minutes)*

Exploring — What does the empty tomb mean? Visual exploration *(5 minutes)*

Music — He has risen *(5 minutes)*

Activity — Preparing for creative confessions and thanksgivings; burning the confessions *(10 minutes)*

Prayer action — Rocket prayer – thanksgiving *(5 minutes)*

Music — Come on and celebrate *(5 minutes)*

Conclusion — Closing prayer and invitation

---

* Ideally, this should be a service at dawn.

Resources

- Outside the church, a small bonfire or brazier
- One firework: a rocket *(see appendix)*
- Votive candles, enough for one each (with a circle of card to catch wax drips)
- Matches and a wooden splint
- Your church's Easter garden, with the stone still covering the entrance to the tomb
- A dish or two of diluted myrrh oil *(see appendix)*
- Two large candles, to be held by volunteers
- A sheet of white cotton or linen
- Music and words
- Two clean, empty halves of an egg shell *(see appendix)*
- Lots of clean sticks: the bags of kindling sold by garages would be ideal
- Lots of sticky labels – address labels or smaller – cut out individually with their adhesive backing
- Biros and felt pens

Leaders

Minimum: 3

- Leader
- Activity Leader
- Prayer Leader

Optimum: 6+

- Leader *(Introduction and Conclusion)*
- Storyteller
- Music Leader
- Explorer
- Activity Leader(s) *(responsible for the bonfire)*
- Prayer Leader(s) *(responsible for the firework)*

Suggestions for additional music

- This is the day that the Lord has made
- Low in the grave he lay
- Jesus Christ is ris'n today

Service

Welcome *As people arrive, distribute the votive candles and gather round the bonfire. Light the Paschal candle from the fire, using a wooden splint. The light is then passed around until everyone's candle is lit. Lead the people into the dark church.*

Introduction In this early morning darkness, we remember the good news of Easter: Jesus has risen from the dead. His light has defeated the darkness of death. Alleluia!

Turn all the lights on. After the hymn, blow out the candles.

Music All in an Easter garden

Storytelling *Gather everyone around the Easter garden, inside or outside the church.*

It was still dark, like this, when Jesus' friends went to his tomb on that first Easter day. Mary Magdalene, Joanna and James' mother, Mary, brought spices for his body, including myrrh.

Pass round the dish of diluted myrrh oil and encourage people to smell it and, if they wish, to rub a little onto their skin.

They made their way through the garden until they found the place. On Friday, Jesus' crucified body had been laid inside the tomb and a big stone had been rolled across to seal the entrance.

Take away the stone.

But when the women reached the tomb, the stone was gone. They found the empty place where Jesus had been laid, but Jesus himself was nowhere to be seen. I wonder what they thought?

Invite responses, valuing all contributions, then light two large candles and invite two volunteers to come forward and hold them.

Suddenly, two shining angels dressed in white appeared in the empty tomb. The women were terrified, but the angels said, 'Why are you looking in a graveyard for someone who is alive? Jesus isn't here: he has risen. Don't you remember how he told you, back in Galilee, that the Son of God would be crucified, and after three days he would rise again?'

Then Mary, Joanna and Mary remembered everything that Jesus had said, and they rushed back to tell the other disciples. Some refused to believe them, but Peter went back to the tomb with them and saw the empty space for himself. He saw the empty linen cloths that had covered Jesus' body.

Pass round the linen cloths.

Then Peter went home, full of amazement.

Exploring *Invite people to return to their places.*

The story of Easter morning focuses on the empty tomb and the empty linen cloths that had contained Jesus' body. The women who brought spices must have been feeling empty, too: they were missing Jesus, whose death had left a gaping hole in their lives. So the story starts with emptiness: Jesus is gone and there is nothing left behind but the tomb. It is like an empty shell – like this.

Show the halves of the empty egg shell and encourage children to come and have a closer look.

If you found this egg shell on the ground, what would you think had happened?

Invite responses, valuing them all. Encourage suggestions that an empty egg shell can mean death (a stolen or fallen egg) or life (a hatched and growing chick).

An egg shell like this is simply empty, but its emptiness can mean very different things. The chick that was inside this egg may have died when the egg fell out of the nest, or been eaten by a predator. Alternatively, the chick inside this egg may have hatched, stretched its wings and gone off to grow and thrive. The emptiness of this egg shell can mean death or life.

The emptiness of Jesus' tomb looked at first as if it meant death and loss: the women thought his body had been stolen; they thought they'd lost their last chance to care for him by preparing his body for the grave. But the angels told them that this emptiness was a sign of life: 'Jesus isn't here: he has risen.'

The good news of Easter is that Jesus turned emptiness and death into the fullness of life for us all. He knows we are not perfect and we all do bad things, so he gave us forgiveness for our wrongdoing. His death took away the life-denying, negative power of sin and gave us new life. Most wonderful of all, his death and resurrection mean that instead of empty nothingness after death, we can enjoy the fullness of eternal life.

Music He has risen

Activity Our Activity today will help us remember that Jesus took away our sins and gave us new life. There are two things to do. First of all, we will say sorry to God for something we have done wrong. We will write or draw whatever it is on a piece of wood, then burn it in the Easter bonfire as a sign that Jesus takes away all our sins. Then we will thank God for something wonderful in our lives, by writing or drawing it on one of these sticky labels. These labels will then be stuck all over a big firework. It is a rocket, so we will send our thanksgiving prayers shooting into the sky in celebration of the fullness of life that God has given us.

Allow plenty of time for people to write their confessions on pieces of wood and their thanksgivings on the sticky labels. Everyone then gathers outside. As they do so, the Prayer Leader sticks all the labels on the rocket and prepares it for launch.

EASTER DAY

Prayer action First of all, let's confess our sins and throw them into this Easter bonfire, as a sign that God takes them all away.

Throw all the wooden confessions onto the bonfire. If you wrote confessions on lolly sticks during the Good Friday service, burn these, too. Then gather at a safe distance from the rocket.

Let us pray.

Almighty God,
we celebrate this Easter day,
we thank you that we are full of life
and we praise you to the skies.

Launch the rocket and watch it explode.

Amen.

Music Come on and celebrate

Conclusion God of Life,
out of the empty tomb
you brought us fullness of life.
May we be witnesses to your glory.
Alleluia!
Amen.

Give notices, announce the next all-age service and invite everyone to the feast.

237

Second Sunday of Easter

Speaking out

Theme	Spreading the good news of Jesus
Scripture	Acts 5:27-32; Psalm 118:14; Psalm 150; John 20:19-31

Running order	Total: 50 minutes
Welcome	Spot the difference *(5 minutes)*
Introduction	Opening the theme
Storytelling	Sketch – Jesus appears to the disciples *(10 minutes)*
Music	Proclaim, proclaim the story *(5 minutes)*
Exploring	How did the disciples change? *(10 minutes)*
Activity	Praise – music and dance *(10 minutes)*
Music	Praise him on the trumpet
Music	Teach me to dance
Prayer action	Sound and silence *(5 minutes)*
Music	Sing it in the valleys *(5 minutes)*
Conclusion	Closing prayer and invitation

Resources

- Three pictures of Peter *(see appendix)*
- Laptop, projector and screen
- A sign or placard: 'A week later'
- Music and words
- Percussion instruments – as many and as varied as possible

Leaders

Minimum: 4

- Leader
- Cast x 3

Optimum: 8

- Leader *(Introduction and Conclusion)*
- Cast x 3 (in modern dress)

  Peter

  Andrew

  Jesus, wearing a white shirt with light trousers. Use face paints to draw wounds in his hands and side
- Music Leader
- Explorer
- Activity Leader
- Prayer Leader

Suggestions for additional music

- Forth in the peace of Christ we go
- Praise him, praise him, praise him

Service

Welcome *As people arrive, display two pictures: Peter after Jesus' arrest, denying Christ, and Peter after the resurrection, preaching to the crowds. Invite them to consider the difference.*

Introduction Today is the first Sunday after Easter. We have begun by comparing these two pictures: they show Jesus' disciple, Peter, before and after Easter. What's the difference?

Invite responses.

There was certainly a big change in Peter, and today we're going to find out why. We know what happened on Good Friday, when Jesus was killed on the cross, and we know what happened on Easter morning, when his disciples found an empty tomb and were told that Jesus had risen from the dead. Some were convinced; others found it hard to believe. Our story today tells us what happened next.

Invite eight non-speaking volunteers to play the additional disciples. Ask them to gather at the front of church with Peter and Andrew.

Storytelling

Peter — Are we all here? *(he looks around and counts)* No Thomas – well, I'm not waiting for him any longer. Andrew, lock the door. *(Andrew mimes doing so: imagine that the door is between the disciples and the congregation)* Is it locked and bolted? *(Andrew nods)* Good. If the religious police find us, they'll kill us. None of us is safe, especially if they know we're talking about Jesus.

Andrew — Peter, I miss him.

Peter — We all miss him.

Jesus — *(suddenly walking in behind them)* Peace be with you.

Peter — Jesus! It's you!

Andrew — It can't be – it must be a ghost!

Jesus — No, I'm not. You can touch me.

He encourages the disciples to grab hold of him.

And look, here are the holes in my hands where the nails went in.

He holds out his hands and the disciples touch them.

And look, here's the hole in my side where the soldier's spear cut me.

He lifts his shirt to show his waist and the disciples move closer for a good look.

Andrew — I saw that happen!

Peter — My Lord, it really is you! Hallelujah!

He hugs Jesus and encourages the other disciples to cheer loudly.

Jesus — Peace be with you. God sent me, so now I'm sending you. I give you God's Holy Spirit. *(he breathes on the disciples)* You have the power to forgive people's sins.

Jesus leaves.

Thomas walks down the aisle and knocks at the door. Andrew unlocks the door and lets him in.

Andrew — Thomas! You've just missed him!

Thomas — Who?

Peter — Jesus! He was here! He's really alive!

Thomas — What?

Andrew — He is! We touched him and saw the holes in his hands, and everything!

Thomas — I don't believe it.

Peter — It's true!

Thomas — Prove it. I'm not believing anything until I see the holes in his hands for myself, *and* put my fingers in the wound in his side.

Thomas sits down with the other disciples. The Leader holds up a sign: 'A week later'.

Peter — Are we all here? *(he looks around and counts)* You as well, Thomas – good. Now lock the door, Andrew. *(Andrew mimes doing so)* Is it locked and bolted? *(Andrew nods)* Rumours about Jesus are spreading and the Temple guards are on the warpath.

Andrew	I wish we could see him again, Peter.
Peter	We all do.
Jesus	*(suddenly walking in behind them)* Peace be with you.
	The disciples cheer; Thomas gawps.
	Now's your chance, Thomas. Here are my hands: give me your finger. See? There's the hole. Look, here's the wound in my side. Go on, touch it.
	Thomas does so.
Thomas	My Lord and my God!
Jesus	So now you've got proof; now you've seen me with your own eyes, you believe in me – is that it? It's even better if people who haven't seen me believe in me. They're blessed.
Music	Proclaim, proclaim the story
Exploring	This story is often referred to as the story of 'Doubting Thomas', because it focuses on the sceptical disciple who wanted proof that Jesus really was alive. This is a bit unfair on Thomas, because when Jesus first appeared, the Bible tells us that he showed all the other disciples the holes in his hands and side. As we saw in our sketch, they had plenty of time to examine the evidence, but Thomas missed that opportunity. He has since been labelled 'Doubting Thomas', but many of the disciples were doubters before they touched Jesus and believed.
	The disciples' shared Easter journey from doubt to faith is particularly clear in Peter's case, as we saw in our 'Spot the difference' pictures. He went from being a terrified disciple-in-hiding, who denied three times that he even knew Jesus, to a bold and confident witness of Christ's resurrection. Peter led the disciples to preach openly about Jesus in Jerusalem, which got them into big trouble with the religious authorities. The chief priests rounded up the disciples and put them in prison, but an angel rescued them and they carried on spreading Jesus' good news in the Temple itself. The chief priests rounded them up again, and this is what happened:

When they had brought them, they had them stand before the council. The high priest questioned them, saying, 'We gave you strict orders not to teach in [Jesus'] name, yet here you have filled Jerusalem with your teaching and you are determined to bring this man's blood on us.' But Peter and the apostles answered, 'We must obey God rather than any human authority. The God of our ancestors raised up Jesus, whom you had killed by hanging him on a tree. God exalted him at his right hand as Leader and Saviour, so that he might give repentance to Israel and forgiveness of sins. And we are witnesses to these things, and so is the Holy Spirit whom God has given to those who obey him.'

Look at how brave Peter has become! In effect, he said to the powerful high priest, 'You're not the boss of me; God is – and you killed his Son!' Peter and the other disciples were doing exactly what Jesus told them to do in our story today. He said, 'God sent me, so now I'm sending you.' Jesus passed on to his disciples his mission to tell people about God.

The journey of Peter and the disciples from doubt to faith, and from faith to action, is our journey, too.

Show the first picture: Peter after Jesus' arrest, denying Christ.

Are we still at the beginning, trying to hide the fact that we believe in Jesus – perhaps even from ourselves?

Show the second picture: Peter and the other disciples examining Christ's hands.

Or are we in the middle, struggling with believing? In our story, Jesus gave his blessing to people like us, people who believe in him without having physically seen him.

Show the third picture: Peter after the resurrection, preaching to the crowds.

We are called to be the kind of disciple Peter became in the end: someone who is brave enough to speak out about their faith and tell people about God.

Activity The words of a psalm sum up the message of today's story: 'The Lord is my strength and my song, and he has become my salvation.'[35] Jesus died and rose again to save us: he is our salvation. He is always with us: he is our strength. Most important of all, we should joyfully tell the world about him: he's not our murmur or our whisper, but our song to be sung out loud for everyone to hear. For our activity today, we will make Jesus our song as loudly and joyfully as we possibly can. Please play any instruments you choose and let's praise God at the top of our voices.

Pull out all the stops for these two hymns! Encourage plenty of hearty singing, percussion playing and even dancing.

Music Praise him on the trumpet

Music Teach me to dance

Prayer action *Pause to let silence settle as the last notes of the previous hymn fade away.*

After our joyful songs of praise, we pause to let peace and quiet gather around us.

Pause.

Jesus said, 'Peace be with you,' and in that peace, his disciples knew him. Let's rest quietly in God's presence and know that he is with us.

Pause.

Risen Lord,
may we know your presence with us now
and believe, like Thomas,
that you are our Lord and our God.
Amen.

---

35. New King James Version.

Music Sing it in the valleys

Conclusion May the peace of Christ
who is and who was and who is to come
be with us all, evermore.
Amen.

Give notices, announce the next all-age service and invite everyone to the feast.

Third Sunday of Easter
The call

Theme	Jesus summons Saul and Peter – and us
Scripture	Acts 9:1-20; John 21:1-19

Running order	Total: 50 minutes
Welcome	Wondering about the bandaged, sleeping figure of Saul *(5 minutes)*
Introduction	Opening the theme
Storytelling 1	Finding Brother Saul – Ananias' tale *(10 minutes)*
Music	Will you come and follow me *(5 minutes)*
Storytelling 2/Activity	The beach barbecue – edible retelling of John 21:1-19 *(15 minutes)*
Exploring	What did God call Saul and Peter to do? *(5 minutes)*
Prayer action	Wake-up call – contemplative prayer with 'Reveille' *(5 minutes)*
Music	You stood there on the shoreline *(5 minutes)*
Conclusion	Closing prayer and invitation

Resources

- A barbecue outside the church
- Matches
- Fish suitable for grilling
- Bread rolls or loaves cut into wedges
- Paper plates
- Baby wipes and kitchen roll for hands
- A bin bag
- Music and words
- 'Reveille', either played live on a trumpet or bugle, or a recording (lots are available on the internet)
- *(Optional)* Sound equipment on which to play 'Reveille'

Leaders

Minimum: 4

- Leader
- Cast x 2
- Activity Leader

Optimum: 7+

- Leader *(Introduction and Conclusion)*
- Cast x 2:
  Ananias, wearing a traditional robe
  Saul, wearing a traditional robe and a bandage around his eyes
- Activity Leader(s)
- Music Leader *(also in charge of 'Reveille')*
- Explorer
- Prayer Leader

Suggestions for additional music

- Heaven shall not wait
- We have a gospel to proclaim

# Service

Welcome *Begin with the actor playing Saul lying down in a prominent spot at the front of the church. As people arrive, invite them to wonder about the bandaged, sleeping figure. Who is he? What has happened to him?*

Introduction (*very loudly*) GOOD MORNING!

Ananias SSSHHHH! (*pointing at the sleeping Saul*) You'll wake him up!

Leader Sorry! Good morning, everyone. We've been wondering about this stranger at the front of the church today. What do you think might have happened to him?

Invite responses, valuing all contributions.

Let's hear what happened.

Storytelling 1

Ananias First of all, let me tell you: three days ago, you wouldn't have caught me in the same room as this man. No way. He may not look like much now, but his name was enough to scare anyone stiff: Saul. He was the chief priest's enforcer, a vicious, single-minded individual who made it his personal mission to hunt down any followers of Jesus and destroy them. He travelled the country with his band of thugs. He sniffed out Jesus' people wherever he went: it was as if he had eyes and ears everywhere, and could follow the sound of a whispered prayer until he cornered another believer. His heavies rounded our people up like cows and herded them back to Jerusalem. God knows what terrible things happened to them there – no one ever saw them again. Men or women, this Saul didn't care. We called him Killer Saul, because he wanted to kill us all – geddit? He breathed threats and murder against us like a dragon breathes fire.

So I know what you're thinking: what happened? Why is Killer Saul in your house, sleeping like a baby? Listen, this story will blow your mind. He was on his way here, to Damascus, ready to hunt down more believers and kill them. He wasn't far away when suddenly, a dazzling light from heaven flashed all around him. He told me this himself: he fell down and covered his eyes, then he heard a voice saying, 'Saul, Saul, why do you persecute me?'

He asked, 'Who are you, Lord?'

The voice replied, 'I am Jesus, whom you are persecuting. Now get up and go to the city, and you'll find out what you've got to do.'

One of his bodyguards told me that he heard the voice, too, but couldn't see anyone. He helped Saul up but Saul had gone blind – they had to lead him into Damascus like a blind beggar. He was blind for three days and they couldn't get him to eat or drink anything: he just sat there, stunned.

Now I was in a safe house in downtown Damascus. We'd had a tip-off that Killer Saul was on his way, so we'd gone into hiding. One night, I was fast asleep when someone called my name: 'Ananias!' The voice was loud and urgent. I leapt up and saw that all my friends were still asleep – then I knew it was God calling me. I said, 'Here I am, Lord,' and God gave me my orders. He said, 'Go to Judas' house on Straight Street and ask for Saul. He's praying and he's just had a vision that a man called Ananias will cure his blindness.'

I started shaking. 'Lord, you can't mean Killer Saul?! I've heard what he's done to your followers in Jerusalem! He'll arrest me and drag me in front of the chief priests! They'll have me killed!'

But God said, 'Go. I've chosen him to tell the world about me.'

What else could I do? I went. All the way there, I was afraid that it was some sort of trap, that Saul's henchmen would grab me as soon as I set foot inside that house. But my feet kept on walking and before I knew it, I was going through the door and there he was: the terrifying Saul was a huddled, bandaged bag of bones who was kneeling and saying the Lord's prayer. Then I knew that God really had sent me there, and that he really had chosen Saul to be a follower of Jesus – one of us. Killer Saul had become Brother Saul. So I touched his shoulder gently and said, 'Brother Saul, the Lord Jesus, who appeared to you on your way here, has sent me so that you may see again and be filled with God's Holy Spirit.'

Saul wakes and jumps up, tearing the bandages from his eyes. He comes forward and puts an arm around Ananias.

Saul And suddenly I could see – more clearly than I had ever done before! Since then I've been resting here and getting my strength back, letting my eyes get used to this new way of looking at the world. I've even been baptised! Now I've got work to do. I'm still visiting every congregation in town, but this time I've got a new message: Jesus is the Son of God!

Music Will you come and follow me

Storytelling 2/Activity *Encourage everyone to gather outside around the barbecue. Share out the grilled fish and toasted bread as you tell the story.*

Today we have a second story, and this one involves a barbecue on the beach. One evening, after Jesus had risen from the dead, Peter and some of the other disciples decided to go fishing, like they used to in the old days before Jesus. In fact, it was while they were fishing that Jesus had first come to them and said, 'Follow me, and I will make you fish for people.' They remembered that as they loaded their old nets into their boat and headed out onto the lake.

They fished all night but didn't catch a single thing. As it started to get light, they could make out a figure on the beach. He shouted to them, 'No luck, lads? Try fishing on the other side of the boat.' So they did, and suddenly their nets were so full of fish that they couldn't haul them in. Then they recognised the man on the beach: it was Jesus!

They piled ashore and dragged the net full of fish with them. Jesus had already got a fire going, and the delicious smells of grilled fish and toasted bread filled the air. Jesus said, 'Come and have breakfast!' and together they shared a feast of fish.

Pause while everybody eats until there is no food left.

When they had all finished, Jesus turned and looked at Peter. 'Peter, do you love me?'

Peter replied, 'Yes, Lord, you know I love you.'

Jesus said, 'Feed my lambs.' Then he said again, 'Peter, do you love me?'

Peter replied, 'Yes, Lord, you know I love you.'

Jesus said, 'Tend my sheep.' Then he said again, 'Peter, do you love me?'

Peter was hurt that Jesus had to ask three times, and he said, 'Lord, you know everything; you know I love you.'

Jesus said to him, 'Feed my sheep. Listen, one day you'll have to go where you don't want to go, just as I did. Follow me.'

Lead everyone back inside the church.

Exploring Both our stories today have shown us what God's call can be like. The story of Saul on the road to Damascus showed us a particularly dramatic and unexpected call: not only was Saul not a Christian, but he hated Christians and was actively working to kill as many as he could. Yet God chose him to do his work, and he became Paul, the leader of the early Church. Paul's story reminds us that God can call *anyone*, even when they least expect it.

Then there was the beach barbecue and Jesus' strange conversation with Peter. He kept repeating the same question: 'Do you love me?' Before the crucifixion, Peter had denied three times that he even knew Jesus. Such a betrayal must have weighed heavily on his heart. On the beach that morning, Jesus gave Peter a chance to start again by cancelling out his three denials with three 'I love you's. Then Jesus repeated the words with which he had first called Peter and the other fishermen from the same beach: 'Follow me.' This story reminds us that God's call doesn't go away, and that Jesus doesn't give up on us: like Peter, we might fail and get things badly wrong, but Jesus will always give us a chance to get back on track.

Saul and Peter experienced different kinds of call, but God called them both to action. Saul's job was to tell the world about Jesus: in the Bible, God says, 'He is an instrument whom I have chosen to bring my name before Gentiles and kings and before the people of Israel.' Peter was handed the job of leading people, caring for them and helping them in Jesus' name. Jesus had described himself as the good shepherd, and by saying 'Feed my lambs' and 'Tend my sheep', he passed his shepherd's responsibility on to Peter.

God continues to call people, and he is calling each one of us. What does he want you to do?

Prayer action

For our prayers today, we will rest in God's presence and listen for his call. To help us, we will hear the trumpet tune called 'Reveille'[36] that is used to wake up soldiers in an army camp. It is literally a call to action: a wake-up call. Let us pray.

Play 'Reveille' and then pause for a short time.

Lord Jesus,
may we hear your wake-up call
and be ready to follow you
wherever you lead us.
Amen.

---

36. Pronounced 'rev-alley'.

Music   You stood there on the shoreline

Conclusion   Heavenly Father,
send us out in the power of your Holy Spirit
to answer your call.
Amen.

Give notices, announce the next all-age service and invite everyone to the feast.

Fourth Sunday of Easter
The Good Shepherd's sheep

Theme	We are the Good Shepherd's flock
Scripture	Psalm 23; John 10:22-30

Running order — Total: 50 minutes

Welcome	Slideshow – green pastures and still waters *(5 minutes)*
Introduction	Opening the theme
Storytelling	Reading Psalm 23 with illustration *(5 minutes)*
Music	The Lord's my shepherd (Townend) *(5 minutes)*
Exploring	Are we like sheep? Considering the video of a shepherd herding 1000 sheep *(15 minutes)*
Activity	Finding the lost sheep before the wolves do *(10 minutes)*
Prayer action	The Lord is my shepherd – tangible prayer with sheep's wool *(5 minutes)*
Music	Love is his word *(5 minutes)*
Conclusion	Closing prayer and invitation

Resources

- Laptop, projector and screen
- Speakers
- Slideshow and picture of sheep *(see appendix)*
- YouTube video of a shepherd herding 1000 sheep *(see appendix)*
- Wolf ears *(see appendix)*
- Hidden around the church, lots of pictures of lambs and/or cuddly toy lambs if you have some *(see appendix)*
- Shepherds' head-cloths and ties x 2
- Music and words
- Sheep's wool – either raw fleece if you can find any, or lengths of natural-coloured woollen yarn

Leaders

Minimum: 1

- Leader

Optimum: 6

- Leader *(Introduction and Conclusion)*
- Storyteller
- Music Leader
- Explorer
- Activity Leader
- Prayer Leader

Suggestions for additional music

- Faithful Shepherd, feed me
- There's a wideness in God's mercy

Service

Welcome — *As people arrive, show the slideshow of green pastures and still waters.*

Introduction — These pictures of beautiful countryside have set the scene for today's service: we are thinking about Jesus, the good shepherd.

Storytelling — *Show the picture of a neat flock of sheep in a meadow, grazing peacefully. Read Psalm 23.*

Music — The Lord's my shepherd (Townend)

Exploring — The psalm we have heard today is very popular because it describes how tenderly God takes care of us. Like a good shepherd, he makes sure that we have everything we need and he protects us from harm. It is very comforting to think of God like this. But how do we feel about thinking of ourselves as sheep? Look at the picture on our screen now: how would you describe these sheep?

Invite responses, valuing all contributions.

Surely we don't have anything in common with sheep, do we? To help us think about this, we'll watch a video of a shepherd herding a thousand sheep. He and his dogs are moving them down from the hills and back home to their farm: it's a journey of six miles across wild Scottish countryside. Let's look at how these sheep behave and wonder, 'Is there anything about them that reminds us of ourselves?'

Show the video clip: it is about seven minutes long.

What did you notice about the way those sheep behaved?

Invite responses.

There was a lot of noise and rushing about, wasn't there? Some sheep were running in the right direction;

others looked confused and went the wrong way. Some got in a panic; some went their own way, off the main path, and some seemed quite determined to make a break for freedom! They headed off over the hills, on their own or as a group.

Whatever the sheep did, the shepherd kept an eye on them all. He sent his dogs to bring back the strays and turn the wayward ones back to the right path. He led them safely home and fastened them securely in their field, behind a big gate.

If we are like sheep with a good shepherd, it is not because we are a mindless flock that trots calmly and obediently in the same direction. It is because we are all individuals, with minds and wills of our own, who nevertheless all belong to Jesus. He wants to lead us safely home to God, however determined we are to break away, strike out on our own or head in the wrong direction entirely. Jesus said this about his followers:

> My sheep hear my voice. I know them, and they follow me. I give them eternal life, and they will never perish. No one will snatch them out of my hand. What my Father has given me is greater than all else, and no one can snatch it out of the Father's hand. The Father and I are one.

What we need to do is trust Jesus, our good shepherd. If we follow him, he will look after us and nothing will take us away from him.

Activity

When Jesus first spoke about his sheep being snatched away, every shepherd who heard him would have known what he meant: wolves. Wherever shepherds in Jesus' time kept their flocks, wolves and other wild animals prowled in the hope of snatching their dinner when the shepherd's back was turned. Our activity today will remind us of the danger those sheep were in. Can I have two volunteers to be wolves?

Bring forward your volunteers and put on their wolf ears.

And can I have two volunteers to be shepherds?

Bring forward your volunteers and put on their head-cloths.

Now, all over the church some lost sheep are hiding. They look like this. *(Hold up a lamb.)* Shepherds, can you find them before the wolves do? Wolves, can you catch lots of tasty lambs for your dinner? Who will get the most? On your marks, get set, GO!

Encourage your wolves and shepherds to hunt all over the church and then to bring back their findings to the front. Count up the sheep and announce whether the wolves or the shepherds have won.

This battle between the shepherds and the wolves reminds us of the dangers faced by sheep and their shepherds in Jesus' time. Shepherds often had to risk their lives to defend their flocks. Another shepherd in the Bible, David, had to kill bears and even lions![37] This is the kind of good shepherd to whom Jesus compared himself. He died to save us: on the cross, he gave his own life so that we could have eternal life with God. This means that even death, the biggest predator of all, cannot snatch us away from him.

Prayer action

Our prayer today will remind us that Jesus is our good shepherd. Please take a piece of this sheep's wool and remember those lively, determined, independent-minded sheep we saw today. Remember the shepherd who led them safely home.

Pass round the sheep's wool and then pause for a short time.

Lord, you are our shepherd and we are your sheep.
Lead us to green pastures and by still waters;
be with us, even in the dark valley of death;
bring us home to be with you for ever.
Amen.

Please keep your piece of sheep's wool to remind you of the good shepherd.

---

37. 1 Samuel 17:34-37.

Music   Love is his word

Conclusion   Jesus, our good shepherd,
lead us out into the world
and never lose sight of us.
Amen.

Give notices, announce the next all-age service and invite everyone to the feast.

Fifth Sunday of Easter
Water of life

Theme	God's love is for everyone
Scripture	Acts 11:1-18; Revelation 21:1-6

Running order	Total: 50 minutes
Welcome	Sharing the tear-and-share bread *(5 minutes)*
Introduction	Opening the theme
Storytelling 1	The well – a parable *(10 minutes)*
Music	Have you heard the raindrops *(5 minutes)*
Storytelling 2	Peter's vision – visual retelling *(5 minutes)*
Activity	Feast of kosher and non-kosher food *(10 minutes)*
Exploring	What kind of distinctions do we make? *(5 minutes)*
Prayer action	Sharing water from the well – contemplative prayer *(5 minutes)*
Music	I'm black, I'm white, I'm short, I'm tall *(5 minutes)*
Conclusion	Closing prayer and invitation

Resources

- Some plates of tear-and-share bread, available from most large supermarkets
- A table at the front of the church
- A large glass bowl and a ladle – something like a punch bowl
- Lots of cups – enough for the cast and congregation
- Music and words
- Five hats – any kind will do
- Two percussion instruments – tambourines or similar
- A table laid with kosher food:
  – cold beef
  – cold chicken
  – flat bread or Matzah
  – fruit and vegetables (for example, olives and dried apricots)
- A table laid with non-kosher food:
  – pork cocktail sausages
  – sliced, cooked black pudding
  – prawns (shelled and cooked)
  – a plate of Coronation Chicken, made with crème fraîche as well as mayonnaise
- Plates and forks

Leaders

Minimum: 7

- Leader
- Cast x 6

Optimum: 12

- Leader *(Introduction and Conclusion)*
- Cast x 6, wearing ordinary clothes:
  Villager 1
  Villager 2/Peter
  Villager 3
  Villager 4
  Stranger
  Son
- Storyteller
- Music Leader
- Explorer
- Activity Leader
- Prayer Leader

Suggestions for additional music

- Spirit of God *(Mallaig Sprinkling Song)*
- Christ's is the world

Service

Welcome — *As people arrive, invite them to share the tear-and-share bread.*

Introduction — Jesus told a lot of stories. They were parables with more than one meaning. Today we are going to begin with a modern parable: it comes from a story by Adrian Plass that needs no introduction because, as he said, 'in the best tradition of parable tellers I shall let it speak for itself.'[38]

Once upon a time, a landowner saw that people were thirsty, so he built them a well.

Place a large bowl of water and a ladle on the table at the front of the church.

Storytelling 1

All villagers	Hooray! Water for everyone!
	Everyone rushes to fill their cups.
Villager 1	Hang on a minute – we need to think about this. We don't want just anyone helping themselves to our water, do we?
All villagers	No!
Villager 1	Let's have a rule: you can only have some water from the well if you're wearing a hat.
Villager 2	OK – sounds fair.
	Everyone goes off and returns to the well wearing a hat. They help themselves to water. Pause while all drink.
Villager 3	You know, we've been doing this for years now but I don't think this hat-wearing is right. I think we need a different rule: you can only have some water from the well if you're playing a musical instrument.
Villager 1	What are you talking about? We've always worn hats! Everyone in our family is a hat-wearer!

---

38. Adrian Plass, *Clearing Away The Rubbish*, Minstrel/Kingsway, 1988. I am indebted to his original parable, which is more nuanced and ends with the landowner himself returning and weeping at the restrictions imposed on the well. Here, I have adapted the story and dramatised it to get a simpler, more Christ-centred message across.

Villager 3	Well from now on, I'm going to be an instrument-player.
Villager 4	Me too!
	The people now return to the well in two distinct groups – hat-wearers and instrument-players who carry percussion instruments. The Son now joins the hat-wearers. There is some squabbling between the groups, but they all help themselves to water. Then a stranger without a hat or an instrument approaches, walking down the aisle.
Stranger	Please can I have some water?
Villager 2	Where's your hat?
Stranger	I don't have one.
Villager 4	Well, where's your musical instrument?
Stranger	I don't have one. But I'm really thirsty.
Villager 1	Sorry – rules are rules.
	One of the hat-wearers, the Son, gives the stranger some water.
Son	Here you go.
Stranger	Oh, thank you!
Villager 2	What are you doing?!
Son	Listen, I'm the son of the landowner who gave you this well.
Villager 1	You? Never!
Son	I am. He sent me to tell you that this water is for everyone.
Villager 3	I don't believe you.
Villager 1	I don't think he can be the landowner's son.
Villager 4	He's a troublemaker – let's get rid of him!
	They bundle him off and carry on helping themselves to water. The stranger leaves. There is even more squabbling between the groups. After a short time, the Son reappears.
Son	I'm back.
Villager 1	You! But I thought you were dead!
Son	Listen: the landowner says that this water is for everyone. So you don't need these hats *(he takes them*

off) and you don't need these instruments *(he takes them away)*. All you have to do is ask for water. Just drink – you needn't be thirsty ever again!

Music Have you heard the raindrops

During the hymn, refill the bowl with fresh water, ready for the Prayer Action.

Storytelling 2 In our parable, the free gift of water was restricted by lots of rules. Jesus and his fellow Jews knew all about rules, because they were an important part of their religious life. Jewish laws about everyday things such as washing and eating clearly marked the difference between the Jews and the non-Jews, or Gentiles.

Bring forward the two tables of food.

Now, here are two different tables of food. Let's imagine that we are a gathering of faithful Jews in Jesus' time, and that we all know the difference between these two kinds of food. First of all, this food *(Indicate the kosher table.)* obeys the Jewish food laws: it is what's called *kosher*. There is beef and chicken, some Passover bread made without yeast, some fruit and vegetables. We know we're allowed to eat these things.

However, *(Indicate the non-kosher table.)* we're not allowed to eat these things. In fact, we're shocked to see them here at all, because our Scriptures tell us that they are unclean. Here are pork sausages: for Jews, pigs are unclean animals. Anything that contains the blood of an animal is forbidden, so this black pudding is definitely out. These prawns are not allowed, and neither is any mixture of meat and milk, so we can't eat this Coronation Chicken, which is chicken in a spicy, creamy sauce. Some exotic food such as snake is also forbidden, although we haven't got any roast adder here today.

Now imagine that Jesus' disciple, Peter, has come to preach to us. This is what he says.

Peter   Listen – I've had a vision! I saw a big tablecloth being lowered down from heaven by its four corners. On it I saw pigs and snakes and all kinds of unclean animals. Then I heard a voice from heaven say, 'Come on, Peter – eat up!' I refused, because I've never eaten anything unclean, but the voice said, 'If God says something is clean and fit to eat, you can't disagree.' This happened three times, and then the tablecloth and all the food disappeared back up into heaven.

I was still reeling from this vision when some men came to see me. They said an angel had told them to bring me to their house, because I had a message that would save them all. Even though they were not Jews like us, the Holy Spirit told me to go with them and not to make it an 'us and them' situation. As I talked, the Holy Spirit came to them, just as it had come to us. God gave them the same gift as he gave us when we believed in Jesus. Then I realised the truth: how can I stand in God's way? He's given good food for us all to eat, and he's given the gift of life to everyone who believes in him – even the Gentiles!

Activity   Peter's news was a double shock to the Jews. First of all, if they followed Jesus, there were no more food rules! They were allowed to eat anything! Let's all join in this feast of kosher and non-kosher food.

Allow plenty of time for people to eat.

Exploring   There was a second shock for Jewish followers of Jesus: God's gift of life was not exclusive to them! Throughout their history, they had been God's chosen people, set apart by him for his special purposes. Now, through Jesus, the gifts of forgiveness and eternal life were being offered to everyone – Jews and non-Jews alike.

Do you remember, in our parable about the well, how people made all sorts of rules about who could have the water? And how the landowner's son insisted that the water in the well was free for everyone? In the Bible, God said, 'To the thirsty I will give water as a gift from the spring of the water of life,' and Jesus made that promise a reality: like a man giving water to anyone who was thirsty, he showed God's love to Jews and non-Jews alike. In Jesus' name, Peter and the first disciples helped all sorts of different people and offered them God's gift of life.

Our parable of the well showed what happened in Jesus' time, but it can also speak to us today. We may look at the divisions between the hat-wearers and the instrument-players and wonder whether we are divided like that, too. We might think about different Christian churches, each with their own way of doing things and their disagreements with each other. We might think about some churchgoers' attitudes to people outside the church, who do something different on a Sunday. We might think about distinctions between 'grown-up' church and 'children's church'. Wherever we see differences of opinion, whenever we think about 'us' and 'them', we need to remember the parable of the well and wonder whether our divisions stop people getting God's water of life. We need to remember what Peter said to himself when God told him to share the good news with those who were not like him at all: 'How can I stand in God's way?'

Prayer action   God said, 'To the thirsty I will give water as a gift from the spring of the water of life.' In our prayers today, we remember that God's gift of life was given freely for us all to share. Let's share this water together now as a sign of that gift.

Serve the water from the altar and invite people to take cups for one another, so that the water is shared around the church.

Let us pray.

Heavenly Father,
we thank you for your water of life.

Encourage everyone to drink.

As we have freely received,
may we freely give.
Amen.

Music I'm black, I'm white, I'm short, I'm tall

Conclusion Almighty God,
send us out into the world to share your good news.
Whenever we are tempted to make
differences and divisions,
may we ask ourselves,
'How can we stand in God's way?'
In Jesus' name.
Amen.

Give notices, announce the next all-age service and invite everyone to the feast.

Sixth Sunday of Easter

Unfinished business

Theme	God's work is still in progress
Scripture	John 5:1-18

Running order	Total: 50 minutes
Welcome	Finishing the jigsaw *(5 minutes)*
Introduction	Opening the theme
Storytelling	Dramatised retelling of John 5:1-18 *(5 minutes)*
Music	Christ is the world's Light *(5 minutes)*
Exploring	What is our unfinished business? *(5 minutes)*
Activity	Finishing the unfinished tasks *(20 minutes)*
Prayer action	Takeaway prayer – workers' badges *(5 minutes)*
Music	We have a gospel to proclaim *(5 minutes)*
Conclusion	Closing prayer and invitation

SIXTH SUNDAY OF EASTER

Resources

- A jigsaw puzzle with 1000+ pieces
- Music and words
- Laptop, projector and screen
- Speakers
- A video showing the living bridges of Meghalaya. The clip is one minute 49 seconds long and can be found on the internet using the following search term: BBC Human Planet living bridges. If your church doesn't have WiFi, you can download clips to use as part of a PowerPoint presentation: see websites such as www.saveyoutube.com for help
- Around the church, lots of different unfinished tasks *(see appendix)*
- Conference badges *(see appendix)*
- Pens

Leaders

Minimum: 4

- Leader
- Readers x 3

Optimum: 9

- Leader *(Introduction and Conclusion)*
- Storyteller
- Readers x 3
  Man
  Jesus
  Accuser
- Music Leader
- Explorer
- Activity Leader
- Prayer Leader

Suggestions for additional music

- God is working his purpose out
- Jesus Christ is waiting

Service

Welcome — *As people arrive, invite them to help finish the large jigsaw puzzle.*

Introduction — This jigsaw puzzle has hundreds of pieces, so it's going to take us a long time to finish. Our theme today is unfinished business and, in our story, Jesus has work to do.

Storytelling — Imagine the scene: we're in Jerusalem, 2000 years ago, near a special pool of water called Bethzatha. It's cool and deep and is said to have healing powers. It is always surrounded by ill people – some blind, some lame, some paralysed. Their relatives bring them, or they crawl here by themselves, hoping that the water will make them better. One man here has been ill for 38 years! He can't walk. He's never reached the water. He is lying on his filthy sleeping mat because he never leaves this place, and everyone has forgotten about him. Now Jesus sees him and knows he's been here a long time.[39]

Jesus	Do you want to be made well?
Man	Sir, I have no one to put me into the pool when the water is stirred up; and while I am making my way, someone else steps down ahead of me.
Jesus	Stand up, take your mat and walk.
Storyteller	Immediately the man is cured! He picks up his sleeping mat and begins to walk away. Now today is the sabbath, when no work of any kind is allowed. As soon as the Jews see the man carrying his mat, they rush to accuse him.
Accuser	It is the sabbath; it is not lawful for you to carry your mat.
Man	The man who made me well said to me, 'Take up your mat and walk.'
Accuser	Who is the man who said to you, 'Take it up and walk'?

---

[39]. The dialogue is taken directly from John's Gospel (NRSV). You may prefer to use a different translation.

Storyteller	But the man shrugs his shoulders. He doesn't know, and now he's lost sight of Jesus in the crowd. Later, in the Temple, Jesus finds him again.
Jesus	See, you have been made well! Do not sin any more, so that nothing worse happens to you.
Storyteller	The man goes back to the Jews and tells them that it was Jesus who made him better. So then the Jews start accusing Jesus of breaking the sabbath by healing people. But Jesus answers them back.
Jesus	My Father is still working, and I also am working.
Storyteller	This makes the Jews even angrier: not only is Jesus breaking the sabbath, but he is also claiming that God is his Father, as if he's God's equal! They are outraged.
Music	Christ is the world's Light
Exploring	The man in our story had been ill for 38 years. He'd waited a very long time for anyone to help him! It seems people were used to ignoring him, as they kept pushing past him to get into the healing pool first. When Jesus asked if he wanted to get well, the man explained how he'd never managed to get down to the pool – he obviously thought that Jesus was just a kind passer-by who was going to help him into the water. Yet without further ado, Jesus cured him completely and he was able to get up and walk. Jesus had clearly decided that this man was someone who needed his help straight away.

That's how the trouble started, because Jesus saw a job that needed doing and he did it, in spite of strict religious rules about doing no work on the sabbath. Jesus argued with the Jews who attacked him for working on the sabbath and said, 'My Father is still working, and I also am working.' His words tell us something very important about God and about ourselves.

First of all, Jesus reminds us that God's nurture and care of his creation – including us – is still a work in progress: it didn't begin and end with the creation of the world and then a day of rest. Ever since, God has been actively involved in his creation, never more so than when he sent his only Son to live as one of us and die for our sake. Father, Son and Holy Spirit continue to be active in the world and in our lives.

Secondly, when Jesus said, 'My Father is still working, and I also am working,' it is a reminder that his work is still unfinished. After his death and resurrection, he left us, his followers, to continue his life-giving work of helping other people and showing them what God is like. We are going to explore what this ongoing work might mean for us, and to help us do this we will look at an inspiring example of some people who are taking care of their own work in progress: they are weaving bridges out of the roots of living trees.

Show the short film of the living bridges of Meghalaya.

These bridges are the work of many lifetimes. They grow stronger as they are nurtured by each generation, and even the smallest root plays its part once it has been woven into place. The bridges enable people to travel and trade, so they are lifelines for the community. Now, think about it: a living, life-giving bridge – could this be a way of describing the church? Jesus has been described as a bridge between heaven and earth,[40] and it is the Church's job to be that living bridge in the world today. Just like the villagers in our film, we are involved in an 'epic project', a creative work in progress that is never finished. Our living bridge will grow and change, but it remains a lifeline to connect people with God. Our job, as a church and as individuals, is to keep that connection strong and growing: whenever we help people and show them God's love in the way we live, we are doing Jesus' work. We are building up his bridge between heaven and earth.

Activity To help us think about Jesus' unfinished business, we will tackle some unfinished jobs in church this morning. Take your time to look at the different areas spread all around the church and find the jobs that are only half-finished. Can you help to get some jobs done?

---

40. This was a recurrent image in the BBC's *The Nativity* (2010).

SIXTH SUNDAY OF EASTER

Allow plenty of time for people to explore the different areas and do some of the jobs.

Prayer action   Our prayers today will remind us that Jesus has given us a job to do. We will each take one of these badges, like the sort worn by shop assistants. *(Show a badge.)* It has a space for your name, and your job description: 'Here to help.' If you like, you can fill in your name. Let's use these badges now as a focus for our prayers.

Hand out the badges and pens. Pause for a moment so that people can fill in their names if they wish.

Let us pray.

God our Father, working all around us,
Son of God, at work within us,
Holy Spirit, at work in the world,
show us what to do –
we're here to help.
Amen.

Please take your badge home to remind you that Jesus needs us all to carry on his work.

Music   We have a gospel to proclaim

Conclusion   Heavenly Father,
send us out into the world
to show your love in all that we say and do,
and so build a living bridge between heaven and earth,
in Jesus' name.
Amen.

Give notices, announce the next all-age service and invite everyone to the feast.

Ascension Day

Being witnesses

Theme	The Ascension and our mission
Scripture	Acts 1:1-11; Luke 24:44-53

Running order	Total: 50 minutes
Welcome	Raising the flag (5 minutes)
Introduction	Opening the theme
Storytelling	Visual retelling of the Ascension (5 minutes)
Music	Meekness and majesty (5 minutes)
Activity	Treasure hunt and putting together the picture story (20 minutes)
Exploring	How can we be witnesses? (5 minutes)
Music	Come, Holy Spirit, come (5 minutes)
Prayer action	'You raise me up' – contemplative prayer (5 minutes)
Conclusion	Closing prayer and invitation

Resources

- Laptop, projector and screen
- Speakers
- Small edible prizes
- Music and words
- A flag and a flagpole *(see appendix)*
- A picture of the disciples looking up at Jesus' Ascension *(see appendix)*
- Hidden around the church, clues for a treasure hunt *(see appendix)*
- The 'treasure': pictures in quarters *(see appendix)*
- Sticky tape and scissors
- A recording of 'You raise me up' by Josh Groban and optional accompanying slideshow *(see appendix)*

Leaders

Minimum: 1
- Leader

Optimum: 6+
- Leader *(Introduction and Conclusion)*
- Storyteller
- Music Leader
- Explorer
- Activity Leader(s)
- Prayer Leader

Suggestions for additional music

- How lovely on the mountains
- Christ triumphant, ever reigning

Service

Welcome — *As people arrive, invite volunteers to help raise the flag to represent Jesus' ascension into heaven.*

Introduction — Today we celebrate Ascension Day. It is 40 days since we celebrated Jesus' resurrection on Easter Sunday. During those forty days, Jesus appeared to his disciples several times and talked to them about God's kingdom. This was the day he finally said goodbye.

Storytelling — Jesus gathered his disciples together for a final briefing. He gave them instructions: 'Don't leave Jerusalem. Wait here for God's promise. Do you remember how John the Baptist baptised people with water? All of you got soaked in the river. Well, in a few days you'll be baptised with the Holy Spirit. You'll be drenched in God's power.'

Of course, there were questions. One disciple asked, 'Lord, what about our nation? When will you give Israel back her power?'

Jesus said, 'That's up to God. He's in charge. But *you* will have power when the Holy Spirit arrives, and you will be my witnesses here in Jerusalem, throughout the Middle East and all over the world.'

Then something extraordinary happened. As they looked at Jesus, he was lifted up into the sky, higher and higher, until clouds hid him from sight.

Show the picture of the disciples gazing at the sky and leave it up on the screen until the end of the Activity.

All the disciples craned their necks to try and see him. Suddenly, two men in white robes appeared beside them. They looked at all the faces tilted upwards and all the eyes squinting into the sun. They said gently, 'Men of Galilee, why are you looking into the sky? Jesus has been taken up into heaven, and one day he will come back in the same way.'

ASCENSION DAY

Music Meekness and majesty

Activity Our story today ended with this image of the disciples searching for Jesus in the sky. Today it's our turn to do some searching of our own, as there's a treasure hunt in the church. There are four different sets of clues: who would like to come and join in the hunt?

Invite four volunteers to come forward and give them the first clues. If you have lots of volunteers, divide them into four teams. Set them off to follow the clues and, when they've reached the end, bring whatever they find to the front. Give each person a small prize when they return.

Now, what have you found? Do you know what it is?

Invite responses. Undo the ribbons, hold up one picture quarter and describe what you can see.

These so-called 'treasures' don't seem to mean much on their own. I wonder if we can work together to make more sense out of them?

Allow plenty of time for your volunteers to look at all the pictures and work out how they fit together. Once you have complete pictures, sticky tape them together and encourage people to try and arrange the pictures so that they tell a story. Then invite your volunteers to hold up the pictures in order and describe them, so that they tell each part of Jesus' story in turn. Applaud your volunteers and ask them to sit down – for now. They will be needed again.

Exploring On Ascension Day, the disciples were left looking up into the sky and wondering, 'Where's Jesus gone?' They asked the same question after they buried him and then, three days later, found an empty tomb. The disciples were busy looking for Jesus, but they were in danger of missing the point. On both occasions, two angels had to spell out the vital news: Jesus wasn't in the grave because he had risen from the dead, and he wasn't in the sky because he had gone up into heaven – and one day he would come back.

In our treasure hunt, our volunteers spent a long time looking for the treasure, but they discovered that finding it wasn't the point. The point was telling the story of Jesus in big, clear pictures. For the disciples who looked for Jesus in the tomb and in the sky, the point was that his story now had its final chapters: Jesus rose from the dead *(Show the picture of the empty tomb.)* and ascended in to heaven. *(Show the picture of the Ascension.)* From heaven, he'll return one day to establish God's kingdom. *(Show the picture of Jesus on his throne.)*

So this is the whole story of Jesus.

Invite your volunteers to line up again with their story pictures in order, and ask them to hold up your last three pictures, too. Alternatively, you could show each of the pictures in turn on the screen.

Just before he left them for good, Jesus told his disciples to be his witnesses. Their job was to tell his story and tell people about his gifts of forgiveness and eternal life. This is our job, too: we need to tell the whole story of Jesus and share his good news.

This sounds simple enough, but why do you think it was hard for the first disciples to tell people about Jesus? What risks did they take?

Invite responses.

What makes it hard for us, today, to tell people about Jesus?

Invite responses.

Jesus knew it would be hard for people to tell the world about him, so he left his disciples with a promise. They would receive the gift of the Holy Spirit – they would be filled with God's power. Soon we will celebrate Pentecost, the day when the disciples received that power, and we'll discover what amazing confidence and abilities it gave them. For now, we need to remember that the disciples' mission is our mission, and their promise is our promise: our job is to tell people about Jesus, and the Holy Spirit will make us strong enough to do it.

Music   Come, Holy Spirit, come

Prayer action   On this Ascension Day, when Jesus was lifted up into heaven, we remember that we too will be raised up after death. Like Jesus, we will join our Father in heaven. We also remember that after his Ascension, Jesus sent us the gift of his Holy Spirit, which makes us stronger than we are on our own. For our prayers today, we will rest in God's presence and listen to a song that reminds us what the Ascension means for us. Let us pray.

Play 'You raise me up' by Josh Groban, accompanied by a slideshow of images.

God our Father,
may your Spirit raise us up to be more than we can be,
and may your Son raise us up to share your eternal life.
Amen.

Conclusion   Jesus, our God and King,
send us out in the power of your Holy Spirit
to tell the world your story.
Amen.

Give notices, announce the next all-age service and invite everyone to the feast.

Seventh Sunday of Easter

A helping hand

Theme	We are never alone – we have God's help
Scripture	Acts 16:16-34; John 17:20-26

Running order	Total: 50 minutes	
Welcome	Drawing around hands *(5 minutes)*	
Introduction	Opening the theme	
Storytelling	Retelling Acts 16:16-34 with sound effects *(10 minutes)*	
Music	You are the King of Glory *(5 minutes)*	
Exploring/Activity	How did Paul and Silas do all those things? Exploring challenges and tasks that cannot be completed by one person alone *(20 minutes)*	
Prayer action	Helping hand – written supplications *(5 minutes)*	
Music	For I'm building a people of power *(5 minutes)*	
Conclusion	Closing prayer and invitation	

Resources

- Paper
- Pencils and pens
- Scissors
- Music and words
- Sound effects *(see appendix)* and equipment to play them on
- Around the church, challenges and tasks that cannot be completed by one person alone *(see appendix)*

Leaders

Minimum: 2

- Leader
- *Voice*/Sound effects technician

Optimum: 6

- Leader *(Introduction and Conclusion)*
- Storyteller
- *Voice*/Sound effects technician
- Music Leader
- Explorer/Activity Leader
- Prayer Leader

Suggestions for additional music

- At the name of Jesus
- Jesus calls us here to meet him

Service

Welcome — *As people arrive, invite them to draw around their hands and cut out their handprints, then leave them on the altar as a way of saying, 'Here I am, Lord.'*

Introduction — Last week, we told the story of Jesus' ascension into heaven: right in front of his disciples, he was taken up into the sky. If you thought that was dramatic, wait till you hear today's story. Listen out for an evil spirit, an angry mob, imprisonment, an earthquake and more!

Storytelling — *The Voice/Sound effects technician is hidden from view.*

This is Luke, reporting live with the latest updates from the Roman colony of Philippi. Paul has been here with his colleagues for several days now, spreading the word about Jesus. Paul is speaking publicly wherever he can – there seems to be no end to this man's courage and determination!

First of all, there was the incident with the slave girl. An evil spirit had given her the ability to tell fortunes. Her handlers were making lots of money by charging people to hear what the future held. When she spotted Paul and the rest of us, she started shouting.

Voice — These men are God's slaves! They're telling you how to be saved! These men are God's slaves! They're telling you how to be saved!

Storyteller — At first, this seemed like good publicity, but –

Voice — These men are God's slaves! They're telling you how to be saved!

Storyteller — – she carried on for days.

Voice — These men are God's slaves! They're telling you how to be saved! These men are God's slaves! They're telling you how to be saved!

Storyteller — Paul got really annoyed.

Voice — These men are God's slaves! They're telling you how to be saved!

SEVENTH SUNDAY OF EASTER

Storyteller　　He shouted to the evil spirit, 'I order you in the name of Jesus Christ to come out of her!' And straight away the spirit left her in peace.

That was when the trouble started. The slave girl's handlers had lost their money-making scheme – they were furious. So they grabbed Paul and his colleague, Silas, and dragged them in front of the magistrates. They accused them of disturbing the peace. An angry mob gathered and there were outbreaks of violence.

Play the sound effect of the angry mob.

The magistrates ordered that Paul and Silas should be severely beaten.

Play the sound of the angry mob, even louder.

Then Paul and Silas were dragged off to prison in chains.

Play the sound of clanking chains.

The jailer locked them in a maximum-security cell and fastened their feet in the stocks.

Play the sound effect of locks and chains.

At about midnight, eyewitnesses report hearing singing and prayers coming from the maximum-security cell, and it sounded as if the other prisoners were joining in.

Play the sound effect of sung prayers.

Shortly after midnight, the earthquake struck.

Play the long sound effect of the earthquake.

The tremor, measuring 4 on the Richter scale, broke open all the prison doors and shook loose everyone's chains. When the jailer came to and saw that every cell was open, he jumped to the obvious conclusion that all his prisoners had escaped – but in fact, every one of them was still there. He told me that he was so amazed, he fell on his knees in front of Paul and Silas and asked, 'Sirs, how do I get saved?'

Paul replied simply, 'Believe in Jesus, and you will be saved – you and your whole family.'

So in the small hours of this morning, the jailer welcomed Paul and Silas into his own home. He cleaned their wounds and fed them, then they baptised his whole family. It's now dawn, and the celebrations are still in full swing.

Play the sound effect of celebrations.

This is Luke, reporting from Philippi at the end of a very eventful night.

Music You are the King of Glory

Exploring/Activity In our story today, Paul and Silas were involved in some amazing events. Can you remember what they were?

Invite responses to elicit the following:
- They got rid of the slave girl's evil spirit
- An earthquake broke open their prison doors, but they didn't run away
- They converted their jailer and baptised his family

What great achievements! Paul and Silas seem like superheroes who can tackle evil spirits, burst open locked doors and even change their enemy's mind. Today we're going to explore how they managed to do all this, and we have an activity to help us think.

In church today, there are a number of challenges and tasks. Take your time to explore them. First of all, try to do them on your own. If you can't, then find someone to help you and see if you can take on the challenges together.

Allow plenty of time for people to circulate and try the activities. Then invite everyone to gather together.

How did you get on with the different challenges?

Invite responses.

These challenges were hard to take on alone: we needed someone else to help us. So did Paul and Silas in our story. They achieved great things, but they weren't working by themselves: God helped them, and

God's power worked through them. Paul got rid of the girl's evil spirit by calling on the name of Jesus Christ. Paul and Silas didn't organise a prison break: they prayed, and the miraculous earthquake broke open their prison doors – although escape wasn't the point, and they didn't run away. Instead, they stayed to convert the awestruck jailer and his family. They baptised them in the name of the Father, and of the Son, and of the Holy Spirit. All these events show that neither Paul nor Silas was a superhero with his own superpowers: they were faithful followers of Jesus who did his work of healing and making disciples, and they did it with God's help.

Our story and our activity have reminded us that we can't always manage by ourselves. Jesus knew this, so before his death he prayed for the followers he would be leaving behind – and that includes us. This is what he asked his Father:

> I ask not only on behalf of these, but also on behalf of those who will believe in me through their word, that they may all be one. As you, Father, are in me and I am in you, may they also be in us, so that the world may believe that you have sent me.

Jesus wanted to make sure that all his followers would continue to share in the closeness he enjoys with God. This means that whenever we can't manage by ourselves, whenever we need God's help, all we have to do is ask.

Prayer action

When we pray, we can ask for God's help for ourselves and for other people. Let's remember those known to us who need God's strength and power in their lives.

Pause for a moment, then encourage everyone to gather around the altar.

Now we will use the handprints we made earlier to help us. Let's write or draw our prayers on the handprints as we ask for God's helping hand.

Allow time for everyone to write or draw their prayers and return their handprints to the altar.

God of power and might,
we bring these people before you now.
May your Holy Spirit help them
and give them strength
in the name of your Son, Jesus Christ.
Amen.

Music For I'm building a people of power

Conclusion Almighty God,
send us out into the world to do your work,
strong in the strength of your power.
Amen.

Give notices, announce the next all-age service and invite everyone to the feast.

Pentecost

Getting the message across

Theme	Communicating by the power of the Holy Spirit
Scripture	Genesis 11:1-9; Acts 2:1-21

Running order	Total: 50 minutes
Welcome	Building a tall tower *(5 minutes)*
Introduction	Opening the theme
Storytelling 1	The tower of Babel – visual retelling *(5 minutes)*
Storytelling 2	Visual and interactive retelling of Acts 2:1-21 *(5 minutes)*
Music	Filled with the Spirit's power *(5 minutes)*
Exploring/Activity	What is made possible by the power of the Holy Spirit? Exploring different ways of communicating the good news of Jesus *(20 minutes)*
Prayer action	The Pentecost megaphone – contemplative prayer and hymn: 'Creator Spirit, come' *(5 minutes)*
Music	Colours of day *(5 minutes)*
Conclusion	Closing prayer and invitation

Resources

- Lots of empty cardboard boxes, taped closed
- (*Optional*) Lego bricks and *Jenga*
- Music and words
- A powerful electric fan, concealed behind a screen or piece of furniture at the front of the church
- 11 sparklers, suitable for indoor use. Many toy shops sell mini ones all year round
- Matches
- A tin bucket with some sand in the bottom
- Pentecost megaphones (*see appendix*)
- Stations around the church, presenting different ways of communicating the good news of Jesus (*see appendix*)

Leaders

Minimum: 1
- Leader

Optimum: 6+
- Leader (*Introduction and Conclusion*)
- Storytellers 1 and 2
- Music Leader
- Explorer/Activity Leader(s)
- Prayer Leader

Suggestions for additional music

- Holy Spirit, truth divine
- Silent, surrendered

Service

Welcome — *As people arrive, encourage them to work together to build a tall tower out of empty cardboard boxes. You could also offer smaller tower-building activities, using Lego or Jenga bricks.*

Introduction — There has been some impressive tower-building in church this morning! It's good to see people working together as they decide how best to build a tower up and make it as tall as possible. Our first story today is about a very tall tower.

Storytelling 1 — Once upon a time, not long after the world began, all the people on earth spoke the same language. They used the same words. Together they settled on a piece of land and made plans. 'Let's make ourselves some bricks,' they said, and everyone agreed. So they made lots and lots of bricks.

Make a line of boxes.

Then they said, 'Let's build ourselves a city, and finish it with a tower that reaches right up to heaven. Then we'll really make our mark. We'll stay together as one people, and we won't be scattered to the ends of the earth.' Everyone agreed, so they worked together to build the city, and they built the tallest tower the world had ever seen.

Add the bricks to the tower that has already been started.

But God looked down from heaven and saw what the people were doing. He said, 'They are one people and they speak the same language, and look what they've managed to do together. This is only the beginning: now nothing will be impossible for them. I can't have that.' So God went down and mixed up their language so that it became many different languages, and he scattered the people to the ends of the earth.

Then there was confusion among the people, and confusion led to arguments. They couldn't agree, and they wouldn't work together, so in the end the city and the tower were left unfinished. Because of the people's confused babble, the place became known as Babel.

Storytelling 2

The tower of Babel is an ancient story that tries to explain why there are different races with different languages spread all over the world. Our second story today adds a new chapter to the old tale of Babel, and I need some volunteers to help me tell it.

Ideally, you need 11 volunteers, although five would do. Gather them together at the front of the church.

Now, you are Jesus' disciples. You're hiding in a locked room in Jerusalem because you don't want the Roman soldiers to get you. They killed Jesus on the cross, but you know that Jesus has come back from the dead. He has visited you several times. A few days ago, you saw him go back up into heaven. The soldiers are waiting to arrest anyone who so much as mentions the words 'Jesus' and 'God' in the same sentence, and that's why you're in hiding. The door is locked and bolted, so you're safe for now.

The hidden fan is turned on and aimed at the group of volunteers.

But what's happening now? There's a powerful wind rushing inside this place! It's filling the whole house!

Turn the fan off and hand out the 11 sparklers.[41] Light them one by one and encourage your volunteers to hold them up high.

Now what's happening? Fiery lights are appearing above each one of you!

When the sparklers are out, gather them up quickly in the sand bucket.

Now you all feel very different. Whatever has just happened, you feel full of strength and power. Suddenly,

---

41. If you only have five volunteers, give them two sparklers each and hold one yourself.

you can't wait to tell people about Jesus! You want to shout his name from street corners!

Give each volunteer a Pentecost megaphone.

You rush into the streets and shout out a message for everyone to hear: 'Jesus is God!'

Encourage your volunteers to shout, 'Jesus is God,' through their megaphones, and spread around the church.

Now something even more amazing is happening! You're talking to a crowd of people from all over the world *(indicate the congregation)* – they're from Rome, Egypt, Arabia, Libya, Greece, Asia, Judea and more places besides. You lot are from Galilee, but suddenly you're speaking in loads of different languages, telling people about Jesus in words that everyone here can understand! Surely, that's impossible – no one has ever seen or heard anything like it!

Applaud your volunteers and ask them to sit down.

Music Filled with the Spirit's power

Exploring/Activity Today we are celebrating Pentecost, when God sent his Holy Spirit to Jesus' disciples. It was the Holy Spirit who appeared as a rushing wind and then as tongues of fire, and it was the Holy Spirit who inspired the disciples to risk everything and tell people the good news about Jesus. It was the Holy Spirit who gave them their extraordinary ability to speak different languages, so that everyone in that multiracial crowd could understand them.

Think back for a moment to our story of the tower of Babel. God saw that everyone spoke the same language and said, 'This is only the beginning: now nothing will be impossible for them,' and that is why he confused their speech and made lots of different languages. On the day of Pentecost, God overturned that situation by giving the disciples the power to speak so that everyone could understand them. It's a fresh start, as if God is saying once more, 'This is only the beginning: now nothing will be impossible for them.' But what is it that began at Pentecost? What does the Holy Spirit make possible?

What began at Pentecost was the Church. It didn't have a building: 'the Church' was the group of disciples who had been given the job of telling the world about Jesus. Jesus had promised that he would send his Holy Spirit to help them. When they received the Holy Spirit at Pentecost, the first thing he enabled them to do was communicate with lots of different people.

Today, we are the Church and we have the job of telling the world about Jesus. We still need the Holy Spirit's help to get that message across to lots of different people. This morning we are going to look at what that might mean. How can we speak in different languages so that everyone can understand us? Around the church building are lots of different ways of communicating Jesus' good news. Let's take our time to explore them.

Encourage everyone to explore the different stations around the church.

Prayer action

We've looked at lots of different ways of getting Jesus' message across, but the story of Pentecost reminds us that we can't communicate effectively without the help of God's Holy Spirit. He inspires us, he motivates us and he translates in the space between us and those we're trying to reach. In our story, the Holy Spirit was like the megaphones that made the disciples' words loud enough to be heard.

Show a megaphone.

For our prayers today, we will consider these Pentecost megaphones. Please pass them around, as we ask for the Holy Spirit's help in getting Jesus' message across.

Sing 'Creator Spirit, come' and pass around the megaphones. Children may be encouraged to sing through them.

Spirit of God,
inspire us and communicate through us.
Be our Loud Hailer, our Translator, our Go-Between.
Amen.

Music Colours of day

Conclusion Heavenly Father,
send us out into the world,
and by the power of your Holy Spirit
may we share your good news with everyone we meet,
in Jesus' name.
Amen.

Give notices, announce the next all-age service and invite everyone to the feast.

Ordinary time

Trinity Sunday

Together

Theme	Unity – three Persons, one God; many people, one Body
Scripture	Romans 5:1-5; John 16:12-15

Running order	Total: 50 minutes
Welcome	Making paper chain people (*9 minutes*)
Introduction	Opening the theme
Music	Holy, holy, holy! Lord God almighty (*5 minutes*)
Storytelling	Jesus' parting words (*1 minute*)
Exploring/Activity	What is the Trinity? Making a giant three-personed God paper chain (*20 minutes*)
Music	Bind us together, Lord (*5 minutes*)
Prayer action	Human chain – active prayer (*5 minutes*)
Music	This day God gives me (*5 minutes*)
Conclusion	Closing prayer and invitation

Resources

- One or more long strips of paper, cut into a paper chain of people *(see appendix)*
- A giant strip of paper for a giant three-person chain *(see appendix)*
- Felt pens
- Two pairs of big scissors
- Three big stickers: 'Father', 'Son' and 'Holy Spirit'
- Sticky tape
- A couple of big tables pushed together for the drawing activity
- Music and words
- One large candle with three wicks, or three separate candles in one candle-holder
- Votive candles, each with a circle of card to catch wax drips
- Matches
- *(Optional)* Glitter, metallic pens or gold and silver self-adhesive paper for the portrait of God

Leaders

Minimum: 2

- Leader
- *Jesus*

Optimum: 5+

- Leader *(Introduction and Conclusion)*
- *Jesus*
- Music Leader
- Explorer/Activity Leader(s)
- Prayer Leader

Suggestions for additional music

- Father most holy, merciful and loving
- I bind unto myself today
- Praise God, from whom all blessings flow

Service

Welcome — *As people arrive, invite them to make a self-portrait by colouring in one of the figures in the paper chain.*

Introduction — Today is Trinity Sunday, when we celebrate the wonderful mystery of our God who is three Persons, yet one God. He is God the Father, God the Son and God the Holy Spirit.

Music — Holy, holy, holy! Lord God almighty

Storytelling

Leader — Between the Last Supper and Jesus' arrest, there was just enough time for some last-minute instructions. Jesus promised his followers that he would not leave them on their own: he would send them a special helper to guide them, keep them company and give them strength. The special helper was God's Holy Spirit and this is what Jesus said about him.[42]

Jesus — I still have many things to say to you, but you cannot bear them now. When the Spirit of truth comes, he will guide you into all the truth; for he will not speak on his own, but will speak whatever he hears, and he will declare to you the things that are to come. He will glorify me, because he will take what is mine and declare it to you. All that the Father has is mine. For this reason I said that he will take what is mine and declare it to you.

Exploring/Activity — Jesus' words show the relationship between the Son, the Father and the Holy Spirit. 'All that the Father has is mine,' Jesus said to his followers, and the Holy Spirit 'will take what is mine and declare it to you.' God the Father, God the Son and God the Holy Spirit share everything and work together, because they are three Persons of the same God. This is what we call the Trinity.

---

42. These words are taken from John's Gospel (NRSV). You may prefer to use a different translation.

The Trinity has always been a mind-boggling fact. It makes us wonder, 'How can God be three Persons *and* one God at the same time?' It makes us ask questions like, 'What's the difference between the Father, the Son and the Holy Spirit?' It makes us search for something to compare it to, such as a clover leaf which is a single leaf with three separate parts.

Today we're going to try a new way of exploring the Trinity. First of all, I need a volunteer to help me. It's a big job: who would like to be God?

Invite your volunteer forward and ask him/her to lie down in a star-jump shape on the triple-folded lining paper you have prepared. Ask another volunteer to come and draw round the body, making sure that the hands and feet reach over the edge of the paper. Only draw round the outside of each leg, so that the finished shape looks like someone wearing a robe. (This will allow more room for artistic licence later.) Add a halo shape around the head. Then give each of your volunteers a pair of scissors and ask them to cut out the body shape carefully, making sure that they cut through all three sheets of paper. Do not cut around the hands or feet, so that the three figures will stay joined when you unfold them. Hold up the finished single figure.

This is our artist's impression of God. It's just an outline so far, but it can show us something important.

Unfold the single figure to reveal the three joined figures. Ask your volunteers to hold up the chain as you stick a label on each halo: 'Father', 'Son' and 'Holy Spirit'.

This is the Trinity: one God, made up of three Persons. Here are God the Father, God the Son and God the Holy Spirit. Each one is distinct, but they are all made of the same substance, just as these three figures are all cut from the same piece of paper. They are three persons and one God. Now, together, we are going to give this artist's impression of the Trinity a little more shape. Let's gather round and add some colour and detail.

Encourage everyone to gather round the drawing tables. This is an opportunity for some interesting discussion of what the Father and the Holy Spirit might look like – even what gender they might be. You could remind people about biblical representations of divine presence, including dazzling light, fire, a bright cloud, wind and a dove. Allow plenty of time for discussion and collaborative drawing, then display the finished Trinity portrait.

This is our picture of our three-in-one God. The interconnected figures remind us that the Trinity relationship is about belonging together and sharing; however, this relationship isn't just about God. It involves us, too. God wants to share everything that he is with us: through his Son he reached out to us, and through Jesus and his Holy Spirit, God remains connected to us. The Bible says,

> we have peace with God through our Lord Jesus Christ, through whom we have obtained access to this grace in which we stand; and we boast in our hope of sharing the glory of God . . . God's love has been poured into our hearts through the Holy Spirit that has been given to us.

So God's peace, love and glory are ours to share because of Jesus. This means that our Trinity picture is not quite finished: God the Father, Son and Holy Spirit are joined together as one, but now we need to show that God is connected to all of us.

Invite volunteers to help you stretch out the paper chain of people that was created at the beginning of the service. Using sticky tape, join the hands of the first and last figures to the hands of the Trinity and hold the chain out to form an outward-facing circle (so that people can see their self-portraits, and so that it makes the next point about an outward-facing church).

This is our finished Trinity picture. It shows togetherness: here are three Persons who are one God, joined in love to lots of people who are one Body – the Body of Christ. That's us. This Trinity picture also tells us about sharing: God wants to share his love with us, and it's our job to share his love with each other. This circle is outward-looking because God wants us to share the good things that he has given us with the people outside our church, too. There is room for everyone in God's love.

Music — Bind us together, Lord

Prayer action — *Hand out the votive candles and invite everyone to form a circle at the front of church, or around the church if you have a large congregation.*

On this Trinity Sunday, we remember that we are joined in love to our three-personed God.

Light the three candles (or the candle with three wicks).

We pray for ourselves and for our church, that we might work together and share God's love with the world.

Pass the light around the circle from candle to candle.

God of Love,
bind us together
and make us one with you,
in Jesus' name.
Amen.

Music — This day God gives me

Conclusion — May the love of God unite us,
may the peace of Christ enfold us
and may the power of the Holy Spirit inspire us.
Amen.

Give notices, announce the next all-age service and invite everyone to the feast.

Proper 4

In charge

Theme	God's authority
Scripture	Galatians 1:1-12; Luke 7:1-10

Running order	Total: 50 minutes
Welcome	Being in the Roman army – video clip *or* dressing up *(5 minutes)*
Introduction	Opening the theme
Storytelling	The centurion's tale *(10 minutes)*
Music	Our God is a great big God *(5 minutes)*
Activity	Erecting a tent with and without an instructor *(15 minutes)*
Exploring	Who's in charge? *(5 minutes)*
Prayer action	Marching orders – contemplative prayer *(5 minutes)*
Music	Father, I place into your hands *(5 minutes)*
Conclusion	Closing prayer and invitation

Resources

- *(Optional)* Clip from *Horrible Histories* *(see appendix)*
- Items of Roman armour *(see appendix)*
- Music and words
- A small dome tent or beach tent. Place the different components around the church and give the bag with the instructions to the Leader
- Unlit tea lights, laid out at the front of the church in the shape of an arrow pointing down the aisle
- Matches and tapers

Leaders

Minimum: 3

- Leader
- *Centurion*
- Activity Leader

Optimum: 6

- Leader *(Introduction and Conclusion)*
- *Centurion*, wearing Roman costume
- Music Leader
- Activity Leader
- Explorer
- Prayer Leader

Suggestions for additional music

- To God be the glory
- Be still, for the presence of the Lord

Service

Welcome — *To begin the service, play the* Horrible Histories *clip: 'Surviving in the Roman Army.' If you can't show this clip, then invite children to dress up as Roman soldiers – they can then be your volunteers.*

Introduction — Our service today is about who's in charge. In Jesus' time, the ruling superpower was the Roman Empire, and Roman soldiers were very clear about who was in charge.

Invite five volunteers forward to dress up as each of the following as you name them. Line them up in front of you. The ordinary centurion is your Storyteller.

Top of the heap was the Roman emperor – the most powerful man of all.

Dress your emperor in a purple cloak.

The emperor chose his legionary commanders.

Dress your commander in an item of armour.

Each legion of the Roman army had senior centurions.

Give your senior centurion a sword.

They were in charge of the ordinary centurions.

Give the centurion (your Storyteller) a sword.

The centurions gave orders to their seconds in command,

Give your second in command a rolled-up scroll.

and they told the ordinary soldiers what to do.

Give the soldier a shield.

Our story today is told by a man who has spent his life as part of this power structure. He is the centurion.

PROPER 4

The centurion steps forward to tell (or read) his story.

Storytelling

My name is Marcus Fabius Strabo. My rank is Decimus Princeps Prior – commander of the third century of the tenth cohort. I serve the Emperor of Rome. I head the occupying army here in Galilee: my mission is to enforce Roman rule and keep the peace.

I am based in Capernaum and, I have to say, I'm proud of the work I've done here. I've tried hard to respect the people and treat them fairly. The Jewish elders and I are on good terms, because in the end we all want the same thing: a peaceful town that does well for itself. I'm fond of their people; I respect their God-fearing ways. It was a pleasure for me to build their synagogue for them so that they could worship their God in peace.

I knew I could call on the community to help me when my right-hand man fell seriously ill. He's called Afer and he has been my slave since I became a centurion. Frankly, I don't know what I'd do without him. In the army, if a job needs doing, I'm used to giving orders and getting it done, but I didn't know what to do about Afer. It looked as if he was going to die. That's when I heard about Jesus and his healing miracles. Without delay, I sent my friends, the Jewish elders, with a message for him: 'My servant is close to death. Please come.'

I waited. Afer was looking worse and worse, but I was sure that Jesus could make him better. I looked outside and saw Jesus heading towards my house – then I suddenly realised what I was asking. I really didn't deserve to have Jesus under my roof – after all, I wasn't one of his people, I was just a man at his wits' end, asking for help. So I sent my friends with a second message for Jesus, in which I tried to explain my position. The message was, 'Lord, don't put yourself out for me, because I don't deserve to have you in my house. All you need to do is give the order, and my servant will get better. I am a man who has to carry out the orders of my commanding officers, and I am in charge of the soldiers under me, so if I say to one of

305

them, 'Go there,' he goes, and if I say to another, 'Come here,' he comes. If I say to my slave, 'Do this,' he does it.'

My friends delivered my message. I waited. The next thing I knew, Afer was awake and asking for water. Within the hour, he was up and about, looking like his old self. Jesus had cured him! I thought I was the man in charge here. Now I know that God is, and Jesus is acting with his authority.

Music — Our God is a great big God

Activity — Our story today was about being in charge. Many of us don't like the idea of someone being in charge of us – if we feel that someone is ordering us around without good reason, we might protest, 'You're not the boss of me!' Our activity today will help us think about what life can be like without anyone in charge.

Invite some volunteers forward and explain that you want them to put up a tent – but you've lost the instructions, you don't know where some of the bits are and you don't know how they all fit together. Encourage the volunteers to hunt for the pieces of tent and start to work out how they might fit together. Let them struggle for a bit before you bring on the Leader.

Leader — It's OK! I've found the instructions and I know how this tent works. I know what you need to do.

Give clear, ordered instructions to the volunteers, perhaps by assigning them different responsibilities (for tent poles, inner and outer tent). Make sure that things are done in the right order and oversee the successful erection of the tent.

Activity Leader — Which was easier: putting up the tent on your own, or following the instructions of someone who knew exactly what they were doing?

Invite responses from your volunteers.

Exploring — In our story today, the centurion knew exactly how authority worked and he recognised Jesus' power. He had no doubt that Jesus' orders would be obeyed and that if he said, 'Let him be cured,' the slave would be cured. The Bible tells us that Jesus was amazed by the centurion and held him up as an example, saying to the crowd around him, 'I tell you, not even in Israel have I found such faith.' He was not a Jew, and not someone Jesus' followers would have thought of as 'one of us', yet the centurion was a shining example of faith because he was someone who totally believed that God was in charge.

The Bible records the lives of other people who shared this strong faith. In the New Testament we learn about Paul, the man who was once a persecutor of Christians and who went about 'breathing threats and murder against the disciples of the Lord'[43] until the day Jesus spoke to him in a flash of blinding light. His life changed forever and he started spreading the good news of Jesus all around the Mediterranean, where he founded the first churches. Paul knew very well that God was in charge of his life, and no one else: he described himself bluntly as 'Paul an apostle – sent neither by human commission nor from human authorities, but through Jesus Christ and God the Father, who raised him from the dead'. Paul recognised that following Jesus was about letting God be the boss, no matter how some people reacted. He asked some unfaithful followers, 'Am I now seeking human approval, or God's approval? Or am I trying to please people? If I were still pleasing people, I would not be a servant of Christ.'

Paul and the centurion in our story both set us an example to follow. They remind us that God is in charge and even if, like the centurion, we feel that we are someone who doesn't deserve God's attention, our job is to accept his authority over us. Our activity reminded us of the messes we can get ourselves into if we try to manage something all by ourselves, with no one in charge; it was so much easier to get that tent up when someone who knew what they were doing took control. God loves us, he knows what he's doing and

---

43. Acts 9:1.

he is in charge. All we have to do is ask, 'What do you want me to do?'

Prayer action The centurion in our story was a soldier who understood Jesus' authority because he knew about following orders. If we are like Jesus' soldiers, ready for action, then we must wait for our orders. As we light up this arrow that points the way forward, we wonder which way God wants us to go.

Light all the tea lights to form the shape of an arrow.

As we pray, let's ask God a question: 'What do you want me to do?' The answer may not come today, and it may not come in a way we expect, but for now we will rest in his presence and simply listen.

Pause for a short time of quiet.

God, Ruler of all,
may we always listen for your word
and do your will,
in Jesus' name.
Amen.

Music Father, I place into your hands

Conclusion All-powerful God,
send us out into the world to do your will.
May we trust in you,
never forgetting that you are in charge.
Amen.

Give notices, announce the next all-age service and invite everyone to the feast.

Proper 5

Help!

Theme	Helping the poor
Scripture	Luke 7:11-17

Running order	Total: 50 minutes
Welcome	Finding the money *(10 minutes)*
Introduction	Opening the theme
Storytelling	Reading Luke 7:11-17 with mime *(5 minutes)*
Exploring	Why did the widow need Jesus' help? *(5 minutes)*
Activity	Invited speaker with props/visual aids *(15 minutes)*
Music	Christ's is the world *(5 minutes)*
Prayer action	God, our Shelter – parachute prayer *(5 minutes)*
Music	Jesus' love is very wonderful *(5 minutes)*
Conclusion	Closing prayer and invitation

Resources

- *NB Advance planning needed: invite a guest speaker (see appendix)*
- Hidden around the church, lots of copper coins totalling 5p less than the price of a loaf of bread and a pint of milk
- At the front of the church, a cheap loaf of white sliced bread and a pint of milk, each marked with a large price label
- Music and words
- At the front of the church, a table for the son to lie on
- A single sheet and a smaller sheet (e.g. cot size)
- A bag or purse full of coins (use the copper coins from the opening activity)
- A round loaf of bread or a large pitta bread
- A parachute: brightly coloured play parachutes are available from Amazon and are a great resource to buy. Alternatively, you could borrow one from a local primary school

Leaders

Minimum: 6

- Leader
- Guest speaker
- Cast x 4

Optimum: 10

- Leader (*Introduction and Conclusion*)
- Guest speaker
- Storyteller
- Cast x 4 (in traditional dress)
  Jesus
  Widow, with her head covered
  Son
  Woman
- Music Leader
- Explorer
- Prayer Leader

Suggestions for additional music

- When I needed a neighbour
- God is the giver of love

Service

Welcome *As people arrive, invite them to look all around the church for the copper coins you have hidden. They can then count up what they have found and see whether there is enough money to buy the bread and milk you have for sale.*

Introduction Our opening activity today was a small reminder of what it can be like if you don't have enough. Some of us need no reminding. There are people all over the world and in our community who find it hard to make ends meet. In Jesus' time, when no government help was available, many people were at risk of falling into poverty. Here's just one story.[44]

Storytelling Soon afterwards [Jesus] went to a town called Nain, and his disciples and a large crowd went with him.

Jesus walks down the aisle. At the front of the church is the son, lying uncovered on a table, and the widow. She has her head covered and is weeping. A second woman is supporting her.

As he approached the gate of the town, a man who had died was being carried out. He was his mother's only son, and she was a widow; and with her was a large crowd from the town.

Jesus opens his arms and hugs the widow.

When the Lord saw her, he had compassion for her and said to her, 'Do not weep.'

Jesus steps towards the son and touches his hand.

Then he came forward and touched the bier, and the bearers stood still. And he said, 'Young man, I say to you, rise!'

There is a pause, then the son sits up and looks about him. The mother and the woman are astonished.

---

44. The text is taken directly from Luke's Gospel (NRSV). You may prefer to use a different translation.

The dead man sat up and began to speak, and Jesus gave him to his mother.

Jesus takes him by the hand and leads him to his mother. They hug each other. The friend falls to her knees, then raises her arms to the heavens.

Fear seized all of them; and they glorified God, saying, 'A great prophet has risen among us!' and 'God has looked favourably on his people!' This word about him spread throughout Judea and all the surrounding country.

Exploring In our story, before Jesus brought the widow's son back from the dead, the Bible makes a point of telling us how Jesus felt: 'He had compassion for her.' Her grief was obvious, but today we're going to find out why he felt particularly sorry this widow.

Bring forward your widow.

An ordinary woman in Jesus' time had little independence. Until she got married, she lived with her parents and her father was in charge of her. After her marriage, her husband looked after her. He provided her with a home.

Invite two volunteers to stretch out a sheet above the widow's head, like a canopy.

Her husband earned money.

Give the widow a bag of coins.

He made sure that there was enough to eat.

Give the widow a loaf of bread.

Her job was to bring up the children and look after the household. Now, if her husband died, she would have to go and live with her brother or grown-up son, because it was not proper for a woman to live on her own. It was a male relative's job to look after her. So she would live in someone else's home.

Change the sheet for a smaller one.

She would have to share whatever money and food there was.

The widow gives away half her money and half her bread.

But at least she would have a roof over her head and someone to provide for her. In our story, this woman's husband died and she was looked after by her only son. When her son died, she had no one to look after her. She had nowhere to live.

Take away the sheet.

She had no money and no food.

Take away the rest of the money and the bread.

She had nothing. This is why Jesus felt so sorry for her, and why he made a miracle happen. That day, he saved two lives: the life of the son who had died and the life of his widowed mother who depended on him.

Our story shows us Jesus' concern for the poorest of the poor – for those who had no one else to help them – and it is our job to follow his example. Our guest today will tell us about people who need our help.

Introduce your speaker.

Activity *This is an opportunity for people to hear about the work of a local, national or international charity, and learn what they can do to help.*

Music Christ's is the world

Prayer action *Gather everyone in an empty space to form a large circle around the folded parachute.*

Today we will pray for everyone who needs help. We will use this parachute in our prayers because it's like God's love: *(Start to unfold the parachute.)* it's huge, it stretches in all directions and our job is to spread it out so that it reaches everyone.

Spread out the parachute and invite everyone to hold it around the edge.

We will be doing two things with this parachute as part of our prayers. First, we will hold it up like a canopy; then, we will turn it into a tent.

Practise both these manoeuvres. The first simply involves everyone raising their arms above their heads so that the parachute catches air inside it and then gently settles to the ground. The tent (or 'mushroom') requires a bit more co-ordination and agility: after a count of three, people raise their arms, lifting the parachute over their heads, and then sit down inside it with their bottoms on the edge of the parachute.[45] *This forms an air bubble that holds up the tent.*

Let us pray.

Make the canopy.

God, our Shelter, may you look after us all.

Make the tent.

Guard, protect and shelter
all those in need.
May we do our best to help,
in Jesus' name.
Amen.

Music Jesus' love is very wonderful

Use the parachute for the actions that go with this song: lift up the chute for 'so high'; move in to form a tighter circle and hold the chute down low for 'so low'; stretch it out wide for 'so wide'.

---

45. See www.woodlands-junior.kent.sch.uk/parachute for excellent photographs and explanations of these manoeuvres. If you have an elderly congregation, you could either invite the children alone to use the parachute, or you could simply make the canopy and say the whole prayer as the parachute settles to the ground.

Conclusion   Heavenly Father,
send us out into the world, ready to help people.
Keep our eyes open to see the needs around us
and give us the strength to do what we can.
Amen.

Give notices, announce the next all-age service and invite everyone to the feast.

Proper 6

Forgiven

Theme	God's unconditional grace
Scripture	Galatians 2:15-21; Luke 7:36–8:3

Running order Total: 50 minutes

Welcome	Foot/hand massage *(10 minutes)*
Introduction	Opening the theme
Storytelling	Dramatisation of Luke 7:36–8:3 *(10 minutes)*
Music	I'm accepted, I'm forgiven *(5 minutes)*
Activity	Writing/drawing confessions *(10 minutes)*
Exploring	How are we forgiven? *(5 minutes)*
Prayer action	Takeaway prayer – receiving forgiveness *(5 minutes)*
Music	God forgave my sin in Jesus' name *(5 minutes)*
Conclusion	Closing prayer and invitation

Resources

- Equipment for hand/foot massage *(see appendix)*:
  - large bowls
  - jugs of warm water
  - small towels
  - dishes of light olive oil, with some drops of fragrant essential oil added
- A table and two chairs at the front of the church
- Plain white envelopes (enough for one each) with a 'FORGIVEN' card sealed inside each one *(see appendix)*
- Pens, pencils and felt pens
- Music and words
- Two large red signs for the debtors:
  - '50 denarii'
  - '500 denarii'
- Three signs (two of them double-sided):
  - 'I've done bad things'
  - '£2500/I've done very bad things'
  - '£25,000/I've done terrible things'

Leaders

Minimum: 8

- Leader
- Volunteer to give hand/foot massage
- Cast x 6

Optimum: 11+

- Leader *(Introduction and Conclusion)*
- Volunteer(s) to give hand/foot massages
- Cast x 6:
  Simon the Pharisee, wearing rich robes
  Jesus, wearing a white tunic
  Woman, wearing brightly coloured robes and carrying a perfume bottle. She begins the service sitting in the congregation
  Creditor, wearing a rich cloak or head-cloth
  Debtors x 2, wearing plain head-cloths
- Music Leader
- Explorer
- Activity/Prayer Leader

Suggestions for additional music

- Forgive our sins as we forgive
- Amazing grace

Service

Welcome — *As people arrive, invite them to receive a hand or foot massage.*

Introduction — We hope you have enjoyed your warm welcome in church this morning. A foot or hand massage feels wonderful, and lots of people pay for the privilege of being pampered in this way. Today it is our free gift to you. In the story we are about to hear, Jesus is given a gift like this.

Storytelling — *Jesus walks down the aisle to where Simon is waiting by a table and chairs at the front of the church.*

Simon — Jesus, you are most welcome to my house. Dinner is almost ready.

Jesus — Thank you, Simon.

Simon — Do have a seat. *(gesturing at the congregation)* I'm afraid we have a bit of a houseful. We Pharisees feel it is our duty to allow the poor and needy into our homes.

Jesus — No problem.

Jesus sits. The woman rushes from her place in the congregation. Crying, she starts to pour ointment on Jesus' feet and massage them. Neither she nor Jesus reacts to Simon's next speech.

Simon — *(aside, to the congregation)*

You know, if this man were really a prophet, he'd know who this woman is. She's a sinner, and if you ask me, Jesus shouldn't let that sort of person get too close.

Jesus — Simon, let me tell you a story.

Simon — Of course, Teacher.

Jesus — Once upon a time there was a man who had lent money to two people. One owed him 50 denarii and the other owed him 500 denarii.

The creditor and the two debtors enter. The debtors hold signs with '50 denarii' and '500 denarii' written in red.

Neither of them had any money to pay him back. *(the debtors shake their heads)* So the man cancelled both their debts.

The creditor takes their signs and tears them up. Both creditors freeze, as if stunned.

Which one do you think was more grateful?

The first debtor shakes the creditor's hand; the second debtor flings his arms around the creditor's neck and hugs him.

Simon   Well, the one who owed more money, I suppose.

Jesus   You're right. *(the creditor and debtors leave)* Now, look at this woman. I came to your house tonight, but you didn't offer me a bowl of water for my feet. Now she has washed my feet with her own tears! You didn't even kiss my cheek, but she's been kissing my feet since the moment I sat down. You didn't give me oil for my hair, but she's been massaging perfume into my feet all this time. So listen, her sins – which were many – have been forgiven, and that's why she's shown me such love and gratitude. Your sins – such as they are – have also been forgiven, but you've not done much wrong, so you've less cause to be grateful. *(to the woman, helping her to her feet)* Your sins are forgiven. Your faith has saved you; go in peace.

She hugs him just as the forgiven debtor hugged the creditor, then leaves.

Music   I'm accepted, I'm forgiven

Activity   Our double story today was all about forgiveness: Jesus forgave the woman for her sins, and he told the story of the man who forgave his debtors. We all need forgiveness, because none of us is perfect. We are all capable of getting things wrong, making a mess of things and hurting other people, but we know we can come to God and have all our sins taken away. We can say sorry, be forgiven and start afresh.

This morning, we will have an opportunity to say sorry to God. Please take one of these cards and write or draw on it anything you'd like to say sorry for. No one else will read it: this is your chance to get these things off your chest.

Allow plenty of time for people to write or draw their confessions.

Exploring

Keep your confessions close to you – we will come back to them later.

Now we are going to look more closely at our story, to find out what we need to do in order to be forgiven. The people in our story had a great deal to be forgiven for.

Bring forward the woman and the two debtors.

We don't know exactly what the woman had done wrong, but she had a bad reputation.

The woman shows her sign: 'I've done bad things'.

In fact, she had done so many bad things that the Pharisee didn't think Jesus ought to let himself be touched by 'that sort of person'.

The debtors show their signs: '£2,500' and '£25,000'.

Then there were the people with debts to pay. In today's money, the first person owed £2500 and the second owed £25,000.[46] They needed to have their debts written off, but Jesus wasn't really talking about money: he used these two as examples of people who had done lots of bad things for which they needed forgiveness. Jesus used these amounts to represent the wrong they had done.

The debtors turn over their signs to read, 'I've done very bad things' and 'I've done terrible things'.

Now, the question is this: in our story, did you hear any of these people say, 'I'm sorry' or 'Please forgive me'?

Invite responses.

And yet they were all forgiven. The debtors didn't even have to ask, and the woman wasn't washing Jesus' feet to earn forgiveness: she knew she was already forgiven

---

46. A denarius was a day's wage for a manual labourer. For these modern figures, I have assumed a denarius = about £50 (an eight-hour day @ £6.08 per hour.) Adjust these figures as necessary, in line with the current minimum wage.

PROPER 6

and she was saying thank you. Jesus said, 'Her sins – which were many – have been forgiven, and that's why she's shown me such love and gratitude.'

This story shows us that God's forgiveness is ours already. It doesn't depend on whether we deserve it, or whether we've earned it, or even whether we say sorry: Jesus died for our sins and we are forgiven. This was radical news for the Jews of Jesus' time, because they believed that they were made good by strict obedience to God's laws. If this were really the case then, as the leader of the early Church bluntly put it, Christ would have died for nothing. In fact, Christ died so that everyone could be saved through God's grace, which he offers to us all, no matter what we've done.

Prayer action For our prayers today, we will use the confessions we made earlier. We are ready to offer them to God and say sorry, but before we do so, let's look at them more closely. You have written and drawn your confessions on envelopes: it's time to tear open these envelopes and see what is inside for you.

Pause while everyone does so and discovers the card that reads: 'FORGIVEN.'

Before you thought of a single confession, before you put pen to paper and before you offered those confessions to God in prayer, God's forgiveness was already there, just waiting for you to receive it. Let us pray.

Loving Father,
we receive this forgiveness through your Son,
Jesus Christ.
We thank you for this fresh start and this new life.
Amen.

Please take your card away with you and keep it in a purse or wallet to remind you that you are forgiven.

Music God forgave my sin in Jesus' name

Conclusion Loving Lord,
send us out to tell the world
about your amazing grace.
Amen.

Give notices, announce the next all-age service and invite everyone to the feast.

Proper 7

Earthquake, wind and fire

Theme	God's presence and power
Scripture	1 Kings 19:1-15a; Luke 8:26-39

Running order	Total: 50 minutes
Welcome	Viewing the pictures of wind, rockfalls and fire *(5 minutes)*
Introduction	Opening the theme
Activity	Making props for the story *(10 minutes)*
Storytelling 1	Interactive retelling of Elijah's encounter in the wilderness, with props *(10 minutes)*
Music	Dear Lord and Father of mankind *(5 minutes)*
Storytelling 2	The Gerasene swineherd's tale *(5 minutes)*
Exploring	How does God help people who need him? *(5 minutes)*
Music	Be still, for the presence of the Lord *(5 minutes)*
Prayer action	Cry for help – calling on God in the noise and silence *(5 minutes)*
Conclusion	Closing prayer and invitation

Resources

- A slideshow of pictures: strong winds, rockfalls and wildfire *(see appendix)*
- A laptop, projector and screen
- Three craft tables, with equipment for making the following: *(see appendix)*
  - wind-makers
  - rocks
  - fire streamers
- Some pitta bread
- A few cups of water
- Music and words

Leaders

Minimum: 2

- Leader
- *Swineherd*

Optimum: 7+

- Leader *(Introduction and Conclusion)*
- Activity Leader(s)
- Storyteller
- *Swineherd,* wearing muddy wellies, jeans and an old T-shirt
- Music Leader
- Explorer
- Prayer Leader

Suggestions for additional music

- Be still, my soul
- Walk with me, O my Lord

Service

Welcome — *As people arrive, show a slideshow of pictures: strong wind, rockfalls and wildfire.*

Introduction — Our opening slideshow has given us a taste of the dramatic events that we'll hear about in our first story today. There will be a whirlwind, an earthquake and wildfire! Before we can tell this story together, I'm going to need your help.

Activity — *Encourage people to gather around the three craft tables. There are three props to choose from: wind-makers, rocks and fire streamers. Allow plenty of time for people to make something.*

Storytelling 1 — *Gather everyone around, in a circle if possible, with their props ready. Tell them to listen out for the right moment to use them.*

This is a story about a great prophet called Elijah. God chose him to be his spokesperson: it was Elijah's job to tell the truth to powerful people, but this was very dangerous. He battled against wicked rulers, unfaithful people and the prophets of a false religion. When the queen of Israel threatened to kill him, Elijah was afraid. He decided that he'd had enough and he ran off into the desert.

There, he asked God to let him die. He couldn't see any point in carrying on. Elijah lay down and fell asleep, but God sent an angel to keep him alive: the angel brought fresh bread and water.

Pass round the bread and water.

The angel kept bringing him food and water until he was strong enough to travel. Elijah went to Mount Horeb and found a cave to sleep in. God's voice came to him there and said, 'What are you doing here, Elijah?'

Elijah replied, 'I've worked as hard as I can for you, God. Now your people have turned their backs on you, given up their worship and killed your prophets. I'm the only one left, and I'm next.'

God said, 'Go and stand on the mountain. I am coming.' Then there was a howling and a whistling, and a powerful WIND whipped the air. It was strong enough to make the earth shiver.

Encourage everyone to use their wind-makers and to make the sound of a howling wind.

But God was not in the wind.

The wind stops.

Then there was a rumbling and a trembling, and a mighty EARTHQUAKE shook the mountain. It was violent enough to throw rocks from the mountain-top.

Encourage everyone to stamp their feet and roll their rocks into the middle of the circle.

But God was not in the earthquake.

The earthquake stops.

Then there was a crackling and a roaring, and a fierce WILDFIRE ripped around the mountain. It was hot enough to cook the rocks.

Encourage everyone to wave their fire streamers in the air and around the rocks.

But God was not in the fire.

The fire stops.

After the fire, there was a sound of sheer silence.

Pause for a moment of silence, then speak very quietly.

In the silence, there was a still, small voice. God said, 'What are you doing here, Elijah?'

Elijah sighed and said, 'I've worked as hard as I can for you, God. Now your people have turned their backs on you, given up their worship and killed your prophets. I'm the only one left, and I'm next.'

God said, 'Go. It's time to go back.'

Music Dear Lord and Father of mankind

Storytelling 2

Swineherd

Listen – wait till you hear what I've just seen! Sorry to come in here smelling of pigs, but I've been out with them in the fields all morning. Swineherd, that's my job. Don't usually do much more than give the boss' pigs their grub, then sit down and keep an eye out for trouble. We're in quiet fields by the lake – there's never any trouble. But that was before today . . .

It started when I heard the shouting. That nutter from the city had found his way out here – you know, the one who goes around starkers, yelling random stuff at people? Folk say that evil spirits have got hold of him. I thought he hung around the city graveyard, and last I heard they'd chained him up like a dog, but he'd obviously done a runner because he was out in my boss' fields, screaming and foaming at the mouth. He was scaring the pigs.

I was just wondering whether I'd have to tackle him myself when I saw a boat pull up on the shore. Several blokes got out of it. One looked familiar. Anyway, as soon as the nutter saw this particular man, he threw himself down on the ground. Then I heard a weird voice coming out of his mouth, saying, 'What are you going to do to me, Jesus, Son of God? Please, don't hurt me!' Jesus – that was the bloke's name. Anyway, he was saying something I couldn't quite catch, and then he put his hands on the nutter and shouted, 'Evil spirits, I order you to come out of this man! Go and take hold of those pigs instead.'

'You what?!' I thought. 'Leave my boss' pigs out of this!' Then I saw the nutter flopping about like a fish, and suddenly the pigs went mental. Never seen anything like it. Crazy, they were – they started running round in circles, then they legged it downhill towards the lake. I ran after them, screaming and yelling, but it wasn't any good. They were out of control: they rushed off the edge of the cliff and into the water. Every last one of them – drowned.

I legged it myself, then. I ran straight into town and got my mates to come and see. I'd need back-up if I was going to explain to the boss what had happened to his pigs. When we got back to the lake, there was Jesus, calm as you like, sitting there having a conversation with someone. When I got closer, I realised it was the madman – except he didn't look mad any more. He had put some clothes on, and he was sitting next to Jesus, listening and asking questions. He looked as sane as anyone.

By now, there was quite a crowd, and we were all completely freaked out, I can tell you. It was too much to take in: what had happened to those pigs? What had happened to the madman? Who *is* this Jesus? Just what kind of powers does he have? We're not his people, and we don't want anything to do with him, so we asked him to leave. I'm pleased to say he went. He left the man he'd cured to tell everyone what had happened to him. Now I've just got to work out what I'm going to tell my boss about his pigs.

Exploring   Both our stories were so full of dramatic events that we might have lost sight of the people caught in the middle. First there was the prophet, Elijah, who was lonely, frightened and in despair. Then there was the man who had been taken over by evil spirits, who was either chained up like an animal or left to run wild: it is hard to imagine how lonely he must have been feeling. Our question today is this: how does God help people who need him?

God came to both these desperate people when they needed him, and when he came, there were some extraordinary happenings: in the desert there was a whirlwind, an earthquake and a wildfire; in the fields by Lake Galilee, pigs went mad and drowned themselves. It would be easy for us to think that God is only present in our lives if he arrives with such noise and drama. However, if we look more closely at each story, we notice something interesting. In Elijah's story, the Bible is quite clear that 'God was not in the wind' and 'God was not in the earthquake' and 'God was not in the fire.' God came to Elijah in 'a sound of sheer silence' and he spoke in 'a still, small voice.'[47] He gave him simple instructions about what to do next. In the story of the man possessed by evil spirits, the wild behaviour of the pigs distracts our attention from where God is: sitting next to a man who, for the first time in years, is in his right mind. All the noisy fury of the evil spirits has left him and he is quiet, still and sane.

Both these stories suggest that although God has the power to make big, dramatic things happen, he often comes quietly to help those who need him, when people are looking elsewhere. His contact is direct and personal, like the still, small voice that spoke to Elijah and the quiet closeness that Jesus shared with the man he had healed. So when we ask for God's help, we needn't expect earthquakes and thunderbolts; instead, we need to listen for God's quiet voice and wait for his gentle touch.

Music Be still, for the presence of the Lord

Prayer action Whenever we need God's help, we can pray. In a moment of quiet, let's think about the help we need, and remember those known to us who need God's help.

Pause.

Our prayers today are going to be one big, noisy cry for help. Hold all your prayers in your heart and when I say, 'Let us pray,' we'll all take a deep breath and pray with one word: 'HELP!' You can shout it as loud as you like, or say it quietly. Now we pray for everyone who needs God's help. Let us pray.

---

47. 1 Kings 19:12 (NKJV).

	All	**HELP!**
		Pause.
Prayer Leader		In the sheer silence after the noise, we rest in God's presence and listen.
		Pause for a short time.
		Amen.

Conclusion Almighty God,
as we go out into the world,
may we know your presence and power.
Speak through the earthquake, wind and fire,
O still, small voice of calm.[48]
Amen.

Give notices, announce the next all-age service and invite everyone to the feast.

---

48. J. G. Whittier, 'Dear Lord and Father of mankind'.

Proper 8

What to do?

Theme	Jesus' urgent and all-important call
Scripture	Luke 9:51-62

Running order	Total: 50 minutes
Welcome	Making 'To do' lists *(5 minutes)*
Introduction	Opening the theme
Storytelling	Visual retelling of Luke 9:51-62 *(5 minutes)*
Music	Follow me *(5 minutes)*
Exploring	How does Jesus call his followers? *(5 minutes)*
Activity	Deciding between Urgent/Non-Urgent and Important/Unimportant *(20 minutes)*
Prayer action	Sirens – emergency prayer *(5 minutes)*
Music	All that I am *(5 minutes)*
Conclusion	Closing prayer and invitation

Resources

- Large sticky notes
- Pens
- A display board at the front of church
- A slideshow of pictures *(see appendix)*
- Laptop, projector, screen and speakers
- A giant Venn diagram *(see appendix)*
- All around the church, hide props, sound effects and pictures for the Urgent/Important Activity *(see appendix)*
- A siren sound effect (police/ambulance). There are many internet sites offering free downloadable sound effects, e.g. www.partnersinrhyme.com

Leaders

Minimum: 2

- Leader
- IT technician *(for Storytelling and Prayer)*

Optimum: 6+

- Leader *(Introduction and Conclusion)*
- Storyteller
- Music Leader
- Explorer
- Activity Leader(s)
- Prayer Leader

Suggestions for additional music

- Will you come and follow me
- We are marching

Service

Welcome — *As people arrive, give each person a large sticky note and a pen. Invite them to make a 'To do' list for the day or week. Gather all the lists on a board at the front of church.*

Introduction — If we look at the lists of jobs we've collected here, we can see what a lot of things we have to do in our daily lives. The people in Jesus' time must have been even busier than us in some ways, because they lived and worked in close-knit communities where family members depended on one other. People grew their own crops, made their own food and even buried their own dead. Here's what happened when Jesus visited a small village.

Storytelling — Jesus knew that his time was drawing near. He was on a fixed course for Jerusalem.

Show the sign pointing to Jerusalem.

He sent messengers ahead. They went to a Samaritan village to prepare accommodation for him, but when he got there, no one in that anti-Jewish place welcomed him, because he had set his sights on Jerusalem.

Show the picture of the locked door.

His disciples, James and John, were outraged. They asked if they should pray for a fire to destroy the village.

Show the picture of fire.

But Jesus was already back on the road, and he told them not to overreact. They pushed on together to the next village. They met someone who said to Jesus, 'I'll follow you wherever you go.'

Jesus answered, 'Foxes have their dens,

Show the picture of the fox cubs in the den and the birds in the nest.

and birds have their nests, but there's no shelter for God's Son.' He pressed on towards Jerusalem.

Show the sign pointing to Jerusalem.

On his way, Jesus called out to a man, 'Follow me!' But the man said, 'I've got to bury my father first.'

Show the picture of a Jewish funeral.

Jesus answered, 'That's a job for those you leave behind: you've got to go and tell people about God's kingdom.'

A woman said, 'I'll follow you, Lord! I've just got to go and say goodbye to my family first.'

Show a family embracing.

Jesus said to her, 'No one who tries to walk my way while looking over their shoulder is fit for God's kingdom.' He kept on walking, following his fixed course for Jerusalem.

Show the sign pointing to Jerusalem.

Music Follow me

Exploring In the story we've just heard, Jesus is clearly a man on a mission. The Bible says more than once, 'he set his face to go to Jerusalem.' He's very focused: he knows he will be arrested and killed once he gets to the city, but he's determined to follow God's plan. We can imagine him striding purposefully along, like an important person in a TV drama who marches down long corridors, with assistants firing questions at him as he walks.

Jesus' sense of purpose comes across in his response to his followers. James and John ask whether they should summon a fire to destroy the Samaritan village: Jesus dismisses such an over-the-top reaction before giving two would-be followers some particularly harsh instructions. One must leave his dead father before the funeral, and another is told off for wanting to say goodbye to her family. Jesus says, 'No one who tries to walk my way while looking over their shoulder is fit for God's kingdom.' The thought of not saying goodbye to our family might shock us, but Jesus' Jewish followers would have been more horrified at the thought of leaving the dead unburied. Jewish law ruled that burying the dead, especially a parent, took precedence over everything else – even the worship of God and the study of his word. Jesus is making demands on his followers that are even more important and urgent than this.

This story shows how Jesus wants us to follow him. Here, as when he called the fishermen from their nets, Jesus calls people to drop everything and come. Whether or not we take this literally, these stories make us question our priorities: what is most important to us? What urgently needs our attention? Our activity today will help us think about some of the things that are important in our lives, and whether they are the same things that urgently demand our attention.

Activity *Lay out the giant Venn diagram and explain briefly what it shows (it should be self-explanatory).*

Around the church today, we have lots of different pictures, objects and sounds. Can you find them all and think where we might place them on this diagram?

Hold up the ringing phone.

For example, a ringing phone might sound like it needs answering right now, so it seems urgent, but I can see that it's a cold call, so it's not that important.

Place the phone on the 'urgent' section, then hold up the plant.

Watering this plant is important because it will die if I don't, but it doesn't need watering now this minute, so it's important but not urgent.

Place the plant on the 'important' section, then hold up the picture of the chip pan.

This chip pan is bubbling over and if I don't do anything, it will catch fire: this is important AND urgent.

Place the picture on the 'important and urgent' section.

Take your time now to think about where the other pictures, objects and sounds might belong: which ones are urgent, which are important and which are both? You may like to write or draw your own ideas, too.

Allow plenty of time for people to look, think and discuss. When everything has been placed, and further ideas have been added, invite people to explain the choices they have made. Remember, you're not looking for the 'right' answer, but for thoughtful engagement.

Some of these were obvious to us, and some were trickier to decide: how do we know whether a ringing doorbell is important until we open the door? It could be a man offering us double glazing or it could be our best friend in tears. Sometimes the situation is not as it first appears: paramedics are taught that if they find two people in a car crash and one is screaming for help and the other is lying there in silence, they must help the silent one first because their injuries may be more life-threatening than those of the person who is demanding attention. In this case, both casualties are important, but the silent need is more urgent than the cry for help.

In our story, Jesus showed that following him was both important and urgent. It took precedence over everything else. So today, let's wonder about the 'To do' lists we made at the beginning of the service, and take this question away with us: do we put Jesus first in our lives?

Prayer action   Sometimes our need for God becomes both important and urgent. When we are in crisis or in despair, when everyone else has let us down, then we turn to him.

However, prayer should be our top priority, not our last resort. Our prayers today will begin with a siren – the noise that tells everyone to get out of the way, because an emergency vehicle is coming through. May this sound remind us that we regularly need to clear everything else out of the way so that our prayers can come through.

Play the sound of the siren.

Let us pray.

Almighty God,
we pray in silence for all those who urgently need your help.

Pause.

We pray for those whose needs are silent or forgotten.

Pause.

May help come to all those in need.
We ask this in Jesus' name.
Amen.

Music All that I am

Conclusion Lord Jesus,
send us out into the world to follow you.
With your eyes may we see
what is urgent and important.
Amen.

Give notices, announce the next all-age service and invite everyone to the feast.

Proper 9

The God Squad

Theme	The disciples' mission
Scripture	Luke 10:1-11, 16-20

Running order	Total: 50 minutes	
Welcome	Drawing a big map of your community *(10 minutes)*	
Introduction	Opening the theme	
Storytelling	Discipleship Dos and Don'ts *(5 minutes)*	
Music	Go forth and tell! *(5 minutes)*	
Exploring	How can we follow in the disciples' footsteps? *(5 minutes)*	
Activity	Decorating peace candles *(15 minutes)*	
Prayer action	Peace candles – house blessings *(5 minutes)*	
Music	Peace is flowing like a river *(5 minutes)*	
Conclusion	Closing prayer and invitation	

Resources

- A large, long sheet of lining paper, spread out on a couple of long tables. Draw a basic outline map of your community: a few main roads and one or two landmarks
- Lots of felt pens and pencils
- Small pillar candles to decorate, enough for one each *(see appendix)*
- Candle pens *(see appendix)*
- Music and words
- Two signs: 'Do' and 'Don't'. Print these words in big bold letters on two pieces of card. Suspend each card from a piece of tape or ribbon, so it can be worn around the neck

Leaders

Minimum: 2
- Leader
- *Jesus*

Optimum: 7+
- Leader *(Introduction and Conclusion)*
- Storyteller
- *Jesus*, wearing white
- Music Leader
- Explorer
- Activity Leader(s)
- Prayer Leader

Suggestions for additional music

- Forth in the peace of Christ we go
- Like a mighty river flowing

Service

Welcome *As people arrive, invite them to help draw a big map of your community. They could add whole streets, or simply draw in their own houses.*

Introduction This morning, we've been creating a picture of the buildings and streets we know well. If Jesus had drawn a map like this, it would have been even bigger, because he travelled around lots of towns and villages in Galilee and beyond. Today we'll be thinking about the seventy disciples he sent out to those places to do his work: you might call them the God Squad.

Storytelling Jesus chose seventy more disciples to go on ahead of him in pairs to every town and village on his route. He gave them clear instructions for their mission.

Jesus There's lots of work to do, and not many people to do it, so I'm sending you. You are the God Squad. Now listen carefully: here is a list of dos and don'ts.[49]

Jesus puts on the 'Do' sign and the Storyteller puts on the 'Don't' sign.

Go on your way.

Storyteller Don't stay put.

Jesus Carry no purse, no bag, no sandals.

Storyteller Don't spend ages getting ready and packing everything you think you might need.

Jesus Greet no one on the road.

Storyteller Don't waste time on social niceties.

Jesus Whatever house you enter, first say, 'Peace to this house!' And if anyone is there who shares in peace, your peace will rest on that person; but if not, it will return to you.

Storyteller Don't waste time trying to work out whether people are for you or against you – wherever you go, pray for God's peace and trust God to work in people's hearts.

---

49. Jesus' words from this point are taken directly from Luke's Gospel (NRSV). You may prefer to use a different translation.

Jesus	Remain in the same house, eating and drinking whatever they provide, for the labourer deserves to be paid.
Storyteller	Don't move about from house to house, looking for an accommodation upgrade.
Jesus	Whenever you enter a town and its people welcome you, eat what is set before you; cure the sick who are there, and say to them, 'The kingdom of God has come near to you.'
Storyteller	Don't be picky about what you eat or who you help. Get on with curing anyone who is sick. Don't make long speeches.
Jesus	But whenever you enter a town and they do not welcome you, go out into its streets and say, 'Even the dust of your town that clings to our feet, we wipe off in protest against you. Yet know this: the kingdom of God has come near.'
Storyteller	Don't try to punish or fight those who don't welcome you – just move on. But don't forget to give them the same message: 'The kingdom of God has come near.'
Jesus	Whoever listens to you listens to me, and whoever rejects you rejects me, and whoever rejects me rejects the one who sent me.
Storyteller	It's not all about you: people are choosing whether or not to accept God's offer.
Jesus	See, I have given you authority to tread . . . over all the power of the enemy; and nothing will hurt you.
Storyteller	Don't gloat over the things that God's power enables you to do; instead, be glad that you will be with him in heaven.
Music	Go forth and tell!
Exploring	In our story today, Jesus sent out seventy disciples. Some people think the number symbolises the nations of the world that are listed in the Bible's Creation story:[50] the message is that Jesus sent out his disciples to every corner of the earth. So the instructions he gave

---

50. Genesis 10.

them, in first-century Galilee, may have something to say to us here in church today. Jesus began by saying, 'There's lots of work to do, and not many people to do it, so I'm sending you. You are the God Squad.' He was talking to us, too! What can we learn from his list of dos and don'ts?

First of all, he told us to be on the move, travelling light. Some of us may live and worship in the same place for most of our lives, but we too can be ready for change and prepared to move forward as a church. Jesus told us to be active people who focus on doing God's work, like his disciples who busied themselves with healing and helping. We don't need to make long speeches: the disciples arrived with a few words of peace and afterwards informed people that they had encountered God's kingdom – that was all. Everything in between was action, not words. Not everyone will accept God's offer, but Jesus emphasised that his disciples shouldn't dwell on rejection or take it personally: people will choose for themselves whether to listen to the good news or not.

This is a very active, practical kind of discipleship. We need to think about whether we work like this, and whether our church follows the example of those early disciples. Are we on the move, or are we standing still? Are we getting things done, or are we worrying about what we need and what we should say? Now, as we think about these big questions, we will do something practical to help people around us. The disciples arrived in someone's home and said, 'Peace to this house!' Today we will make peace candles to offer to people in our community, so that we can spread the message of God's peace.

Activity *Invite people to gather around the craft tables and decorate candles with the word 'Peace' and appropriate patterns. Remember that these candles will be given away as gifts from the church.*

Prayer action *Bring forward the map of your community and lay it out at the front of church.*

Heavenly Father,
we ask for your peace on this community.
May you bless all the homes and businesses within it,
the people who live and work here
and those who are passing through.

Invite everyone to bring forward their candles and place them on the map. (They will be blessed but not lit.)

May you bless these candles
and make them signs of your peace
wherever their light shines.
May your peace be upon us all
in Jesus' name.
Amen.

Please take your candle away with you and give it to someone else as a sign of Christ's peace.

Music Peace is flowing like a river

Conclusion Lord Jesus,
send us out to help people in your name.
May we communicate your peace
and spread the good news of your kingdom.
Amen.

Give notices, announce the next all-age service and invite everyone to the feast.

Proper 10

The good Samaritan

Theme	Loving our neighbours
Scripture	Luke 10:25-37

Running order Total: 50 minutes

Welcome	Viewing images of the Jericho road *(5 minutes)*
Introduction	Opening the theme
Exploring	Meeting the characters *(10 minutes)*
Storytelling	Dramatisation – the story of the good Samaritan *(5 minutes)*
Music	When I needed a neighbour *(5 minutes)*
Activity	Who is our neighbour? Visual representation *(15 minutes)*
Prayer action	Pouring oil – active prayer *(5 minutes)*
Music	Brother, sister, let me serve you *(5 minutes)*
Conclusion	Closing prayer and invitation

PROPER 10

Resources

- Laptop, projector and screen
- A slideshow of images and/or video footage of the Jerusalem–Jericho road *(see appendix)*
- Four stations around the church, introducing the four characters: *(see appendix)*
  - the injured man
  - the Priest
  - the Levite
  - the Samaritan
- Music and words
- A chair and table at the front of the church
- The good Samaritan's bag *(see appendix)*
- A big sheet of card
- Pens and pencils
- Newspapers and magazines
- Scissors
- Glue sticks
- Some dishes of olive oil

Leaders

Minimum: 6

- Leader
- Cast x 5

Optimum: 10

- Leader *(Introduction and Conclusion)*
- Explorer
- Cast x 5: *(for costume details, see appendix)*
  Injured man
  Priest
  Levite
  Samaritan
  Innkeeper, carrying a cup of water
- Music Leader
- Activity Leader
- Prayer Leader

Suggestions for additional music

- Help us to help each other, Lord
- Take my hands, Lord

Service

Welcome — *As people arrive, show images and/or video footage of the Jerusalem–Jericho road.*

Introduction — Today we will be telling one of Jesus' best-known stories: the parable of the good Samaritan. Even if you don't know the story, you probably have an idea that it's about helping people. If you lend someone a hand, you might be described as 'a good Samaritan'; you may know about the organisation called Samaritans, whose volunteers provide a listening service for people in crisis. But for Jesus' Jewish audience, this story was a shock. A good Samaritan? That was a contradiction in terms. For us, it would be like hearing about 'a good racist' or 'a good terrorist'. Let's find out a bit more about the Samaritan and the other characters we'll meet in our story.

Exploring — *Encourage people to visit the four stations, so that they get to know the injured man, the Priest, the Levite and the Samaritan.*

Now we know a bit more about the people in our story, let's find out what happened. The events take place on the road from Jerusalem to Jericho. We saw pictures of this road as we came into church this morning: how would you describe it?

Invite responses.

Travellers heading to and from the big city often had money with them, so thieves used to lie in wait by the side of the road. Muggers had plenty of places to hide amongst the rocks, and plenty of heavy stones with which to attack unsuspecting travellers. When Jesus announced that his story was about a man travelling from Jerusalem to Jericho, his listeners knew precisely the road he was talking about. They must have sucked their teeth and said to each other, 'I wouldn't do that journey on my own. Only last week, my cousin was attacked in broad daylight.' Sure enough, the man in Jesus' story was attacked, beaten up, robbed and left for dead. So our story begins with a body on the road.

Storytelling

The injured man collapses at the front of the church, groaning.

Man Urrgh...

The priest is walking down the aisle. He reaches the body and hesitates.

Priest Oh!

He hesitates, then walks in a wide curve around the body and exits.

Man Urrgh...

The Levite walks down the aisle. He spots the body and stops.

Levite Ah.

He peers more closely and is disgusted by what he sees.

Eeuch!

He dithers for a moment, looks at the spotless clothes he is wearing, then he too gives the man a wide berth and exits.

Man Urrgh...

The Samaritan walks down the aisle. He spots the body and sighs sadly.

Samaritan Aah.

He goes closer and looks at the body.

Oh...

He takes the man's pulse.

Mmm.

He strokes the man's forehead. The man wakes with a start.

Man Aargh!

Samaritan Sshhh.

The Samaritan takes some strips of cloth from his bag and two little bottles of wine and oil. He pours these on the man's wounds and ties the bandages. The man cries out in pain; the Samaritan makes soothing 'Sshh' and 'Mmm' noises.

Come.

The Samaritan helps the man to his feet. The Samaritan grunts with the effort and the man winces. Together they struggle to the chair and table in front of the altar. The innkeeper arrives and the Samaritan hands over some coins.

Take care of him. I'll be back in a few days and I'll repay whatever else you spend on food and medicine.

The innkeeper nods. He hands over some water and the Samaritan helps the man drink. He then leaves.

Man   *(feeling more comfortable at last)* Aaah!

Music   When I needed a neighbour

Activity   Jesus used this story to illustrate one of the most important commandments: love your neighbour as you love yourself. He asked his audience, 'Which of these three, do you think, was a neighbour to the man who fell into the hands of the robbers?' The answer, of course, is the one who took pity on him – the Samaritan. This story shows that to love your neighbour, you don't have to agree with him or even like him: remember that Jews and Samaritans hated one another. What matters is that you help your neighbour, whoever he or she is.

Today we will explore who our neighbours are. We will cover this big sheet of card with the pictures or names of everyone we might describe as a neighbour. You could start with your actual neighbours, and name the people who live next door to you. You could draw your friends and family. Who else might you include?

Allow plenty of time for people to write names or draw portraits. Encourage people to cut out faces from magazines and newspapers, too, to encourage understanding of our national and international 'neighbours'. Hold up the finished display.

All these people are our neighbours. Some are people we don't know at all; some are hard to like; some don't like us. Today's story reminds us that these feelings are irrelevant: loving our neighbours means doing whatever we can to help them.

Prayer action   The good Samaritan helped the injured man by pouring oil on his wounds. Today we will use oil in our prayers.

Hold a dish of oil and anoint one of your fellow leaders as you speak.

Take this dish of olive oil, turn to your neighbour and use a little oil on the tip of your finger to make the sign of the cross on his or her palm. As we reach out to each other like this, may we pray for the strength to love our neighbours by helping other people.

Pass round the dishes of olive oil and pause while people anoint each other's palms.

Loving Lord,
may we be good Samaritans
who help our neighbours
in Jesus' name.
Amen.

Music   Brother, sister, let me serve you

Conclusion   God of Love,
send us out in your name
to love you
and to love our neighbours
as we love ourselves.
Amen.

Give notices, announce the next all-age service and invite everyone to the feast.

Proper 11

Martha and Mary

Theme Putting Jesus first

Scripture Luke 10:38-42

Running order Total: 50 minutes

Welcome — Finding the provisions (5 minutes)

Introduction — Opening the theme

Storytelling — Martha's chores and Mary's choice – edible retelling (10 minutes)

Music — To be in your presence ('My desire') (5 minutes)

Exploring — What can we learn from Jesus' treatment of Martha and Mary? (5 minutes)

Prayer action — Laying aside our worries and distractions – offertory prayer (5 minutes)

Activity — 'Choosing the better part' – activities to help people sit still and listen to God (15 minutes)

Music — Be the centre of my life (5 minutes)

Conclusion — Closing prayer and invitation

Resources

- Lots of ingredients for the feast, hidden all around the church *(see appendix)*
- A table
- Plates, bowls and butter knives
- A bowl of warm soapy water
- A towel
- In every pew or row of seats:
  - small pieces of paper
  - pens and pencils
- A collection plate
- Music and words
- Listening stations around the church *(see appendix)*

Leaders

Minimum: 1

- Leader

Optimum: 6

- Leader *(Introduction and Conclusion)*
- *Martha*, wearing a tunic and head-cloth
- Music Leader
- Explorer
- Prayer Leader
- Activity Leader

Suggestions for additional music

- I will worship
- Take this moment

ALL-SORTS WORSHIP

Service

Welcome *As people arrive, tell them you have just discovered that there's going to be a big party and you've got to get the food ready: can they help you find the ingredients which are stored all round the church?*

Introduction Have you found everything we need to make the party food?

Encourage people to bring all the provisions forward and place them on the table at the front of the church.

Our story today begins with a woman in a panic. Her name is Martha and she's the older sister of Mary and Lazarus. She's just heard that Jesus is coming to dinner, along with all his disciples! They'll all need feeding, so that's why she's been rushing around getting extra food out of storage. Let's find out what happens.

If you are playing Martha, put on your tunic and head-cloth now.

Storytelling *Gather everyone around the table and ask for some volunteers to help get the food ready.*

I've got such a lot to do! Jesus has just arrived. There's all this food to prepare and I'm in charge of the kitchen. First things first: clean hands.

Martha washes her hands and passes the bowl and towel around to her helpers.

Now, there are lots of jobs that need doing. Jesus and his friends are hungry and I don't want to keep them waiting. We need my sister Mary in here, too. *(calling)* Mary! MARY!

Wait briefly for an answer, then shake your head. Hand around the food and – as if instructing kitchen servants – explain what needs peeling, what needs chopping, what needs laying out on plates, etc.

I hope there's going to be enough food! Jesus is a wonderful friend and I want to make a special effort for him.

Give more instructions concerning food preparation.

Have any of you seen Mary? She's supposed to be helping.

Invite responses.

Excuse me – I'm going to find my little sister and get her to give us a hand.

Leave for a moment and return, looking furious.

I don't believe it! She's just sitting there, listening to Jesus! He's talking to his friends and followers as usual, telling stories and teaching, but that's men's talk – what does my sister think she's doing? We need her in here!

Continue chopping, angrily.

This is no good: I'll get Jesus to make her help. She'll listen to him. It's not fair that she should leave all this food for me to organise.

Storm off. The volunteers continue preparing the food until you return.

Guess what? He won't tell her to come and help! He said, 'Mary has chosen the better part, which will not be taken away from her.' 'The better part'?! No one would get any dinner if *I* chose 'the better part'! What about feeding people, looking after them, making them feel welcome? Isn't that important?

Continue chopping, even more angrily. Gradually slow down and become thoughtful.

Although . . . he did seem to care about what I have to deal with. He looked at me really kindly and said, 'Martha, Martha, you are worried and distracted by many things.' He could tell I was stressed. *(pause)* He always seems to know how I'm feeling. Then he said, 'There is need of only one thing,' and he talked about Mary choosing 'the better part'.

Pause in thought.

It makes me wonder whether all this panicking over a perfect feast might not be the most important thing. Jesus is here, now, in my house, and I want to spend time with him. I'm starting to think that my sister has got the right idea.

Pause.

Do you know what? I think we should leave all this. Let's go and hear what Jesus has to say.

You and your volunteers leave the table and exit. Invite everyone to return to their seats.

Music To be in your presence ('My desire')

During the hymn, move the table of food to the back of the church, ready for the post-service feast.

Exploring Poor Martha! When we think of her rushing around in the kitchen and Mary sitting quietly with Jesus, we can all sympathise with her cry of 'It's not fair!' Sometimes we feel like Martha, too: many of us know what it's like to be so busy that we haven't got time to think. We might wish that in our story, Jesus had sent Mary into the kitchen to help, or had rolled up his sleeves and given Martha a hand himself. However, he sympathised with Martha, yet defended Mary's right to sit and listen to him: he said, 'Martha, Martha, you are worried and distracted by many things; there is need of only one thing. Mary has chosen the better part, which will not be taken away from her.' What can we learn from Jesus' response to Martha and Mary?

Jesus stood up for Mary because she had chosen to listen to him and learn from his teaching. This was not usual for a woman: Martha described Jesus' discussion as 'men's talk' because religious teaching in the synagogue took place in a room where only men were allowed. The proper place for women in a traditional Jewish household was where Martha busied herself: in the kitchen, preparing the food for the guests. However, Jesus didn't tell Mary to take her 'proper place' in the kitchen, and by saying that she had chosen 'the better part', he even recommended that Martha join her sister. Furthermore, he said that Mary's choice would 'not be taken away from her', either by her sister or by the male disciples, who may have been tut-tutting about the woman who dared to sit with them. This story shows that Jesus ignored the restrictions that his society placed on women and treated Mary and Martha as human beings with spiritual needs. In listening to him, both Mary and his male disciples chose 'the better part.'

They chose the better part and so should we. It's time to stop rushing around like Martha. However much we have to do and however we are restricted by other people's expectations of us, we should make time to sit and listen to Jesus, as Mary did.

Prayer action

For our prayers today, we will lay aside our worries and distractions for a time. Whatever is bothering you and whatever you have got to do today, draw it or write it down on one of these pieces of paper.

Pause while everyone does this.

Now we will leave these worries and distractions in God's hands by placing them in this collection plate. Like Martha's chores, they won't go away, but for now we will leave them with God.

Pass round the collection plate and place it on the altar.

Gentle Lord,
take these worries and distractions from us
and give us Time Out with you.
Amen.

Activity Now we have a chance to 'choose the better part' ourselves. Around the church are different activities to help us all sit still and listen to God. Take your time and make the most of this opportunity.

Allow plenty of time for everyone to explore the different listening stations.

Music Be the centre of my life

Conclusion Loving Lord,
as we go out into the world
to be busy Marthas who get things done,
may we never forget to be Marys
who choose to spend time with you.
Amen.

Give notices, announce the next all-age service and invite everyone to the feast that Martha and the volunteers prepared earlier.

Proper 12

Teach us how to pray

Theme	The Lord's Prayer; how to pray
Scripture	Luke 11:1-13

Running order	Total: 50 minutes
Welcome	Writing in the book of prayers *(9 minutes)*
Introduction	Opening the theme
Storytelling 1	Reading Luke 11:2-4 *(1 minute)*
Activity	Multisensory exploration of the Lord's Prayer *(10 minutes)*
Music	Our Father (Caribbean) *(5 minutes)*
Storytelling 2	Sketch – the persistent friend *(5 minutes)*
Music	Seek ye first the kingdom of God *(5 minutes)*
Exploring	How should we pray? *(5 minutes)*
Prayer action	Lucky-dip prayers *(5 minutes)*
Music	Lord Jesus Christ *(5 minutes)*
Conclusion	Closing prayer and invitation

Resources

- Your church's book for prayer requests. If you don't already use a book like this, buy an attractively bound notebook and a good pen. Use it in the service and then leave it out in your church, perhaps by the visitors' book or votive candles
- Several pens
- Music and words
- Laptop, projector, screen and speakers
- A recording of Nat King Cole singing 'Let There Be Love' (search iTunes and YouTube)
- A short slideshow of visual aids (*see appendix*)
- Matches and tapers
- A cloth bag (or two, if you have a large congregation)
- Lots of plain ping-pong balls, ideally enough for one each (*see appendix*)
- A signpost (*see appendix*)
- A microphone/radio mic for Sam
- Hide the following props around the church:
    - a box of votive candles, enough for one each
    - a plate or two of pitta bread pieces
    - some holding crosses
    - a large heart, cut out of red card

Leaders

Minimum: 2
- Leader
- *Sam*

Optimum: 7
- Leader (*Introduction and Conclusion*)
- Storyteller
- *Sam*, unseen and amplified
- Music Leader
- Explorer
- Activity Leader
- Prayer Leader

Suggestions for additional music

- Abba, Father, let me be
- Father God, I wonder
- Lord of all hopefulness

Service

Welcome — *As people arrive, invite them to write in your church's book of prayers.*

Introduction — Today we will be thinking about how to pray. Even Jesus' own disciples needed help: they saw that Jesus regularly went off by himself to pray, and they wanted to learn how to talk to God. They said, 'Lord, teach us to pray.' Here is Jesus' answer.

Storytelling 1 — *Read Luke 11:2-4.*

Activity — Jesus taught his disciples the prayer we call the Lord's Prayer. It appears in two Gospels, and we have just heard the shorter version. Whether we know the Lord's Prayer off by heart, or whether we've never heard it before, it will help us to take a fresh look at what this prayer is saying.

Display the prayer from Luke 11:2-4 on the screen.

First of all, we are to call God 'Father' – except the Bible uses the word 'Abba', which means 'Daddy'. We are not talking to a strict Victorian father figure when we pray: we are like little children calling, 'Daddy!' Look at how a toddler holds out his arms for his daddy to pick him up:

Hold your arms out in an open, upwards-facing gesture.

This is how we call on God. We say, 'Daddy!'

Encourage everyone to hold out their arms in the same gesture.

Then we say, 'Hallowed be your name.' This means we worship and honour everything about God. In church, we often use candlelight in our worship: can anyone find lots of candles for us all to light?

Encourage volunteers to locate the box of votive candles and hand them out. Light a few with tapers and then pass the light around.

This candlelight, like a halo, is a reminder of God's holiness: hallowed be his name.

Then we say to God, 'Your kingdom come.' God's kingdom has been described as 'God's way of doing things',[51] and that way is love. Somewhere in the church today there is a big red heart. When you've found it, we'll hear a song that reminds us what God's kingdom is all about.

Encourage volunteers to locate the heart. Hold it up as you listen to Nat King Cole singing 'Let There Be Love'.

The aim of God's kingdom is simply this: let there be love.

Ask people to blow out their candles.

Then the Lord's Prayer moves on to a request: 'Give us each our daily bread.' Can you find some bread in church for us all to share?

Encourage volunteers to find and distribute the bread so that everyone has some to eat.

This part of the Lord's Prayer is about what we need. Bread is a staple food, one of life's essentials, and we pray that we will have enough for today: not more than we can eat, and not a hoard that will last us a month, but simply *enough*. It is a prayer not only for bread, but for all our essential needs.

Then we pray, 'Forgive us our sins.' None of us is perfect, and we are all capable of hurting people, getting things wrong and messing things up. We need forgiveness so that we can leave behind the weight of sin, sorrow and regret, and live. The cross reminds us that Jesus died to cancel out all our sins and give us life.

Pass round the holding crosses.

---

51. Keith White in *Through the eyes of a child*, ed. Anne Richards and Peter Privett, Church House Publishing, 2009, p.48

Hold these smooth crosses in your hands and remember that because of Jesus' sacrifice on the cross, we are forgiven. We have found new and everlasting life.

Pause while the crosses are handed around.

Then there is a reminder that we may offer forgiveness as well as receive it. 'Forgive us our sins, for we ourselves forgive everyone indebted to us.' It's hard to forgive someone who has hurt your feelings, or who has borrowed something without paying you back, or who has said something unkind about you, but just as we need forgiveness, the people who have wronged us need forgiving, too. When we share the Peace in church, it's a reminder that we need to love and forgive each other. Let's share the Peace together now by shaking hands.

Encourage everyone to move around the church, shaking hands with each other.

Then there is a closing prayer: 'Do not bring us to the time of trial.' In the longer version of the Lord's Prayer, this is 'Lead us not into temptation, and deliver us from evil.'

Show the signpost.

We know that there may be trouble ahead for any of us: this prayer asks for God's help. We pray both that bad things won't happen to us, and that we ourselves won't make bad choices.

So this is the Lord's Prayer. Who would like to help me show each of its parts?

Invite your volunteers forward – you will need a minimum of four. They will need to hold the candle, heart, bread, holding cross and signpost. One should have free hands to share the Peace with another volunteer, and to demonstrate the Abba gesture: it would be lovely if this volunteer could be a father with a small child.

We call on God as Abba, Daddy.

A volunteer holds out his arms in the praise gesture (or cuddles his child).

God is hallowed.

A volunteer holds up the lighted candle.

We pray for his kingdom to come.

A volunteer holds up the heart.

We ask for our daily bread

A volunteer holds up the bread.

and for our sins to be forgiven.

A volunteer holds up a holding cross.

We forgive each other.

Two volunteers shake hands.

Finally, we pray that God will keep us safe.

A volunteer holds up the sign post.

Amen.

Music   Our Father (Caribbean)

Storytelling 2   After Jesus taught his friends the Lord's Prayer, he went on to talk to them –

There is a loud knocking at the door.[52]

He went on to talk to them about how God answers –

There is an even louder knocking at the door.

Excuse me a moment.

Go to the door and call out.

Who is it? What do you want?

---

52. Sam will be heard but not seen. He/she could be in the vestry or a side chapel, with a microphone.

Sam	*(unseen, amplified)* It's your mate, Sam! Can you lend us some tea and biscuits? An old school friend has just turned up, and I haven't got anything in the house!
Storyteller	I can't – I'm in the middle of a service here! Everybody's sitting here waiting for me to tell them what Jesus said about prayer. I can't go running around looking for tea bags! *(returning to the congregation)* Now, where was I? Ah yes – Jesus taught his friends the Lord's Prayer, then he went on to talk to them about how God answers prayer. He –

There is a loud, prolonged knocking at the door.

I think I'm going to have to deal with this. Excuse me. *(calling, as you walk off)* Coming! I should have some biscuits here somewhere . . .

Music — Seek ye first the kingdom of God

Exploring — When Jesus talked about how to pray, he used the example we have just seen: a friend keeps knocking at your door and won't go away. Even if you're busy, even if it's very late at night, you eventually give them what they're asking for. Their persistence pays off. This story tells us two very important things about prayer. Firstly, we have to keep trying, we have to keep knocking on God's door; secondly, God will answer our prayers. The answer may not come straight away, and it may not come in the way we expect, but our loving Father will respond.

We began our service with the disciples' request: 'Lord, teach us to pray.' So what did Jesus teach them – and us?

Show the picture of the toddler in his/her dad's arms with the title, 'CHILDLIKE'.

We should pray like little children talking to our loving Father.

Pause for a moment, then show the words of the prayer from Luke 11:2-4 with the title, 'SIMPLE'.

We should pray simply.

PROPER 12

Pause for a moment, then show the picture of the hand knocking on the door with the title, 'PERSISTENT'.

We should keep praying and never give up.

Pause for a moment, then show the words from Luke 11:9.

Jesus said that God will answer our prayers: 'Ask, and it will be given to you; search, and you will find; knock, and the door will be opened for you.'

Prayer action Now that we have thought about how to pray, our prayers today will be a simple lucky dip. In this bag are lots of ping-pong balls. Each ball has a word on it to suggest a prayer. If you pick out a ball marked 'THANK YOU', thank God for something good in your life. If you pick out a ball marked 'PLEASE', yours will be an asking prayer: bring before God anyone who is in need. If your ball says 'SORRY', remember something that was your fault and ask God to forgive you. Finally, if your ball says 'WOW!', think of something amazing that God has done, and pray in awe and wonder. Let us pray.

Take a ball yourself and then pass the bag around the congregation. Once everyone has a ball, pause for a short time.

Almighty God, your glory wows us into silence.

Pause.

We are sorry for the times we have let you down; may you forgive us.

Pause.

Please walk alongside those in need; may you give them strength.

Pause.

For all your great goodness, we say,
'Thank you, thank you, thank you, Lord.'
Amen.

Music Lord Jesus Christ

Conclusion For our closing prayer, we will say together the Lord's Prayer in the form we know best.

Display the words on the screen.[53]

All **Our Father in heaven,
hallowed be your name.
Your kingdom come,
your will be done,
on earth as in heaven.
Give us today our daily bread.
Forgive us our sins,
as we forgive those who sin against us.
Lead us not into temptation,
but deliver us from evil.
For the kingdom,
the power and the glory are yours.
Now and for ever.
Amen.**

Give notices, announce the next all-age service and invite everyone to the feast.

---

53. Use the modern version or whichever version is used in your church.

Proper 13

Lots and lots

Theme	Turning away from greed and towards God
Scripture	Psalm 107:1-9; Luke 12:13-21

Running order	Total: 50 minutes
Welcome	A slideshow of glossy images of consumer goods (*5 minutes*)
Introduction	Opening the theme
Storytelling	Visual retelling of the parable of the rich fool (*5 minutes*)
Music	Firmly I believe and truly (*5 minutes*)
Activity	'The conveyor belt' – remembering all the prizes (*20 minutes*)
Music	Love is his word (*5 minutes*)
Exploring	Does God absorb our attention? (*5 minutes*)
Prayer action	Meditation montage (*5 minutes*)
Conclusion	Closing prayer and invitation

Resources

- Laptop, projector, screen and speakers
- A slideshow of glossy images of consumer goods *(see appendix)*
- A meditation montage based on Psalm 107 *(see appendix)*
- Boxes of corn *(see appendix)*
- A sheet
- A deck chair with cushions
- A fancy drink (e.g. with a curly straw and a little umbrella)
- A plate with a cake
- Music and words
- Prizes for 'The conveyor belt' game *(see appendix)*
- A small screen with a chair in front of it
- Two tables: one behind the screen and one next to it
- A kitchen timer
- *(Optional)* Music to play during the game

Leaders

Minimum: 4
- Leader
- *Rich man*
- Activity helpers x 2

Optimum: 9
- Leader *(Introduction and Conclusion)*
- Storyteller
- *Rich man*
- Activity Leaders x 3
- Music Leader
- Explorer
- Prayer Leader

Suggestions for additional music

- Be the centre of my life
- Take my life, and let it be

Service

Welcome — *As people arrive, show the slideshow of glossy images of consumer goods.*

Introduction — I'm sure we all saw something we'd like in our opening slideshow. What caught your eye?

Invite responses.

Today we will be thinking about all the stuff we have and all the stuff we wish we could afford. Jesus had something to say about this. He was talking to a crowd when someone shouted, 'Teacher! Tell my brother to divide the family inheritance with me.' This was someone who wanted his fair share of the family fortune: no doubt there had been arguments and the brothers had fallen out over the money. The man who wanted Jesus to intervene had clearly reached the end of his tether. Jesus didn't get involved in that particular family's case: instead, he told a story.

Storytelling — Once upon a time there was a rich man.

The rich man enters.

His land produced crops in abundance.

The rich man spreads out all the boxes of corn around him.

He thought to himself, 'Where am I going to put all this grain? I haven't got enough room in my barns!' Then he had an idea. 'I know! I'll pull down my old barns and build some new, super-size barns! Then I can store all my grain and all my possessions, too!' He imagined the luxury barns he would build.

Invite volunteers to spread out a large sheet like a roof. The rich man piles up all the boxes of corn underneath it.

The rich man said, 'Then I can say to myself, "You've got plenty of goods stored up for many years to come: relax, eat, drink and be happy!"'

Ask your volunteers to carry on a cushioned chair, a fancy drink and a plate with a cake. The rich man reclines, eats and drinks.

But God said, 'You fool!

The rich man sits bolt upright.

Tonight you're going to die. Then who will your possessions belong to?' The rich man didn't answer.

The rich man runs off down the aisle, looking scared.

Music Firmly I believe and truly

Activity Jesus spelled out the moral of his story: 'Take care! Be on your guard against all kinds of greed; for one's life does not consist in the abundance of possessions.' Our activity today is going to help us explore what Jesus meant.

Who remembers the old TV show called *The Generation Game*? *(Invite a show of hands.)* It was a very popular game show in which families took on different challenges to compete for a prize. The final challenge was 'The conveyor belt': the contestant watched lots of prizes moving along a conveyor belt, then had to remember as many items as possible. There was one prize that was always on the conveyor belt: who can remember what it was?

Elicit the response, 'Cuddly toy!'

Today I need a volunteer to try and remember all the prizes on our own version of the conveyor belt.

Bring a volunteer forward. Sit him/her in front of the screen, behind which are your two helpers and all the prizes.

(To the volunteer.) Now, lots of different things are going to pass in front of you and you've got to remember as many as possible. I'm afraid you won't be able to take home all the prizes you name – but you will win the

cuddly toy, if you remember it! *(To the congregation.)* In the original show, the audience helped by shouting things out, so you all need to try and remember the prizes you see.

If using music, start it now. Call out the prizes as they are carried in front of the volunteer.

Now, you have one minute to see what you can remember.

Start the timer and as the volunteer lists the prizes, your helpers bring them out from behind the screen and pile them on the table. Encourage the congregation to shout out prizes, too. At the end of the time, the helpers show any prizes that are left. Applaud the volunteer and give him/her the cuddly toy.

Didn't she/he do well?

Music Love is his word

Exploring We began today's service with Jesus' story about a greedy farmer. The moral was, 'Take care! Be on your guard against all kinds of greed; for one's life does not consist in the abundance of possessions.' Now, the man in our story wouldn't have thought of himself as greedy: his bumper crop was grown on his own land and was the result of his own hard work. He had earned his riches. However, Jesus wasn't talking simply about his wealth, but his attitude towards it. His mind was full of the huge piles of possessions he would store away for himself, and he daydreamed about a long, happy life in which he would have nothing to do but eat, drink and relax. He had no thought for anything or anyone else. God brought him back to reality by reminding him that he wouldn't live for ever, and that he couldn't take his possessions with him when he died.

Now think back to 'The conveyor belt' game. We were completely focused on the prizes. We tried to find ways of remembering them, of holding on to them with our minds. Then, during the one-minute challenge, our brains were busy trying to retrieve as many prizes as possible. This was only a game, but it might make us wonder about how much attention we give to the stuff we own and the stuff we want.

Let's remember the pictures we saw at the beginning of the service. Do we tend to focus on the thought of something new that we've always wanted? Are we constantly looking to upgrade our pieces of technology? Jesus was challenging his listeners, and us, to think about how much of our attention is absorbed by our possessions. His message is insistent: 'one's life does not consist in the abundance of possessions' – in other words, there is more to life than stuff. He said of the rich man in his story, 'So it is with those who store up treasures for themselves but are not rich towards God.' The man was so focused on hoarding his wealth that he neglected the riches of a relationship with God. An existence that is focused on God is rich because it is rooted in love and full of life – and it leads to eternal life.

Perhaps the man in the crowd, who first asked Jesus the question about his inheritance, went away wondering whether he really wanted to sacrifice his relationship with his brother for the sake of money. It is good for all of us to reconsider our attitude to the stuff we own and the stuff we want: for now, we will forget it all and let God absorb our attention.

Prayer action *Play the meditation montage based on Psalm 107.*

Conclusion God of Love,
as we go out into the world,
may we seek the riches of a relationship with you,
in Jesus' name.
Amen.

Give notices, announce the next all-age service and invite everyone to the feast.

Proper 14

Are you ready?

Theme	Being ready to accept God's invitation to his kingdom
Scripture	Psalm 50:1-8, 23; Luke 12:32-40

Running order	Total: 50 minutes
Welcome	Lighting candles and lanterns *(5 minutes)*
Introduction	Opening the theme
Storytelling	Sketch – Who's ready? *(5 minutes)*
Music	I'm accepted, I'm forgiven *(5 minutes)*
Activity	Decision-making challenge: in or out? *(20 minutes)*
Exploring	How can we be ready? Visual exploration *(5 minutes)*
Prayer action	After-dinner mints – thanksgiving prayer *(5 minutes)*
Music	One more step along the world I go *(5 minutes)*
Conclusion	Closing prayer and invitation

Resources

- Candles and lanterns
- Matches and tapers
- Two sleeping bags
- A torch
- A coat and wellies for Camper 1
- A hand bell
- Music and words
- A large square and a large circle, marked out on the floor in masking tape
- Lots of simple party food on plates
- Boxes of after-dinner mints – enough for everyone to have one chocolate each (Don't buy supermarket own-brand mints unless they come with little envelopes)
- In every pew or row of seats:
    - little pieces of card that are the same size as the mints
    - pens and pencils

Leaders

Minimum: 3

- Leader
- Cast x 2

Optimum: 7

- Leader (*Introduction and Conclusion*)
- Cast x 2:
    Camper 1, wearing Cub/Scout/Brownie/Guide uniform
    Camper 2, wearing pyjamas
- Music Leader
- Activity Leader
- Explorer
- Prayer Leader

Suggestions for additional music

- There's a place where the streets shine
- Have faith in God, my heart

Service

Welcome *As people arrive, invite them to light candles and lanterns as a sign of their prayer.*

Introduction Our service today is all about being ready for God. Jesus promised his disciples that one day he would come back to earth. On that day, he will take charge of everything: he will judge who has done right and who has done wrong, and he will establish God's kingdom for ever. Jesus said to his disciples, 'Make sure you're ready for me!' He told a story to make his point clear, and today we're going to tell an updated version.

Storytelling *Two Cubs/Scouts/Brownies/Guides are in sleeping bags at the front of church.*

Camper 1	Wake up! Wake up!
Camper 2	What is it?
Camper 1	Tonight's the night we're having a midnight feast!
Camper 2	I'm not sure it's tonight.
Camper 1	I think it is and I want to be ready, just in case.
Camper 2	I'm tired.
Camper 1	Come on, get up! We've got to get ready! I need my coat and my boots. *(puts coat and boots on, then starts to search)* Where's my torch? Have you seen my torch?
Camper 2	I'm sleepy.
Camper 1	Ah – here it is. *(turns on torch)* I'm all ready! Come on, you'll miss the midnight feast!
Camper 2	I won't – I think it's tomorrow night.

The Leader rings a bell.

Leader	*(voice off)* Wake up! Wake up! The midnight feast is starting! Come and get it!
Camper 1	It's right now! I'm off!
Camper 2	But I'm not ready! I don't want to be left out!

The first camper leaves.

Don't go without me!

Music I'm accepted, I'm forgiven

Activity In our story, the person who wasn't ready ended up missing out on the feast. Jesus used a story like this to explain what will happen when his kingdom comes at the end of time: anyone who isn't ready for God will be left out and left behind. We all know what a horrible feeling that is. It hurts if we miss a party or if we are left out of a treat. Jesus used this experience to describe what it's like being separated from God.

However, the other person in our story was ready and so was able to join in the feast. We know how good it feels to be included in a treat and to be part of the fun. Jesus used this experience to describe what it's like being close to God and part of his kingdom.

So Jesus' story showed what it's like to be either close to God or separated from him. This closeness to God is also known as heaven, or belonging to his kingdom; separation from God has been called hell. However, we don't end up in one situation or the other by accident or as a result of harsh judgement: we choose whether we join in God's feast or exclude ourselves from it. The most important thing is that God *wants* us all to join in: Jesus said, 'It is your Father's good pleasure to give you the kingdom.'

Our activity today will help us explore this idea. First of all, I need lots of volunteers.

Bring your volunteers forward.

On the floor you can see that there's a big square and a big circle. You've got to choose which one you want to stand in. All I can tell you is that one of these places is 'In' and the other is 'Out' – but you've got to decide for yourselves which is which. Now choose where you'd like to go.

Let your volunteers dither for a moment.

Now I'm going to make your choice a bit clearer. Here's a question for you: if someone hurts you, should you get your own back? If you think the answer is yes, you should get your own back, then stand in the square. If you think the answer is no, getting your own back is wrong, then stand in the circle.

The volunteers move.

And just in case anyone still hasn't decided, I can tell you that there will be a feast for anyone who is in the circle. Have you all definitely decided where you'd like to be?

Bring in party food for everyone in the circle to share.

If anyone else would like to come and join the feast, feel free!

Encourage the rest of the congregation to come and share the feast.

Exploring So what have we learned today about being ready for God's kingdom?

Bring forward Camper 1.

Our well-prepared camper reminds us to be ready by having faith. Faith shines in the darkness like a torch, lighting our way to God.

Camper 1 turns on the torch.

Our activity reminded us that we need to make a choice: are we going to do things God's way, or not?

Indicate the circle and the square.

Finally, our feast reminded us that God wants everyone to join in, and it's never too late to choose his way.

Prayer action Our prayers today will help us to choose God's way. In these words from Psalm 50, God calls us to have thankful hearts:

PROPER 14

> Those who bring thanksgiving as their sacrifice honour me;
> to those who go the right way I will show the salvation of God.

Today we will thank God for the good things in our lives. Please write or draw your thanksgiving prayers on these little pieces of paper.

Allow time for people to do so.

By thanking God, we honour him and show that we are doing things his way – we are getting ready to enter his kingdom. Please exchange your thanksgiving prayer for a sweet treat, to remind you that God wants us all to join him at the feast.

Demonstrate by taking out a little after-dinner mint envelope, placing your prayer in it and then eating the chocolate. Pass round the boxes of chocolates and encourage people to do the same.

Generous Father,
we thank you for all the good things you have given us here and now
and for the promise of eternal life hereafter.
Amen.

Music One more step along the world I go

Conclusion Heavenly King,
send us out into the world in faith,
ready to choose your way
and enter your kingdom.
Amen.

Give notices, announce the next all-age service and invite everyone to finish the feast.

Proper 15

'Sit down, you're rocking the boat!'

Theme	When Jesus brings upheaval, not peace
Scripture	Luke 12:49-56

Running order	Total: 50 minutes
Welcome	Listening to 'Sit Down, You're Rockin' The Boat' *(5 minutes)*
Introduction	Opening the theme
Activity	Dressing the Roman soldier and the Messiah *(10 minutes)*
Storytelling	Interactive performance of Jesus' challenging words: Luke 12:49-53 *(5 minutes)*
Music	O Lord, all the world belongs to you *(5 minutes)*
Exploring	Does Jesus bring peace on earth? Visual and interactive exploration *(15 minutes)*
Prayer action	Sit down, stand up – active prayer *(5 minutes)*
Music	Stand up, stand up for Jesus (words by Jean Holloway*) *(5 minutes)*
Conclusion	Closing prayer and invitation

* In *Anglican Hymns Old and New* (Kevin Mayhew, 2008)

Resources

- A recording of 'Sit Down, You're Rockin' The Boat' from *Guys and Dolls*, (available on YouTube and from iTunes)
- Equipment to play it on
- A Roman soldier costume *(see appendix)*
- A white robe
- Promises about the Messiah *(see appendix)*
- A lightweight table
- Lots of copper coins or foreign coins
- *(Optional)* An old-fashioned set of balancing scales
- Music and words
- Information stations about the following people: *(see appendix)*
  – Martin Luther King, Jr
  – Dietrich Bonhoeffer
  – Óscar Romero
  – Sheila Cassidy
  – Sara Miles

Leaders

Minimum: 2
- Leader
- *Jesus*

Optimum: 7
- Leader *(Introduction and Conclusion)*
- Activity Leader
- Storyteller
- *Jesus* (a confident actor)
- Music Leader
- Explorer
- Prayer Leader

Suggestions for additional music

- Fight the good fight
- Inspired by love and anger

Service

Welcome — *As people arrive, play a recording of 'Sit Down, You're Rockin' The Boat'.*

Introduction — Our opening song has introduced today's theme for us. If someone tells you not to rock the boat, they mean, 'Calm down, stop making a fuss, don't cause trouble, don't make a scene.' In Jesus' time, it was particularly important not to rock the boat. Let's find out why.

Activity — When Jesus lived in Galilee, the Romans were in charge: the Roman Empire reached all around the Mediterranean. This was a time of relative peace and stability which has become known as the Roman Peace. However, this Peace required the Roman army to protect and defend it. Can I have a volunteer to be a Roman soldier?

Bring your volunteer forward.

All around the church there are clothes, armour and weapons for this Roman soldier: can anyone help me find them and kit him out?

Other volunteers find all the clothes, armour and weapons and help to dress the soldier.

This soldier is ready for anything. His job is to keep the Roman Peace. He won't stand for unruly crowds or upstarts challenging the people in power. If there is a riot, he'll protect himself with his shield. If he has to round up troublemakers, he'll threaten them with his sword. If he has to march prisoners to their execution, he'll need these good, strong sandals on his feet. He's ready to nail rebels and criminals to wooden crosses: he has big muscles and the right tools for the job. He'll do whatever it takes to keep the Roman Peace.

This soldier reminds us that the peace imposed by Rome was kept in place by violence and fear. However, the Jews were looking forward to a different kind of peace: the peace brought by God's Chosen One, his Messiah. Can I have my actor who's going to play Jesus?

Invite your actor forward.

Now, I need white robes for this Messiah, and a collection of the promises made about him. Can you help me find them?

Volunteers find the robes and the promises. Dress your actor in the robes.

Here are the Bible's promises about Jesus, the Messiah.

Invite your volunteers to read out the promises they have found.

Our Christmas cards often carry the words 'Peace on earth' because this was the promise of the Messiah. The Jews of Jesus' time must have longed for peace to come through God's love rather than the force of the Roman Empire, so they had great hopes that Jesus would make such peace a reality. This is the background of our story today.

Storytelling   Jesus was travelling around the towns and villages in Galilee, preaching, teaching and healing. Wherever he went, huge crowds followed him: people wanted to listen to him, be healed by him and see for themselves whether he really was the Messiah. The Bible tells us that the crowd in today's story 'gathered by the thousands, so that they trampled on one another'.[54] Let's set the scene: can you all stand up and make the sound of a big, unruly crowd? It's rather like a football crowd. Let's make some noise!

Encourage loud cheering and shouting.

In a moment, we will hear what Jesus has to say. I want you to keep this noise going until he raises his hand to speak, like this.

Encourage more shouting until you raise your hand to quieten the noise.

---

54. Luke 12:1.

Jesus will ask a question: he'll say, 'Do you think that I have come to bring peace to the earth?' At that point, we'll all shout, 'YES!' Let's practise. 'Do you think that I have come to bring peace to the earth?'

Encourage everyone to shout, 'YES!'

Now let's start cheering as Jesus gets ready to speak.

Encourage cheering and shouting as Jesus walks down the aisle. He raises his hand to speak.[55]

Jesus	I came to bring fire to the earth, and how I wish it were already kindled! I have a baptism with which to be baptised, and what stress I am under until it is completed! Do you think that I have come to bring peace to the earth?
All	YES!
Jesus	No, I tell you, but rather division! From now on, five in one household will be divided, three against two and two against three; they will be divided: father against son and son against father, mother against daughter and daughter against mother, mother-in-law against her daughter-in-law and daughter-in-law against mother-in-law.
Music	O Lord, all the world belongs to you
Exploring	Jesus' words are shocking, because we're used to thinking of him as 'gentle Jesus, meek and mild', the Prince of Peace. However, if we look at the evidence of what he said and did during his life, we can see that he was not always peaceful and he did bring division. He was someone who rocked the boat.
	First of all, Jesus caused the kind of family divisions he described when he said, 'They will be divided: father against son and son against father, mother against

---

[55]. Jesus' words are taken directly from Luke's Gospel (NRSV). You may prefer to use a different translation.

daughter.' Jesus divided the Jews who believed he was the Messiah from those who didn't believe, and this would certainly have caused rifts within families. Many fathers would have wept to see their sons turning their backs on the faith of their ancestors; many children would have been furious with their parents for denying that Jesus was the true Messiah. This kind of division was predicted by the old man who once met the baby Jesus in the Temple and who said: 'This child is destined for the falling and the rising of many in Israel, and to be a sign that will be opposed so that the inner thoughts of many will be revealed.'[56] When Jesus began his ministry, people had to decide what they really believed and whether they were for him or against him.

Then there were the crowds. We have made some noise ourselves this morning, but that's nothing compared to the noise of thousands of hot, excited, argumentative followers, all pushing and shoving through narrow streets to get a glimpse of Jesus. Local authorities became uneasy about this man who seemed to be stirring up trouble and starting riots.

Jesus also challenged the religious leaders who were responsible for keeping the peace among the Jewish people. In public, in front of a crowd of thousands, he called them hypocrites![57] Even worse, he caused a scene in the Temple itself in Jerusalem, when he found people treating it like a market place.

Lay out the table with the coins on it.

This is what he did.

Jesus storms down the aisle, throws over the table and shouts.

Jesus   My house shall be a house of prayer
         but you have made it a den of robbers![58]

---

56. Luke 2:34-35.
57. Luke 12:1.
58. Luke 19:46

Explorer　For the Jewish leaders, Jesus was trouble with a capital T. For the Roman governor, he was responsible for disturbing the peace. No wonder these people joined forces to get rid of him!

Jesus is still rocking the boat today. In his name, Christians all over the world stand up for what they believe by challenging powerful people and disrupting the way things are. Around the church we have information about some brave and inspiring individuals: let's take some time to learn more about them.

Allow plenty of time for people to visit the information stations about Martin Luther King Jr, Dietrich Bonhoeffer, Óscar Romero, Sheila Cassidy and Sara Miles.

Prayer action　We begin our prayers today by sitting down.

Everybody sits, including you.

As we sit, we think about those who have worked to change the world in Jesus' name, and we ask God what needs to change in our society today.

Pause.

We remember before God all the feelings, pressures and practical concerns that persuade people to sit down and stop rocking the boat.

Pause.

Now we will stand up.

Everybody stands.

We remember those who have dared to stand up and rock the boat, and we pray for the courage to stand up for what we believe.

Pause.

Jesus, may we stand up in your name
and work to make our world a better place.
Amen.

Music Stand up, stand up for Jesus (words by Jean Holloway)

Conclusion Almighty God,
send us out into the world
to run with perseverance the race marked out for us,
looking to your Son, Jesus Christ.
Amen.

Give notices, announce the next all-age service and invite everyone to the feast.

Proper 16

God unlimited

Theme — Don't underestimate God – be open to what he can do

Scripture — Jeremiah 1:4-10; Luke 13:10-17

Running order — Total: 50 minutes

Welcome	Unlimited prayer – making a paper chain *(10 minutes)*
Introduction	Opening the theme
Storytelling 1	Dialogue – Jeremiah's call *(5 minutes)*
Music	My God is so big *(5 minutes)*
Storytelling 2	Interactive sketch – Jesus heals the crippled woman *(5 minutes)*
Exploring/Activity	How does God work in our lives? The chocolate challenge *(15 minutes)*
Prayer action	'There's nothing that God cannot do' – gesture prayer *(5 minutes)*
Music	Give thanks *(5 minutes)*
Conclusion	Closing prayer and invitation

Resources

- Lots of strips of coloured paper for the paper chain
- Sticky tape
- Scissors
- Pens
- Two large signs: 'GASP' and 'CHEER'
- A king-size chocolate bar
- A tray
- A plate
- A knife and fork
- A hat
- A scarf
- Gloves
- A dice
- Music and words

Leaders

Minimum: 5

- Leader
- Cast x 4

Optimum: 9

- Leader *(Introduction and Conclusion)*
- Cast x 4:
  Leader of the synagogue, wearing a rich robe/cloak
  God/Jesus, wearing white
  Crippled woman, wearing a head-cloth and using a walking stick
  Jeremiah/Voice (in the congregation), wearing a head-cloth
- Music Leader
- Explorer
- Activity Leader
- Prayer Leader

Suggestions for additional music

- Amazing grace
- Come, Lord, to our souls come down

Service

Welcome — *As people arrive, invite them to write their prayers on strips of paper and add them to an ever-growing paper chain of prayers.*

Introduction — How long is our paper chain of prayers so far?

Invite volunteers to stretch it out.

If we had an infinite supply of paper, we could go on making this paper chain of prayers for ever, because there's no limit to the number of prayers we can offer. Today we will be thinking about the fact that God has no limits. We begin with the story of a reluctant prophet.

Bring forward Jeremiah.

His name is Jeremiah and he tried to limit God's plans for him by protesting that he wasn't cut out to be God's spokesman. However, God was having none of it, as we'll hear in the following conversation.[59]

Storytelling 1

God — Before I formed you in the womb I knew you,
and before you were born I consecrated you;
I appointed you a prophet to the nations.

Jeremiah — Ah, Lord God! Truly I do not know how to speak, for I am only a boy.

God — Do not say, 'I am only a boy';
for you shall go to all to whom I send you,
and you shall speak whatever I command you.
Do not be afraid of them,
for I am with you to deliver you.

God reaches out with two fingers and touches Jeremiah's mouth.

Now I have put my words in your mouth.
See, today I appoint you over nations and over kingdoms,

---

[59]. This dialogue is taken directly from Jeremiah (NRSV). You may prefer to use a different translation.

to pluck up and to pull down,
to destroy and to overthrow,
to build and to plant.

Music   My God is so big

Storytelling 2

Leader
: Our next story requires some participation on your part. Let's practise.

The Leader holds up the 'GASP' and 'CHEER' signs and encourages the congregation to respond.

Now wait for your moment to take part in our story.

Leader of the synagogue
: We are gathered in our synagogue on this holy Sabbath day to hear the word of God and listen to the teaching of his rabbis. Are we all seated? Men and boys here *(indicate the main body of the church)* and women and girls separate in the balcony above? *(indicate an area high up).* Then let us begin. Our rabbi today is Jesus of Nazareth.

Jesus
: Let me tell you a story. A man owned a vineyard and in it there was a fig tree. He went to see whether there was any fruit on it, but –

Crippled woman
: *(hobbling down the aisle)* Help me!

The service Leader holds up a sign – 'GASP' – and encourages the people to respond. The congregation gasps.

Leader of the synagogue
: Excuse me, madam, I think you're looking for the balcony.

Crippled woman
: *(ignoring him)* Jesus of Nazareth, help me!

Jesus
: Come here.

The service Leader holds up a sign: 'GASP'. The congregation gasps.

Leader of the synagogue
: Really!

Jesus lays his hands on the woman's back.

Jesus
: Woman, you are cured.

She stands straight up, stretches and jumps for joy.

Crippled woman
: I'm better! Praise the Lord! Thank you! God has made me better!

	The service Leader holds up a sign: 'CHEER'. The congregation cheers.
Voice	*(from the congregation)* Me next! Me next!
Leader of the synagogue	Now look, don't get excited. Today is the Sabbath, and the law is quite clear: DO NO WORK. There are six days when work ought to be done: if you need healing, come and be cured then, and not on the Sabbath.
Jesus	You hypocrite! Don't you untie your donkey and give it some water on the Sabbath? This woman, a daughter of Abraham, has been suffering for 18 years: shouldn't she be freed from her pain on the Sabbath?
	The service Leader holds up a sign: 'CHEER'. The congregation cheers.

Exploring/Activity

In both our stories, people tried to impose limits on God's power and restrict his ability to work in the world. Of course, they failed and God did exactly what he wanted to do.

Bring forward Jeremiah.

First of all, there was Jeremiah. God had big plans for him: he wanted a spokesman to tell the truth to his people, however hard it might be for them to hear. Jeremiah complained that he was too young; he objected that he was no good at public speaking and wouldn't know what to say. He clearly had no confidence in his own ability to do the job. Nevertheless, God promised his help and protection and gave Jeremiah the words he needed.

In the end, Jeremiah worked as God's spokesman for 40 years, preaching to his people at a time when they were under attack from powerful enemies. He constantly told them to turn back to their God, but they ignored his warnings. In the end, Jerusalem was invaded, the Temple was destroyed and God's people were deported. Jeremiah never stopped reminding them that God would not forget them and that he would make a new covenant, or promise, with them. That promise became a reality with the birth, death and resurrection of Jesus, hundreds of years later.

Bring forward the leader of the synagogue.

In our gospel story, the crippled woman ignored the rules of the synagogue by approaching Jesus directly in the men-only area. This was reason enough for the leader of the synagogue to turn her away, but then he tried to enforce God's own law about doing no work on the Sabbath. It's as if he expected God to work only during office hours! Jesus healed the woman anyway and argued passionately that this was the right thing to do.

Both of our stories are about God getting things done in spite of people's attempts to put obstacles in his way. Our activity today will help us think about this.

Hold up the big bar of chocolate.

Who would like to eat some of this chocolate?

Invite responses.

That's fine – but you can only eat some chocolate if you throw this dice and get a six. Then you've got to put on this hat, this scarf and these gloves. Oh, and by the way, you can only eat the chocolate with a knife and fork.

Invite volunteers forward to form a circle. Place the chocolate bar on a large plate on a tray with the knife and fork. Put the hat, scarf and gloves next to the tray. Pass the dice around and as soon as someone throws a six, they take on the chocolate challenge. Keep passing the dice as they do so: as soon as someone else throws a six, they take over. When you have played for long enough, stop the game and divide any remaining chocolate between the volunteers who haven't had any.

Even though our volunteers had to work with all those restrictions, such as the gloves and the cutlery, they still managed to eat some chocolate! They were quite determined to overcome all the obstacles in their way.

God works like this. He is determined to work in our lives, regardless of the obstacles we put in his way. He worked through Jeremiah in spite of his spokesman's reluctance and lack of confidence. Jesus healed the crippled woman in spite of strict religious laws, showing that God doesn't always obey his own rules! In our own lives, we can expect God to work through unexpected people – even us. He might work in surprising, challenging or inconvenient ways. We must never underestimate God's ability to get things done; instead, we need to be open to his limitless possibilities. Imagine what he could do!

Prayer action

Our prayer today is inspired by the words of our first hymn: 'My God is so big, so strong and so mighty, there's nothing that he cannot do'. We will use the following actions: let's practise them together now. First there is a 'stop' gesture.

Hold your hand out with a flat palm, as if stopping traffic. Encourage everyone to do the same.

Then there is a 'holding' gesture, as if you're trying to catch running water in your hands.

Cup both your hands together. Encourage everyone to do the same.

Finally there is the 'reaching' gesture, as if you're trying to stretch your arms around a very big tree trunk.

Stretch your arms out and encourage everyone to do the same.

Let us pray.

Almighty God,
forgive us for the times we have tried to stop you,

Make the 'stop' gesture.

through weakness, fear or the desire to control.

Make the 'holding' gesture.

Your power is so great that none can contain it;
your grace overflows like a river bursting its banks.

Make the 'reaching' gesture.

Your might is beyond anything we can encompass.
May our hearts and minds stay open
to your limitless possibilities.
In Jesus' name.
Amen.

Music Give thanks

Conclusion God unlimited,
send us out into the world with confidence,
trusting that with you, nothing will be impossible.
Amen.

Give notices, announce the next all-age service and invite everyone to the feast.

Proper 17

At the top table

Theme	Exalting ourselves and being humbled
Scripture	Jeremiah 2:4-13; Luke 14:1, 7-14

Running order	Total: 50 minutes
Welcome	Musical chairs *(5 minutes)*
Introduction	Opening the theme
Activity	Setting the scene for the banquet *(5 minutes)*
Storytelling	Interactive retelling of Luke 14:1, 7-14 *(5 minutes)*
Music	Brother, sister, let me serve you *(5 minutes)*
Exploring	How do we exalt ourselves and how can we humble ourselves? Collective brainstorm *(15 minutes)*
Prayer action	Visual and written prayers for the forgotten and unloved *(10 minutes)*
Music	He is exalted *(5 minutes)*
Conclusion	Closing prayer and invitation

Resources

- Some chairs set up for a game of musical chairs
- Music and equipment to play it on
- A long table at the front of the church with a number of chairs around it
- Shiny stars, each with sticky tack on the back:
  – a big gold star
  – two small gold stars
  – two small silver stars
- Music and words
- A long sheet of lining paper with the title, *'How do people exalt themselves?'*
- Marker pens
- A slideshow of two pictures:
  – a natural spring (search Google Images)
  – a leaky, patched bucket (criss-cross an old bucket or water butt with lines of duct tape, fill it with water, surround it with a puddle, then photograph it)
- Laptop, projector and screen
- Gold star stickers
- Prayer stations *(see appendix)*

Leaders

Minimum: 2

- Leader
- *Jesus*

Optimum: 7

- Leader *(Introduction and Conclusion)*
- Activity Leader
- Storyteller
- *Jesus*
- Music Leader
- Explorer
- Prayer Leader

Suggestions for additional music

- A new commandment I give unto you
- Christ's is the world

Service

Welcome *As people arrive, invite volunteers to take part in a game of musical chairs.*

Introduction In our game of musical chairs, everyone was scrambling for a seat. In our story today, Jesus has something to say about a rather more polite tussle over seats at a grand dinner. Let's set the scene.

Activity *Stand behind the long table at the front of the church.*

If you've eaten a meal at a wedding reception, you will have seen an arrangement like this: this is the top table, where the most important people sit. At a wedding, it's the bride and groom. If this was a royal feast, the king or queen would sit here. The most important place at this table is in the middle: let's give it a big gold star.

Stick a big gold star on the seat in the middle.

The second most important places are either side of this seat: let's give them smaller gold stars.

Stick smaller gold stars on the seats either side.

Next to them are the other important places: they get silver stars.

Stick silver stars on the two seats either side.

The people down at the ends are the least important – they don't get any stars at all. Now, can I have some volunteers to take their places at this feast? Where would you like to sit?

Encourage volunteers to come forward and choose their places. Hopefully there will be some competition for the best seats!

PROPER 17

Storytelling This is what happened at a dinner Jesus went to, hosted by the leader of the Pharisees – a very important man. Everyone wanted the best seat at *his* table. Jesus told them all a story.[60]

Jesus When you are invited by someone to a wedding banquet, do not sit down at the place of honour, in case someone more distinguished than you has been invited by your host; and the host who invited both of you may come and say to you, 'Give this person your place', and then in disgrace you would start to take the lowest place.

The Storyteller goes to the person in the big-gold-star seat.

Storyteller I'm sorry, but someone more important than you needs to sit here. Please could you move down to the end?

They move to a seat at the end of the table (find them another chair if necessary).

Jesus But when you are invited, go and sit down at the lowest place, so that when your host comes, he may say to you, 'Friend, move up higher'; then you will be honoured in the presence of all who sit at the table with you. For all who exalt themselves will be humbled, and those who humble themselves will be exalted.

Go to someone at the end of the table.

Storyteller Excuse me, you need to be in the place of honour, sir/madam. Would you like to sit here?

Seat them in the big-gold-star seat.

Jesus When you give a luncheon or a dinner, do not invite your friends or your brothers or your relatives or rich neighbours, in case they may invite you in return, and you would be repaid. But when you give a banquet, invite the poor, the crippled, the lame, and the blind. And you will be blessed, because they cannot repay you, for you will be repaid at the resurrection of the righteous.

Music Brother, sister, let me serve you

---

60. Jesus' words are taken directly from Luke's Gospel (NRSV). You may prefer to use a different translation.

Exploring

Jesus told his story to make his listeners realise that they shouldn't behave as if they were more important than anyone else.

Show the chair with the gold star.

You'll remember that everyone wanted the place of honour at the top table, and Jesus shocked his important host by telling him that he should invite the least valued people in his community: the poor, the crippled, the lame and the blind. The Pharisees definitely felt they were more important than such people, but Jesus told them, 'All who exalt themselves will be humbled, and those who humble themselves will be exalted.'

'Exalt' is a grand, old-fashioned word that doesn't sound as if it has anything to do with us – or does it? If I exalt myself, it means I make myself out to be more important, more special, than someone else. Today we're going to explore together some of the ways in which people can exalt themselves over others.

Show the roll of paper: How do people exalt themselves?

How do people exalt themselves? We are thinking about the everyday things people do to make themselves look important and make others feel small: for example, pushing in front of a queue, showing off about money or bullying someone.

Write down these three ideas.

Take some time now to come and add your own ideas to this big sheet of paper.

Encourage people to come forward and write or draw their ideas, then read some out.

We may try hard not to behave like this, but there is a second way in which we exalt ourselves, and that is by acting as if we can do better than God, as if we can manage without him. This is what happened in the

Old Testament, when God's people turned away from him and started worshipping false gods: the priests, lawmakers and rulers started doing things their own way, rather than God's way. Through his spokesman, Jeremiah, God said this:

My people have committed two evils:
they have forsaken me,
the fountain of living water,
and dug out cisterns for themselves,
cracked cisterns
that can hold no water.

God compared himself to a fountain of living water, like this.

Show the picture of the natural spring.

This image showed that God's people were getting above themselves. Instead of relying on his life-giving fountain, they tried to make their own cistern or reservoir to hold water. They didn't do a very good job: it was cracked and leaky, and the water in it quickly became stagnant.

Show the picture of the broken bucket.

This is what we end up with when we try to do something all by ourselves, without relying on God's help. A wise man once pointed out that, while we might talk about needing God's help, 'we seem to press on notwithstanding with our man-made programmes.'[61] We might abandon a church project because there is not enough money, or there aren't enough people to help, but when has a committee ever given up its agenda because God's Holy Spirit has failed to arrive?

We have looked today at the ways in which we exalt ourselves. Jesus' message was clear: instead of exalting yourselves, humble yourselves. If we consider the two areas we have been looking at, we will see that 'humbling ourselves' can mean two things.

---

61. John V. Taylor, *The Go-Between God*, SCM Press, 1972, p.5. I have paraphrased his argument here, as well as quoting from it.

Show the picture of the broken bucket.

Being humble means realising that we can't do without God – we can't manage things better without his help. It's no good trying to make our own cracked water containers.

Show the picture of the natural spring.

We need to keep turning back to God's spring for his living water.

Being humble also means realising that we're not more important or more special than other people.

Bring forward the seat with the gold star.

We don't deserve the best seat at the top table: we're *all* equally special to God.

Hand round the gold star stickers and invite everyone to take one.

Prayer action In our prayers, we usually bring before God those people who are closest to us. Today, as we remember that we are all special to God, we will pray for those we tend to forget, for those who are 'out of sight, out of mind' and for those who may have no one else to pray for them. Take your time to remember them now, by visiting the prayer stations around the church. In each place, please write or draw something as a sign of your prayer, or simply leave one of these gold stars, as a reminder that these people are just as special to God as we are.

Allow plenty of time for people to visit the stations.

Let us pray.

Lord of the overlooked, the unloved and the forgotten, we pray for these, your children.
Amen.

Music   He is exalted

Conclusion   Almighty God,
send us out into the world to walk humbly,
knowing we are all special in your sight.
May we exalt you rather than ourselves,
knowing we can do nothing without you.
Amen.

Give notices, announce the next all-age service and invite everyone to the feast, which should be laid out on the top table.

Proper 18

Giving our all

Theme	Following Jesus costs everything we have
Scripture	Psalm 139:1-7, 12-18; Luke 14:25-33

Running order	Total: 50 minutes
Welcome	Guesstimates – counting the cost *(5 minutes)*
Introduction	Opening the theme
Storytelling 1	Reading Psalm 139:1-7, 12-18 *(3 minutes)*
Activity	Making clay self-portraits *(15 minutes)*
Music	O God, you search me *(5 minutes)*
Storytelling 2	Jesus' words in Luke 14:25-33 *(2 minutes)*
Exploring	How much of ourselves are we willing to give? Creative exploration with clay *(10 minutes)*
Music	I am a new creation *(5 minutes)*
Prayer action	Clay models – offertory prayer *(5 minutes)*
Conclusion	Closing prayer and invitation

Resources

- A list of things to 'guesstimate', on paper or on a screen *(see appendix)*
- Pens
- A quantity of Model Magic, enough for everyone in the congregation to have some *(see appendix)*
- Music and words
- Clay tools or other things for making marks and indentations, such as plastic cutlery

Leaders

Minimum: 2

- Leader
- *Jesus*

Optimum: 7

- Leader *(Introduction and Conclusion)*
- Storyteller
- *Jesus*, wearing white
- Music Leader
- Explorer
- Activity Leader
- Prayer Leader

Suggestions for additional music

- All that I am
- I will offer up my life

Service

Welcome — *Display or hand out the list of 'guesstimates'. As people arrive, invite them to estimate the cost of undertaking the different projects.*

Introduction — 'My problem is, they just don't understand me!' This complaint is sometimes made by teenagers about their parents, or by married couples about each other. However, if we are lucky enough to be loved and understood by someone who knows everything about us, warts and all, we can sometimes feel a bit exposed. We might even complain, 'My problem is, they *do* understand me!' We will begin today's service with some words from the Bible that remind us how well God knows us. Listen out for those mixed feelings: it's wonderful and also unnerving to be so thoroughly understood.

Storytelling 1 — *Read Psalm 139:1–7, 12–18.*

Activity —
For it was you who formed my inward parts;
you knit me together in my mother's womb.
I praise you, for I am fearfully and wonderfully made.

These lovely words remind us that God knows us intimately: he is our creator who gave us form, life and breath. To help us think about how we are all the work of his hands, we are going to do something creative ourselves.

Show the Model Magic.

This is air-drying clay. Take a large handful and see if you can make a model of yourself. Make it as detailed as possible so that we can all recognise your self-portrait.

Allow plenty of time for people to make their clay self-portraits. You could invite people to show their finished pieces.

Music — O God, you search me

Storytelling 2

Leader — Our second story today is challenging. Jesus was surrounded by huge crowds wherever he went, and one day he turned to them and said this.[62]

Jesus — Whoever comes to me and does not hate father and mother, wife and children, brothers and sisters, yes, and even life itself, cannot be my disciple. Whoever does not carry the cross and follow me cannot be my disciple. For which of you, intending to build a tower, does not first sit down and estimate the cost, to see whether he has enough to complete it? Otherwise, when he has laid a foundation and is not able to finish, all who see it will begin to ridicule him, saying, 'This fellow began to build and was not able to finish.' Or what king, going out to wage war against another king, will not sit down first and consider whether he is able with ten thousand to oppose the one who comes against him with twenty thousand? If he cannot, then, while the other is still far away, he sends a delegation and asks for the terms of peace. So therefore, none of you can become my disciple if you do not give up all your possessions.

Exploring — At the start of our service, we made some 'guesstimates' of the sort Jesus described, when we planned how much it would cost us to keep a pet or go on a particular journey. This is a practical way of going about things, but Jesus turned it into a stark challenge: 'How much will it cost you to follow me?' he asked. 'How much are you willing to give up?' His words were deliberately shocking: when he said, 'If you don't hate your family, you can't be my disciple,' he made people ask themselves whether they could really love Jesus more than their own families. He was not telling them to hate others; rather, to love him more – to love him above all else. When he said, 'You can't be my disciple if you don't give up all your possessions,' he was telling those around him to love him more than everything they owned.

---

62. These words are taken directly from Luke's Gospel (NRSV). You may prefer to use a different translation.

This is a challenge for us, too. How much will our faith cost us? How much of ourselves are we willing to give? To help us think about this, we need to take our clay self-portraits that we have made with care, just as God lovingly made us.

Everyone holds their clay self-portraits, including you.

Jesus often told his disciples that following him was all about love – loving God and loving one other.[63] Let's represent that love in our lives: how much of your clay self-portrait can you spare to make a heart shape?

Pull off a little bit of clay from an inconspicuous part of your self-portrait and make it into a tiny heart shape. Encourage everyone else to do the same.

How big is the heart you've made?

Invite people to show their tiny heart shapes.

We've each given up just a little bit of ourselves and we've made these tiny, fragile hearts. However, Jesus' words in today's story show that he won't settle for just a bit of us: he wants us to give everything up for him – for love. Can you reshape all your clay into a heart shape?

Roll your own self-portrait into a ball and remake it into a heart shape, then encourage everyone else to do the same. Hold up your own heart shape.

This is still me, but I've been remade in the image of God's love – and this heart is big and strong. I'm going to make it look like me again by marking my self-portrait on this heart. Come and use these clay tools so that you can do the same.

Encourage everyone to make or mark their self-portrait on their clay heart, either in relief or with lines and indentations.

---

63. See Matthew 22:36-40; John 13:34, 35.

Music   I am a new creation

Prayer action   Jesus told people that they had to be prepared to give up everything if they were going to follow him. We might ask ourselves whether we are prepared for such a cost. For our prayers today, we will rest in God's presence and wonder how much of our lives we give to him. We will offer our new heart-shaped self-portraits as a sign of our prayer. In your own time, please come forward and lay your self-portrait on the altar.

Pause for a moment, then lay your own clay heart on the altar and encourage others to do the same.

O Lord, you have searched us and known us.
You know how much of ourselves
we are willing to give to you.
Hold us in love
and make us new.
Amen.

Conclusion   Loving Lord,
give us the courage to count the cost,
then follow you
and give you our all.
Amen.

Give notices, announce the next all-age service and invite everyone to the feast.

Proper 19

Lost and found

Theme	God wants us to repent and return to him
Scripture	Exodus 32:7-14; 1 Timothy 1:12-17; Luke 15:1-10

Running order	Total: 50 minutes
Welcome	Giant jigsaw puzzle *(5 minutes)*
Introduction	Opening the theme
Storytelling	The lost sheep and the lost coin – interactive retelling *(10 minutes)*
Music	I have a friend *(5 minutes)*
Activity	Treasure hunt *(10 minutes)*
Exploring	How do we get lost and found by God? *(10 minutes)*
Prayer action	Missing puzzle piece – takeaway prayer *(5 minutes)*
Music	Come on, let's get up and go *(5 minutes)*
Conclusion	Closing prayer and invitation

PROPER 19

Resources

- A jigsaw puzzle with very large pieces: a child's floor puzzle is best. Before using it, make sure it contains all the pieces, then remove one and hide it somewhere safe at the front of the church
- A number of sheep's ears for dressing up (see appendix)
- A shawl
- Ten x 10 pence pieces: hide one of them in a dark corner of the church where a volunteer will find it
- A broom
- A torch
- Music and words
- Chocolate coins, enough for at least one each, hidden in one area of the church (separate from the main congregation) or in the church grounds
- A bowl of miscellaneous pieces of jigsaw puzzles, enough for one each (use incomplete puzzles or jigsaws from charity shops)
- Four pictures, shown on screen or as large hard copies. Search Google Images:
  - a golden calf
  - hands or feet in shackles and chains
  - the Promised Land (any beautiful view of a distant landscape will do)
  - St Paul
- (Optional) Laptop, projector and screen

Leaders

Minimum: 1

- Leader

Optimum: 6

- Leader (Introduction and Conclusion)
- Storyteller, wearing a head-cloth and holding a staff or crook
- Music Leader
- Activity Leader
- Explorer
- Prayer Leader

Suggestions for additional music

- There's a wideness in God's mercy
- The gracious invitation stands

Service

Welcome *As people arrive, invite them to help fit together the giant jigsaw puzzle until there is only one piece left to find.*

Introduction Can anyone find our missing puzzle piece?

Invite responses.

All we need is that one last piece – where can it be? We'll have to find it later. Our theme today is 'Lost and found'. Jesus told two stories about losing something that is very precious, then finding it again.

Storytelling I'm going to need your help to tell both these stories. The first one is about a flock of sheep: who would like to be a sheep?

Bring your volunteers forward and give them all sheep's ears. You put on a head-cloth and hold a staff or crook.

I am your shepherd and you are my little flock. You're my livelihood: every single one of you is precious to me. Each day I lead you out into the countryside so you can find the best grass to eat.

Encourage your volunteers to spread out around the church.

I try to keep an eye on all of you, but sometimes one of you gets lost. Which one of you would like to be the lost sheep?

Choose one of your sheep and encourage him/her to find a really good hiding place somewhere around the church while you pretend to go to sleep. Remind him/her not to come when you call – you will have to find your lost sheep.

I've had a little nap in the shade, and now it's time to gather up my flock and take them home. Sheep! Where are you, sheep?

All your sheep return, apart from the one who is hiding. Count them.

Oh no! My little sheep is missing! You will all have to stay here while I go and find him/her!

Hunt for the missing sheep. If he/she is hard to find, encourage the congregation to shout out 'Warmer!' or 'Colder!' to help you. When you find the sheep, encourage everyone to cheer.

Hooray! I've found my lost sheep!

Applaud all your sheep volunteers and ask them to sit down. Take off your head-cloth and put down your crook.

Our next story is about a woman who is counting up all her savings. She has ten valuable silver coins: they are all she has in the world.

Wrap a shawl around your head and take out nine ten pence pieces. (You have already secreted the tenth somewhere in the church.)

One, two, three, four, five, six, seven, eight, nine – nine? I had ten! Where's my last coin? Has anyone seen a silver coin? I can't believe I've lost it! Can someone help me sweep the floor, in case I dropped it there?

Bring forward a volunteer to come and use the broom.

Can someone take this torch and look in all the dark corners?

Bring forward a volunteer to come and use the torch.

Can anyone find my lost silver coin?

Encourage everyone to search until someone finds it, then encourage cheering.

Hooray! We've found it!

Music I have a friend

Activity Both our stories were about finding lost things. To help us think about how much the shepherd wanted to find his lost sheep, and how much the woman wanted to find her lost coin, we are going to find something, too. Lots of gold and silver chocolate coins have been hidden all around this part of the church.[64] *(Indicate the area.)* Can you find one for yourself? When you have found one, eat it and then leave the rest for other people to find. You could help them search!

Encourage everyone to search for the missing chocolate coins. When they have all been eaten, gather everyone together.

Exploring

In the stories we told today, Jesus compared God to the shepherd who found his sheep and the woman who found her money; he compared us to the lost sheep and the lost coin. Our question is this: how do we get lost and found by God?

When Jesus told these stories, he talked about sin. He said, 'There will be more joy in heaven over one sinner who repents than over ninety-nine righteous people who need no repentance.' We are all sinners because none of us is perfect and we can all do bad things, whether by accident, on purpose or by failing to do the right thing. When we sin, we separate ourselves from God. He is still there, loving us and looking out for us, but we have turned away from him. We have got lost.

We're in good company: the Bible is full of examples of people getting themselves lost like this.

Show the picture of the golden calf.

A long, long time ago, God rescued his people from slavery in Egypt, under the leadership of Moses. He parted the Red Sea for them and led them to freedom. You would have thought that after all their adventures, the people would have trusted in God, right? Wrong. While Moses was in the presence of God at the top of a mountain, the people on the ground wondered what had happened to him and doubted they would see him again. They wanted a god they could get close to, so they made a statue of a golden calf and called it a god. They worshipped it and even made sacrifices to it!

---

64. Or outside the church, in the grounds.

Show the picture of the hands or feet in shackles and chains.

Many years later, a man called Saul also rejected God's truth. He was a very strict Jew who hated all followers of Jesus. He used to hunt them down and have them killed for blasphemy. The Bible says he went about 'breathing threats and murder against the disciples of the Lord'[65] and he described himself as 'a persecutor, and a man of violence.'

These people got things badly, dramatically wrong: God's people started worshipping an idol and Saul killed Jesus' followers. They were lost sheep who were very lost indeed – yet God found them all.

Show the picture of the Promised Land.

He led his people to the land he had promised them: a land of their own, 'flowing with milk and honey.'[66]

Show the picture of St Paul.

Saul was dramatically converted when Jesus spoke to him in a blinding flash of light. He became Paul, a leader of the early Church, whose letters are now part of the Bible itself. His words are those of a lost sheep who was, wonderfully, found:

> I received mercy because I had acted ignorantly in unbelief, and the grace of our Lord overflowed for me with the faith and love that are in Christ Jesus . . . Christ Jesus came into the world to save sinners – of whom I am the foremost. But for that very reason I received mercy, so that in me, as the foremost, Jesus Christ might display the utmost patience, making me an example to those who would come to believe in him for eternal life.

These stories of people who were lost and found show us that however lost we are, God wants to find us, too. Do you remember how keen we were to find the chocolate coins in our treasure hunt? Do you

---

65. Acts 9:1.
66. Exodus 33:3.

remember how the shepherd longed to find his sheep, and how anxious the woman was to find her lost coin? These feelings suggest that God looks for us with urgent, anxious longing. He wants to find us and gather us in. Sometimes he will wait for us, as he waited for his people in the wilderness to turn back to him. Sometimes God will find us even when we don't want to be found, like Paul. Whatever happens, we know that if we are lost, he will never stop looking for us until he finds us.

Prayer action Do you remember the jigsaw we tried to finish at the beginning of the service? There was just one piece missing – and here it is. I've found it at last.

Place the missing piece in position.

For our prayers today, we remember that God wants to find us, whoever we are and whatever we've done. We are his missing puzzle piece. As we think about this, please come forward and receive a puzzle piece to take away with you. Keep it somewhere safe, such as your purse or wallet, to remind you that you are the one God is looking for.

Invite people to come forward and take a puzzle piece.

We remember those things we have done that have separated us from God, and we say sorry for them in our hearts.

Pause.

Ever-seeking God,
we are sorry for getting lost.
Find us where we are
and bring us home to you.
Amen.

Music Come on, let's get up and go

Conclusion God of the lost and found,
send us out into the world
to follow your way.
Though we will get lost,
may we trust that you will always find us.
Amen.

Give notices, announce the next all-age service and invite everyone to the feast.

Proper 20

God or money?

Theme	How we use our money and serve God; fair trade
Scripture	Amos 8:4-7; Luke 16:1-13

Running order	Total: 50 minutes
Welcome	Listening to 'Money' by Pink Floyd *(5 minutes)*
Introduction	Opening the theme
Storytelling	Retelling the story of the dishonest manager, with mime *(5 minutes)*
Music	Inspired by love and anger *(5 minutes)*
Exploring	What did Jesus say about money? Illustration using Monopoly *(10 minutes)*
Activity	Learning about fair trade *(15 minutes)*
Prayer action	'Faithful in a very little' – prayer with pennies *(5 minutes)*
Music	God is the giver of love *(5 minutes)*
Conclusion	Closing prayer and invitation

Resources

- A recording of 'Money' by Pink Floyd (or 'Money Makes The World Go Round' from *Cabaret*)
- Equipment to play it on
- Music and words
- A game of Monopoly in progress *(see appendix)*
- Fair trade stations around the church *(see appendix)*
- A bowl full of pennies, enough for one each

Leaders

Minimum: 6

- Leader
- Cast x 5

Optimum: 10+

- Leader *(Introduction and Conclusion)*
- Cast x 5:
  Jesus, wearing white
  Rich boss, wearing a suit and carrying a letter
  Manager, wearing a suit
  Debtors x 2, each carrying a long sheet of paper
- Music Leader
- Explorer
- Activity Leader(s)
- Prayer Leader

Suggestions for additional music

- Heaven shall not wait
- Take my life, and let it be

Service

Welcome — *As people arrive, play 'Money' by Pink Floyd (or 'Money Makes The World Go Round' from* Cabaret*).*

Introduction — Our service today is about a fact of life: money. Whether we've got lots, just enough or hardly any, we can't avoid dealing with it. Jesus had a lot to say about money, and this is a modern version of one story he told.

Storytelling

Jesus — Once upon a time there was a rich boss. He employed a manager to look after his business.

The rich boss and the manager enter.

But someone tipped off the boss that his manager was overspending.

The boss opens the letter and looks furiously at the manager.

He said, 'Is this true? Bring me the accounts! I'm not having you ruin my business!'

The boss storms off and the manager holds his head in his hands.

The manager was seriously worried. He thought, 'What am I going to do when he fires me? I'm not strong enough to work with my hands and I'm too proud to beg.

The manager suddenly lights up with a bright idea.

I know! I've got a plan so that when I lose my job, people will owe me – big time!'

The debtors walk on with their long bills.

So he called the people who owed his boss money. He said to the first, 'How much do you owe?'

The first debtor shows the bill.

The man said, 'I owe a thousand pounds.'

The manager said, 'Quick – give me your bill.

He tears the bill in half.

Now you only owe £500.'

The first debtor hugs him and runs off happily.

Then the manager said to the second debtor, 'How much do you owe?'

The second debtor shows the bill.

The man said, 'I owe a thousand, too.'

The manager takes the bill and tears off the top part.

'Let's call it £800.'

The second debtor shakes his hand and walks off happily. The boss walks on and looks at the pieces of the bills. He shakes his head, smiles and shakes the manager's hand.

The boss was impressed by his manager's cunning. 'You sly old dog! That's the kind of sharp business practice I need around here!'

The boss and the manager walk off together.

You see? These dishonest businessmen know how to take care of their future better than God's children do! But you can't buy friends who will get you into heaven.

Whoever is faithful in little things is also faithful in big things; and whoever is dishonest in small ways is also dishonest in a big way. If you haven't used money honestly, who will give you the true riches of God's kingdom? If you haven't been trustworthy with another person's wealth, who will give you wealth of your own? A slave can't serve two masters, because he's bound to hate one and love the other. That kind of divided loyalty just doesn't work. You can't serve God and money.

Music Inspired by love and anger

Exploring Jesus was quite clear about the meaning of his story: you can't serve God and money. The dishonest manager might have sorted out a comfortable life for himself by buying his way into people's good books, but he wasn't going to get into heaven that way. You can't buy or sell your way into God's kingdom.

Whenever Jesus speaks in the Gospels, there is always an audience. On this occasion, his disciples were listening, as well as a whole crowd of 'tax-collectors and sinners'.[67] The money-grabbing tax-collectors certainly needed to be told a thing or two about God and money, but they weren't the only ones. The scribes and the Pharisees were there, too: those ultra-correct Jewish leaders stood back from the rabble and carped at Jesus mixing with 'the wrong sort of people'. Luke's Gospel describes the Pharisees as 'lovers of money':[68] certainly, they were powerful and influential men, and many of them must have relished the wealth such status brought them. When Jesus said, 'You can't serve God and money,' he was talking to them and they knew it. They were the proud guardians of God's law, so they didn't like hearing that their wealth made them unable to serve him. They mocked Jesus' teaching and tried to dismiss it.

However, Jesus wasn't only talking to the 'lovers of money' in the crowd around him that day: his words are relevant to our lives, too. In modern times we have faced the credit crunch, debt crises and the meltdown of entire financial systems; many people are wondering whether, as a society, we have loved money too much.

There is a popular family board game that perfectly illustrates how the love of money works: who knows the game called Monopoly?

Invite responses.

Who would like to come and take part in a Monopoly game with a difference?

Invite four volunteers forward.

We're picking up this game halfway through: all the properties have been sold and lots of houses and hotels have been built. You know the rules: you move round the board and if you land on a property you have to pay money to its owner. These players should be getting worried: for example, if they land on Mayfair with a hotel, they will have to pay £2000! Let's see what happens.

---

67. Luke 15:1-2.
68. Luke 16:14.

The players roll the dice and move until someone lands on a property. Announce how much they owe and to whom.

Now, I said this would be a Monopoly game with a difference. *(Address the property owner.)* Normally, you would take all this money off the other player. However, this time I want you to be kind. You could either ask for less money or you could let them off paying you all together. What are you going to do?

Let the property owner decide: money then changes hands (or not). Continue rolling the dice until the next person lands on a property. Announce how much they owe and to whom.

(Address the property owner.) Now, that player owes you lots of money, but again, I want you to be kind. They're getting short of cash: I want you to give them some of yours. You decide how much.

The property owner hands over some cash.

In normal Monopoly, the point is to take everyone else's money off them until they've got nothing and you've got the lot. Then you're the winner. In our version of the game, these players are letting each other off their debts and giving their money away, just to be kind. They'll never win like that! This just goes to show that you can't be kind and win Monopoly; in the same way, you can't serve God and money.

Applaud your volunteers and ask them to sit down.

Serving God is about love: we are called to love God and love other people – or be kind to them, as we were in our game. If we serve God, then everything we do should show that we love God and love other people. This includes the way we use money. Whether we are dealing with pocket money or an investment portfolio, we can use our money in a good way – a godly way.

Activity

Our Activity will help us discover more about good ways of using the money we have. Every spending choice we make has an impact, and it works like this. If you buy a pair of jeans, you become connected to everyone who has had anything to do with those jeans: the farmer who grew the cotton, the men who wove and dyed the denim, the woman who sewed the jeans together and the people who sold them to the shop. As the buyer of those jeans, you become part of this chain of people, and you support the fair or unfair system that produced the jeans. Around our church today is information about the Fairtrade Foundation, which works for these important things:

- Fair prices
- Decent working conditions
- Sustainable produce, which doesn't harm the land or its people
- A fair deal for farmers and workers in the developing world

Take your time now to explore these different areas.

Allow plenty of time for people to circulate around the different stations.

Prayer action

In our story, Jesus said, 'Whoever is faithful in little things is also faithful in big things; and whoever is dishonest in small ways is also dishonest in a big way.' Today we pray that we will use our money in a good way, whether we have very little or a great deal. As a sign of our prayers, we will use these pennies. Please take one and hold it in your hand.

Pass round the bowl of pennies and encourage everyone to take one.

As we hold this small coin, let's rest in God's presence and bring before him our thoughts and feelings about money.

Pause.

God of all goodness,
all that we have comes from you.

In our buying, selling, spending and saving,
may we put you first, not money.
In Jesus' name.
Amen.

Please keep this penny in your purse or wallet. As it gets mixed up with the rest of your money, may it remind you of your prayer today.

Music God is the giver of love

Conclusion God of Love,
send us out into the world,
wise to the power of money
yet willing to serve you.
Amen.

Give notices, announce the next all-age service and invite everyone to the feast.

Proper 21

Rich and poor

Theme	The use of wealth
Scripture	1 Timothy 6:6-19; Luke 16:19-31

Running order	Total: 50 minutes
Welcome	Lighting candles at the gate *(5 minutes)*
Introduction	Opening the theme
Activity	Preparing the sumptuous feast *(10 minutes)*
Storytelling	The rich man and Lazarus – interactive reading *(10 minutes)*
Music	Brother, sister, let me serve you *(5 minutes)*
Exploring	Who is at our gate? *(10 minutes)*
Prayer action	Empty bowl prayer *(5 minutes)*
Music	When I needed a neighbour *(5 minutes)*
Conclusion	Closing prayer and invitation

Resources

- Tea lights in jam jars or glass tumblers, enough for one each
- Matches and tapers
- Ingredients for a feast *(see appendix)*
- Bowl of water and a towel
- A lightweight table, laid with a luxurious cloth
- A chair
- Rich robes/cloak, including something purple
- A ragged tunic and bandages stained with red food colouring
- An old wooden bowl
- A long tunic and a head-cloth
- Two white sheets
- Two deck chairs
- Glass of iced water
- Fiery streamers *(see appendix)*
- Music and words
- A few cheap, plastic bowls

Leaders

Minimum: 1

- Leader

Optimum: 6

- Leader *(Introduction and Conclusion)*
- Activity Leader
- Storyteller
- Music Leader
- Explorer
- Prayer Leader

Suggestions for additional music

- Heaven shall not wait
- If we only seek peace

Service

Welcome — *As people arrive, invite them to light tea lights in jam jars and leave them at the gates or the door of the church, as signs of their prayers. Make sure there is still room for people to go in and out safely.*

Introduction — Our story today involves a sumptuous feast. Who would like to help me prepare some delicious food?

Activity — *Invite volunteers forward and ask them to wash their hands in the bowl of water. Then explain the various jobs that need doing and set them to work. As each plate for the feast is filled, display it on the table you have draped with a luxurious cloth.*

Storytelling — *Gather everyone round, in a circle if possible.*

Now the feast is prepared, we are ready to tell the story. I will need some volunteers for this, too. First of all, I need a rich man and a poor man; then I will need someone to be Abraham in heaven.

Invite volunteers and assign the roles.

We will bring you each into the story in due course. Let's begin.[69]

There was a rich man who was dressed in purple and fine linen and who feasted sumptuously every day.

Bring forward your rich man and dress him up in rich robes, then seat him comfortably at the table with the feast.

And at his gate lay a poor man named Lazarus, covered with sores, who longed to satisfy his hunger with what fell from the rich man's table; even the dogs would come and lick his sores.

---

69. The story is taken directly from Luke's Gospel (NRSV). You may prefer to use a different translation.

Bring forward your poor man and dress him in rags and bandages, then give him an empty wooden bowl. He lies on the ground opposite the rich man.

The poor man died and was carried away by the angels to be with Abraham. The rich man also died and was buried.

Cover both men with white sheets. Announce that Lazarus went to heaven and the rich man went to hell. Bring forward your Abraham and dress him in a long tunic and a headcloth. He takes off Lazarus' white sheet, lifts him to his feet and supports him. Bring on deck chairs for Abraham and Lazarus. Move the feast table in front of them. Then remove the white sheet from the rich man and invite volunteers to wave fiery streamers around him.

In Hades, where he was being tormented, he looked up and saw Abraham far away with Lazarus by his side. He called out, 'Father Abraham, have mercy on me, and send Lazarus to dip the tip of his finger in water and cool my tongue; for I am in agony in these flames.'

Encourage Lazarus to drink some iced water.

But Abraham said, 'Child, remember that during your lifetime you received your good things, and Lazarus in like manner evil things; but now he is comforted here, and you are in agony. Besides all this, between you and us a great chasm has been fixed, so that those who might want to pass from here to you cannot do so, and no one can cross from there to us.' He said, 'Then, father, I beg you to send him to my father's house – for I have five brothers – that he may warn them, so that they will not also come into this place of torment.' Abraham replied, 'They have Moses and the prophets; they should listen to them.' He said, 'No, father Abraham; but if someone goes to them from the dead, they will repent.' He said to him, 'If they do not listen to Moses and the prophets, neither will they be convinced even if someone rises from the dead.'

Applaud all your volunteers.

Music Brother, sister, let me serve you

Exploring Jesus told this story to a big crowd of people, including poor people who lived on the streets, like Lazarus, and wealthy Pharisees whom the Bible describes as 'lovers of money'. They would have been wearing fine linen, like the rich man. Jesus' listeners would have nodded with recognition at the details in his story. They had seen rich men wearing purple robes, which were coloured with the world's most expensive dye. Purple cloth was like a Rolex watch or a Porsche – it showed off how much money you had. Townspeople were also used to the sight of desperately poor people lying in the streets, as they still do in the poorest parts of the world today. The detail about the dogs licking Lazarus' sores is disgusting, but would have been familiar to Jesus' audience, for whom dogs were not pets but scavengers. They ate rubbish in the street, stole food and licked beggars' wounds.

So Jesus' story about the rich man and the poor man was a real-life story for his listeners, and this made its message even more powerful. It was a story to comfort the afflicted and afflict the comfortable. If you were poor and hungry, you might have been comforted by the vision of a heavenly feast in store for you after your short, unhappy life. However, if you were well off, like the Pharisees, you would have felt decidedly uncomfortable about the threat of hell, from which there was no possibility of help or rescue. The message to Jesus' wealthy listeners was clear: share your wealth with the poor, or you'll be shut out of heaven.

What about us? We may not be as rich as the rich man in Jesus' story, but living in a developed country, most of us are better off than many poor people in the world. We need to think about this story of the rich man who went through his gates every day, in and out, going about his business. Every day he walked past Lazarus, who was begging for food at the gate. With his open sores, he wasn't a pleasant sight. The rich man looked the other way and tried to forget he was there. After a week or so, Lazarus seemed like part of

PROPER 21

the scenery and the rich man didn't give him a second thought. I wonder whether we walk past people like this? Are there people in our own neighbourhood whom we try to pretend aren't there? Who is at *our* gate? In a moment, we're going to go outside to consider our own church gates and the streets beyond. As we do so, let's think about who is outside these gates on a Friday night. Who is there at two o'clock in the morning? Who is there at the start of the day? Let's go and look outside, beyond our gates.

Lead everyone outside and allow time for thinking and discussion in the church grounds. The tea lights you lit around the church door or gates should still be alight, providing a visual focus for reflection. The aim is to encourage awareness of those people in our community whom we tend to overlook. Ideally, this would lead to discussion of ways in which the church could serve the community. When you are ready, lead people back inside.

Today's story told Jesus' wealthy listeners how to treat the poor at their gate, and it speaks to us, too. The message is spelled out in one of the Bible's letters:

> As for those who in the present age are rich, command them not to be haughty, or to set their hopes on the uncertainty of riches, but rather on God who richly provides us with everything for our enjoyment. They are to do good, to be rich in good works, generous, and ready to share, thus storing up for themselves the treasure of a good foundation for the future, so that they may take hold of the life that really is life.

We are comparatively rich: our job, as individuals and as a church, is to share. Doing so will enrich us now and ensure our future with God. As the Bible wonderfully puts it, we will 'take hold of the life that really is life'.

Prayer action Today we will use these empty bowls to help us pray for those who have nothing. Pass them around and hold them in your hands as we pray.

Hand out the bowls. (They will be passed around during the prayer, so people don't need one each.)

We pray for those who don't have enough to eat. We pray for the men, women and children who hold out bowls like these for a few grains of rice, for leftover scraps, for food aid and donations.

Pause.

We pray for those who don't have enough money to live on. We pray for the men, women and children who sit in shop doorways and train stations, holding out bowls like these to beg for a few coins.

Pause.

God of all goodness,
may you lift up the lowly
and fill the hungry with good things.
Amen.

Music When I needed a neighbour

Conclusion Heavenly Father,
send us out into the world
to help the poor at our gate
and share what we have
in Jesus' name.
Amen.

Give notices, announce the next all-age service and invite everyone to the feast, which is the one you prepared for the rich man at the beginning of the service. As people leave the church, the tea lights should still be burning around the door or gates as a reminder of today's story.

Harvest Thanksgiving

Giving life to the world

Theme	Thanking God for his creation and for Jesus, the bread of life
Scripture	John 6:25-35

Running order	Total: 50 minutes (longer with Holy Communion)
Welcome/Activity	Presenting the Harvest offering and making a rainbow of food *(10 minutes)*
Music	Who put the colours in the rainbow? *(5 minutes)*
Introduction	Opening the theme
Storytelling	Jesus is the bread of life – edible retelling *(10 minutes)*
Music	I am the bread of life *(5 minutes)*
Exploring	How does Jesus give life to the world? Edible exploration with breads from around the world *(10 minutes)*
EITHER	
Holy Communion	Beginning at the Creed and using the Prayer action instead of the Intercessions
OR	
Prayer action	Thanksgiving meditation montage – 'What a Wonderful World' *(5 minutes)*
Music	We plough the fields and scatter *(5 minutes)*
Conclusion	Closing prayer and invitation

Resources

- Suggested church set-up: café-style, with jugs of water and glasses on each table (to go with the bread)
- Music and words
- A couple of baskets filled with pieces of bread
- A couple of plates of honey bread (white bread with the crusts cut off, thinly spread with honey and cut into squares)
- Hidden around the church, lots of different kinds of bread from around the world, for example: baguette, ciabatta, naan, chapati, Irish soda bread, German rye bread
- Thanksgiving meditation montage *(see appendix)*
- Laptop, projector, screen and speakers
- *(Optional)* Long scarves or strips of cloth in purple/blue, green, yellow/orange and red, laid out like a rainbow to provide a background for the rainbow of food

Leaders

Minimum: 1

- Leader

Optimum: 6+

- Leader *(Introduction and Conclusion)*
- Activity Leader(s)
- Storyteller
- Music Leader
- Explorer
- Prayer Leader

Suggestions for additional music

- For the fruits of his creation
- Jesus the Lord said: 'I am the Bread'
- God, whose farm is all creation

Service

Welcome/Activity — *As people arrive, invite them to bring forward their Harvest offerings. Encourage them to help you arrange the produce at the front of church to form a huge rainbow of food, curving upwards in stripes from violet to red.*[70]

Music — Who put the colours in the rainbow?

Introduction — Today is our Harvest Thanksgiving, when we thank God for all the good things he has given us, and this glorious rainbow of food reminds us of the wonderful variety of his gifts. Our story today is all about food. Who's hungry?

Storytelling — *Invite people to gather round.*

Our story begins with the leftovers of an all-you-can-eat picnic, miraculously provided by Jesus with just five loaves and two fish. He shared these amongst thousands of hungry people and there was enough for everyone! There was even some bread left over: who would like a piece?

Pass round the baskets of bread and encourage everyone to take some. Allow time for everyone to eat their bread.

The crowds who shared the picnic all followed Jesus. He said, 'You're not following me because of the miracle, but because you're full of bread! Don't work for food that will go mouldy tomorrow, but for the food that lasts forever, which God's Son will give you. He is God's Chosen One.'

The crowds asked, 'How do we do God's work?'

Jesus answered simply, 'By believing in the One he sent.'

Someone in the crowd shouted, 'Go on then – show us a miracle! That'll help us believe in you! Our ancestors ate manna in the wilderness. It was bread from heaven!'

---

[70]. Use the dominant colours of tins and packets to fill up the trickier parts of the spectrum: for example, there aren't many blue foods, but Heinz baked beans tins will give you a strong turquoise colour.

Quick recap: long ago, God's people had indeed survived in the desert on something white and starchy that they called manna, or bread from heaven. It was soft and sweet, a bit like this.

Pass round the honey bread and allow time for everyone to eat.

God provided this miraculous bread from heaven for his people. They lived on it for 40 years.

Now, back to our story today: Jesus said to the crowds, 'That bread from heaven came from God, who gives you the true bread from heaven.'

The crowds cried, 'Give us some! From now on, we only want the sort of bread you're talking about!'

Jesus said, 'I am the bread of life. Whoever comes to me will never be hungry, and whoever believes in me will never be thirsty.'

Music I am the bread of life

Exploring *Invite volunteers to find the different kinds of bread that you have placed around the church and bring them to the front. Ask people to identify the different varieties and where they come from. Pass round all the breads and invite people to try them.*

Bread, bread, bread! People all over the world eat bread as a main part of their diet, and we have sampled some of those different varieties this morning. Our story was full of bread; now, so are we. Bread is important because it is a staple food: rich in carbohydrate and protein, it meets our basic needs for nutrition and energy. In Jesus' time, women made fresh bread every day for their families and people relied on it, especially when other food was in short supply. Wheat or barley grain could be stored for a long time without going mouldy, so no matter what else was scarce, people could always grind some flour and make some bread. Indeed, bread was so vital that Jesus taught his followers to pray, 'Give us this day our daily bread.'

So Jesus chose a powerful image when he described himself as God's bread from heaven that 'gives life to the world'. These words remind us that God provides for us all: just as he fed his people in the wilderness, he gives us food to sustain our bodies, and today's colourful rainbow of food shows how generous his creation is.

When Jesus said, 'I am the bread of life,' he showed that God has given us spiritual food that will last forever and give us eternal life. In the Far East, where people rely on rice rather than bread, some Bible translations describe Jesus as 'the rice of life'. Rice or bread, Jesus is our staple food: we need to turn to him every day and depend on him. He is our survival ration, like life-saving bread and water, and with him we will live forever. As he promised, 'Whoever comes to me will never be hungry, and whoever believes in me will never be thirsty.' The bread we share in Holy Communion reminds us that Jesus is bread from heaven – the bread of life. All we have to do is believe in him.

EITHER

Holy Communion — Begin at the Creed and use the Prayer action instead of the Intercessions, then follow the service as usual.[71]

OR

Prayer action — For our Harvest thanksgiving prayers, we will thank God for the beauty of his creation and the good things he has given us. Let's rest in God's presence as some music and pictures help us to reflect on his goodness.

Play the thanksgiving meditation montage to the soundtrack of 'What a Wonderful World' by Louis Armstrong.

---

71. See the Introduction for details of how to adapt this service to incorporate *Common Worship* Holy Communion.

Life-giving God,
we thank you for the food that strengthens our bodies;
we thank you for your Son, the bread of life, who sustains our souls.
We thank you for giving life to the world.
Amen.

Music We plough the fields and scatter

Conclusion God of Harvest,
give us this day our daily bread
and may we daily depend on Jesus, the bread of life.
Amen.

Give notices, announce the next all-age service and invite everyone to the feast.

Proper 22

There's no place like home

Theme	The longing for home
Scripture	Lamentations 1:1-6; 3:19-26

Running order — Total: 50 minutes

Welcome	Watching the closing minutes of *The Wizard of Oz* (*5 minutes*)
Introduction	Opening the theme
Activity	'Home and Away' tag game (*10 minutes*)
Storytelling	Reading from Lamentations 1:1-6 (*2 minutes*)
Music	Do not be afraid (*5 minutes*)
Exploring	Where is home? Creating a visual display (*15 minutes*)
Prayer action	House of prayer – creative prayer with building bricks (*8 minutes*)
Music	There's a place where the streets shine (*5 minutes*)
Conclusion	Closing prayer and invitation

Resources

- Laptop, projector, screen and speakers
- The closing minutes of *The Wizard of Oz* (available on YouTube) from where Dorothy taps her heels together three times to her closing line, back in Kansas: 'There's no place like home.'
- A large non-slip mat at the front of the church
- A blindfold
- Music and words
- A big board for the display
- Craft and collage materials, for example: old newspapers, catalogues and magazines; felt pens; crayons; colourful stickers; drawing stencils; scissors and glue sticks
- A large supply of *Duplo* or *Mega Bloks*, ideally with a base board and some features that could help build a house, such as a door and windows*
- Plain sticky labels to fit on the side of these bricks
- Pens and pencils

Leaders

Minimum: 1

- Leader

Optimum: 6+

- Leader *(Introduction and Conclusion)*
- Activity Leader
- Storyteller
- Music Leader
- Explorer(s)
- Prayer Leader

Suggestions for additional music

- Faithful One, so unchanging
- Father, I place into your hands

---

* You could try a super-size alternative here: your bricks could be empty cardboard boxes, with prayers written on the sides in marker pen. These would then make a house big enough for children to sit in.

Service

Welcome *Show the final few minutes of* The Wizard of Oz, *from where Dorothy taps her heels together three times to her closing line, back in Kansas: 'There's no place like home.'*

Introduction Which film did our opening clip come from?

Invite responses.

Dorothy in *The Wizard of Oz* had many strange and extraordinary adventures, but she never stopped wanting to go home. In our service today, we will be thinking about the places we call home.

Activity We will begin by playing a game called 'Home and Away'. Who would like to join in?

Invite your volunteers to join you on the mat at the front. Choose one confident volunteer to be blindfolded, then instruct the rest.

Now, this mat is home. This is where you're safe, but you're all going to start the game far away from home, somewhere at the back of church. Your aim is to get home, but this person here will be trying to catch you. If he/she touches you, you're out. If you get home safely, shout 'Home!' To make the game a bit more challenging, we'll blindfold our catcher. *(Tie on the blindfold.)* The rest of you need to creep forward really quietly, so that he/she doesn't hear you! Let's begin: our catcher is guarding your home, and you're all far away.

Encourage your volunteers to get as far away as possible. When they are ready, begin the game. They all creep forward and one by one either reach home or get caught.

Storytelling 'There's no place like home!' said Dorothy, and everyone in our game was keen to get home, no matter who stood in their way. Such a longing for home has been felt by exiled people throughout history. More than 500 years before Jesus was born, the Jews were deported from their homeland. Their capital city,

Jerusalem, was destroyed by an invading army and the Temple was reduced to rubble. God's people lost both their homeland and their spiritual home: for the Jews, Jerusalem was God's holy city and his Temple was the focus of their festivals and regular pilgrimages. Listen to this ancient voice from the Bible singing a funeral song for Jerusalem. The city is sometimes called Zion, and here it's compared to a grieving widow:

Read Lamentations 1:1-4.

Music   Do not be afraid

Exploring   Kansas was home for Dorothy in *The Wizard of Oz*; in our game, home was the mat at the front of church. For the Jews, home was and still is Jerusalem. Home can mean different things to different people, but we know it when we find it. Home is where we are safe, like the mat in our game. Home is a place where we are known and loved, like Dorothy's Kansas. Above all, home is a place where we can be ourselves. In our Bible reading, the grieving voice said, 'no one comes to the festivals': exiled, God's people could no longer make pilgrimages to Jerusalem as they used to do. They could no longer celebrate the festivals that were such a big part of their faith. They couldn't be themselves.

I wonder where home is for us? It may be the house we share with our loved ones; it may be the closeness and warmth we share with our friends. Some people are lucky enough to feel at home in their work. There is a wonderful description of the Church which suggests that it, too, can be our home:

> . . . the Church is first of all a kind of space cleared by God through Jesus in which people may become what God made them to be (God's sons and daughters) . . . It is a place where we can see properly – God, God's creation, ourselves.[72]

---

72. Rowan Williams, 'The Christian Priest Today', quoted by Justin Lewis-Anthony, *If You Meet George Herbert on the Road . . . Kill Him!*, Mowbray, 2009, p.81.

If home is a safe place where we are loved and can be ourselves, this sounds like home. We're going to take some time now to create pictures of the different places we call home. You could draw or make a collage out of different images: whatever you do, try to create a picture of a place that, to you, feels like home.

Allow plenty of time for people to create their pictures. As they are finished, display them all together on a big board. You may like to invite people to comment on the pictures they have produced.

Home is a safe place where we are loved and can be ourselves. We can trust that God, who long ago gave his people the Promised Land, wants us to find our home, too, whatever it may look like and wherever it may be. This morning we heard a voice from the Old Testament, lamenting the loss of home, yet even this voice expressed faith and hope:

> But this I call to mind,
> and therefore I have hope:
> the steadfast love of the Lord never ceases,
> his mercies never come to an end;
> they are new every morning;
> great is your faithfulness . . .
> The Lord is good to those who wait for him,
> to the soul that seeks him.

God wants us to find a place where we can feel at home. If we have already found our home, we should give thanks; if we haven't found it yet, we should wait and hope in faith. Most wonderful of all, we have an open invitation to join God in his eternal kingdom, and that really is a place we can call home.

Prayer action

For our prayers today, we will use bricks to build the simple shape of a home. Let's write or draw our prayers on sticky labels and attach them to these bricks.

Pass around the sticky labels, pens and Duplo or Mega Bloks bricks.

Let us pray.

Heavenly Father,
we pray for the home we love,
for the home we miss,
or for the home we have yet to find.
We pray for those who have lost their homes.

Allow time for people to write or draw their prayer on a sticky label and attach it to a brick. Encourage them to create more than one prayer brick. Then invite people to come forward and, together, build a simple house out of the prayer bricks.

God our Father,
wherever we make our home,
may we find our true home in your love.
Amen.

Music There's a place where the streets shine

Conclusion Loving Lord, Giver of the Promised Land,
thank you for the gift of home
and the promise of your heavenly home.
Amen.

Give notices, announce the next all-age service and invite everyone to the feast.

Proper 23

Thank you!

Theme	The importance of continually thanking God
Scripture	Luke 17:11-19

Running order	Total: 50 minutes
Welcome	Counting blessings (5 minutes)
Introduction	Opening the theme
Storytelling	Sketch – Jesus heals the ten lepers (5 minutes)
Music	Thank you, Lord (5 minutes)
Exploring	Why don't we say always say thank you? Telling the story of St Swithun and the ungrateful monks (10 minutes)
Activity	Making thank-you cards (15 minutes)
Prayer action	Continual thanksgiving – creative prayer with Möbius strips (5 minutes)
Music	Thank you for saving me (5 minutes)
Conclusion	Closing prayer and invitation

PROPER 23

Resources

- Equipment for 'Counting blessings' activity *(see appendix)*
- Ten bandages or rough strips of cloth
- A halo (make one out of gold card or tinsel)
- A bishop's mitre *(see appendix)*
- A monk's cowl. A piece of brown or black cloth draped over the head would do, but it is possible to buy a modern cowl made of fleece material. It's a kind of tubular scarf, often called a snood
- Music and words
- White A4 card, enough to make one thank-you card each
- Lots of good felt pens
- Craft equipment such as stickers, glitter glue, self-adhesive jewels, etc
- Craft tables
- Thank-you strips *(see appendix)*
- Several reels of sticky tape in dispensers, or with lots of pairs of scissors

Leaders

Minimum: 3

- Leader
- Cast x 2

Optimum: 8+

- Leader *(Introduction and Conclusion)*
- Storyteller
- Cast x 2:
  Jesus, wearing a white tunic
  Samaritan, wearing a rough, ragged tunic
- Music Leader
- Explorer
- Activity Leader(s)
- Prayer Leader

Suggestions for additional music

- Thank you for the summer morning
- Praise, my soul

Service

Welcome *As people arrive, encourage them literally to count their blessings by joining in a creative activity. Whether they are threading beads or tying pieces of ribbon, each item represents something for which they thank God.*

Introduction One of the earliest things we are taught as children is the importance of saying 'Thank you.' Our service today is all about saying 'Thank you' to God.

Storytelling In our story, we will meet a group of people who really needed God's help: they were suffering from a terrible skin disease called leprosy. This disease is catching and although it can be treated today, in biblical times there was no medicine that could cure it. The people the Bible calls lepers were left out of normal society. They were seen as untouchable and folk were scared to go near them. One day, Jesus came across a whole group of lepers: who would like to help me tell the story of what happened?

Invite volunteers to come forward – nine, if possible – and give out bandages. Encourage them to bandage each other's limbs.

Now, all of you have leprosy, and you're all in pain, so I want you to walk as if you hurt all over.

Encourage them to practise moving in character.

There's one more sufferer in your group, but you're not talking to him.

Bring on your tenth leper, the Samaritan.

He's a Samaritan, and you all hate the Samaritans. You wish he'd go back to his own people.

Encourage your nine lepers to hiss and shout 'Go home!' at the Samaritan.

PROPER 23

> Now, our story begins with all of you together, outside a village that you're not allowed to enter.
>
> *Group the nine lepers together at the front of the church, with the Samaritan slightly apart.*
>
> Remember, you hurt all over.
>
> *Encourage them to stand in character, then point to the back of the church.*
>
> Look! There's Jesus!
>
> *Jesus starts to walk down the aisle.*

Samaritan — Jesus, Master, have mercy on us!

> *Encourage the other nine to echo these words.*

Jesus — *(arriving at the front)* Go and show yourselves to the priests. Go on, off you go!

Storyteller — What was he talking about? The lepers weren't allowed to go anywhere near the priests! But as they walked away, they started to feel better.

> *Encourage your lepers to start walking down the aisle.*

Their bodies didn't hurt any more. In fact, their skin looked completely clear. They were cured! They all ripped off their bandages and started to cheer.

> *Encourage the lepers to take off their bandages and cheer.*

Nine of the lepers headed off to see the priests. *(encourage your nine volunteers to keep walking)* Only one turned back: the Samaritan.

Samaritan — *(running to the front of church and falling at Jesus' feet)* Thank you! Thank you! Thank you, Lord! Praise God! You've cured me!

Jesus — *(to the congregation)* Didn't I just heal ten people? Where are the other nine? Isn't anyone going to say thank you to God, apart from this foreigner? *(to the Samaritan)* Get up and go on your way; your faith has made you better.

Music — Thank you, Lord

Exploring

In our story, ten people were cured by Jesus, but only one said 'Thank you'. I wonder why the other nine didn't thank Jesus?

Invite responses.

If we're honest, we must admit that *we* don't always say thank you to God, either. Today we're going to think about why this might be, and to help us I'm going to tell you a story. This is a very old story – it was written in English over a thousand years ago![73]

Put on the halo.

This is a story about St Swithun. He lived long ago, in the time we call the Dark Ages. Swithun died and was buried, but that's when his story really began. It all started when a man with a hunchback hobbled on crutches to St Swithun's tomb. He prayed to be made better, and within minutes his back straightened, his hump disappeared and his legs grew strong. It was a miracle!

Word spread and sick people came from all over the country to St Swithun's tomb. Two hundred were cured in ten days, and countless numbers were healed in a year! The churchyard was always full of people with spots and swellings, lumps and lurgies, pain and plague. There were so many people that you could hardly get into the church! Yet within days, they were all healed by St Swithun.

Now, all this healing came to the attention of the Bishop.

Put on the mitre.

The Bishop went to the local monastery and said to the monks, 'Every time St Swithun heals someone, I want you to sing a song of praise. Every time, mind you! You've got to thank God for his goodness.'

---

73. This is my retelling of a story from *Aelfric's Lives of Saints*, Walter Skeat (ed.), Early English Text Society for OUP, 1966.

Put on the cowl.

So every time someone was healed, the monks sang, *(sing to the tune of the Peruvian Gloria)* 'Glory to God! Glory to God! Glory to the Father!' When St Swithun healed someone just as they were sitting down to lunch, they left their food to go cold and sang, 'Glory to God! Glory to God! Glory to the Father!' When they'd just tucked themselves up in bed for the night, St Swithun healed someone so they got up and sang, 'Glory to God! Glory to God! Glory to the Father!' And in the middle of the night, when they were fast asleep, St Swithun healed someone else so they had to get up and sing, *(sing sleepily, rubbing your eyes)* 'Glory to God! Glory to God! Glory to the Father!' When this started happening three or four times a night, the monks decided they'd had enough. 'That's it!' they said. 'This is getting ridiculous! We're singing God's praises at all hours of the day and night!' They gave up their singing and reckoned they wouldn't get found out, because the Bishop was always busy with the king. That's where they were wrong . . .

Put on the halo.

St Swithun himself appeared to the Bishop and said, 'Those monks of yours are slacking off! They see miracles around them every day, but they can't be bothered to thank God! God is not best pleased, I can tell you. He's doesn't like their grumbling or their laziness. Go and tell them to buck up their ideas, or you won't get any more miracles.'

Put on the mitre.

So the Bishop went to the monks and said, 'Listen! I know what you've been up to and it's got to stop. No more of this laziness – I want you on your feet and singing God's praises *every* time someone is healed, do you hear? Or there'll be no food for a week!'

Put on the cowl.

The monks wondered how on earth the Bishop had found out, but of course, they did as they were told. The miracles continued, and every time St Swithun healed someone, day or night, the monks sang, 'Glory to God! Glory to God! Glory to the Father!'

Take off the cowl.

We can sympathise with those grumpy monks, can't we? St Swithun complained, 'They see miracles around them every day, but they can't be bothered to thank God!' They remind us that God surrounds us with an embarrassment of riches. There is so much to say thank you for, sometimes we don't know where to start. We begin to take things for granted and in the end, saying thank you can seem like a chore. The monks had to say thank you so often that it was hard work: they remind us that it's easy to be grateful for a small, one-off act of kindness, but harder to express our thanks for great and ongoing goodness. For example, we can easily thank our parents for a birthday present, but how do we begin to say thank you for the life and upbringing they have given us? God is continually good to us, and we all need to say thank you, over and over again. Our activity today will help us make a start.

Activity *Invite everyone to gather round the craft tables and make a thank-you card each as a way of saying 'Thank you' to God. They can draw on it, write on it and do anything else with it that might help them express their thanks. As the cards are finished, place them on the altar.*

Prayer action The Bible tells us to 'rejoice always, pray without ceasing, give thanks in all circumstances.'[74] For our prayers today, we will make a symbol of never-ending thanksgiving.

Hold up your Möbius strip.

This is called a Möbius strip. It's a simple loop of paper with a twist in it, but it has a never-ending edge. If you run your fingers along one edge without taking them

---

74. 1 Thessalonians 5:16-18.

off, you will find that you never come to the end: your fingers travel on and on along both edges of the paper without stopping.

Demonstrate this by lightly pinching one edge and – with the other hand – drawing the strip smoothly through your fingers, allowing it to twist as it turns.

Take a strip of paper that says 'Thank you' on it and twist it once, then join the ends together with sticky tape.

Allow time for everyone to do this.

Now we will use these strips as we pray. Gently pinch one edge of the paper and use the other hand to pull the strip smoothly through your fingers.

Pause while everyone does so.

God of all goodness,
may we rejoice always,
pray without ceasing
and give thanks in all circumstances,
in Jesus' name.
Amen.

Please take your strip home. May it be a sign of never-ending thanksgiving to remind you always to thank God.

Music Thank you for saving me

Conclusion Generous Lord,
as we go out into the world,
give us eyes to see your goodness,
a heart to give you thanks,
and a voice to sing your praise.
Amen.

Give notices, announce the next all-age service and invite everyone to the feast.

Proper 24

The wrestling match

Theme	Struggling and persevering with God
Scripture	Genesis 32:22-31; Luke 18:1-8

Running order	Total: 50 minutes
Welcome	Wondering about the picture of Jacob fighting with God *(5 minutes)*
Introduction	Opening the theme
Storytelling 1	The wrestling match – combat demonstration with narration *(5 minutes)*
Music	For the days when you feel near *(5 minutes)*
Storytelling 2	Sketch – the persistent widow *(5 minutes)*
Exploring	What do these stories show us about our relationship with God? *(5 minutes)*
Activity	Prayer stations – struggling and persevering with God *(15 minutes)*
Prayer action	Holding on to God – prayer with hand gestures *(5 minutes)*
Music	It's me, O Lord *(5 minutes)*
Conclusion	Closing prayer and invitation

Resources

NB: This service requires advance preparation and rehearsal with two fighters.

- A picture of Jacob wrestling God, on a screen or in hard copy *(see appendix)*
- *(Optional)* Laptop, projector and screen
- Suitable mats for the fight
- A table and chair
- A plate with a large chunk of bread on it
- A blanket and a pillow
- Music and words
- Prayer stations which offer some multi-sensory prayer activities for when we are struggling with God or attempting to 'pray always' *(see appendix)*

Leaders

Minimum: 5

- Leader
- Fighters x 2
- Cast x 2

Optimum: 11+

- Leader *(Introduction and Conclusion)*
- Storytellers x 2
- Fighters x 2 (enthusiasts who practise wrestling or martial arts) *(see appendix)*
- Cast x 2
  Widow, wearing a plain tunic and a head-cloth
  Judge, wearing rich robes
- Music Leader
- Explorer
- Activity Leader(s)
- Prayer Leader

Suggestions for additional music

- Here, O my Lord
- Lord, for the years

Service

Welcome *As people arrive, show the picture of Jacob fighting with God and invite them to wonder about it: who are these two wrestlers? Why are they fighting?*

Introduction Our service today has begun with a puzzle: we've been wondering who these two wrestlers are and why they're fighting. We'll find out in our first story. To help us tell it, we have two people who are trained fighters.

Introduce your two fighters, then ask one to stand aside until he appears in the story.

Storytelling 1 *Bring forward your first fighter.*

Let's tell the story. This is Jacob and he's getting ready for a battle. He stole his twin brother's birthright and tricked their father into blessing him instead of his brother. Now he's in exile and his brother is on the warpath with 400 men by his side. Jacob is terrified, so he prays to God. He says, 'O God of my father and my grandfather, you told me you would look after me! I don't deserve your love and faithfulness, but I'm here now, and my brother's coming to get me. I'm scared – please save me from him! He'll kill me and my whole family. But you said you'd look after me, and give me as many descendants as there are grains of sand on the seashore.'

Jacob sends hundreds of his finest animals as a peace offering to his brother, then he orders his family to go on ahead with all his possessions. He's left alone for the night, thinking about the battle he'll face in the morning.

Bring forward the second fighter.

But the fight comes sooner than Jacob expects: a stranger appears and wrestles with him until dawn.

The two fighters engage and struggle. After a short time, tell the rest of the story as the fight continues.

There is no winner, so they keep on fighting.

The second fighter briefly fells the first with a blow to the hip, then the fight continues.

The stranger hits Jacob's hip and knocks it out of joint, but even though they've been fighting all night, Jacob says, 'I won't let go until you give me a blessing.'

The stranger asks, 'What's your name?'

'Jacob,' he answers.

The stranger tells him, 'From now on, your name will be Israel, because you've struggled with God and with humans and won.'

Jacob says, 'Who are you?'

The stranger replies, 'Do you need to ask?' Then he blesses Jacob.

The fighters hug.

At last, Jacob lets go and the fight is over.

The fighters separate and the second fighter leaves.

Jacob struggles to his feet, because his hip hurts. He says, 'I've seen God face to face and survived!'

Applaud your fighters.

Music For the days when you feel near

Storytelling 2 Our second story is about a different kind of struggle.

Bring forward the widow.

Here is a poor widow who has lost everything to a cheating landlord. She wants justice and she won't give up until she gets it.

Bring forward the judge.

Here is the judge who must decide her case. He's a godless man who respects no one. He's just sitting down to dinner.

The judge sits down to eat. There is a knocking at the door.

Widow — *(behind the door)* Grant me justice against my opponent!

The judge ignores the noise and starts eating.

Widow — Grant me justice against my opponent! Grant me justice against my opponent!

The judge sighs and opens the door.

Grant me justice against my opponent!

Judge — Go away!

He slams the door.

Widow — Grant me justice against my opponent! Grant me justice against my opponent!

Judge — I'm going to bed.

Widow — Grant me justice against my opponent! Grant me justice against my opponent! Grant me justice against my opponent!

The judge lies down under the blanket and puts the pillow over his head.

Grant me justice against my opponent! Grant me justice against my opponent! Grant me justice against my opponent!

Judge — I give up! I don't care what God or anybody else thinks, but this woman keeps bothering me. I'll give her justice so that she doesn't wear me out by coming here day and night.

Exploring — Both our stories today have involved struggle and opposition. In the story of Jacob's fight, he wrestled all night with a stranger who is described as a man, yet whom Jacob recognised as God himself. The Bible also refers to this being as an angel.[75] Whether he was an

---

75. Hosea 12:4.

angel or God in human form, he gave Jacob the special name of God's chosen people: Israel. The exact meaning of the name is uncertain, but it may mean 'struggles with God' or 'perseveres with God'.

The widow persevered in her struggle for justice. She badgered the judge relentlessly until he gave her what she wanted, simply so that she would leave him in peace. Jesus' point in this story was that if a heartless judge can be won over by persistence, then our loving God will be even readier to respond to our persistent prayers. The story is a parable about the 'need to pray always and not to lose heart.'

Both these stories are about struggling with God, persevering in our prayers and never giving up. They remind us that a relationship with God will not always be easy – sometimes it will feel like a wrestling match. Can I have two strong volunteers, please?

Invite your volunteers forward and sit them facing each other across the table, in position for an arm-wrestling match.

When we pray, we reach out towards God. Prayer is a meeting, like this.

Encourage your volunteers to place one hand each palm-to-palm, to form a pair of praying hands.

Sometimes, our relationship with God will feel like close companionship.

Encourage your volunteers to shake hands across the table.

But sometimes we will feel as if we are pushing against God, wrestling with him – like this.

Encourage your volunteers to arm-wrestle until you have a winner.

These wrestling matches with God are the difficult times. In our story, Jacob was torn between fear and faith when he prayed to God, 'My brother will kill me and my whole family. But you said you'd look after me.' Jesus wrestled in prayer just before he was arrested, when he asked to be spared a horrible death, yet obeyed his Father: 'My Father, if it is possible, let this cup pass from me; yet not what I want but what you want.'[76] We may find ourselves wrestling with God whenever we are afraid, or angry about the things we can't change. We push and push against the fact that our loving God has not stopped bad things from happening to us.

Today's stories show us that such struggles will come in our relationship with God, but that we must never give up. Jacob refused to stop fighting until he received God's blessing; the widow persistently called for justice, and Jesus used her as an example of the 'need to pray always and not to lose heart'. Our activity today will introduce us to some ways of praying which may help us when we are struggling and persevering with God.

Activity

Briefly introduce people to the following prayer stations, which offer some multi-sensory prayer activities for when we are struggling with God or attempting to 'pray always'.

- Stress ball: this is for when you are really struggling with God. As you pray, squeeze these stress balls as hard as you can, or bounce these little balls hard on the floor. As you do so, talk to God in your heart about whatever it is that you are finding difficult at the moment.

- The cloud of unknowing:[77] this is for when you feel surrounded by things that you don't understand, or things that seem too big or too difficult for you to get to grips with. On a cloud, write or draw whatever it is that you find hard to understand, then offer it to God in prayer.

---

76. Matthew 26:39.
77. This is the title of an anonymous medieval guide to contemplative prayer. The author recommends that, since God is beyond our intellectual comprehension, we should suspend all thoughts, words and ideas in prayer and simply love God. He describes this as piercing the 'cloud of unknowing' which is between us and God with the 'sharp dart of longing love'.

- Sticky situation: this is another way of praying about difficult things. Take a sticky toffee and chew it. As your teeth wrestle with the toffee, pray to God about whatever you are struggling with in your life.

- Earworm: you know that feeling when you just can't get a song out of your mind? This is called an earworm, and we can use this as a kind of continual prayer. Come and learn this simple chant and let it become your earworm prayer.

- Counting beads: many people use prayer beads to help them pray regularly. Come and say a prayer as you move each bead through your fingers.

- Yo-yo: a yo-yo goes up and down, up and down. We can use this constant, repetitive motion in our prayers. Think about what you need to ask God, and as the yo-yo goes down, pray, 'Please, Lord,' and as it comes back up to your hand, pray, 'Amen.'

Invite people to explore the different prayer stations.

Prayer action

For our prayers today, we will use the hand gestures demonstrated earlier by our arm-wrestlers. Let's practise the different gestures. First, there is the palms-together gesture that represents our meeting with God in prayer.

Place your palms together and encourage everyone else to do the same.

Then there is the friendly hand-shaking gesture, which reminds us how close to God we can sometimes feel.

Hold your hands together as if shaking them and encourage everyone else to do the same.

Then there is the arm-wrestling gesture, with hands clasped together, which reminds us of wrestling with God. Press your hands together hard, as if each hand is fighting the other. This gesture feels like desperate pleading.

Clasp your hands, pushing them together hard, and encourage everyone else to do the same.

We'll use these three gestures in our prayer. We begin with our palms together.

Everyone puts their hands together.

Let us pray.

Loving Lord.
as we pray, we draw closer to you.

Everyone shakes their hands together.

We thank you for your close companionship.

Everyone clasps their hands together hard.

When we struggle against you,
hold on to us as we hold on to you.
When we continually cry to you,
O Lord, hear our prayer.
Amen.

Music   It's me, O Lord

Conclusion   Heavenly Father,
as we go out into the world,
may we pray always and not lose heart,
in Jesus' name.
Amen.

Give notices, announce the next all-age service and invite everyone to the feast.

Proper 25

What has God done for us?

Theme	Appreciating God's goodness and our need for him
Scripture	Psalm 65; Luke 18:9-14

Running order	Total: 50 minutes
Welcome	Blowing giant bubbles *(5 minutes)*
Introduction	Opening the theme
Storytelling 1	Psalm 65 with slideshow *(5 minutes)*
Music	All things bright and beautiful *(5 minutes)*
Storytelling 2	Sketch – the Pharisee and the tax-collector at prayer *(5 minutes)*
Exploring	What does this story tell us about ourselves? *(2 minutes)*
Activity	Prayer stations – adoration and repentance *(18 minutes)*
Prayer action	Gesture prayer – 'Sorry' and 'Wow!' *(5 minutes)*
Music	Amazing grace *(5 minutes)*
Conclusion	Closing prayer and invitation

PROPER 25

Resources

- Bubble swords for blowing giant bubbles (available cheaply from many toy shops, pound shops and newsagents)
- A slideshow with the words from Psalm 65 *(see appendix)*
- Prayer stations which offer some multi-sensory prayer activities for adoration and repentance *(see appendix)*
- Music and words

Leaders

Minimum: 3

- Leader
- Cast x 2

Optimum: 8+

- Leader *(Introduction and Conclusion)*
- Storyteller
- Cast x 2:
  Pharisee, wearing fine robes
  Tax-collector, wearing a plain tunic
- Music Leader
- Explorer
- Activity Leader(s)
- Prayer Leader

Suggestions for additional music

- Thank you for the summer morning
- Praise, my soul, the King of heaven

Service

Welcome — *As people arrive, invite them to blow giant rainbow bubbles as a sign of their prayer.*

Introduction — There's only one thing we can say about these giant rainbow bubbles we've been blowing: 'WOW!' There are times when that's all we can say to God, too. Here is a psalm that looks at what God has done for us and says – in effect – 'Wow!'

Storytelling 1 — *Show the slideshow with the words from Psalm 65.*

Music — All things bright and beautiful

Storytelling 2 — Our second story begins with two people who have come to the Temple in Jerusalem to pray. Here they are.

The Pharisee walks confidently down the aisle and stands squarely at the front. He clears his throat loudly and throws up his arms in a wide gesture of praise. He holds the position, looking upwards and smiling broadly. Now the tax-collector shuffles down the aisle, looking down. He sidles to a seat in the corner and kneels down, putting his head in his hands. Pause for a moment.

(*in a stage whisper*) Let's listen in to their prayers.

Pharisee — Wow, God! I'm really something. I'm a real credit to you. Thank you that I'm not like everyone else: *(he gestures dismissively at the congregation)* I'm far better than the rest of these crooks, trouble-makers and cheats. *(he looks disapprovingly at the tax-collector)* Thank you that I'm nothing like this money-grabbing tax-collector over here. I do everything by the book: I give you ten per cent of everything I earn, and I fast not once but twice a week! Seriously, you've got to be impressed. Amen.

Tax-collector — *(slapping his own forehead, as if at his own stupidity)* God, go easy on me. I've made a mess of everything.[78]

---

78. I am indebted to the vivid retelling of this story in *the street bible* (Rob Lacey, Zondervan, 2003).

Storyteller	Jesus told this story and – in the words of a very modern version of the Bible – he commented, 'I'm telling you, it's the second guy who walks out in God's good books. Anyone who sets themselves up as something special will crash. Anyone who knows his place, and shows it, will get promotion.'[79]
Exploring	This memorable story showed us two very different kinds of prayer. The first was self-centred: the Pharisee focused entirely on his own achievements and treated God like an admiring audience. The second prayer focused on the sinner's need for God's forgiveness: the tax-collector was painfully aware of his own weaknesses and failings. The Bible says that Jesus told this story 'to some who trusted in themselves that they were righteous and regarded others with contempt.' This is the key: they trusted in themselves, like the Pharisee who didn't think he needed God's help at all; unlike the tax-collector, who knew he couldn't do without it. It was the tax-collector who ended up in God's good books. In our psalm today we saw that same trust in God and that same dependence on him: the psalmist praised God who sends the rain, grows the crops and takes our sins away. Both the psalm and our story remind us to appreciate what God has done for us and to acknowledge our need for his mercy. Our activity today will help us to do both these things.
Activity	Today we will be exploring two different kinds of prayer: prayers that look at God's goodness and say 'Wow!' and prayers in which we look at ourselves in God's presence and say, 'Sorry.' *Briefly introduce the following prayer stations, which offer some multi-sensory prayer activities for adoration and repentance:* • 'Wow!' corner: take some time to look at and feel these beautiful things from the natural world and wonder at God's creation.

---

79. *Ibid*, p.325.

- Fragrant prayer: smell these lovely but very different smells and thank God for the power of smells and the memories they stir.
- Rainbow globe: hold this globe in your hand and watch it slowly change through all the colours of the rainbow. Remember how God used the rainbow as a wonderful sign that he would never again destroy the earth.
- The Jesus Prayer: this is a very old Christian prayer. It will remind you of what the tax-collector said in today's story, and it goes like this: 'Lord Jesus Christ, Son of God, have mercy on me, a sinner.' Repeat this simple prayer over and over again, until saying it becomes automatic. It can help you settle into deeper prayer.
- Ice cubes: when we feel bad about having hurt someone or having done something wrong, it can feel cold and hard inside. Hold an ice cube and say sorry to God for something you regret, then drop it in the water and watch it melt, as a reminder that God's love takes all our sins away.
- Cleansing fire: think about something you feel sorry for having done or not done, then take one of these wooden sticks and draw it, write it down or simply write the word 'Sorry'. Add your stick to the coals and later we will burn all these confessions, as a sign that God's love gets rid of our sins.

Invite people to explore the different prayer stations. Towards the end of the time, take the brazier outside and invite everyone to watch as you burn the confessions.

Prayer action

For our prayers today, we will use the gestures we saw in our story. First, there is the forehead slap, also known as the 'facepalm', which the tax-collector used. This gesture shows extreme disappointment, a feeling of 'Oh, no . . .' or as Homer Simpson would say, 'D'oh!' This is how the tax-collector felt about all the things he had done wrong, and this is the gesture we'll use to say 'Sorry' to God.

Encourage everyone to practise this gesture.

Then there is the great big gesture of praise, used hypocritically by the Pharisee when he was praising himself rather than God. We can use this wide open gesture to help us turn to God and praise his goodness: this gesture says, 'Wow!'

Encourage everyone to practise this gesture.

Let us pray.

Heavenly Father,
as we look at the wrongs we have done
and the messes we have made,
we can only say, 'Sorry.'

Make the forehead-slapping gesture.

Please forgive us.

Pause.

When we look around us
at the wonderful things you have done,
we can only say, 'Wow!'

Make the open gesture of praise.

Praise is due to you, O God.

Pause.

Amen.

Music Amazing grace

Conclusion God of all goodness,
may we be truly thankful
for all you have done for us.
In Jesus' name.
Amen.

Give notices, announce the next all-age service and invite everyone to the feast.

All Saints' Day

All join in

Theme	Being part of the Church and the communion of saints
Scripture	Ephesians 1:11-23; Luke 6:20-31

Running order	Total: 50 minutes
Welcome	All Hallows – making glow-stick haloes *(10 minutes)*
Music	O when the saints *(5 minutes)*
Introduction	Opening the theme
Storytelling	Reading Luke 6:20-31 with interactive scene-setting *(5 minutes)*
Activity	'Do to others as you would have them do to you' – creative brainstorm *(10 minutes)*
Exploring	How can we join the saints? Reading *All Join In* by Quentin Blake *(5 minutes)*
Music	I am one voice and I am singing *(5 minutes)*
Prayer action	Circle of light – interactive prayer *(5 minutes)*
Music	Christ is the King! *(5 minutes)*
Conclusion	Closing prayer and invitation

Resources

- Lots of glow-sticks *(see appendix)*
- Circles of white card, about five inches in diameter, with a cross snipped in the middle for the candle *(see appendix)*
- Thin votive candles, enough for one each
- Matches
- Music and words, including the words of 'I am one voice and I am singing', printed or displayed on a screen *(see appendix)*
- Craft tables
- Felt pens, pens and pencils
- A copy of *All Join In* by Quentin Blake *(see appendix)*
- *(Optional)* Laptop, projector and screen

Leaders

Minimum: 4

- Leader
- *Jesus*
- Music Leaders x 2

Optimum: 8

- Leader *(Introduction and Conclusion)*
- Storyteller
- *Jesus*, wearing white
- Music Leaders x 2 (voices 1 and 2 in the 'I am one voice' song)
- Activity Leader
- Explorer
- Prayer Leader

Suggestions for additional music

- For I'm building a people of power
- In our day of thanksgiving
- There's a place where the streets shine

Service

Welcome — *As people arrive, invite them to make their own halo out of glow-sticks.*

Music — O when the saints

Introduction — Today we celebrate all the saints. 1 November is All Saints' Day: it used to be called All Hallows, and so the day before it is All Hallows' Eve – or Hallowe'en. The two days are complete opposites: Hallowe'en explores the dark and devilish, while All Hallows celebrates light and holiness, which is why we began by making these glowing haloes. In our story today, Jesus deals with opposites, too. He talks about who will be blessed, like the saints, and who will be full of sadness, or 'woe'.

Storytelling — We need to set the scene for our story, because when Jesus speaks in the Bible, he always has an audience. Today, we are the crowd around Jesus in first-century Galilee. Let's see what the Bible says about us.

Consult Luke 6:17-19.

We're in a level place with Jesus: imagine a big dusty field. There's a great crowd of disciples: that's more than just twelve, that's all those of us who follow Jesus from town to town in Galilee. *(Indicate several rows of your congregation.)* Let's say that's all of you. You're a mixed bunch: some of you are poor men and women who have led hard lives, farming other people's land. You're hungry and tired. Some of you have made a good living as dishonest tax-collectors: you've made lots of money but you've lost all your friends. Jesus is starting to make you think that there's more to life than money. For all of you, Jesus is the most exciting person you've ever met, and you can't wait to see what miracle he'll perform next. You've already seen him cure a leper and a paralysed man; now many of you are hoping that he'll cure you, too.

What you particularly love about Jesus is the way that he seems to enjoy spending time with ordinary people

ALL SAINTS' DAY

like you. He's not like those Pharisees, who look down their noses at you. In fact, he stands up to your religious leaders and tells them that they've got it all wrong! It's music to your ears. You call yourselves Jesus' disciples. It's not been easy for you: some of you fishermen have left profitable businesses behind. Some of you have been disowned by your Jewish families. Some of you have lost friends and made enemies because you believe that this teacher from Nazareth is the Son of God.

(Address the rest of the congregation.) But there are many more people in this crowd today. The Bible tells us that there's a great multitude from all Judea, Jerusalem, and the coast of Tyre and Sidon. Word about Jesus has been spreading, and some of you have travelled for over a week to get here! *(Address those at the back of the church.)* You at the back have had the longest journey of all, across mountainous deserts, but you're here now and you're trying to see Jesus over the heads of all these people. *(Address one group of people.)* You want to hear what Jesus has to say: you've heard that his teaching is life-changing. *(Address another group of people.)* You've come because you want Jesus to heal you. You've heard that one touch from him can cure leprosy or get rid of evil spirits!

Encourage everyone to stand.

Here's Jesus!

Bring forward your actor.

All of you are pushing forward, trying to touch him.

Encourage everyone to crowd forward, creating a bit of noise and bustle.

Shh – let's hear what he has to say!

Jesus   *Address the crowd with Jesus' words from Luke 6:20-31.*

Activity

If we were the first people to hear those words, on that hot afternoon in Galilee, I wonder what we'd think? If you were poor and hungry, what would you think?

Invite responses.

If you were rich and well-fed, like the tax-collectors, what would you think?

Invite responses.

What would you think if you were a disciple who had been bullied because he followed Jesus?

Invite responses.

Jesus ended with an instruction for all his disciples, including us: 'Do to others as you would have them do to you.' The examples he gave sounded difficult, such as loving your enemies, turning the other cheek and giving to everyone who begs, but the consistent message is that we should meet people with love – not with hate, or revenge, or rejection, but love.

Today we will think about practical ways in which we might love other people by 'doing to others as we would have them do to us.' *(Hold up the circles of card.)* We will cover these circles of card with our suggestions: for example, you could write down ideas such as 'Say sorry to someone I have upset' or 'Offer a cup of tea to the next homeless person I meet.' You could also draw your ideas about loving others: for example, you could simply draw the sign of a kiss with an X, or you could draw a picture of two very different people hugging, such as a Man United fan and a Man City fan.[80]

Encourage everyone to gather round the craft tables and write or draw their ideas on the circles of card. You may like to invite people to share their ideas before they return to their places, taking their cards with them.

---

80. Change these teams to local rivals, as appropriate.

ALL SAINTS' DAY

Exploring On All Saints' Day we remember the faithful men and women of God who have gone before us, and our question is this: how can we be more like the saints? We have been thinking of ways in which we can meet people with love and so follow Jesus' instruction, 'Do to others as you would have them do to you.' It is easy to see how turning our backs on hate, grievance and revenge would make our lives happier and our world a better place, but Jesus promised even more: 'Your reward will be great, and you will be children of the Most High.' If we make our lives all about love, God will recognise us as one of his own. The people we call saints are those whose lives have been defined by their love for God and for other people. The more we try to meet people with love, the more we become like saints ourselves, and we can look forward to what the Bible calls 'the riches of [Christ's] glorious inheritance among the saints.'

As well as setting us an example of love, the saints remind us of our connection with each other. The Bible describes Jesus as the head of the Church, and the Church as his body; as members of that body, we are connected to each other and to him. The saints are part of the body of Christ, too, and we believe that when we pray, the whole Church and the saints in heaven join us in our prayers. Being part of the Church means joining this whole body of believers, and there is a lovely children's story that will help us remember this.

Read All Join In *by Quentin Blake.*

The saints remind us that when we follow Jesus, we are not alone: we are part of the body of Christ, and we are connected to the saints and our fellow Christians all over the world, across time and in heaven. So what do we do? We all join in!

Music I am one voice and I am singing

Prayer action *Encourage people to gather in a circle that reaches all around the church. They need to be wearing their glow-stick haloes and carrying their circles of card from the Activity. Pass* *round the thin votive candles (unlit) and invite people to push them through the hole in the centre of their card. When everyone is ready, turn out the lights.*

For our prayers today, we remember the saints. We remember that we are called to meet people with love, and that this is how we can become like saints ourselves.

Let us pray.

Light your candle and pass the light to the people either side of you in the circle. Pause while the light is passed around the circle.

Heavenly Father,
we pray with the saints,
whose lives shone with the light of your love.
May we all join in
and share this light in all that we say and do.
Amen.

Pause for a moment, then turn on the lights and blow out the candles. Invite people to return to their places and suggest that they take their votive candles home with them, as a reminder of today's service.

Music Christ is the King!

Conclusion God of Love,
send us out into the world
to do to others as we would have them do to us,
in Jesus' name.
Amen.

Give notices, announce the next all-age service and invite everyone to the feast.

Fourth Sunday before Advent

Putting things right

Theme	Saying sorry and making amends
Scripture	Isaiah 1:10-18; Luke 19:1-10

Running order	Total: 50 minutes
Welcome	Prayer leaves on Zacchaeus' tree *(5 minutes)*
Introduction	Opening the theme
Storytelling	Sketch – Dinner at Zacchaeus' house *(10 minutes)*
Music	Zacchaeus was a very little man *(5 minutes)*
Exploring	What can we learn from Zacchaeus? *(5 minutes)*
Prayer action	Newspaper confessions *(5 minutes)*
Activity	Papier mâché *(15 minutes)*
Music	I'm accepted, I'm forgiven *(5 minutes)*
Conclusion	Closing prayer and invitation

FOURTH SUNDAY BEFORE ADVENT

Resources

- At the front of church, a step ladder with prayer tree attached *(see appendix)*
- Prayer leaves *(see appendix)*
- Pens and pencils
- Music and words
- Strips of old newspaper
- Felt pens
- A large plastic bowl containing watery glue (made with warm water, to speed up the pulping process)
- An old wooden spoon
- A wipe-clean craft table
- A large aluminium platter (available cheaply from supermarkets)
- A bowl of warm soapy water and a towel

Leaders

Minimum: 4

- Leader
- Cast x 3

Optimum: 9

- Leader *(Introduction and Conclusion)*
- Storyteller
- Cast x 3:
  Woman, wearing a tunic and a head-cloth
  Zacchaeus (shorter than your other actors), wearing rich robes
  Jesus, wearing a white tunic
- Music Leader
- Explorer
- Prayer Leader
- Activity Leader

Suggestions for additional music

- Dear Lord and Father of mankind
- We turn to you

Service

Welcome — *As people arrive, invite them to write or draw a prayer on a sycamore leaf and attach it to Zacchaeus' tree.*

Introduction — Our opening prayers today have added leaves to a sycamore tree. This tree plays a part in today's story: let's find out what happened.

Storytelling — *(in the style of a royal wedding commentator)* Good morning. You join us here on a fine day in Jericho. Crowds are lining the streets in anticipation, because Jesus is expected to come through the town later today. Some people have been camping out all night to make sure they are in the best place to see him when he arrives. Madam, may I ask how long you've been here?

Woman — Since daybreak. I wouldn't miss Jesus for the world! I've tidied my house just in case, because I've heard that sometimes he just invites himself for dinner. I'm not worthy, of course, but I'd be so thrilled if he chose *my* house!

Storyteller — Now I've just been told that Jesus has in fact arrived in Jericho! The whole crowd is on its feet, hoping to catch a glimpse of him.

Encourage the congregation to stand. Zacchaeus climbs his step ladder behind the tree.

People are so desperate to see Jesus today that one rather short man has even climbed a sycamore tree to get a better look! Does anyone know him?

Woman — Oh, *him*. We don't have anything to do with *him*: that's Zacchaeus, the chief tax-collector. He's filthy rich – he makes all his money from fleecing us ordinary, hard-working citizens. Everyone hates him.

Storyteller — Oh – I see. *(an awkward, throat-clearing pause)* At last, here's Jesus! I can just see him over the heads of the crowd!

Jesus walks down the aisle until he draws level with the step ladder.

Jesus — Hey, Zacchaeus! Hurry up and get down – I've got to come to dinner at your house today.

FOURTH SUNDAY BEFORE ADVENT

Zacchaeus	Coming! *(as he climbs down)* My Lord, that would be such an honour!
Woman	Huh! He's going eat a sinner's food! Fancy going to *his* house when there are so many good people to choose from!
Zacchaeus	*(standing in front of Jesus)* Look, Lord, I'll give half of everything I own to the poor, and if I've cheated anyone of anything, I'll pay them back four times over.
Jesus	Today this man has been saved, because he's one of God's people, too. The Son of God has come to find and save anyone who's lost.
Music	Zacchaeus was a very little man
Exploring	No one likes paying taxes, but in Jesus' time, tax-collectors were particularly hated because they were cheats. They added their own bonuses on top of the official taxes, so they got rich at the expense of the poor. Zacchaeus was especially unpopular because he was a chief tax-collector: he organised all the taxes in the region, and all the unfair extras, so as a result he was – as the woman in our story said – filthy rich. No wonder people grumbled when Jesus chose to have dinner at Zacchaeus' house instead of at the home of an honest, God-fearing, local citizen.
	Zacchaeus was no fool. He must have been as astonished as anyone when Jesus singled him out and invited himself for dinner. He knew what he'd done wrong, and he knew why people were grumbling: everyone in town hated his dishonest business dealings. So before he welcomed Jesus into his home, he put things right. He didn't just say he was sorry – he publicly proposed a plan of action: he'd give half his wealth to the poor, and if he had cheated anyone of anything, he'd pay them back four times over. People in the crowd must have started doing their sums when they heard that! Who among them hadn't been cheated by Zacchaeus over the years?
	In response to Zacchaeus' plan for making amends, Jesus announced that he was saved, and that this was

the Son of God's mission – to save the lost, to forgive the sins of the sinful. This explains why he walked down the main street in Jericho and called, 'Hey, Zacchaeus!' He'd come to find the biggest sinner in town and give him the opportunity to receive forgiveness.

Zacchaeus was forgiven not simply because he was sorry for his wrongdoing, but because he did his best to put things right, by giving his money to the poor and repaying more than he had stolen. He sets us an example of what we should do when we have done something wrong: say sorry *and* do our best to put things right. In the Old Testament, God gave the same message to his people who had turned away from him and done lots of very bad things. Through his spokesman, Isaiah, he told them how much he hated their wrongdoing, and gave them these clear instructions:

> Wash yourselves; make yourselves clean;
> remove the evil of your doings
> from before my eyes;
> cease to do evil,
> learn to do good;
> seek justice,
> rescue the oppressed,
> defend the orphan,
> plead for the widow.

For God's people then and for us today, God's command is the same: 'cease to do evil, learn to do good.' This may mean making a change in our own lives, as Zacchaeus did; Isaiah's words suggest that we should also tackle injustice, oppression and inequality in the world around us. We need to ask ourselves, 'What can we do to put things right?'

Prayer action For our prayers today, we will say sorry for what we have done wrong. Please take a piece of this old newspaper and write or draw your confession on it. Let's say sorry to God.

Pass round the newspaper strips and felt tip pens. Pause while everyone writes or draws their confession.

We remember that Zacchaeus turned his wrongdoing into something good, so today we will make something useful out of these confessions. We will turn them into pulp and use them as papier mâché. As we ask God to take away our sins, we will tear our confessions up and add them to this watery glue mixture so that our words, and the paper strips they are written on, start to dissolve.

Invite everyone to come forward and add the torn-up pieces of their confessions to the bowl of watery glue and stir them in with the big spoon. The felt pen should start to run and dissolve as the mixture is stirred.

Let us pray.

Forgiving Lord,
may you take away our sins
and dissolve them in your love,
in Jesus' name.
Amen.

Activity

Now we will use this papier mâché to make a big collection plate or serving dish. Our confessions will become something that encourages us to give.

Invite volunteers to gather round the craft table and help make the big plate out of papier mâché, by smoothing layers on top of a large aluminium platter. Allow time for people to wash their hands afterwards.

Music

I'm accepted, I'm forgiven

Conclusion

Almighty God,
as we go out into the world,
strengthen us so that we may we stop doing wrong
and learn to do the right thing,
in Jesus' name.
Amen.

Give notices, announce the next all-age service and invite everyone to the feast. Leave the papier-mâché plate in a warm place to dry, then apply several layers of varnish and use it in future all-age services, either as a collection plate or as a dish for serving food at the feast.

Third Sunday before Advent
Conviction

Theme	Christian persecution
Scripture	Job 19:23-27a; 2 Thessalonians 2:1-5, 13-17

Running order Total: 50 minutes

Welcome	Fingerprints *(5 minutes)*
Introduction	Opening the theme
Storytelling	Persecuted Christians – Paul's words of comfort, with visual aids *(5 minutes)*
Music	Be bold, be strong *(5 minutes)*
Exploring	What did Christian persecution mean in Paul's time? What does it mean today? *(5 minutes)*
Activity	If it were a crime to be a Christian, what evidence would convict you? Collecting evidence; a scavenger hunt *(20 minutes)*
Prayer action	Candles and barbed wire – visual intercessions *(5 minutes)*
Music	Grant us the courage, gracious God *(5 minutes)*
Conclusion	Closing prayer and invitation

Resources

- A long strip of lining paper
- A pad of ink
- Baby wipes for fingers
- Laptop, projector and screen
- Pictures for visual aids *(see appendix)*
- A piece of card and a marker pen (for drawing the fish symbol)
- Music and words
- Evidence bags. Use large zip-lock freezer bags and stick a large label on each one that reads 'EVIDENCE'
- Pieces of A5 paper
- Pens, pencils and felt pens
- Hidden all over the church, Christian fish symbols made from different materials (e.g. drawn; knitted; modelled from pipe cleaners, building bricks, clay, etc)
- A circle of barbed wire
- Tea lights
- Matches and tapers

Leaders

Minimum: 1
- Leader

Optimum: 6+
- Leader *(Introduction and Conclusion)*
- Storyteller
- Music Leader
- Explorer
- Activity Leader(s)
- Prayer Leader

Suggestions for additional music

- How sweet the name of Jesus sounds
- Forth in the peace of Christ we go

Service

Welcome — *As people arrive, invite them to make a set of fingerprints as a way of saying, 'Here I am, Lord.'*

Introduction — Our service today is about conviction. If you have a conviction, it can mean two things: you have a strong belief, or you have been found guilty of a crime. Nearly 2000 years ago, the first Christians had both kinds of conviction, because their faith in Jesus could get them arrested, put in prison and even killed.

Storytelling — First of all, we have a curious object to look at. What do you think this might be?

Invite people to respond to the picture of the metal book. Ask such questions as:

- What do you think this is made of?
- How old do you think it might be?
- What do you think the lines and squiggles are?
- If we were able to make out any words, what language might they be in?

These questions are ones that experts have been asking themselves, and people are still trying to discover all the answers. Metal notebooks like this one have come to light in Jordan in recent years. They are made of sheets of lead and are covered in what looks like code and some scraps of ancient languages such as Hebrew. Strangest of all, some of them are closed on all sides by metal rings. People have wondered whether these books were made by the earliest Christians as a secret record of their faith. They sound like the book that was described with longing by Job in the Old Testament:

> O that my words were written down!
> O that they were inscribed in a book!
> O that with an iron pen and with lead
> they were engraved on a rock for ever!
> For I know that my Redeemer lives.

However, most experts now agree that the metal books found in Jordan are fakes, but it is easy to believe that such coded Christian records might exist. For example, we know that the first Christians used the sign of the fish as a secret symbol.

Show the sign of the fish.

This sign marked Christian meeting places and tombs. Some people think that Christians used it as a code for recognising each other. If you met a stranger on the road, you could draw this sign in the sand:

Draw an arch (the top half of the fish).

The stranger might look confused, or he might finish the sign.

Complete the fish symbol.

If he did, you knew that he was a fellow Christian and not someone looking to report you to the police.

Secret signs and codes like this remind us that the first Christians were constantly in danger of being arrested and killed, simply because they believed in Jesus and wouldn't keep quiet about it. They needed lots of support and encouragement in their dangerous situation. This is what Paul, the leader of the early Church, wrote to Christians in Greece. They had suffered a lot but remained faithful.

> But we must always give thanks to God for you, brothers and sisters beloved by the Lord, because God chose you as the first fruits for salvation through sanctification by the Spirit and through belief in the truth. For this purpose he called you through our proclamation of the good news, so that you may obtain the glory of our Lord Jesus Christ. So then, brothers and sisters, stand firm and hold fast to the traditions that you were taught by us, either by word of mouth or by our letter.

> Now may our Lord Jesus Christ himself and God our Father, who loved us and through grace gave us eternal comfort and good hope, comfort your hearts and strengthen them in every good work and word.

Music   Be bold, be strong

Exploring   Paul's message to the Christians in Greece was, 'Be bold, be strong.' Why did they need to be strong? What exactly were they up against?

Show the picture of the crucifixion.

After Jesus' execution by the Romans, anyone who preached in his name risked the same fate. The Bible tells us that Jesus' enemies went about 'breathing threats and murder against the disciples of the Lord.'[81] In short, there was a manhunt.

Show the picture of an angry crowd.

There were also riots against Christians, because the Jews were angry that Jesus was being called God; the Romans were angry that Jesus, rather than their emperor, was being called king, and ordinary citizens were angry that the peace of their towns and cities was being disturbed. In Greece, people described the first Christians as 'these people who have been turning the world upside down',[82] and they wanted to get rid of them. Many were put in prison.

Show the picture of a prison cell.

Many were tortured and killed.

Show the picture of a sword.

Not many of us here today would think of going to church as a dangerous activity. However, the dangers faced by the first Christians are still being faced by Christians in some parts of the world today.

Show the picture of the burning church in Egypt.

---

81. Acts 9:1.
82. Acts 17:6.

THIRD SUNDAY BEFORE ADVENT

For example, in Egypt, churches have been set on fire. In one case, when thousands of Christians protested, soldiers attacked them, killing at least 30 people and injuring over 300.[83]

Show the picture of the crowd of Egyptian Christians.

In Uganda, a teacher lost his job and his family because he converted to Christianity. He was imprisoned on a false charge. Yet he founded a Christian school which teaches children of all faiths and he is working to help people in the area grow better crops to feed themselves.[84]

Show the picture of Ugandan children farming.

Stories like these show us that many Christians in the world do not have the freedom we enjoy. They take risks that we might find hard to imagine, simply by believing in Jesus.

Activity

Today we have a big question to think about: if it was a crime to be a Christian, what evidence would convict you? Here are lots of police evidence bags. What might you write, draw or find to put in them? For example, is having a fish symbol on your car enough evidence to prove that you are a Christian? If you think it is, then draw one and put it in an evidence bag. Are there things in church that prove we believe in Jesus? Would you put a hymn book in an evidence bag? Or perhaps it is something we say or do that is the real proof. Can you write or draw something that proves a person is a Christian?

Allow plenty of time for people to engage with the big question. Some might prefer to write and draw; others will want to put physical objects, such as a cross or a service book, in evidence bags. Encourage younger children to find the fish symbols you have hidden all over church and place them in evidence bags, too. When plenty of evidence bags have been filled, invite people to explain what they have chosen and encourage discussion.

---

83. Source: Amnesty International report, 2011: *Broken Promises – Egypt's military rulers erode human rights.*
84. Source: *Compass Direct News,* Open Doors UK & Ireland.

Prayer action Today we will pray for Christians everywhere who are threatened because of their belief in Jesus Christ. We pray for their leaders and their churches.

Pause.

We pray for people of every faith and none who are threatened because of what they believe. We pray for prisoners of conscience everywhere.

Encourage everyone to come forward and place a candle inside the circle of barbed wire, then light it as a sign of their prayer.

God of power and might,
comfort all these people,
give them good hope
and strengthen them in every good work and word,
through Jesus Christ.
Amen.

Music Grant us the courage, gracious God

Conclusion Lord Jesus,
send us out into the world to follow you.
Give us the courage of our convictions.
Amen.

Give notices, announce the next all-age service and invite everyone to the feast.

Remembrance Sunday

Peace be with you

Theme	Nothing can separate us from God's love
Scripture	Romans 8:31-39; John 14:27

Running order	Total: 60 minutes
Act of Remembrance	The laying of wreaths and the two minutes' silence *(15 minutes)*
Welcome	The National Anthem *(5 minutes)*
Introduction	Opening the theme
Activity	Lighting candles of remembrance *(10 minutes)*
Storytelling	Reading Romans 8:31-39 *(5 minutes)*
Exploring	What can separate us from God's love? Interactive exploration with Tug of War *(10 minutes)*
Music	Christ is the world's Light *(5 minutes)*
Prayer action	Peace poppies – visual prayers *(5 minutes)*
Music	Make me a channel *(5 minutes)*
Conclusion	Closing prayer and invitation

Resources

- Music and words
- Votive candles and candle stands
- Matches and tapers
- A long, strong rope for the Tug of War. It must not break! Ask a local school's PE department if you can borrow one
- A white tunic
- Seven large white peace poppies *(see appendix)*

Leaders

Minimum: 9

- Leader
- Reader
- Prayer helpers x 7

Optimum: 14

- Leader *(Introduction and Conclusion)*
- Readers x 2
- Music Leader
- Activity Leader
- Explorer
- Prayer Leader
- Prayer helpers x 7 to bring forward the prayer poppies. I suggest you approach the uniformed organisations in advance

Suggestions for additional music

- Eternal Father, strong to save
- We will lay our burden down
- I vow to thee, my country

Service

Act of Remembrance — The laying of wreaths and the two minutes' silence.

Welcome — The National Anthem

Introduction — Welcome to our service of remembrance. This morning we remember all those who have died in the service of their country, and those who are still fighting for justice and freedom in our name. You are invited to come forward and light a candle for anyone you are thinking of today.

Activity — *Allow plenty of time for people to light candles of remembrance. If you have a very large congregation, it may be best to organise this like Communion, so that people come forward in turn and light candles before the altar (and perhaps before a side altar, too).*

As we remember all those who have died in war, and all those whose lives have been touched by conflict, it can be hard to find the right words. So our Bible reading today begins with an apt question: 'What then are we to say about these things?'

Storytelling

Reader 1	What then are we to say about these things?
Reader 2	If God is for us, who is against us? . . . Who will separate us from the love of Christ?
Reader 1	Will hardship, or distress, or persecution, or famine, or nakedness, or peril, or sword?
Reader 2	. . . No, in all these things we are more than conquerors through him who loved us.
Reader 1	For I am convinced that neither death, nor life,
Reader 2	nor angels, nor rulers,
Reader 1	nor things present, nor things to come,
Reader 2	nor powers, nor height, nor depth,
Readers 1 and 2	nor anything else in all creation, will be able to separate us from the love of God in Christ Jesus our Lord.

Exploring

These words were written by Paul, the leader of the early Church. Living in a time when Christians were a persecuted minority, he was a man who knew about danger, struggle and conflict. He considered the question, 'Who will separate us from the love of God in Christ Jesus?' It's as if Jesus' love is a strong rope that connects us with God.

Show the rope.

Let's see what that might look like. Can I have two volunteers?

Invite two volunteers forward and dress one in a white tunic. Get them to hold one end of the rope each.

This person represents you and me *(Indicate your first volunteer.)* and this person represents God. *(Indicate your volunteer in white.)* A strong rope joins them together: this rope is like Jesus' love, because it connects us with God.

Now, Paul gave us a long list of all the things that seem capable of separating us from God, and he began with experiences we associate with war: hardship, distress, persecution, peril and the sword. Can I have some volunteers to represent those things? Are they strong enough to separate us from God?

Invite some volunteers to come up and form sides for the tug of war: they should line up in front of your first two volunteers.

Then Paul mentioned famine and nakedness: hunger and poverty too often affect the ordinary people who are caught up in conflict, but are they strong enough to separate people from God's love?

Invite two more volunteers up to join the tug of war.

Then Paul gets to the deepest questions of all: can death separate us from God's love? Can powerful people in this world or powers beyond our understanding? What about things that might happen in the future: can they separate us from God's love? Paul lists all these things: death, life, angels, rulers, things present, things to come, powers, height, depth and – just in case he'd missed anything out – anything else in all creation. I'm going to need lots more volunteers.

Line all your volunteers up.

Now, are any of these strong enough to break the bond of love between God and us? Will the rope break?

Begin the tug of war and let them struggle for a bit. (Your first two volunteers hold the rope but don't join in.) It's not about which side wins, it's about showing that the rope will not break. Applaud your volunteers' efforts.

This is Paul's conclusion and his message to us, today: ABSOLUTELY NOTHING can separate us from the love of God in Christ Jesus our Lord. Jesus' love is like an unbreakable rope that connects us to God. This truth can comfort and strengthen us when we feel as if we have nothing else to hold on to. Since God will never stop loving us, we have nothing to fear; if we take this to heart, it will give us peace. This was Jesus' promise to his disciples, and he says the same to us:

> Peace I leave with you; my peace I give to you. I do not give to you as the world gives. Do not let your hearts be troubled, and do not let them be afraid.

Music   Christ is the world's Light

Prayer action   God holds this war-torn world in his hands and looks with love on his suffering people. Today we pray for peace. After each prayer there will be a pause as a white peace poppy is brought forward. In that time of quiet, we offer our own prayers in silence. Let us pray.

God of peace,
we pray for all those who have died in war.

Pause. The first poppy is brought forward and laid down.

May they rest in peace.
We pray for all those who are fighting in conflicts around the world.

Pause. The second poppy is brought forward and laid down.

May they achieve peace.
We pray for all those who suffer as a result of active service.

Pause. The third poppy is brought forward and laid down.

May they find peace.
We pray for ordinary people caught up in conflict.

Pause. The fourth poppy is brought forward and laid down.

May peace be with them.
We pray for those who live and work in war zones.

Pause. The fifth poppy is brought forward and laid down.

Give them that peace which the world cannot give.
We pray for those who grieve or wait for news.

Pause. The sixth poppy is brought forward and laid down.

May they know Christ's peace in their hearts.
We pray for those in power who strive for peace.

Pause. The seventh poppy is brought forward and laid down, completing the shape of the cross.

May you bless their peacemaking.
We offer these prayers in Jesus' name.
Amen.

Music Make me a channel

Conclusion Heavenly Father,
send us out into the world
with your peace in our hearts,
knowing that nothing can separate us
from your love.
Amen.

Give notices, announce the next all-age service and invite everyone to the feast.

Second Sunday before Advent

It's not fair!

Theme	Longing for justice and waiting for the Last Judgement
Scripture	Malachi 4:1-2a; 2 Thessalonians 3:6-13; Luke 21:5-19
Running order	Total: 50 minutes
Welcome	Weighing objects on the balancing scales *(5 minutes)*
Introduction	Opening the theme
Storytelling	Sketch – 'It's not fair!' *(5 minutes)*
Music	O Lord, the clouds are gathering *(5 minutes)*
Activity	Writing on the protest wall/placard *(15 minutes)*
Exploring	What does the Bible say about fairness? Dramatic exploration *(10 minutes)*
Prayer action	Balancing scales – active prayer *(5 minutes)*
Music	Make me a channel of your peace *(5 minutes)*
Conclusion	Closing prayer and invitation

Resources

- A set of balancing scales *(see appendix)*
- A collection of objects to weigh on the scales (use items ordinarily found around church, such as a candle, a hymn book, a service sheet, etc)
- Music and words
- A toy, for use as a prop: use a doll/Lego figure/iPod, etc, depending on the age and gender of your actors
- A protest wall/placard *(see appendix)*
- Marker pens/giant chalks
- A clapper board *(see appendix)*
- A stick of white chalk
- A small towel soaked in red food colouring for the casualty to hold to his/her leg
- A blanket
- A tie, to use as a tourniquet
- A mobile phone
- In every pew or row of seats:
  - small cards or pieces of paper
  - pens

Leaders

Minimum: 3

- Leader
- Cast x 2

Optimum: 7

- Leader *(Introduction and Conclusion)*
- Cast x 2, wearing ordinary clothes:
  Child 1/Casualty
  Child 2/Helper
- Music Leader
- Activity Leader
- Explorer
- Prayer Leader

Suggestions for additional music

- Judge eternal, throned in splendour
- Heaven shall not wait

Service

Welcome — *As people arrive, invite them to experiment with weighing and balancing different objects on the scales.*

Introduction — The scales we have been using this morning are a very old symbol of justice: they represent the balancing of truth and fairness. Scales like these hang on courtroom statues all over the world, but justice isn't only about what happens in court. Justice is what we call for every time we say, 'It's not fair!' This is our theme today, and our story might seem rather familiar.

Storytelling

Child 1 — Have you seen my *toy*?[85]

Child 2 — No.

Child 1 — Are you sure?

Child 2 — No – I mean, yes.

Child 1 — You've got it, haven't you? Where is it?

Child 2 — I dunno.

Child 1 — *(searching frantically, then finding it)* Aha! I knew you'd taken it! *(looking closely)* But hang on – it's broken!

Child 2 — It's not my fault!

Child 1 — Yes it is! You took it without asking and now you've broken it! Why does this always happen to me? *(calling)* Mum!

Child 2 — I didn't mean to. It just sort of broke.

Child 1 — Just wait till Mum finds out. *(calling)* MUM! It's not fair – this was a present. *(calling)* MUM! You're going to be in so much trouble when Mum gets here.

Child 2 — *(crying)* That's not fair! It wasn't my fault it broke! You're always getting me into trouble!

Music — O Lord, the clouds are gathering

---

[85]. Substitute doll/Lego figure/iPod etc, depending on the age and gender of your actors.

SECOND SUNDAY BEFORE ADVENT

Activity 'It's not fair!' How many of you have said or heard that recently?

Invite responses.

When we're children, we're always on the look-out for things that aren't fair, and it's one of those strong feelings that never leave us. When bad things happen to us, we might think, 'Why me? It's not fair!' When we look at the world around us, we can get really angry at the unfairness of life: we see rich people getting richer and poor people getting poorer. Every time we watch *Comic Relief* or *Children In Need*, we see countless examples of how unfair life is for some people: for the children in Africa who die of preventable diseases, or for the young people in this country who are reduced to living on the streets.

Today we are going to have a chance to protest about things that aren't fair. Here is our protest wall/placard: take your time to write on it anything that you think is unfair. It might be about you, about those close to you or about events in the wider world.

Allow plenty of time for people to think and write, then share some of the contributions.

Exploring

Explorer We can see that there are lots of things we find unfair. We are not alone in our protests: the Bible is full of complaining voices. The Psalms direct many angry questions at God, like these:

Child 1 How long, O Lord? Will you forget me for ever?
How long will you hide your face from me?
How long must I bear pain in my soul,
and have sorrow in my heart all day long?
How long shall my enemy be exalted over me?[86]

Explorer This bitter complaint might remind us of the cross child in our sketch who shouted, 'Why does this always happen to me?' God's answer comes in part

---

86. Psalm 13:1, 2.

through his prophets, who predict what will happen at the end of the world:

Child 1   See, the day is coming, burning like an oven, when all the arrogant and all evildoers will be stubble; the day that comes shall burn them up, says the Lord of hosts, so that it will leave them neither root nor branch. But for you who revere my name the sun of righteousness shall rise, with healing in its wings.

Explorer   This describes the Day of Judgement, which is a threat for the wrongdoer but a promise for those who have been wronged: on that last day, God will sort everything out and give people exactly what they deserve. In our sketch, there was a similar threat: 'You're going to be in so much trouble when Mum gets here.'

So we might wonder where that leaves us and the unfairness we have been complaining about today. Do we just have to stand by and let it happen while we wait for God to put everything right in the end? We have a short sketch to help us think about this question, and there are two alternatives to choose from.

Hold up a clapper board: Take 1.

Casualty   *(collapsing on the floor, with the blood-soaked towel clutched against his/her leg)* Help! Help! I've cut my leg really badly!

Helper   Oh no! Let me phone an ambulance for you! *(dialling)* Hello? I need an ambulance please. There's a person with an injured leg. I'm in *[give your church's address]*. It's OK – the ambulance is on its way.

Casualty   I'm bleeding!

Helper   I know. The ambulance is on its way.

Pause.

Casualty   My leg really hurts!

Helper   It won't be long now.

Casualty   I'm really cold!

Helper   I'm sure the ambulance will have a blanket for you when it gets here.

The casualty passes out.

Hold up a clapper board: Take 2.

Casualty	*(collapsing on the floor, with the blood-soaked towel clutched against his/her leg)* Help! Help! I've cut my leg really badly!
Helper	Oh no! Let me phone an ambulance for you! *(dialling)* Hello? I need an ambulance please. There's a person with an injured leg. I'm in *[give your church's address]*. It's OK – the ambulance is on its way. *(into the phone)* What can I do to help? *(listens and nods)*
Casualty	I'm bleeding!
Helper	I know. We need to tie something tight around your leg, like this. *(he uses a tie as a tourniquet)* Now we need to get you lying down with your leg up. *(he helps the casualty into this position)* There.
	Pause.
Casualty	My leg really hurts!
Helper	Let me see what I can do. *(going back to the phone)* Hello? Are you still there?
Casualty	I'm really cold!
Helper	Can you hear that? *(listens and nods – then to the casualty)* Here you are – you need a blanket. I'll stay with you until the ambulance comes.
	He tucks the casualty up in a blanket and holds his hand.
	The ambulance will be here soon.
Explorer	Which version of the sketch did you like best?
	Invite responses and ask people to explain their choices.
	This sketch shows us what we need to do when we see something unfair or unjust in the world around us. We can't simply wait for God to sort everything out for us: there are things we can do to help here and now. God himself set us an example, because he could have stayed in heaven and waited until the end of the world to make things better; instead he became a human being – Jesus – and gave his life to help us here on earth. It's our job to follow in Jesus' footsteps and do what we can to make this world a better, fairer place for everyone. The leader of the early Church, Paul, gave this simple advice: 'Brothers and sisters, do not be weary in doing what is right.' This is what we need to do.

Prayer action In our prayers today, we remember those who long for justice and those who are struggling with the unfairness of life. Please write or draw your prayer, then place it in these scales of justice.

Allow time for everyone to do so.

God of Justice,
we bring these people before you now.
Help us to balance truth and fairness
in our lives and in our world.
May we do what is right
in Jesus' name.
Amen.

Music Make me a channel of your peace

Conclusion God of Love,
send us out into the world,
hungering and thirsting for righteousness.
May we help your kingdom come.
Amen.

Give notices, announce the next all-age service and invite everyone to the feast.

Christ the King

Our God and King

Theme	Jesus is King and Lord of all
Scripture	Psalm 46; Colossians 1:11-20; Luke 23:33-43

Running order	Total: 50 minutes	
Welcome	Making crowns *(10 minutes)*	
Introduction	Opening the theme	
Activity	Finding, making and exploring the images that tell us about Christ the King *(10 minutes)*	
Storytelling	Visual retelling of Luke 23:33-43 *(5 minutes)*	
Music	The King is among us *(5 minutes)*	
Exploring	What kind of king is Jesus? Visual and interactive exploration *(10 minutes)*	
Music	Let all the world in every corner sing *(5 minutes)*	
Prayer action	'Be still, and know that I am God' – contemplative prayer with crown *(5 minutes)*	
Conclusion	Closing prayer and invitation	

CHRIST THE KING

Resources

- Craft tables
- Equipment for making crowns *(see appendix)*
- All around the church, things to find, make and explore that tell us about Christ the King *(see appendix)*
- Christ the King lists *(see appendix)*
- Music and words
- A large candle
- Several smaller candles or tea lights, enough to make a circle around the special crown *(see appendix for third bullet point, above)*
- Matches and tapers

Leaders

Minimum: 1

- Leader

Optimum: 6+

- Leader *(Introduction and Conclusion)*
- Activity Leader(s)
- Storyteller
- Explorer
- Music Leader
- Prayer Leader

Suggestions for additional music

- King of kings, majesty
- Rejoice, the Lord is King!

Service

Welcome — *As people arrive, invite them to make and decorate their own crowns.*

Introduction — We've started by making crowns because today we are celebrating the festival of Christ the King. We will be thinking about what kind of king Jesus is, and wondering what his kingship means for us.

Activity — All around the church this morning there are lots of different things to find, make and explore: they all tell us something about Christ the King. Please take a list and see how many of these things you can find or do.

Hand out the lists. You might suggest that people work in families or all-age teams. Collect all the items together at the front, then gather people around for the Storytelling, in a circle if possible.

Storytelling — We're going to use some of these things to help us tell our story today. First of all, there's this splendid king's crown.

Hold up the special crown.

Before Jesus was born, the Jewish people were waiting for their Saviour, God's Chosen One, who would be their King. It's as if they had a crown like this, all ready for when the right person came along. When Mary was told by an angel that she was going to have a baby, she learned that he was God's Son and that he was going to be the King of the Jews. This crown would be his.

Place the special crown in the centre of the circle.

The title of King never left Jesus. It gave the Romans a reason to kill him, because they thought he was their emperor's rival. When the Roman soldiers arrested Jesus, they laughed about having a king in their power. They bullied him by forcing him to wear a crown made of thorns.

Place the crown of thorns in the centre of the circle.

CHRIST THE KING

They even labelled his cross with a sign for everyone to see: 'King of the Jews'.

Place the cross with the sign in the centre of the circle.

The soldiers nailed him to the cross and laughed at him. They said, 'If you're the King of the Jews, save yourself!'

There were two criminals nailed to crosses beside Jesus. One of them shouted, 'If you're our Saviour the King, then save yourself and us!'

But the other one said, 'Aren't you afraid of talking to God like that? We're guilty and we're being punished for what we did, but this man hasn't done anything wrong.' Then he turned to Jesus and said, 'Jesus, when you get to your kingdom, remember me.'

Jesus replied, 'Believe me when I say that today, you'll be with me in heaven.'

Music   The King is among us

Exploring   Now we're going to look at all the things we have found and made, to help us discover more about what kind of king Jesus is. First of all, there was his title before he was even born: King of the Jews.

Hold up the special crown.

This title was where the trouble started, because King Herod didn't like the idea of having a rival king. So he tried to kill the baby Jesus by murdering all the baby boys in Bethlehem, but Jesus escaped with Mary and Joseph.

Then, as we heard in our story, the title 'King of the Jews' gave the Romans a reason to kill Jesus. Their emperor was in charge and he didn't like competition.

Hold up the crown of thorns and the cross with the sign.

So they killed him under the sign that read, 'King of the Jews'.

However, being King of the Jews was only the beginning of Jesus' power. His resurrection showed that he is stronger even than death, and that he has the power to give us eternal life with God. The Bible gives us a detailed description of Jesus' power, and this is illustrated by the rest of the things we have been collecting this morning. First of all, the Bible says that Jesus 'is the image of the invisible God' – in other words, he shows us what God is like. Can you find a picture of Jesus?

Bring forward the picture of Jesus.

Because of Jesus, we can say that we know God. Then we learn that Jesus is 'the firstborn of all creation' – he has the most important place in creation. Who has found the world that God created?

Bring forward the globe and switch the light on.

Jesus was with God before any of this world came into being. The description goes on: in Jesus

> all things in heaven and on earth were created, things visible and invisible, whether thrones or dominions or rulers or powers—all things have been created through him and for him. He himself is before all things, and in him all things hold together.

No matter what forces there are in the universe, and no matter how powerful people become on earth, they can never be as powerful as Jesus. Has anyone found pictures of powerful people and the places where they work?

Bring forward the pictures of the White House, etc.

Then Jesus' power comes closer to home: 'He is the head of the body, the church' – that's us. Jesus is in charge of us, too. Has anyone made a picture of the church that they'd like to show us?

CHRIST THE KING

Show the pictures of the church.

Jesus is in a unique position of power, because he rose from the dead: 'he is the beginning, the firstborn from the dead, so that he might come to have first place in everything.' Who made a model of the empty tomb that Jesus left behind when he rose from the dead?

Show the empty tomb.

Because of Jesus, we can have life after death. The Bible goes on to say that in Jesus 'all the fullness of God was pleased to dwell'. God made himself completely human when he was born as Jesus, and Jesus is God, entirely. Has anyone found the baby Jesus in the manger?

Bring forward the baby in the manger.

Finally, through Jesus, 'God was pleased to reconcile to himself all things, whether on earth or in heaven, by making peace through the blood of his cross.' Jesus' death means that we can join God in eternity: the cross was like a bridge between earth and heaven. Who did some balancing this morning that took you from 'earth' to 'heaven' by way of the cross?

Invite a child to walk along the balancing beam.

So we have discovered that Jesus wasn't just King of the Jews: he is King of us, King of our church and King of everything in heaven and earth. He is our God and King.

Music — Let all the world in every corner sing

Prayer action — *Place the special crown as a focal point for prayer. Position a large candle inside it and smaller candles in a circle around it.*

We've been thinking about some very big things today, such as heaven and earth and time and space. We might be left thinking, 'So what does this mean for me?' The Bible spells it out: God simply says, 'Be still,

ALL-SORTS WORSHIP

and know that I am God!' So today we will sit in stillness and know that Jesus is our God and King. He is in charge of everything, and nothing is more powerful than him. Let us pray.

Light all the candles and pause for a moment of quiet.

Jesus, our God and King,
we worship you.
Amen.

Conclusion Jesus is our King and we can all have a place in his kingdom. If you made a crown at the beginning of the service, put it on now to remind you that the King wants us all to be with him.

People put on their crowns.

Jesus, remember us when you come into your kingdom.
Amen.[87]

Give notices, announce the next all-age service and invite everyone to the feast.

---

87. You may like to end with the Taizé chant that uses these words.

Appendix

Resources for Activities

First Sunday of Advent

Fig tree illustration
Print the double-sided leaves on green card and cut out. Print the double-sided sun picture on white card and cut out. You may like to enlarge these visual aids to A3.

Timeline
You will need a 5m long roll of paper – lining paper is ideal. Draw a horizontal line along the length of the paper and mark it at 10cm intervals. Label the marks from 1–46.

Numbers 1–24, cut out of paper
Print on white paper and cut out.

Third Sunday of Advent

Charity information
Many resources can be downloaded from the internet, or obtained directly from organisations and charities such as the United Nations, Amnesty International, the Fairtrade Foundation, Traidcraft, Oxfam, Christian Aid,

Save the Children and many others. Provide information from local charities, too. Select eye-catching pictures and simple, factual information to display around the church. You may like to enlist the help of local charity representatives – such as the Mother's Union – for this service: they could provide their own display and literature.

Boo!

So what should we do?

Two cards with the crowd's lines
Print each on A4 then enlarge to A3 and stick onto a piece of card.

Title: 'So what should we do?'
Print on A4 then enlarge to A3. Cut out the words and stick them on the display you produce during the Activity.

Roman armour
English Heritage or National Trust shops attached to Roman sites usually stock Roman armour and toy weapons for dressing up. You could also try toy shops and fancy dress stores.

Christmas Eve

A flame headdress
Cut flame shapes out of red and yellow card or paper and attach to a circlet of card, like this. Add a second flame to the back of the circlet and staple the points of the flames together, so that they stand up.

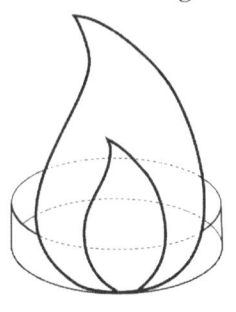

A very large map of the world
A great resource is the giant, brightly coloured, plastic floor mat in the children's game, *Globe Trotting*, produced

by the Early Learning Centre. If you can't get hold of this, you could stick some large pieces of card or lining paper together and paint on the outlines of continents and countries with a thick brush.

First Sunday of Christmas

The contents of Jesus' family campsite
You need items which suggest a makeshift pilgrim's camp in the Middle East – rugs and cloths for a Bedouin-style tent, plus any of the following: an iron cooking pot, wooden spoons and bowls, hessian sacks, sticks for firewood, a traditional terracotta oil lamp, some sand and pebbles on the ground. You could also throw in anything that might suggest a hastily abandoned family campsite, such as a leather sandal, some dropped grapes or a couple of child's wooden bricks.

Speech bubbles
Make lots of copies on A4 paper and cut out. Leave a pile in each pew or row of seats.

Epiphany

Treasure hunt items: gold, frankincense and myrrh
For the gold, use gold chocolate coins, hidden individually around the church. Frankincense in granular form is available from church suppliers and, often, gift shops connected to religious houses and cathedrals. Spoon some granules into small organza bags or tiny plastic bags, which you can then hide. Myrrh is sold as an essential oil: it can be found with aromatherapy oils in health shops. Wrap the little bottle in shiny paper and hide it.

A copy of *Three Wise Women* by Mary Hoffman
(Frances Lincoln, 1999) This lovely story complements the story of the wise men's visit. It has been in and out of print: if you need a second-hand copy, it should be available from Amazon and elsewhere.

Insert for each gift tag

Make several copies, cut around each circular text and stick one inside each gift tag.

First Sunday of Epiphany

Meditation montage based on Isaiah 43:1-7

This is a slideshow of images, shown with lines from Isaiah 43:1-7 either with the images or in between them. (See service for details of images.) The aim is to encourage reflection and deepen our understanding of God's promises here. The best computer programs for creating slideshows are PowerPoint for PCs and Keynote for Macs. Look on the internet for copyright-free images, for example at www.shutterstock.com or www.dreamstime.com.

Second Sunday of Epiphany

Two speech bubbles

Enlarge a copy of each to A3 and stick it on a piece of card, then cut out the speech bubble.

Fourth Sunday of Epiphany

Knitted heart

Ask a confident knitter in your congregation to knit a simple heart shape in stocking stitch. It must be big enough to be clearly seen by all: about A4 size should be fine. Explain how it will be used, so that your knitter understands why it needs to be easy to unravel (and also so that they are not upset when this happens!). The last stitch should not be tied off, and – most importantly – the wool should not be cut. Instead, the heart should remain attached to the ball of wool so that there will definitely be enough to stretch around your congregation.

APPENDIX

Equipment for roses/crosses
You will need:

- Balsa wood modelling sticks, often sold as 'candy floss sticks'. These are available online, for example from eBay. Take one third of your supply and cut them in half: these will make the cross beams.
- Green felt pens, for colouring in the stems.
- Red tissue paper or crepe paper for the petals.
- Sticky tape to fix the flower to the stem.
- Scissors.
- Green cotton for fixing the cross beam to the stem.
- *Optional:* green paper for leaves.

Petals can be cut or torn, then folded or scrunched around the top of the stem and attached with sticky tape. Several layers will make a full-blown rose.

Heart-shaped pieces of paper
Make several copies on red A4 paper and cut out.

Candlemas

Silhouettes of two pigeons
Copy twice onto A4 card and cut out.

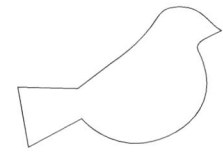

Sky lanterns
These Chinese flying lanterns make a spectacular display if launched together, especially at night. Most sky lanterns are quite large, so a pack of ten should provide plenty of space for people to write their prayers. They are becoming widely available: I have seen them in toy shops and even in a local newsagent's. The internet is probably your best source, especially if you are concerned about the environment: fully biodegradable, metal-free sky lanterns are now available. For example, see www.skylanterns4u.co.uk.

Proper 1 **A large box covered with fish shapes**
This is a stylised way of suggesting a large catch. Cut lots of simple fish shapes out of tin foil and glue them all over the box, leaving a little space in between each fish. Fill the box with the heavy carrier bags (see below), then tape the lid shut and stick more fish over the top. When the glue is dry, you may like to pick out individual outlines with a black permanent marker.

Before the service, set up the boat and place the first net loose inside it. Place the second net behind you, at the back of the boat, with the heavy box of fish pinning it down. Drape blue fabric around the boat so that it hides the second net and the box.

Lots of small paper carrier bags with handles
These are the sort used to carry takeaway sandwiches. They are available cheaply in bulk, for example from Amazon.

Proper 2 **Roman armour**
Items of Roman armour are available from shops attached to Roman sites, especially those run by English Heritage. Toy shops and fancy dress shops may also sell them.

Video clip of Narayanan Krishnan
You will find this inspiring clip on YouTube: search for 'Narayanan Krishnan – Feeding the hungry, nourishing the soul.' The clip is just over two minutes long. If your church doesn't have WiFi, there are internet sites that will help you download YouTube clips to use as part of a PowerPoint presentation, for example:
www.saveyoutube.com

A rose ready for planting
Buy a rose with bare roots that is suitable for planting in very early spring. As long as the ground is not frozen, you should be able to plant it outside; otherwise, plant it temporarily in a large container. For 24 hours before planting, soak the roots in water. Dig a hole or prepare the container, making sure that the roots will not be cramped. Make a small mound of earth at

APPENDIX

the bottom on which the rose will 'sit', so that the roots drape naturally downwards. During the service, hold the rose in place while people fill in the soil firmly, and then water the area thoroughly.

Proper 3

Joseph's story in pictures.
Display the following on a screen.

- Joseph in his multicoloured coat.
- Joseph in chains.
- Overflowing baskets of food.
- The hungry brothers with empty bowls.
- Joseph facing the brothers, remembering himself in chains.
- Joseph embracing his brothers.

Jesus' email from HQ
Either display on a screen *or* make enough copies for everyone to have one.

Pictures of people from the crowd in Galilee
Print off each one and enlarge to A3, then mount it on a large piece of card or board.

- Angry man, complaining about the Romans
- Angry woman, fuming about an insult in the marketplace
- Angry man, fighting over fishing nets
- Angry man who has had his coat stolen

Second Sunday before Lent

Illustrations for the story, shown as a slideshow
Search the internet for free, downloadable, copyright-free images, for example at www.shutterstock.com and www.dreamstime.com. Create a slideshow in PowerPoint for PCs or Keynote for Macs. For images of God, Adam and Eve, classical art is probably your best source – for example, the famous image of God

523

touching Adam, from the Sistine Chapel ceiling. Alternatively, you could use images from the Brick Testament: see www.thebricktestament.com for Bible illustrations made from Lego. The story of Adam and Eve is beautifully depicted[88] (although you should avoid the final picture, which is rather explicit).

Animal outlines

The idea is that you use the green creatures to fill in the shape of continents and the blue creatures to fill in the seas. White animals go at the top and bottom, at the poles.

- Polar animals
  Make one copy on white paper.
- Sea creatures 1 and 2
  Make one copy of each on blue paper.
- Land animals/birds 1 and 2
  Make one copy of each on green paper.

Sunday next before Lent

A shining tabard

Make a basic sandwich board out of two large sheets of card and some tape over the shoulders. The back can be plain; the front should be shiny gold, silver or hologram card. On this, people will stick strings of sequins in a radiating pattern. Moses will wear this for the first story, and Jesus will wear it, initially under his robe, for the second story.

Stone tablets

Cut two classic tombstone shapes out of thick cardboard and paint both grey. You will need to prop them up during the shadow play, so that their outline is visible as Moses chisels.

---

88. Go to http://www.bricktestament.com/genesis/the_garden_of_eden/01_gn02_04-05.html

High-visibility letters, spelling out 'THE GLORY OF GOD'

Cut the letters out of stiff cardboard: make them about 1 inch wide and several inches high. Cover one side with strips of high-visibility reflective tape (white or gold – available from hardware shops and Amazon).

Hide all but one G in dark hiding places in church, such as under pews, behind pillars and inside the pulpit. When the letters are arranged on the altar, have something there for them to lean against, such as a row of hymn books.

Craft tables with equipment for making high-visibility crosses

As with the letters above, you will need:

- High-visibility reflective tape
- Stiff cardboard crosses, about one inch wide and several inches high
- *Optional:* sequins and glitter glue

Ash Wednesday

Sackcloth and ashes

A helpful grocer may have a hessian sack you could use; otherwise, you could cut up an old 'bag for life' made of jute. You only need enough fabric to drape around your penitent's shoulders. For the ashes, the usual practice is to burn last year's palm crosses: one cross yields enough ash to make the sign of the cross on about ten foreheads. You will need a little extra, as people will get some on their hands at the beginning, and your penitent will use some, too.

First Sunday of Lent

Clip from *Harry Potter and the Deathly Hallows Part 2*

Go to Scene Selection, scene 26. Begin the clip when Harry, Ron and Hermione walk outside onto the ruined bridge (1hr 47:04) and end the clip when the scene fades to black (1hr 49:33).

Pictures and objects to suggest modern temptations

- Pictures of sleek modern technology: smartphones, iPads, games consoles, cars, etc. (look for glossy brochures or catalogues)

- Beauty products (empty bottles and boxes or glossy ads from magazines)
- Famous labels. Copy and paste from the internet and enlarge to A5 size, for example: Harrods, Prada, Versace, Burberry, DKNY, Hunter, Superdry, Animal
- Packaging for luxury food (chocolates, wine, etc.) or pictures from food magazines
- Picture of a limousine
- Pictures of skyscrapers
- Picture of the Twitter followers counter
- Picture of the Facebook friends counter
- A bank statement showing lots of money
- A very large cheque
- A CEO's business card
- Child's letter to God:
  Dear God,
  OK. I kept my half of the deal. Where's the bike?
  Bert [89]

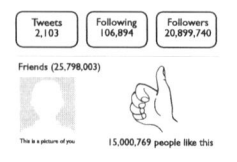

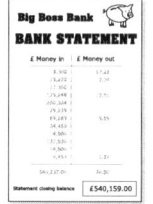

Second Sunday of Lent

Hourglass or home-made sand timer; equipment for making sand timers

Sturdy, colourful hourglasses by Tickit Timers are available from educational suppliers and Amazon. To make a home-made sand timer, use two empty, dry water bottles:

1. Using a funnel, pour some fine, dry sand into one bottle.
2. Cut a circular piece of card that exactly fits over the neck of one bottle and make a clean hole through it.
3. Stick the circle of card to the top of one bottle with sticky tape.
4. Stand the second bottle on top of the first and bind the necks together firmly with sticky tape.
5. Turn the bottles over and watch the sand run through.

An incense burner

Use any kind of incense burner that you can hold: this could be anything from incense sticks with something

---

[89]. From *Children's Letters to God*, Fontana, 1976.

to catch the hot ash, to a thurible with charcoal and granular incense. The incense will not need to burn for very long.

Two age counters
Use two A5 spiral bound notepads. Turn each one through 90 degrees so that the spiral binding runs across the top, then open it to the first double page. You will be writing big, bold numbers on the uppermost pages, so that your volunteers can flip down the pages as you count Abram's and Sarai's years.

For Abram: On the upper half of your first double page, write '100'. Then on each subsequent upper page, write numbers counting backwards to 76. This will be the first page your Abram volunteer shows.

For Sarai: On the upper half of your first double page, write '91'. Then on each subsequent upper page, write numbers counting backwards to 67. This will be the first page your Sarai volunteer shows.

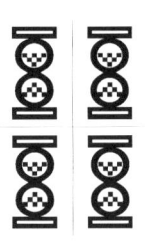

Copies of the computer's hourglass picture, enough for one each.
Copy and cut into quarters.

Third Sunday of Lent

Slideshow of wilderness pictures with sound effects
This is a computer-generated slideshow of pictures, created in PowerPoint on PCs and Keynote on Macs. Look on the internet for copyright-free, high-quality images, for example at www.dreamstime.com. If you register on the site, you can access a large number of images to download for free, as well as others for which the site charges a fee. Useful search terms: 'Wilderness' and 'Israel desert'.

Sound effects can also be downloaded free from the internet, for example from www.partnersinrhyme.com. Here, you are aiming for the sound of howling wind in the desert – listen for something that sounds suitably lonely and desolate.

The Annunciation

A slideshow of extraordinary pictures of nature and Christ's incarnation

For this and the pictures below, create a computer-generated slideshow in PowerPoint for PCs or Keynote for Macs. Look on the internet for images, particularly www.dreamstime.com where you can register as a user and download free, high-quality images.

This slideshow will be used twice: once as people arrive, and again during the prayers. For this slideshow you will need the pictures to change automatically and stop on the last but one slide. During the prayers only, you should then move to the last slide with a click.

- *Slide 1 – any number you like*: extraordinary pictures of nature, from the very big (planets and galaxies) to the very small (pictures from the Hadron collider), and including anything weird and wonderful: a butterfly emerging from a chrysalis, Niagara Falls, the spiral pattern of a sea shell, luminous deep sea fish, a volcano erupting, unfurling ferns, etc. Include one picture of the baby Jesus in the manger.
- *Last slide:* 'Here I am, the servant of the Lord; let it be with me according to your word. Amen.'

Pictures to illustrate the Annunciation story

For this slideshow you will need the pictures to change only when you click them. Use Google Images, particularly for pictures of Mary, King David, Jesus on his throne (search term: 'King Jesus') and the Holy Spirit – there are a wide variety of interpretations. If your church has Wi-Fi, before the service use Google Maps to locate Nazareth with a pin, then zoom right out to view the whole earth: this is your first image. Then you can gradually zoom in to the Middle East, Galilee and Nazareth. Your slideshow will then begin with the picture of Mary. You will need the following pictures for the Storytelling and also for the Exploring:

- The Earth from space
- The Middle East
- Galilee

- Nazareth
- Mary
- King David on his throne
- Jesus on his throne in eternity
- The Holy Spirit
- Mary kneeling before the angel

Items for the 'Wow! Corner'

- The baby in the manger: one from a Nativity set would be ideal.
- Beautiful natural objects with interesting colours, patterns, textures or smells, for example: seashells, polished wood, driftwood, feathers, fresh herbs, pebbles, semi-precious stones, leaves, flowers, etc. Hide them all around the church before the service begins.

Fifth Sunday of Lent

A bottle to represent Mary's bottle of nard

For the thick, creamy nard, I suggest using a large measure of creamy bubble bath – the sort with a glossy sheen would be ideal. For the bottle, take a suitable plastic bottle (such as a squeezy ketchup bottle with a wide neck). A day or two before the service, cover the bottle in some Model Magic by Crayola (a bright white air-drying clay). Then fill the bottle with the bubble bath and seal it with Model Magic, extending the clay beyond the neck of the bottle and pressing the edges together. This seal should smash safely but effectively at the right moment. Leave the bottle to dry for at least 24 hours.

An incense burner and granular incense

If your church does not own an incense burner, a neighbouring church may be able to lend you one. Alternatively, burners and incense are available from church suppliers and, often, gift shops connected to religious houses and cathedrals. Also check websites such as www.incense-man.co.uk. Ideally the incense you use should contain some spikenard.

Three stations around church:

- *Hand-washing:* use two jugs of warm water, one soapy and one clean. Hold the person's hand over a large bowl and pour over water from each jug in turn. Have a supply of small hand towels or paper towels.
- *Foot-washing:* as above.
- *Hand massage:* use dishes of very light olive oil, perhaps with a drop of lavender oil added. There are useful videos on YouTube showing how to give a hand massage: leaders may like to view one beforehand.

Palm Sunday

Worship flags

These are beautiful resources for worship and well worth making or buying. For each one you will need:

- A piece of dowel
- A semicircle of shiny, floaty fabric – e.g. organza, polyester shiny fabrics, lycra foil, metallic lamé, poly habotai

For this service, the flags need to be particular colours. Each features its own emblem, which should be sewn on as a motif or drawn on with fabric pens:

- Jesus: white flag with a gold crown
- First Pharisee: black flag with red cross
- Second Pharisee: red flag with black crown of thorns
- Pilate: red flag with black laurel wreath and/or Roman eagle
- Herod: black flag with red crown

For the large size, the fabric should be 180cm long and 90cm wide; the dowel should be 90cm long.

Fold over slightly less than half the length of the fabric to form a narrow hem. Sew it across the top and down the side, leaving it open at the bottom so it forms a sleeve for the dowel. Insert the dowel and make sure that there is enough left sticking out of the end of the sleeve for you to hold.

APPENDIX

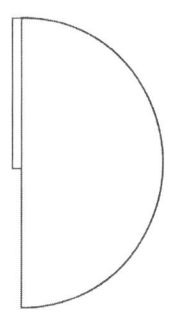

These flags are at their best when in motion. They can be quite spectacular when used in dance, like this:

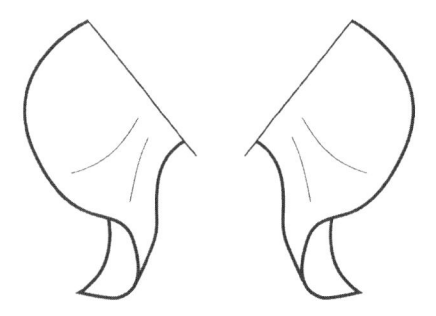

For further pictures, information and videos of dancing with flags, search the internet for 'worship flags'. See especially www.wingsofpraise.com. A UK supplier I can recommend is Kingdom Dance Resources: see www.kingdomdance.co.uk.

Equipment for making the crowd's flags
These will be triangular pennants. Prepare beforehand by cutting and hemming the triangles; then fold over the base of each triangle and sew it along two sides to form a narrow sleeve for the stick. Leave it open at the bottom.

People will use the templates to help them decorate their pennants with either a dove (outlined in blue) or a palm leaf (coloured in green). Then they will insert the balsa wood stick in the sleeve to complete their flag.

Pattern templates
Make a few copies of each.

Maundy Thursday

Ingredients for making unleavened bread (Matzah)

This bread is easy and very quick to make: in fact, according to Jewish tradition, kosher Matzah must take no longer than 18 minutes from the moment the ingredients are mixed to the end of baking. First, preheat your oven to its highest temperature, then:

1. Mix one part water to three parts flour and form a small ball of dough.
2. Roll out the dough very thinly.
3. Put it on a lined baking sheet and prick it all over with a fork.
4. Bake for 2–3 minutes.[90]

Good Friday

News stations of the cross

The idea is to present a collection of multi-media stations, telling the story of the crucifixion as if it were happening in modern times. If it were, it would be featured in news footage, in shaky pictures from eyewitnesses' cameras, on the front pages of newspapers and on the internet.

This is a great IT challenge for a youth group or some keen teenagers in your church, as they can use downloaded clips, their own videos and camera pictures, and put it all together using their knowledge of the conventions of rolling TV news coverage. Here are some straightforward suggestions for each station to get you (or your technology experts) started:

Station 1: Condemned
A series of mobile phone camera close-ups of handcuffs, angry crowds, cheering crowds, pointing fingers – as when a controversial criminal is bundled into a police van after a trial.

Station 2: Surrounded
Sound effects of a large and angry crowd. These may be downloaded from the internet as isolated sound effects, for example from www.partnersinrhyme.com.

---

90. Source: Judaism.about.com 'How to make Matzah'.

Alternatively, use the sound track from news footage of modern popular uprisings. Play the sound effects through headphones so that visitors to the station can hear them in turn.

Station 3: Stripped
A cloak contained in a large, clear, sealed plastic bag, labelled like a police evidence bag: 'Property of prisoner 7842: Jesus of Nazareth.'

Station 4: Killed
A tabloid-style front page with the headline, 'KILLED!' and a picture of Jesus on the cross.

Station 5: Buried
Pictures of the sealed stone tomb (either still or video – extreme close-ups of the church Easter garden, perhaps?) with a red bar across the bottom, as in rolling news coverage, and the words: 'Jesus buried today'.

If you are not holding an all-age service on Easter Day, you will need one more station, to be displayed at the end of the service:

Station 6: Alive!
This could be a short (one minute) video and voiceover or a simple slideshow with an audio track. It should suggest rolling news coverage featuring pictures of the empty tomb and the discarded linen cloths, and the words of eyewitnesses, such as: 'I went there first thing this morning and his body was gone!' 'He's alive! An angel told me!' 'What have they done with him?'

Lolly sticks
These are available from most places that sell craft materials, including pound shops. They are also available cheaply from the kitchenware shop, Lakeland, in packs of 100.

Easter Day

A rocket
If you have a large congregation, use more than one. In the past I have managed to keep one or two rockets back from the 5 November celebrations for use at Easter.

However, out of season, they are best purchased online: there are many sites to choose from. Given that this may well be a dawn display, take note of the sound level guidelines on the packets: this should help you achieve maximum sparkle with minimum bang!

A dish or two of diluted myrrh oil
Myrrh is sold as an essential oil, valued for its antiseptic properties. It can be found with aromatherapy oils in health food shops. For this service, you will need to add a drop or two of myrrh to some light olive oil.

Two clean, empty halves of an egg shell
A chicken's egg is fine, although a duck's egg would be a larger visual aid. Even better would be a wild bird's discarded egg shell, which you may be lucky enough to find at this time of year.

Second Sunday of Easter

Three pictures of Peter
During the Welcome, show pictures 39 and 41 alternately. During the Exploring, show pictures 39, 40 and 41 in turn, as described in the script.

Fourth Sunday of Easter

Slideshow and picture of sheep
For the slideshow, use PowerPoint for PCs or KeyNote for Macs. There are some beautiful pictures available to download free from www.dreamstime.com if you register as a user; your own photographs of local places would also be good. Your aim is to show green pastures and still waters – lots of calming images of countryside, with no sheep just yet.

For the picture of sheep, look for a neat flock in a meadow, grazing peacefully.

YouTube video of a shepherd herding 1000 sheep

Search YouTube for 'Bearded Collie sheepdogs driving one thousand sheep'. It is the first video listed and lasts about seven minutes. If your church does not have internet access, you should be able to download the clip: there are several sites that explain how to do this, for example www.saveyoutube.com (Google 'youtube converter').

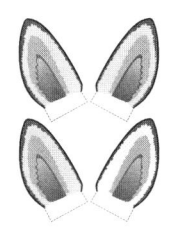

Wolf ears

You will need two cheap plastic Alice bands. Print the ears onto grey card and cut out, then wrap the tabs around an Alice band and secure with sticky tape so that the ears point straight up. For deluxe wolf ears, you might like to cover both the band and the ears with grey fur fabric.

Hidden around the church, lots of pictures of lambs and/or cuddly toy lambs if you have some

Make several copies on A4 paper and cut out along the straight, solid lines. Hide them well so that the wolves and shepherds really have to hunt!

Sixth Sunday of Easter

Around the church, lots of different unfinished tasks

The aim is to provide interactive stations with practical things that people can do to help: some are straightforward chores, and others may make them think about the church's mission in the world. Here are some suggestions:

Half-made sandwiches

- Some half-buttered bread and an open pot of jam
- Some plates and knives

Sweeping up

- A small area covered in breadcrumbs, half of which have been swept up
- Dustpan, brushes and a bin

Food bank

- A cardboard box labelled 'Food Bank Donations'
- A pile of non-perishable groceries, a few of which have been loaded into the box

Recycling

- A pile of clean but mixed recyclable material (tin foil, plastic bottles, cardboard, old clothes – nothing sharp or breakable)
- Bags/boxes into which some of the stuff has been sorted

Sorting coins

- A heap of 5p, 2p and 1p pieces, some of which have been sorted into piles

Unfinished story

- Several Bibles, including children's editions, each with a bookmark placed after the Nativity story in Luke's Gospel, for anyone to continue reading (either to themselves or aloud to others)
- Some cushions or beanbags

Dirty water

- Eight bottles of water, one of which has mud in it
- A sign: '884 million people lack access to safe water supplies; that's one in eight people.'[91]
- A collection plate with a few coins in it

Welcome mat

- A carpet square with felt letters spelling 'WELCOME', only the first three of which have been stuck on
- Some PVA glue and glue spreaders

Conference badges

These are clear plastic badge holders with an attached clip or safety pin and space to hold a removable name card. They are available cheaply from eBay and Amazon. Prepare the cards beforehand by pasting the insert on the card.

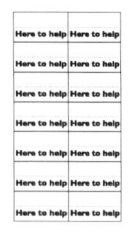

---

91. UNICEF/WHO 2008.

APPENDIX

Ascension Day

A flag and a flagpole
If your church already has both, there will be no shortage of young volunteers to help you raise the flag. Alternatively, you could buy a telescopic flag pole online: see www.windcreations.co.uk, where you can buy a 3m telescopic windsock flag pole and a plain white flag for under £10. If you created flags for the Palm Sunday service, Jesus' white flag with gold crown would be perfect for today.

Picture of the disciples looking up at Jesus' Ascension
Display this picture on the screen.

Hidden around the church, clues for a treasure hunt
You will need four different sets of clues: I suggest using sticky notes in different colours or shapes. On each one, draw a simple picture of something in your church and add a more cryptic written clue underneath. For example, you might draw the organ pipes and write, 'You need both hands and both feet to play me.' Then stick the next clue on the organ, and so on. The last clue leads to one pile of picture quarters, tied with ribbon (see below).

The 'treasure': pictures in quarters

These pictures are basically a visual representation of the Creed, with one or two additions. Print off each picture and enlarge onto A3 card. You may also like to display them all on the screen as a slideshow, as described in the Exploring.

537

PICTURES 46–51 ONLY: Cut each picture into quarters and put the quarters into four separate piles. Shuffle each complete pile and tie it up with a ribbon: each treasure hunt will lead to one of these.

PICTURES 52–54 remain whole, to be used in the Exploring.

A recording of 'You raise me up' by Josh Groban and optional accompanying slideshow
This is available from iTunes and on YouTube. You could simply play the music track. If you wish, you could simultaneously display the words on a screen, or the words accompanied by some meditative images appropriate for Ascension Day, for example: clouds, blue skies, sunlight streaming through clouds, etc.

Seventh Sunday of Easter

Sound effects
These are available online (for example from www.partnersinrhyme.com). You could also produce several of these sound effects live if you had a small group of vocal volunteers and some props such as chains and heavy pieces of wood.

- An angry mob
- Clanking chains
- Locks and chains
- Sung prayers or hymn-singing (a few unaccompanied voices)
- An earthquake (prolonged rumble with the noise of screaming, collapsing buildings, etc.)
- Celebrations

Challenges and tasks that cannot be completed by one person alone
Think of chores with which you always need help, and the kind of games you might play in teams at parties or as a team-building exercise. Some will be self-evident, while others may need an explanatory notice. Here are some ideas:

- *Beanbag toss*
  Try to throw a collection of beanbags into a loose sack from some distance away. It's a lot easier if a partner holds the sack open and moves to catch the beanbags.

- *Snap*
  Try playing this card game single-handed.

- *Balancing ball*
  Try to carry an orange between two chopsticks, or a football between two bamboo poles, and transport it from a table to a bucket. It's a lot easier if you have a partner, and together you hold the sticks or poles parallel, so that the orange or ball balances on them.

- *Sheets*
  Try folding a big double sheet neatly on your own.

- *Beach tent*
  Try putting up a small beach tent or dome tent on your own.

- *Plaiting*
  Have bunches of three long strips of fabric and challenge people to plait them. It's a lot easier if you have a partner to hold the end of the plait taut as you work.

- *Pin the tail on the donkey*
  Clearly, this is a lot easier if you have a non-blindfolded partner to guide you!

- *Obstacle course*
  If you have a lot of space in church, you could make an obstacle course with empty cardboard boxes. Challenge people to make their way through it blindfolded and alone: again, this is much easier if you have a guide to lead you by the hand or call out directions.

- *One hand clapping*
  A Zen challenge: can you clap with one hand, or do you need someone to work with so that you can clap your hands together?

- *Measuring height/length*
  Try to measure a person's height or the distance between two points with a floppy tape measure.

Pentecost

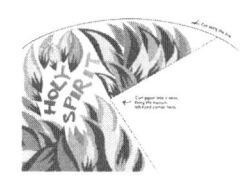

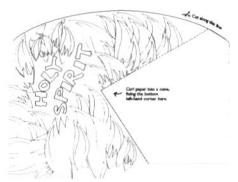

Pentecost megaphones

You will need between 5 and 11 copies, depending how many volunteers you expect. *Either* print off the coloured version and enlarge onto A3 card, *or* print off the black-and-white version, enlarge onto A3 card and enlist the help of some children to colour in the flames. Construct the megaphones by cutting out and rolling into a cone shape as marked, then secure with sticky tape.

Stations around the church, presenting different ways of communicating the good news of Jesus

These stations will display some things that you have already used in church, and others that you might think about using one day. I've suggested different categories of communication, such as written and sensory. Think of this as a brainstorming session to come up with fresh ways of sharing the gospel. Here are some ideas:

- *Written* – display some different versions of the Bible, for example *the street bible* by Rob Lacey (Zondervan 2003)

- *Spoken* – In a quiet corner, one of the leaders tells a Godly Play story

- *Visual* – on a laptop or iPad, display the *Glo Bible* (an interactive and visual version of the Bible, available from Amazon)

- *Sensory* – make a display or a story bag of tactile objects that tell a Bible story, for example: a toy ark with animals, a large tray of water and an olive branch

- *Active* – planting cress seeds on damp cotton wool, laid out in strips to spell J-E-S-U-S

- *Edible* – lay a table with unleavened bread, grapes and grape juice

- *Technological* – show a three-minute video from YouTube: 'If Jesus were born in times of Google, Facebook and Twitter.' It is a brisk and entertaining retelling of the Nativity using modern social media.

Trinity Sunday

One or more long strips of paper, cut into a paper chain of people

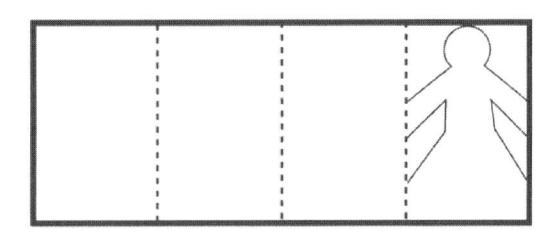

Use a long strip cut from a sheet of lining paper. Make it about A5 width. Fold it up forwards and backwards so that you have a thick block of paper. Cut out the shape of a person, with a robe-like shape instead of legs so that people can draw someone wearing trousers or a skirt, or in a wheelchair, etc. Remember not to cut along the vertical edges of the hands and hem.

A giant strip of paper for a giant three-person chain
This is the same principle as the paper chain above. Cut three x 2m strips of lining paper and stick them side by side, lengthways, with masking tape. Then fold them one behind the other so that only the top sheet is visible: your volunteer's outline will be drawn on this one.

Proper 4

Clip from *Horrible Histories*
This one-minute clip is available on YouTube – search for 'Horrible Histories Surviving in the Roman Army'. It makes the point perfectly, as well as being historically accurate and very funny. If your church doesn't have internet access, you can download a YouTube clip to use as part of a PowerPoint presentation: for example, go to www.saveyoutube.com

Items of Roman armour
Many items are available from English Heritage shops attached to Roman sites; toy shops may also stock some swords and helmets. Alternatively, you could make your own, or ask your local Primary school if they have anything left over from a project on the Romans. You will need the following:

- A purple cloak
- An item of armour (helmet or breastplate)

- Two swords
- A shield
- A rolled-up scroll of paper, tied with a red ribbon

These are the bare essentials for this service. It would be good, though, if you could find more for your Storyteller to wear, such as a red tunic, a belt, sandals and other items of armour.

Proper 5 Guest speaker

This is an opportunity for people to hear about the work of a local, national or international charity, and learn what they can do to help. For example, if your church sponsors a particular overseas mission, you could invite a missionary to speak; you could ask a representative of your local food bank or someone who works with homeless people in your area. You could tie this service in with a current national fundraising campaign.

Tell your speaker that they will be speaking to an all-age congregation and suggest that a multi-media approach would be welcome: still pictures and video clips are great, as are physical objects for people to handle, such as the contents of a food bank box or a life-saving mosquito net. Ask your speaker to spell out clearly what people can do to help.

Proper 6 Equipment for hand/foot massage

There are lots of helpful videos on the internet showing how to give a hand or foot massage. Your volunteers should practise beforehand so that they know what they are doing. Feet and hands should be washed thoroughly before being massaged. Useful essential oils are lavender or peppermint. You may like to give your congregation some advance notice of this service's activity, so that people can come with extra-clean feet if they would like a foot massage!

If you have a local beauty parlour that offers foot, hand and even head massages, you could invite them to give their services for free: I know of one church that was able to offer professional Indian head massages thanks to an arrangement like this.

Plain white envelopes with a 'FORGIVEN' card sealed inside each one

Standard small white business envelopes (113mm x 163mm) are probably best for this activity, especially because they have an opaque lining: you don't want the card inside to be seen until the Prayer Action. Print off the 'FORGIVEN' cards on A4 card and cut them out, making sure you have enough for everyone to have one each, then seal them inside the envelopes. During the Activity, you will hand out the sealed envelopes (describing them as 'cards') for the written or drawn confessions.

Proper 7

A slideshow of pictures: strong winds, rockfalls and wildfire

Use PowerPoint for PCs or Keynote for Macs. There are some great pictures available for free at www.dreamstime.com, if you register as a site user. Search for pictures or video footage of tornadoes and hurricanes, landslides and rockfalls, forest fires and fire close-ups. Try to avoid obviously urban or tropical settings because your aim is to set the scene for Elijah in the wilderness.

Three craft tables, with equipment for making the following:

Wind-makers

- Sheets of thin A3 card (or bigger)
- Make giant versions of hand-held paper fans: place the card landscape-wise and make vertical pleats all along it, then pinch the bottom of the pleats together and fold up the bottom edge to form a fan shape.

Rocks

- Newspaper
- Old manila envelopes
- Scissors
- Sticky tape or brown parcel tape

Make boulders by scrunching up newspaper into a dense ball, then cover the ball with pieces of old manila envelope (turned inside-out so that the blank side is showing). Hold each rock together with lavish quantities of sticky tape or brown parcel tape.

Fire streamers
- Short pieces of dowel, bamboo canes or candy floss sticks
- Lots of red, orange and yellow crepe paper
- Scissors
- Sticky tape

Cut or tear the crepe paper into long flame-like strips and attach to the top of the sticks with sticky tape.

Proper 8

A slideshow of pictures
Use PowerPoint for PCs or Keynote for Macs. There are some great pictures available for free at: www.dreamstime.com, if you register as a site user. You will need the following pictures, in this order:
- A sign pointing to Jerusalem
- A locked door
- A fire (close-up)
- Split screen: fox cubs in a den/birds in a nest
- A sign pointing to Jerusalem (repeat)
- A Jewish funeral
- A family embracing
- A sign pointing to Jerusalem (repeat)

A giant Venn diagram

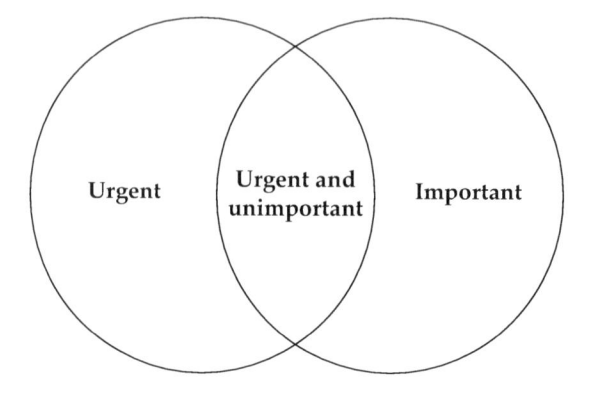

Urgent | Urgent and unimportant | Important

APPENDIX

On a large piece of lining paper or a giant piece of card, draw a diagram like this. Lay it out on the floor at the beginning of the Activity.

Props, sound effects and pictures for the Urgent/Important Activity

You will need:

- A mobile phone, ready to play a demonstration ringtone
- A small pot plant
- A picture of a bubbling chip pan (on CD-ROM)

You will also need to give people lots of different things to consider when deciding what is urgent, important or both. Here are some suggestions:

- An alarm clock, ringing
- A birthday present
- A wedding invitation
- A teapot and a mug on a tray
- A Bible with a bookmark in it
- A book of prayers
- An advert for a shop's sale, reading 'BUY NOW!' or 'EVERYTHING MUST GO!'
- An advert for 'this season's must-haves' or 'essential homewares'
- A doorbell sound effect
- A few current newspaper headlines
- Pieces of paper, some felt pens and marker pens (for people to add their own ideas)
- Pictures (on CD-ROM). Print off one copy of each:
  – a crying child
  – a bath overflowing
  – two friends having a cosy chat
  – a text/email alert
  – Jesus' command

545

Proper 9   **Small pillar candles to decorate; candle pens**

I recommend buying cheap white household candles (not tea lights or long tapering dinner candles). These can be decorated with special pens containing colourful liquid wax. Candle pens are available from the arts and crafts catalogue, Yellow Moon: see www.yellowmoon.org.uk.

This service could open up further mission possibilities for your church: as well as delivering peace candles to homes in your community, you could also deliver prayer cards more widely. Many churches pray for every street in their community in turn: each week, church volunteers deliver cards to the relevant households, explaining that prayers will be said and inviting particular prayer requests.

Proper 10   **A slideshow of images and/or video footage of the Jerusalem–Jericho road**

Use PowerPoint for PCs or Keynote for Macs. There are some great pictures available for free at www.dreamstime.com, if you register as a site user. Search the internet for pictures or video footage: there are lots of good still pictures and many amateur videos taken by pilgrims. You might like to start your slideshow with a picture of a modern signpost in the desert, pointing to Jerusalem in one direction and Jericho in the other.

Four stations around the church, introducing the four characters

The injured man

- Your actor, lying down in a torn tunic and covered with fake blood and bruises
- An empty purse by his side
- A sign: 'Unclean!' Print off and enlarge

The priest

- Your actor playing the priest
- 'The Priest' pictures and information cards. Print off one copy of each and cut out the cards
- *(Optional)* An incense burner with incense

APPENDIX

The Levite

- Your actor playing the Levite
- 'The Levite' pictures and information cards. Print off one copy of each and cut out the cards
- *(Optional)* A scroll of Scripture

The Samaritan

- Your actor playing the Samaritan
- 'The Samaritan' pictures and information cards. Print off one copy of each and cut out the cards

Costume details

The above stations explain how your actors should be dressed: as far as possible the Priest, the Levite and the Samaritan should resemble their pictures. The innkeeper wears a plain tunic. For the fake injuries, blend dark eye-shadow and lipstick to make bruises. Red food colouring is useful as fake blood.

The good Samaritan's bag

This is a simple cloth bag containing the following:

- Strips of white cotton cloth or bandages
- A little bottle of olive oil
- A little bottle of grape/apple juice
- A few coins

Proper 11

Lots of ingredients for the feast

Choose things that suggest a middle Eastern feast, and that need some chopping, peeling or laying out on plates or in bowls, for example:

- Olives (to be put on cocktail sticks)
- Pitta bread (to be cut in half)
- Oranges (to be peeled and divided into segments)
- Feta cheese (to be cut into cubes)
- Grapes (to be pulled off the stalks)
- Mint leaves (to be chopped)
- Plain yoghurt (to be mixed with the mint leaves)

Listening stations around the church

These are multi-sensory ideas to encourage quiet attentiveness. Be creative! Each station needs a short explanatory sign (on CD-ROM – print off on card). Here are some ideas:

- *Seashell*
  Provide some fairly large seashells, suitable for listening to the sound of the waves.

  > **Listen hard for the sound of the sea.**
  > When you pray, try to be still, stay quiet and listen hard to God in the same way.

- *Chill zone*
  Create a really comfortable area in the church where people can relax: for example, use rugs, bean bags, cushions and even a small tent. You might like to play some calming music.

  > **'Be still and know that I am God.'**

- *The disappearing candle*
  This station will need matches and adult supervision. Provide some birthday candles, each pushed through a small circle of card to catch any wax drips. Light the candles and encourage people to stay still and watch as the candles burn down to nothing. (Half a birthday candle takes about five minutes – push the other half through the card and hold on to it.)

  > **Watch the candle disappear...**

- *Hourglass*
  Many schools now use colourful sand timers that you may be able to borrow. Alternatively, you could buy your own, for example from Amazon, supplied by TickIT Educational Products. Encourage people to sit and contemplate the slow passing of time as they rest in God's presence.

  > **Spend some time with God.**

- *Singing bowl/bell*
  The singing bowl is used as a meditation aid in Eastern religions. It may be found in shops which sell clothing and ornaments from India and the Far East. It looks like a metal pestle and mortar. You rub the outside rim of the bowl with the wooden beater, firmly and slowly, and a bell-like note wells out of the bowl, growing and fading as you 'stir' the sound. Ask for a demonstration in the shop! It

  > **Listen to the ringing sound as it fades away, then keep listening to the silence.**

APPENDIX

requires some practice, but the effect is startling and unearthly.[92] Alternatively, you could use a hand bell.

Encourage people to sound the singing bowl or bell and listen as the note fades away – then keep on listening.

- *Still waters*
  Find a beautiful picture of still water and either print it off or display it on a screen: for example, a still lake with the reflection of mountains or a peaceful forest pool. See www.dreamstime.com for pictures. Encourage people to sit and contemplate the soothing image.

> The Lord is my shepherd, I shall not want. He makes me lie down in green pastures; he leads me beside still waters; he restores my soul.

Proper 12

Short slideshow of visual aids

Create this on a laptop, using PowerPoint for PCs and Keynote for Macs. For pictures, look on the internet, especially at www.dreamstime.com, where you can download images for free if you register as a site user. For the Bible verses, copy and paste from the website *oremus Bible Browser*. You will need the following slides, in this order:

1. 'Father, hallowed be your name.
   Your kingdom come.
   Give us each day our daily bread.
   And forgive us our sins,
   for we ourselves forgive everyone indebted to us.
   And do not bring us to the time of trial.'
   (Luke 11:2-4)

2. A picture of a toddler in his/her dad's arms, with the title, 'CHILDLIKE'.

3. The same prayer as slide 1, this time with the title, 'SIMPLE'.

4. A picture of a hand knocking on a door, with the title, 'PERSISTENT'.

5. 'Ask, and it will be given to you; search, and you will find; knock, and the door will be opened for you.'
   (Luke 11:9)

6. The Lord's Prayer (modern version, or whichever you use in your church)

---

92. See my website www.clairebentonevans.com for a picture and further information.

549

Lots of plain ping-pong balls,[93] **enough for one each**
These are available in bulk fairly cheaply from sports shops and Amazon. Coloured balls would be lovely, but they are much more expensive than white. Whichever you buy, make sure they are completely plain: some have large brand names on them. Divide them into four batches and label them as follows, using a permanent marker:

– PLEASE
– THANK YOU
– SORRY
– WOW!

A signpost
Make a simple signpost, like this:

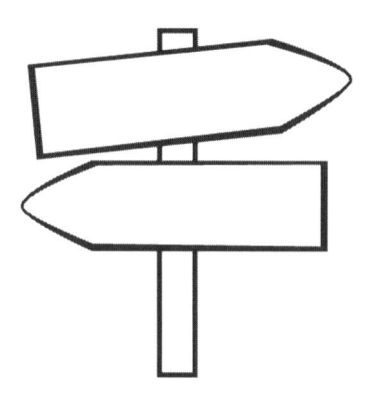

You could use a broom handle or a plank of wood for the pole, then make the signs out of heavy brown cardboard and stick them on with parcel tape. Mark each sign with a large question mark.

Proper 13   **A slideshow of glossy images of consumer goods; meditation montage based on Psalm 107**
For both these slideshows, use PowerPoint for PCs or Keynote for Macs. There are some great pictures available for free at www.dreamstime.com, if you register as a site user. Choose a range of consumer goods that will appeal to all ages, from top-of-the-range cars, designer clothes and luxury homewares to smartphones, the latest computer games and the most popular toys. For the meditation montage, create a simple

---

93. Thanks to my son Tobias for the novel idea of 'lucky-dip' prayers.

slideshow of images to encourage contemplation of God's goodness, featuring some verses from Psalm 107, for example:

> O give thanks to the Lord, for he is good;
> for his steadfast love endures for ever.
> Let them thank the Lord for his steadfast love,
> for his wonderful works to humankind.
> For he satisfies the thirsty,
> and the hungry he fills with good things.
> Let those who are wise give heed to these things,
> and consider the steadfast love of the Lord.
> *(Verses 1, 8, 9, 43)*

Copy and paste text from *oremus Bible Browser*. Images could include wonders of the natural world, clean running water and pictures of abundant growing food such as fruit or sweetcorn. You may like to add some suitably reflective music as a soundtrack.

Boxes of corn
Print off lots of copies of the corn on yellow paper. Find some empty cardboard boxes, then tape them closed and cover the front side of each one with pictures of corn, so that together the boxes suggest an abundant harvest.

Prizes for 'The conveyor belt' game
If you remember *The Generation Game*, you will know that the prizes were generally rather basic household goods, such as a toaster or a fondue set. Collect anything you like from your house or church, as long as it is easy to carry and not too valuable: you are looking for an eclectic assortment of about 20 items. None of these things will be given away. You will, however, need to include a cuddly toy to give away as a prize.

Set up and run the game as follows. Pile your prizes on the table behind the screen. Your two helpers form a human conveyor belt: they take it in turns to parade each item out from behind the screen, in front of the volunteer and back behind the screen again.

Proper 15

A Roman soldier costume

You will need as full a costume as you can manage: ideally, a tunic, a belt, a pair of sandals, a shield, some armour and a sword or dagger. You could also include a small hammer to tuck into the belt. Fancy dress shops and toy shops may have many of these things; alternatively, shops attached to Roman heritage sites usually sell cheap items for dressing up. Most primary schools do a project on the Romans at some point, and it would be worth asking if they have any props or costumes you could borrow.

Promises about the Messiah

Print off one copy of each and hide them around the church.

> By the tender mercy of our God, the dawn from on high will break upon us, to give light to those who sit in darkness and in the shadow of death, to guide our feet into the way of peace.
> *Luke 1.78-79*

> When Jesus was born, the angels sang: 'Glory to God in the highest heaven, and on earth peace among those whom he favours!'
> *Luke 2.14*

> For a child has been born for us, a son given to us; authority rests upon his shoulders; and he is named Wonderful Counsellor, Mighty God, Everlasting Father, Prince of Peace. His authority shall grow continually, and there shall be endless peace for the throne of David and his kingdom. He will establish and uphold it with justice and with righteousness from this time onwards and for evermore.
> *Isaiah 9.6-7*

Information stations about the following people

For each station, you will need an information box (on CD-ROM – print off one or more copies on card). You will also need three pictures: the person, a map of the country or city they are associated with and a picture to show what (or whom) they opposed. All these pictures are available on the internet: search Google Images and see below for further information.

Martin Luther King, Jr
- Picture of Martin Luther King, Jr
- Map of the USA
- Picture of racial segregation (Google 'race segregation USA' images)

Dietrich Bonhoeffer
- Picture of Dietrich Bonhoeffer
- Map of Germany
- Picture of Hitler addressing crowds of Nazis (Google 'Hitler rally' images)

APPENDIX

Óscar Romero
- Picture of Óscar Romero
- Map of El Salvador
- Picture of military repression (Google 'El Salvador Revolutionary Government Junta' images)

Sheila Cassidy
- Picture of Dr Sheila Cassidy
- Map of Chile
- Picture of the names or faces of Chile's 'Disappeared' (Google 'Pinochet's Dictatorship' images)

Sara Miles
- Picture of Sara Miles (see www.saramiles.net)
- Map of San Francisco
- Picture of a poor area of San Francisco (Google 'San Francisco Housing Projects' images and look for one that shows poor housing)

Proper 17

Victims of torture

Prisoners

Homeless people

The Disappeared (missing people who may have been killed)

Victims of natural disasters

Refugees

Prayer stations

Search the internet for pictures: for example, visit www.dreamstime.com for free, downloadable, copyright-free images. At each station, there should be:

- A sign (on CD-ROM)
- A picture to illustrate the prayer intention (suggestions below)
- Pens and small pieces of paper
- Gold star stickers

1. Prisoners

Find a picture of empty prison buildings, wire fences or prisoners in orange uniforms.

2. Victims of torture

Choose a picture that is symbolic rather than graphic: for example, some shackles or a roll of barbed wire.

3. 'The Disappeared'

Find a picture of lots of photographs of faces, for example of 'the Disappeared' in Pinochet's Chile.

4. The homeless
Find a picture of someone begging or sleeping on the street.

5. Refugees
Search Google Images for a wide selection of pictures.

6. Victims of natural disasters
Find a picture of a relatively recent natural disaster that is no longer in the news – for example, the Haiti earthquake.

Proper 18

A list of things to 'guesstimate', on paper or on a screen

Make sure you offer a range that is appropriate for all ages, for example:

- How much would it cost you to travel to London and back? (substitute another city if you live in or near to London)
- How much would it cost you to feed a dog or a cat for a year?
- How much would it cost you to buy the latest iPhone?
- How much would it cost you to buy every *Lego Star Wars* set/*Littlest Pet Shop* figure/book in the *Beast Quest* series? (substitute the latest collecting craze here)

A quantity of Model Magic

Model Magic is a bright white, lightweight, air-drying modelling clay which is not at all messy to use, unlike traditional clay. It can be bought from children's craft suppliers, for example www.crafts4kids.co.uk.

Proper 19

A number of sheep's ears for dressing up

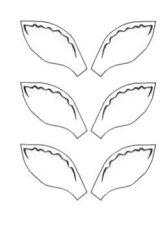

Make as many as you like, depending on how many volunteer sheep you expect. You will need some cheap plastic Alice bands: many chemists and pound shops sell these. Copy the sheep ears template onto cream or white A4 card, cut out the ears and wrap the tabs around the Alice bands, securing them with sticky tape so that the ears stand out at the appropriate angle. If you are feeling adventurous, you could try making the ears out of fur fabric instead.

Proper 20

A game of Monopoly in progress

Set up the game for four players. Share out the money unequally, leaving some in the bank. Group the properties by colour and share them out in batches between the players. Distribute all the houses and hotels on the board, making sure that Mayfair and Park Lane both have hotels.

Fair trade stations around the church

You need a different display to illustrate each of the aims of the Fairtrade Foundation:

- Fair prices
- Decent working conditions
- Sustainable produce, which doesn't harm the land or its people
- A fair deal for farmers and workers in the developing world

An abundance of information and resources is available from the Fairtrade Foundation website (www.fairtrade.org.uk). If you have a Fairtrade representative in your church, you might like to invite him or her to prepare these stations, and perhaps include some edible Fairtrade produce. Many schools now have Fairtrade groups, too: you could invite them to help with this service. At the 'Fair prices' station, include a sign with the quotation from Amos (on CD-ROM).

The need for fair prices is not new. Centuries ago, God's people were exploiting the poor and God spoke to them through his prophet, Amos: 'Hear this, you that trample on the needy, and bring to ruin the poor of the land... buying the poor for silver and the needy for a pair of sandals, and selling the sweepings of the wheat.'
Amos 8:4, 6

Proper 21

Ingredients for a feast

You will need food for a finger buffet that needs a little assembling by your volunteers, but not too much, for example:

- Cocktail sausages (spear with cocktail sticks and arrange on a plate)

- Fruit salad (chop and mix easy-to-cut fruit, such as bananas, grapes, plums, peaches and strawberries, and pile in a glass bowl with some fruit juice)
- Slices of French bread (butter them and arrange on a plate)
- Cucumber and tomatoes (chop them and arrange on a plate)
- Ready-made fairy cakes (ice them and arrange on a plate)
- *(Optional extra)* Lots of *Ferrero Rocher* chocolates, piled in a gleaming pyramid!

Fiery streamers

These are two-foot lengths of bamboo cane or similar, with strips of red, yellow and orange crepe or tissue paper, torn into rough flame shapes and attached with sticky tape. For this service, you will only need three or four streamers.

Harvest Thanksgiving

Thanksgiving meditation montage

Create a simple slideshow, using PowerPoint for PCs or Keynote for Macs. Include Louis Armstrong's 'What a Wonderful World' as a soundtrack. A good site for free, downloadable pictures is www.dreamstime.com (you will need to register as a site user in order to access the free images). For this slideshow, choose pictures that show the abundance and variety of food grown in the world, such as vast fields of American corn, apple trees loaded with fruit, rice fields, grapevines etc. Your last three pictures should show 'Jesus, the Bread of Life': use this as a search term for Google Images and select the following:

- A depiction of Jesus feeding the 5000
- A depiction of Jesus breaking bread (for example, at the Last Supper)
- An image of the bread and wine of Holy Communion

APPENDIX

Proper 23 **Equipment for 'Counting blessings' activity**
Choose one or more of the following:

- Assorted beads or buttons to thread onto thin bead wire
- Dry macaroni to thread onto pieces of string or uncooked spaghetti
- Coloured ribbons or pieces of wool to tie onto a piece of netting
- Small pebbles with which to build a cairn

A bishop's mitre
The mitre's shape is based on the flames that appeared at Pentecost, so you can adapt the flame crown that is used in the Christingle service – namely, a simple band with two flame shapes attached and stapled at the point (see page 518). The shape of the mitre is slightly squarer, like this:

Thank-you strips
Make enough copies on A4 paper for everyone to have one strip each. Cut them out before the service begins.

Proper 24 **A picture of Jacob wrestling God**
Search Google Images with the search terms 'Jacob wrestles God' and 'Jacob wrestles angel'. There are lots of striking images to choose from. It is probably easiest to display the picture on a screen; however, if you live near a major art gallery, you may be able to buy postcards of a famous painting of this scene: for example, the National Galleries of Scotland own Paul Gauguin's 'The Vision after the Sermon (Jacob wrestling with the Angel)'.

Fighters

You are looking for enthusiasts of any age who practise wrestling or martial arts, who would be willing to demonstrate their combat skills as part of the Storytelling. Approach your local sports centre for details of local clubs and ask them for volunteers. You will need to borrow the appropriate mats and arrange for a practice in church beforehand, so that your fighters understand the story and their role within it.

Prayer stations

These stations offer some multi-sensory prayer activities for when we are struggling with God or attempting to 'pray always'.

Stress ball

- Some stress balls (squeezable palm-sized balls, available from Amazon)
- Some small bouncy balls (these can be bought cheaply from newsagents and pound shops)

The cloud of unknowing

- Some small pictures of clouds (on CD-ROM: make several copies and cut out along the straight, solid lines)
- Pens and pencils

Sticky situation

- A bowl of really chewy toffees

Earworm

- *Either* your Music Leader, ready to teach people the Taizé chant, 'O Lord, hear my prayer'
- *Or* a recording of this chant and the words, so that people can sing along

Counting beads

- *Either* some simple beads threaded in a loop
- *Or* some rosaries, with your Prayer Leader to teach people how to use them

Yo-yo
- Lots of cheap yo-yos, available from the 'Party Supplies' section of big supermarkets

Proper 25 **Slideshow with the words from Psalm 65**

Create a simple slideshow, using PowerPoint for PCs or Keynote for Macs. You may like to choose a suitable piece of music as a soundtrack. A good site for free, downloadable pictures is www.dreamstime.com (you will need to register as a site user in order to access the free images). For this slideshow, combine words from the psalm with appropriate images, for example:

Praise is due to you, O God, in Zion . . .
O you who answer prayer!
(A picture of a person praying, or praying hands)
To you all flesh shall come.
. . . you forgive our transgressions.
(A depiction of Christ on the Cross)
By awesome deeds you answer us with deliverance,
O God of our salvation;
(A picture of the empty tomb)
By your strength you established the mountains . . .
(A picture of mountains)
You silence the roaring of the seas . . .
(A picture of stormy seas)
Those who live at earth's farthest bounds are awed by your signs;
(A picture of a solar eclipse or the northern lights)
you make the gateways of the morning and the evening shout for joy.
(A picture of a beautiful sunrise or sunset)
You visit the earth and water it,
you greatly enrich it;
(A picture of pouring rain)
the river of God is full of water;
(A picture of a fast-flowing river)
you provide the people with grain . . .
(A picture of wheat grain in sacks)
You water its furrows abundantly,
settling its ridges,
(A picture of a ploughed field)

softening it with showers,
and blessing its growth.
(A picture of green shoots)
You crown the year with your bounty;
(A picture of abundant harvest produce: search Google Images for 'cornucopia')
The pastures of the wilderness overflow,
the hills gird themselves with joy,
(A picture of a wildflower meadow)
the meadows clothe themselves with flocks,
(A picture of a meadow full of sheep)
the valleys deck themselves with grain,
(A picture of a ripe wheatfield)
they shout and sing together for joy.

These images are suggestions only: choose any you like that will help people reflect on the psalm.

Prayer stations
These offer some multi-sensory prayer activities for adoration and repentance.

'Wow!' corner
- Lots of natural objects that are lovely to look at and hold, for example: shells, pebbles, driftwood, feathers, conkers, polished wood, seed heads (for example, a fully grown sunflower head), autumn leaves, etc. Display them attractively on a table draped with a beautiful cloth (I use a length of red and gold sequinned sari).

Fragrant prayer
- Fresh herbs
- Whole spices such as nutmeg, cinnamon and ginger root
- Various essential oils, diluted in small dishes of water

Rainbow globe
- A 'colour change ball'. This is a resource which is well worth hunting for, because it never fails to make people of all ages pause and wonder. It is an opaque white ball, slightly larger than a tennis ball,

APPENDIX

with a tiny switch set into its base. When you switch it on, it softly glows red, then gradually changes colour through the spectrum. It is marketed as a 'colour change ball': mine came in a pack of three, with a battery charger, from the Christmas lights section of B & Q. Something similar has been sold by Argos as 'Colour change LED lights'. Search the internet for 'colour change balls', or check out shops and garden centres that sell night lights, mood lamps, novelty gifts or Christmas/outdoor lights. Ideally, you should have several colour change balls for this prayer station.

The Jesus Prayer
- Copies of the Jesus Prayer on small cards for people to memorise and take away with them

Ice cubes
- A bag of ice cubes
- A glass bowl full of hand-hot water

Cleansing fire
- A small brazier or barbecue with a few pieces of charcoal in the bottom (unlit)
- Lots of lolly sticks, available cheaply in bulk from Lakeland
- Felt pens
- Lighter fluid
- Matches
- Inside the church, lay the fire with the confessions, then carry it outside to light it.

All Saints' Day

Lots of glow-sticks

These are best bought online in bulk, for example from www.glowsticks.co.uk. Here, you need the product called 'glow bracelets', usually available in tubes of 100 with plastic connectors supplied in the tube. Three 8-inch glow-sticks should make one adult halo (two glow-sticks for small children), although you may like to provide extra in case people would like to weave two or more rings together to make a thicker halo.

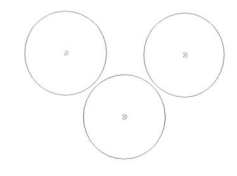

Circles of white card
Copy onto white A4 card and cut out enough for one each. Snip a small cross in the middle.

The words of 'I am one voice and I am singing'
This powerful and moving song is by Dom Eaton (© 1990 Small Change). It is a particular favourite with the Scouting Movement. You can find the lyrics online (Google 'I am one voice Don Eaton lyrics'), for example at www.gscmchorus.org/song/one-voice-singing/ (click on Lyric Sheet and Audio Recording). The first verse should be sung as a solo, the second as a duet; the whole congregation joins in from the third verse onwards.

A copy of *All Join In* by Quentin Blake
(Jonathan Cape Ltd, 1990)
This simple rhythmic story is enhanced by Quentin Blake's entertaining pictures. If possible, display these on a screen as you read the story, or simply show the spectacular last double-page spread. For this service, you will need the first part of the story, from 'When Sandra plays the trumpet . . .' to 'But the very best of all is when we ALL JOIN IN.' Skip 'The Hooter Song' and the other short stories and jump straight to the second 'All Join In' story at the end of the book: it begins, 'When we're cleaning up the house we ALL JOIN IN.'

Fourth Sunday before Advent

A stepladder with prayer tree attached
Choose some long, bare twigs or thin branches and tie them to both sides of the stepladder. Make sure you leave room for Zacchaeus to climb up and down safely. Use brown wool and criss-cross it all over the wood and around the sides of the ladder. People can then tuck their prayer leaves behind the wool, rather than fiddling about trying to tie the leaves on.

Prayer leaves
Make plenty of copies on green A4 paper and cut out.

APPENDIX

Third Sunday before Advent

Pictures

You will need the following pictures, in this order. I have given specific web locations for some; for the rest, try www.dreamstime.com for free, high quality images (you will need to register as a site user to download the free images).

- A metal book: search Google Images for 'Jordan metal books'. Choose an image (or make a montage of several images) showing some details of the markings on the lead pages
- The Christian sign of the fish
- A depiction of the crucifixion
- An angry crowd
- A prison cell or barred window
- A Roman sword
- The burning church in Egypt: see www.thedailynewsegypt.com/thugs-behind-imbaba-church-fire-says-fact-finding-committee.html. Scroll down to the end of the article for this picture
- The crowd of Egyptian Christians: see www.thedailynewsegypt.com/thugs-behind-imbaba-church-fire-says-fact-finding-committee.html. This picture is at the top of the article
- A picture of Ugandan children farming (for lots of pictures, see karlarleen.blogspot.co.uk/2012/03/children-farming-gods-way.html)

Remembrance Sunday

Seven large white peace poppies[94]

Print off two copies and cut out seven poppies. Number them 1-7 on the back and give them out to your prayer helpers. Explain that after each prayer intention, they will bring their poppies forward in turn and lay them down to form the shape of the cross.

---

94. The white 'peace poppy' can be controversial when worn instead of the red poppy, because it may be seen as an anti-military, pacifist statement. In this context, where people will presumably be wearing red poppies and laying wreaths of red poppies as usual, the white poppy should be an acceptable symbol of our prayers for peace.

Second Sunday before Advent

A set of balancing scales

Either borrow a set of traditional balancing scales with weights (many schools use these) or make your own: see the internet for instructions, for example 'Build your own Scales' on YouTube. This suggests taking the bottom halves of two 2-litre fizzy drink bottles and suspending them from a coat hanger to make a simple set of scales; other websites suggest more deluxe versions.

Protest wall/placard

- *Either* use a very large, plain piece of brown cardboard and mark it with the outline of bricks
- *Or* make a simple, large placard by attaching a piece of white board to a sturdy wooden batten

Clapper board

- *Either* make your own out of black card
- *Or* print off the CD-ROM picture and stick it onto a piece of card. Cut off the stripy top edge and reattach it, using sticky tape as a hinge, so that you can clap it down at the start of each scene. Write 'Scene 1 Take 1' in white chalk, then rub out the last '1' and replace it with '2' for the second version of the sketch

Christ the King

Equipment for making crowns

Here are some suggestions:

- Wide bands of gold or yellow card
- Scissors
- Sticky tape or stapler
- Stick-on jewels or self-adhesive coloured foam shapes
- Glue
- Sequins
- Cotton wool (for ermine trim)

Things to find, make and explore that tell us about Christ the King

Position these all around the church. The bullet points below indicate the resources you will need.

A special crown
- A grand crown made out of gold card (undecorated)
- The crown-decorating materials people used at the beginning of the service

Clear away any half-made crowns and any used materials, then place the special crown in the middle of the craft tables for people to decorate lavishly.

A crown of thorns
- A circlet made of brambles
- A pair of bramble-proof gloves for picking it up

A sign: 'King of the Jews'
- A large, rough wooden cross (such as many churches use at Easter)
- A sign made out of hardboard: 'King of the Jews'
- Some strong nails
- A couple of hammers

People will hammer the sign onto the cross.

A depiction of Jesus
- A depiction of Jesus (search Google Images and choose a simple dark-haired, dark-eyed portrait)

A globe
- A child's illuminated globe, plugged in and switched on (available from Amazon, Early Learning Centre and others)

Pictures of the White House, 10 Downing Street and those in power
- Search Google Images or newspaper sites – print off these images in hard copy

Pictures of the church
- Paper
- Pencils, rubbers and felt pens

Invite people to make a picture of the church. You could encourage teenagers to photograph the church on their mobile phones instead.

The empty tomb
- Materials for your church's Easter Garden

People will create a model of the empty tomb, as used on Easter Day, according to your church's custom.

The baby Jesus in a manger
- A baby doll, wrapped in blankets
- A manger or wooden fruit box, filled with straw

The bridge between earth and heaven
- Green and/or brown fabric or cushions
- Blue and/or white fabric or cushions
- A large cross shape: this could be made out of bricks laid end-to-end, or one long plank of wood with two shorter planks either side for the cross beam

Lay out the green/brown fabric at the foot of the cross to represent earth, and the blue/white fabric at the top to represent heaven. The cross shape will be used as a balancing beam by small children who will walk along it from 'earth' to 'heaven'.

Christ the King lists
Make enough A5 copies for everyone.

Index by theme

Christian seasons

Advent	Get ready! (First Sunday of Advent)	28
	The voice in the wilderness (Second Sunday of Advent)	34
	What should we do? (Third Sunday of Advent)	40
	It's you! (Fourth Sunday of Advent)	46
Christmas	God is with us (Christmas Day)	62
The Church year	Epiphany	82
	Candlemas – Festival of Light	116
	Ash Wednesday	160
	The Annunciation	198
	Palm Sunday	214
	Maundy Thursday	220
	Good Friday	226
	Easter Day	232
	Ascension Day	274
	Pentecost	288
	Trinity Sunday	296
	All Saints' Day	474
God our Father	Water of life (Fifth Sunday of Easter)	260
	A helping hand (Seventh Sunday of Easter)	280
	In charge (Proper 4)	302
	God unlimited (Proper 16)	392
Jesus Christ	Missing! (First Sunday of Christmas)	68
	You are my Son (First Sunday of Epiphany)	88
	Good news for the poor (Proper 2)	132
	Shining bright (Sunday next before Lent)	152
	The Good Shepherd's sheep (Fourth Sunday of Easter)	254
	Unfinished business (Sixth Sunday of Easter)	268
	Forgiven (Proper 6)	318
	'Sit down, you're rocking the boat!' (Proper 15)	384
	Christ the King	510

The Kingdom of God	God's plan (Second Sunday of Christmas)	76
	Are you ready? (Proper 14)	378
Being called	Fish galore! (Proper 1)	124
	The call (Third Sunday of Easter)	246
	What to do? (Proper 8)	334
Being disciples	One body (Third Sunday of Epiphany)	104
	The greatest gift (Fourth Sunday of Epiphany)	110
	The challenge of love (Proper 3)	140
	Sweet-smelling feet (Fifth Sunday of Lent)	206
	Speaking out (Second Sunday of Easter)	238
	Help! (Proper 5)	310
	The God Squad (Proper 9)	342
	Giving our all (Proper 18)	408
'Teach us how to pray'	Teach us how to pray (Proper 12)	362
	Thank you! (Proper 23)	450
	The wrestling match (Proper 24)	458
	What has God done for us? (Proper 25)	468
Difficult times	In the wilderness (Third Sunday of Lent)	184
	Conviction (Third Sunday before Advent)	488
	It's not fair! (Second Sunday before Advent)	502
Repentance and forgiveness	Me! Me! Me! (First Sunday of Lent)	168
	Lots and lots (Proper 13)	372
	Putting things right (Fourth Sunday before Advent)	482
Old Testament stories	Waiting for God (Second Sunday of Lent)	176
	Earthquake, wind and fire (Proper 7)	326
	There's no place like home (Proper 22)	444
Gospel stories, miracles and parables	Water into wine (Second Sunday of Epiphany)	96
	The good Samaritan (Proper 10)	348
	Martha and Mary (Proper 11)	354
	At the top table (Proper 17)	400
	Lost and found (Proper 19)	414
	God or money? (Proper 20)	422
	Rich and poor (Proper 21)	430

INDEX BY THEME

Special occasions Christingle (Christmas Eve) 54
Pets' service (Second Sunday before Lent) 146
Mothering Sunday 190
Harvest Thanksgiving 438
Remembrance Sunday 496

Also by Claire Benton-Evans

All-sorts Worship – Year A

Complete all-age services for every Sunday of Common Worship Year A

This is the ideal book for creative, fun, real all-age worship which creates a sense of belonging in your church.

Product code: 1501234

All-sorts Worship – Year B

All-sorts Worship contains complete services for every Sunday of Common Worship Year B, which are designed to include people of 'all sorts and conditions of life', meaning that the whole congregation worships together and nobody is tidied away.

Product code: 1501237

www.kevinmayhew.com

All-Sorts Prayer

Creative prayers for all ages

Uses symbols, actions and sensory experience to provide adaptable and original prayers for an all-age, 'all-sorts' congregation.

Product code: 1501223

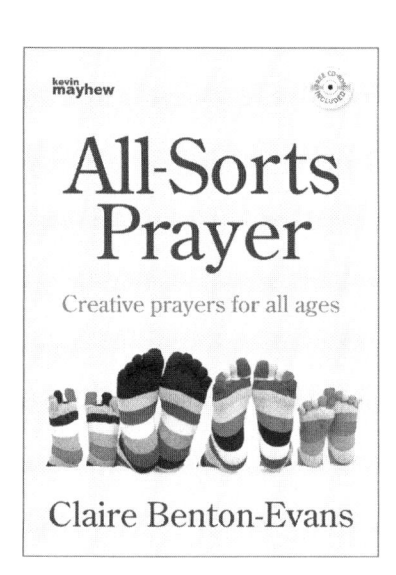

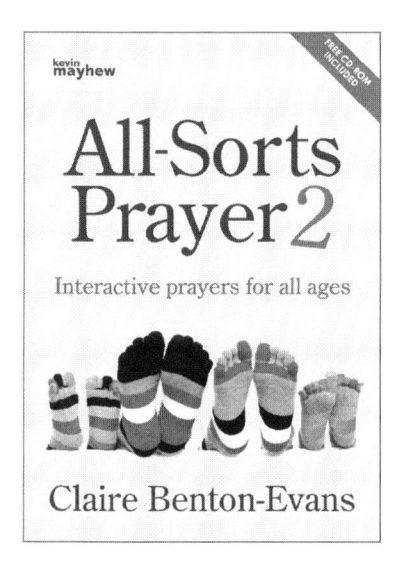

All-Sorts Prayer 2

Interactive prayers for all ages

All-Sorts Prayer 2 offers a fresh collection of seasonal prayers for the Church's special occasions. Have you ever found yourself thinking, 'Help! I've got to produce informal intercessions for this week's Harvest Festival'? If so, then this is definitely the book you need.

Product code: 1501305

www.kevinmayhew.com

One for All – Book 1

Complete services for every Sunday of the year, designed to include everyone so nobody is tidied away.

One for All is the themed version of *All-sorts Worship* Year A and is the ideal book for creative, fun, all-age worship which creates a sense of belonging in your church.

Product code: 1501239

One for All – Book 2

Complete services for the whole church family.

Product code: 1501294

www.kevinmayhew.com